Robert Mills, Architect

ROBERT·MILLS

Robert Mills, Architect

Edited by John M. Bryan

The American Institute of Architects Press

Washington, D.C.

This publication and the complementary exhibition "Robert
Mills: Designs for Democracy" were made possible by a generous contribution from the Otis Elevator Company. Additional
funding was provided by the National Endowment for the Arts,
the National Endowment for the Humanities, and the Graham
Foundation for Advanced Studies in the Visual Arts.

The American Institute of Architects Press
1735 New York Avenue, N.W.
Washington, D.C. 20006

The Octagon
The American Architectural Foundation, Washington, D.C.

Printed in Canada
93   92   91   90   89   5   4   3   2   1

Library of Congress Cataloging-in-Publication Data

Robert Mills, architect.

   1. Mills, Robert, 1781-1855—Criticism and interpretation.
2. Architecture, Modern—19th century—United States.
I. Bryan, John Morrill.
NA737.M5R64 1989   720'.92'4   88-35000
ISBN 1-55835-019-5
ISBN 1-55835-023-3 (pbk.)

Design and production by Market Sights, Inc.
Set in Berkeley by Unicorn Graphics, Washington, D.C.
Printed by D. W. Friesen, Altona, Manitoba, through Four
Colour Imports, Ltd., Louisville, Kentucky

Cover illustration:
County Records Office (Fireproof Building) (1822–27),
Charleston, South Carolina. (South Carolina Historical
Society)

CONTENTS

HONORARY

COMMITTEE FOR

THE ROBERT MILLS

EXHIBIT

Mr. Harold L. Adams, FAIA
Mr. Robert McC. Adams
Mr. Charles H. Atherton, FAIA
Mr. Preston Bolton, FAIA
Mr. Richard G. Boxall
Mr. and Mrs. Benjamin E. Brewer, Jr.
Mr. Kevin C. Cassidy
Miss Betty Lou Custer, FAIA
Mr. and Mrs. Thomas J. Eyerman
Mr. Richard J. Fasenmyer
Mr. Winthrop W. Faulkner, FAIA
Ms. Mildred Friedman, Hon. AIA
Mr. James B. Holderman
The Honorable Ernest F. Hollings, Hon. AIA
Mr. James A. Horstman
Mr. Hugh Newell Jacobsen, FAIA
Mr. Russell L. Jordan, AIA
Mr. Roger G. Kennedy
Mr. A. Eugene Kohn, FAIA
Mr. Karl J. Krapek
Mr. C. James Lawler, AIA
Ms. Maya Lin

Mr. Alan J. Lockman
Mr. Terrence M. McDermott
Mr. K. Donald Menefee
Mr. Set Charles Momjain
Mr. John O'Neil
Mr. and Mrs. Ted P. Pappas
Mr. I. M. Pei, FAIA
Mrs. Maureen Quimby
The Honorable Arthur Ravenel, Jr.
Mr. William A. Rose Jr., FAIA
Mr. F. Max Schuette
Ms. Laurinda H. Spear, AIA
The Honorable Floyd Spence
Mr. Frederic A. Stoner
Mr. James L. Thomas, AIA
The Honorable Strom Thurmond
Mr. James D. Tittle, FAIA
The Honorable Morris K. Udall
Mrs. Frankie Welch
Mr. George M. White, FAIA
Dr. Don W. Wilson

ROBERT L. ALEXANDER   is professor of art history at the University of Iowa and senior editor of the Papers of Robert Mills.

JOHN M. BRYAN   is associate professor of art history at the University of South Carolina. He is associate editor of the Papers of Robert Mills and guest curator of the exhibit "Robert Mills: Designs for Democracy."

DOUGLAS E. EVELYN   is deputy director of the National Museum of American History, Smithsonian Institution, and project director of the Papers of Robert Mills.

PAMELA SCOTT   is associate editor of the Papers of Robert Mills and editor of the microfilm edition of the Papers of Robert Mills.

FOREWORD

he Washington Monument is America's most well-known memorial. Robert Mills (1781–1855), creator of the monument, has remained relatively unknown beyond a small group of scholars and specialists. This book marks the first comprehensive study of his work and influence in more than fifty years.

Robert Mills's buildings, writings, and career deserve further study and attention for many reasons. As Thomas Jefferson's protégé, Mills was the first native-born American to train for an architectural career. Unlike many of his contemporaries, he never studied architecture abroad. With the encouragement of Jefferson, he made a study tour of the northeastern states, became familiar with architectural books, and trained in the office of Benjamin Henry Latrobe.

This American training and his early professional experience provided him with a deep understanding of America's ideals and aspirations during a critical period in the transformation of this country from a fundamentally agrarian society to one characterized by intense nationalism, mercantile capitalism, government bureaucracy, expanding population, and urbanization.

Mills helped define and shape the architectural symbolism of the early republic. He adapted and reinterpreted classical architecture and successfully established his version of the Greek Revival as the style most expressive of the new American political system. By 1836 his reputation was such that he was appointed by President Andrew Jackson to the post of federal architect, and for the next sixteen years he was responsible for the design or supervision of numerous government buildings, including the Treasury Building and the Patent Office. In addition to fulfilling his federal responsibilities, he contributed to the development of the architectural profession in the United States and worked actively as an author, cartographer, and engineer.

Working in a time when travel and communication presented significant difficulties, Mills was prolific, even by today's standards. He designed more than 160 projects, including churches, hospitals, universities, jails, courthouses, private residences, and monuments. In order to convey his ideas to clients and builders, whom he might never meet, he produced booklets that explained his designs and enabled him to conduct a truly national practice.

Mills's practical and theoretical delineation of the architect's responsibilities is his most important contribution to the profession, and this definition of the profession, drawn from his strong social conscience, extended well beyond the design of individual buildings and the supervision of construction. He understood the architect's obligation to serve not only the specific client but also the broad needs of the public. Thus throughout his career he wrote extensively advocating the development of canals, waterworks, railroads, and bridges and the reclamation of swampland as a means of improving the general welfare of his fellow citizens.

The American Architectural Foundation is pleased to be involved with this publication and the Robert Mills exhibition for many reasons. First, the material on Mills's work previously available was inadequate, and this book incorporates valuable new research. Second, since its founding, the

American Institute of Architects has appealed to the government and the public for a commitment to high quality in all public buildings, sculptures, bridges, parks, monuments, and other works commensurate with this nation's high ideals. Finally, this book and exhibition provide a better understanding of the contribution made by one of America's earliest and foremost architects and demonstrate that architecture at its best is an instrument for the public good.

This book is an outgrowth of a historical editing project, the Papers of Robert Mills, organized in 1984 by the Smithsonian Institution. We are grateful to the editors of the Mills papers—Dr. Robert Alexander, John M. Bryan, Douglas E. Evelyn, and Pamela Scott—all of whom have contributed thoughtful essays to the volume. We are particularly indebted to Mr. Bryan, who skillfully and energetically took on the responsibilites of author, volume editor, and guest curator for the exhibition "Robert Mills: Designs for Democracy," sponsored by the American Architectural Foundation.

This book has benefited beyond all reasonable expectation from many professional colleagues. At the AIA Press, John R. Hoke, Jr., AIA, Joel Stein, and Janet Rumbarger have played key roles bringing the book out on schedule and in this very handsome format. The American Architectural Foundation staff dedicated themselves to this endeavor for several years. All who appreciate this book and the exhibition owe a debt of gratitude to them. Judith S. Schultz, curator of the Foundation's exhibition programs, championed the project and was the driving force behind it. Nancy Davis, director of the Octagon, Sherry Birk, curator of the Prints and Drawings Collection, Marilyn Montgomery and Sherri Lee in the development office, and Raymond P. Rhinehart, vice president for public programming, all greatly assisted toward the success of the project. Betty Jean Musselman and Paula Dravec provided precise administrative talents. We are also grateful to Gretchen Smith Mui, the volume's consulting editor, and designer Marilyn Worseldine.

The encouragement we received from the American Institute of Architects was led by immediate past president Ted P. Pappas, FAIA, and President Benjamin E. Brewer, Jr., FAIA. Winthrop W. Faulkner, FAIA, chairman of the Octagon Society, provided valuable support. Finally, we would like to thank Thomas J. Eyerman, FAIA, RIBA, chairman of the Board of Regents of the American Architectural Foundation, for his commitment to directing Foundation resources to scholarship that advances public understanding of architecture.

We owe much to our sponsors—the National Endowment for the Arts, the National Endowment for the Humanities, the Graham Foundation, and the Otis Elevator Company. Their generosity allowed the book and exhibition to be accomplished without compromise or shortcuts.

The ultimate judges of our success will, of course, be those of you who come into contact with both this book and the exhibition. We are grateful for your interest and trust that it will be not only rewarded but also heightened to explore the vast landscape of achievement and challenge that is architecture.

James P. Cramer, Hon. AIA
President
The American Architectural Foundation

obert Mills has long been recognized as a major American architect, but heretofore the lack of an extensive, accessible collection of primary materials has hampered research concerning his career. Specialized studies have initiated the process of attribution and analysis in recent years. In 1982 "Robert Mills, the Years of Growth," a symposium organized by Dr. Robert L. Alexander at the Henry Francis du Pont Winterthur Museum, gave focus to current research and resulted in the creation of the Papers of Robert Mills, with Dr. Alexander as senior editor, John M. Bryan and Pamela Scott as associate editors, and Douglas E. Evelyn as project director. The editors, sponsored by the University of Iowa, the University of South Carolina, the Smithsonian Institution, the National Endowment for the Humanities, and the National Historical Publications and Records Commission, have collected, collated, indexed (and in many cases transcribed) some 3,500 manuscripts. This material provided the data needed to develop a detailed portrait of Mills's personal and professional life. Drawing on these documents, the following essays treat major aspects of his training and work as an architect, engineer, cartographer, and author. The complete papers will be published by Scholarly Resources and will contain facsimiles of documents cited here; Pamela Scott, editor of the microfilm edition, is preparing an index and guide that will make this material accessible.

Team effort—the norm in scientific research—is all too rare in the humanities, but this book reflects the collective work of the editors of the Papers of Robert Mills, all of whom have shared in the acquisition and tedious transcription of thousands of pages of unpublished manuscript material. My first expression of gratitude is therefore to colleagues Robert L. Alexander, Douglas E. Evelyn, and Pamela Scott. Among them, the major burden—the management and processing of the central file—has fallen on Pamela Scott. Researchers using the Mills papers are in her debt.

Our work has depended on access to manuscript collections. For their help and the interest they have taken in the project, I am especially grateful to the following archivists and librarians: George Barringer and Nicholas B. Scheetz, Georgetown University; J. Jefferson Miller, Museum and Library of Maryland History; Louis L. Tucker and Ross Urquhart, Massachusetts Historical Society; Herman Elstein, Mount Holly, New Jersey; Peter J. Parker, Historical Society of Pennsylvania; Catherine E. Sadler, Charleston Library Society; David Moltke-Hansen, Harlan Greene, and Susan Walker, South Carolina Historical Society; James Conway, Bunker Hill Monument Association; Roger Moss, The Athenaeum, Philadelphia; Gregory A. Johnson, Alderman Library, University of Virginia; Dean Krimmel, The Peale Museum; William Gullison, Tulane University; Charles F. Penniman, The Franklin Institute; the staff of the Perkins Library, Duke University; the staff of the Southern Historical Collection and Manuscripts Department, University of North Carolina; Lynn Barron, Roger Mortimer, Ellen Tillett, Virginia Weathers, Daniel Boice, and Lester Duncan, Thomas Cooper Library, University of South Carolina; Allen Stokes, Herbert J. Hartsook, and Eleanor M. Richardson, South Caroliniana Library, University of South Carolina;

Charles Lee, Charles Lesser, Robert Mackintosh, and the staff of the South Carolina Department of Archives and History; Woodrow Harris, South Carolina Department of Mental Health; Lucille Showalter, Maritime Society, New London, Connecticut; William Elder, Baltimore Museum of Art; Frank L. Horton, Bradford L. Rauschenberg, and Rosemary N. Estes, Museum of Early Southern Decorative Arts, Winston-Salem, North Carolina; Sara D. Jackson, National Historical Publications and Records Commission; Anthony Wrenn, American Institute of Architects; Florian H. Thayn and Anne-Imelda Radice, Office of the Architect of the Capitol; and C. Ford Peatross, Prints and Photographs Division, Library of Congress. For an initiation into the mysteries of historical editing, I wish to thank Richard Sheldon of the National Historical Publications and Records Commission, Elizabeth S. Hughes of the Papers of Dwight David Eisenhower, and David R. Chesnutt of the Papers of Henry Laurens.

In addition to grants noted by Mr. Cramer in the foreword, funding has been provided by the South Carolina Committee for the Humanities and the South Carolina Arts Commission. I also wish to thank the Palmetto Society for Heritage Conservation and its president, Walton McLeod, for an important grant. I shall always be grateful to John O'Neil, chairman of the art department of the University of South Carolina, for his constant support. For the forebearance of my fellow art historians at the university—Charles R. Mack, Beverly Heisner, and Annie-Paule Quinsac—I am equally thankful.

The reader benefits, as I have, from reviews and conversations with Jeffrey A. Cohen, Papers of Benjamin Henry Latrobe; Lee Nelson, National Park Service; William Pierson, Williams College; James M. Goode, former keeper of the Smithsonian Castle; and Pamela Scott. Beyond specific instances cited in the notes, earlier research by Gene Waddell, Rhodri Liscombe, and Douglas Harnsberger has meant much to me. Throughout the project conservation of the drawings has been a primary goal, and most of this has been accomplished by Kendra Lovette and the Conservation Department of the National Archives.

Here we bring together much of what has been learned during the compilation of documents and drawings. The support and participation of the American Institute of Architects, the Foundation, the AIA Press, and the Octagon are especially gratifying, for Robert Mills often asserted that he was the first American to train specifically for a career in architecture. It was his most insistently repeated claim to fame.

Finally, on a personal note, I wish to express appreciation to Douglas and Martha Evelyn, Anthony and Jacqueline Merrill, and Frank and Mary Beth Dorsey for providing a home away from home during research trips. My gratitude to Bill Toal, a friend, and Martha, my wife, words cannot convey.

John M. Bryan

PLATES

Credits

Plates 1 and 22—South Carolina Historical Society;
plates 2, 5, and 6—Maryland Historical Society; plate
3—American Architectural Foundation; plates 4, 11,
12, and 18—National Archives; plates 7, 8, 9, 10,
and 17—South Carolina Department of Archives and
History; plates 13, 14, and 15—Georgetown
University; plate 16—Col. Harvey Anderson; plates
19, 20, and 21—First Presbyterian Church, Augusta,
Georgia.

Plate 1
Front elevation, County
Records Office (Fireproof
Building) (1822–27),
Charleston, South Carolina,
c. 1828.

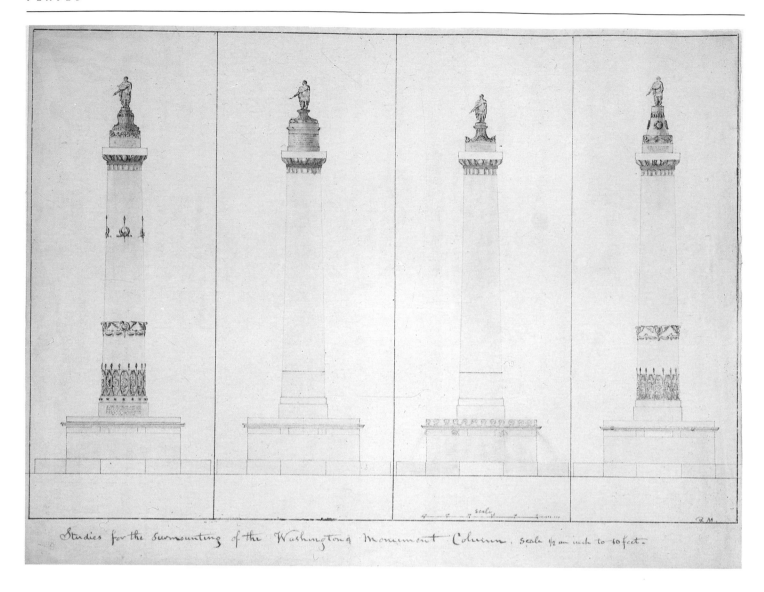

Studies for the surmounting of the Washington Monument Column, scale ½ an inch to 10 feet.

Above: Plate 2
Sketches of the Washington
Monument, Baltimore,
Maryland, c. 1815.

Below: Plate 3
Elevation and working
drawing of the east wing,
U.S. Patent Office,
Washington, D.C.,
1849–50.

Opposite: Plate 4:
Washington National
Monument (1845–52;
completed 1879–84),
Washington, D.C.

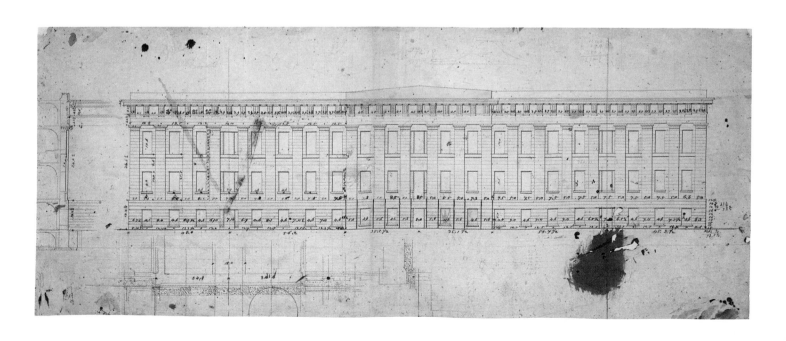

SKETCH OF

WASHINGTON

Pantheon.
Plan.

NAT^L: MONUM^T:

BY

ROB^T: MILLS,

ARC^T.

Plate 5
"Elevation of the Principal
Fronts," Washington
Monument, Baltimore,
c. 1814.

Plate 6
Section showing stairs within
the column, Washington
Monument, Baltimore,
c.1814.

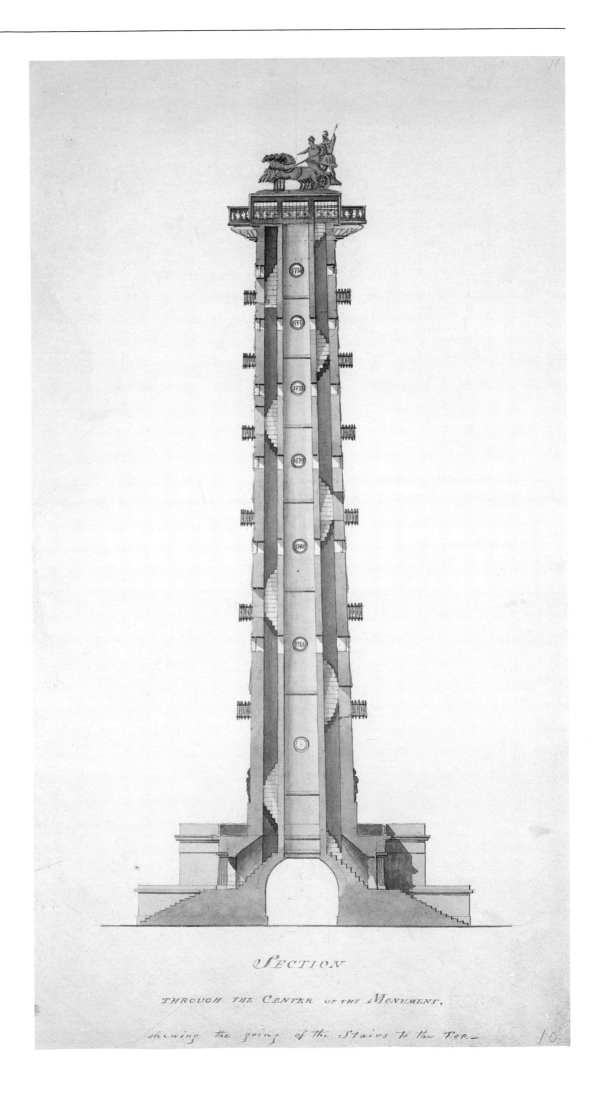

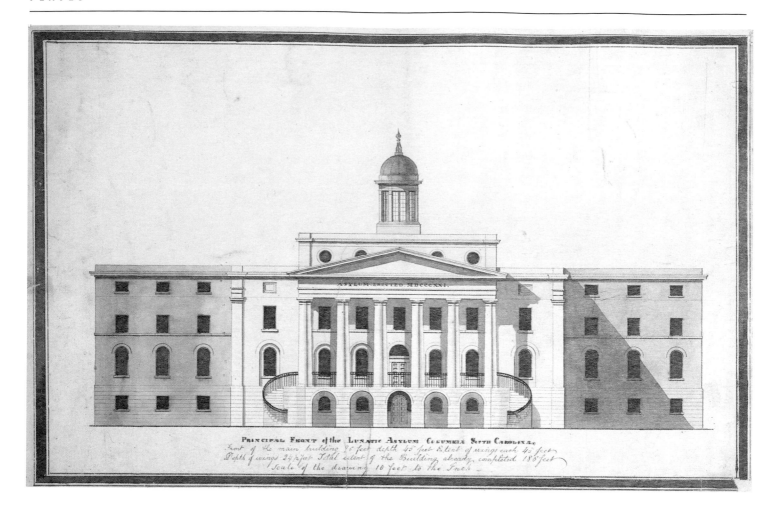

PRINCIPAL FRONT of the LUNATIC ASYLUM COLUMBIA SOUTH CAROLINA.
Front of the main building 95 feet depth 45 feet Extent of wings each 45 feet
Depth of wings 24 feet Total extent of the Building already completed 185 feet
Scale of the drawing 10 feet to the Inch

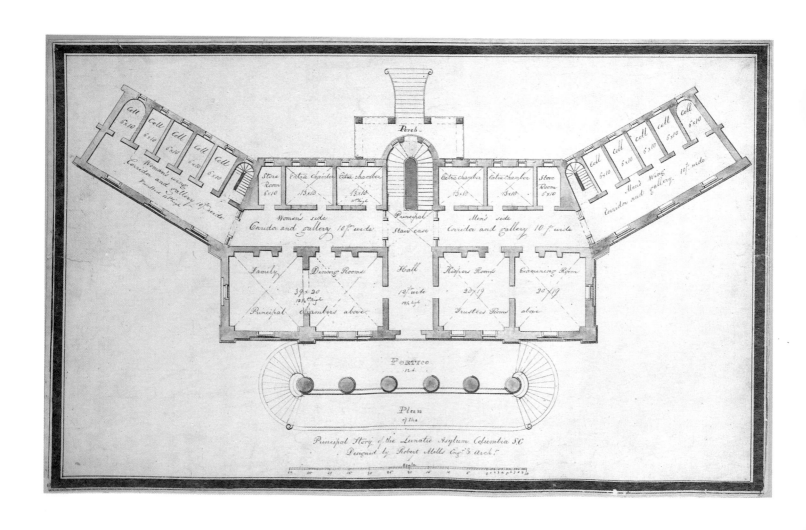

Plan of the
Principal Story of the Lunatic Asylum Columbia SC
Designed by Robert Mills Eng'r & Arch't

Elevation of the Back or South front of the Lunatic Asylum
The Cells or Chambers are all disposed on the front—

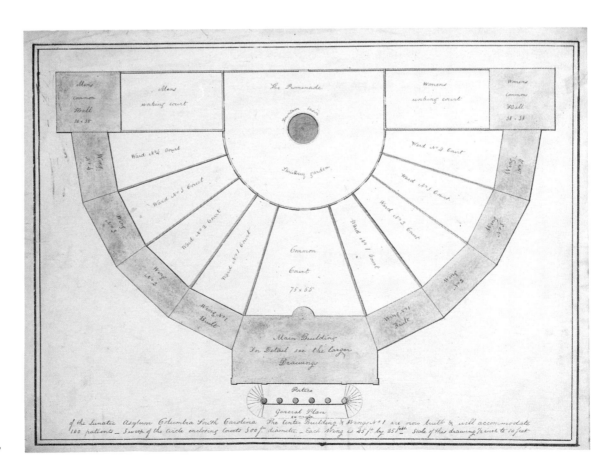

Opposite top: Plate 7
Principal elevation, South
Carolina Asylum
(1822–28), Columbia,
South Carolina, c. 1822.

Opposite bottom: Plate 8
Plan of the principal floor,
South Carolina Asylum,
c. 1822.

Above: Plate 9
Rear elevation,
South Carolina Asylum,
c. 1822.

Right: Plate 10
Plan of wings and courtyards,
South Carolina Asylum,
c. 1822.

Plate 11
Perspective of the proposed
Smithsonian Institution,
Washington, D.C., 1841.

of the Smithsonian Institution agreeably to the Design

Plate 12
View of building and
grounds, Smithsonian
Institution, 1841.

Picturesque View of the Building,
and Grounds in front.

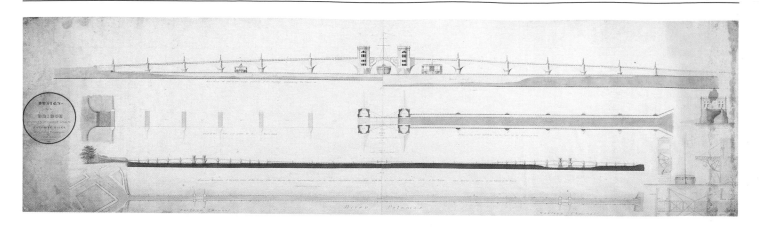

Plate 13
Potomac River Bridge,
Arlington, Va.,
to Washington, D.C.,
1852.

Plate 14
Detail, Potomac River
Bridge, 1852.

*Opposite: Plate 15
Details, Potomac River
Bridge, 1852.*

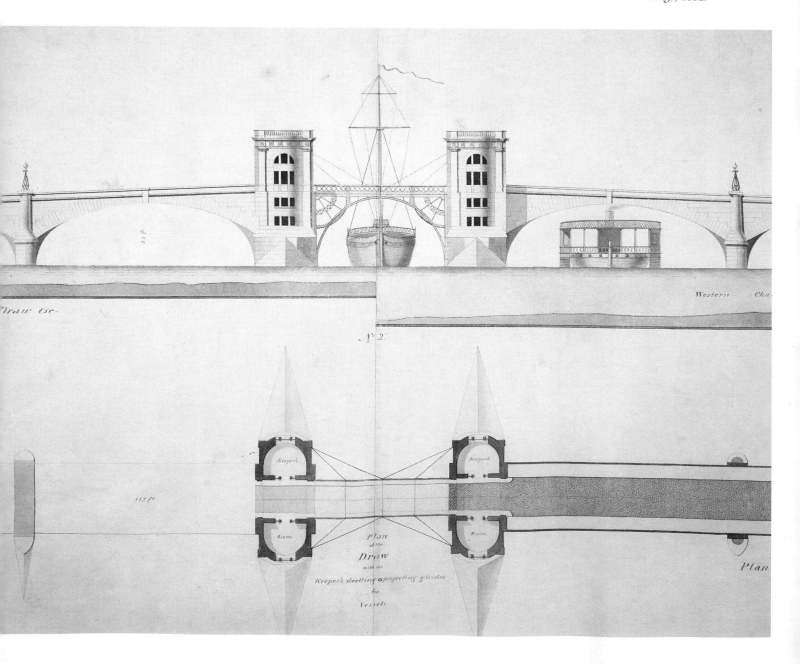

Level Cov

Elevation of the entrance on the Draw fro
the Bridge.
N.º 4

Section
shewing the working
apparatus of the
Draw as with the
Draw open.

Elevation shewing half the draw Close

N.º 3

Room con-
taining the
working app
aratus of the
Draw

Virginia

Shore

Virginia

Top: Plate 16
Front elevation,
South Carolina College,
Hugh Smith, 1802.

Bottom: Plate 17
Composite drawings,
South Carolina College,
1802.

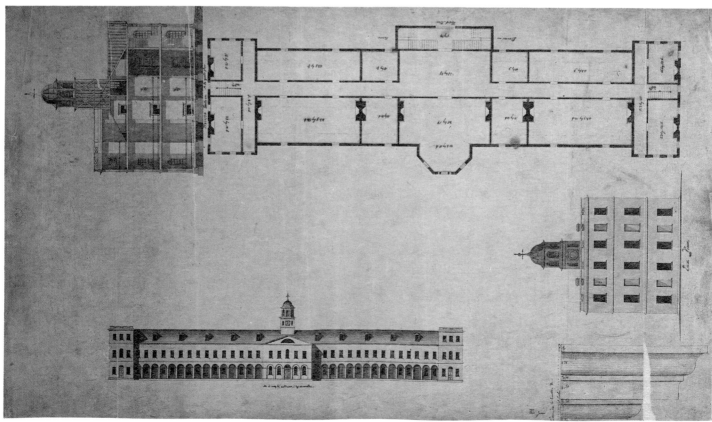

Plate 18
North and south elevations,
Library and Science
Building (1838–40), U.S.
Military Academy, West
Point, New York, 1839.

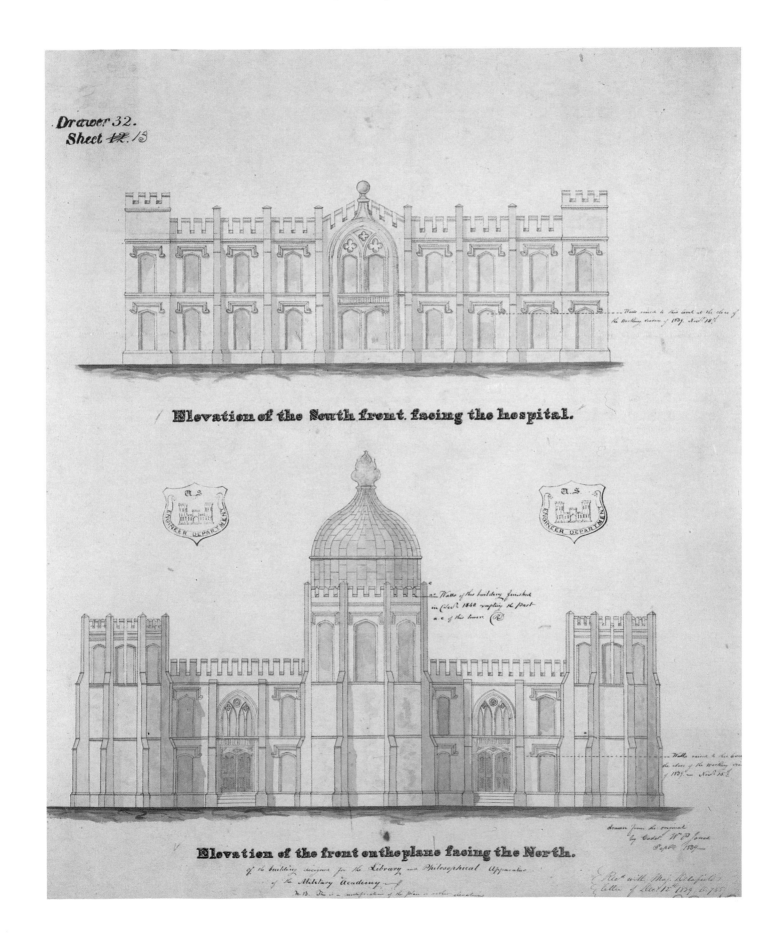

Elevation of the South front. facing the hospital.

Elevation of the front on the plane facing the North.

Façade

or

Principal Front of the Church.

Scale 10 ft to ½ inch

PLATES

Opposite: Plate 19
Principal front, First
Presbyterian Church
(1807–12), Augusta,
Georgia, 1807.

Top: Plate 20
Section looking toward the
pulpit, First Presbyterian
Church, 1807.

Bottom: Plate 21
Section looking from the
pulpit, First Presbyterian
Church, 1807.

Sections looking towards the Pulpit.

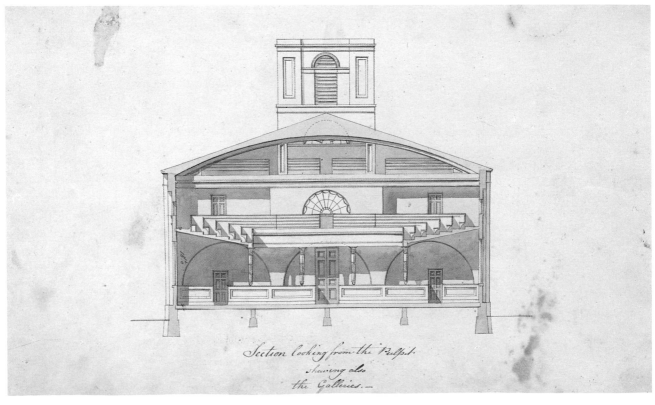

*Section looking from the Pulpit.
shewing also
the Galleries.—*

Plate 22
Front elevation,
Kershaw County Courthouse
(1825–26), Camden, South
Carolina, c. 1828.

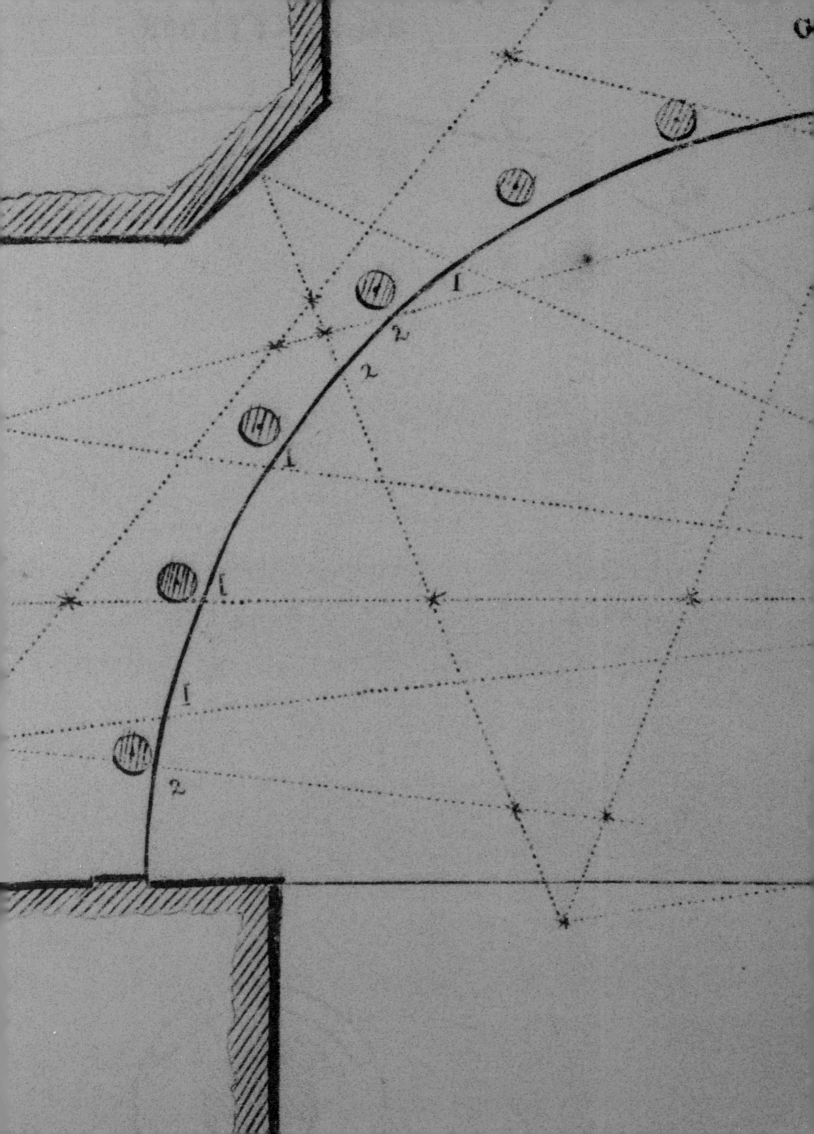

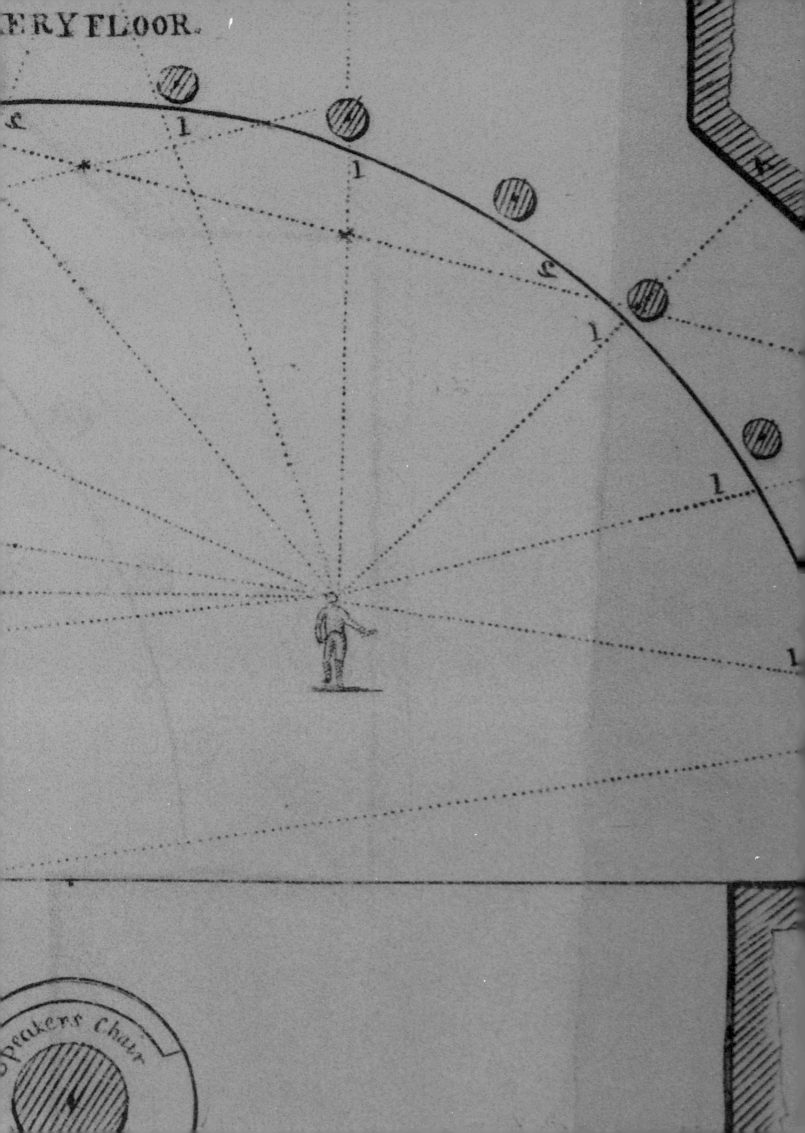

Speakers Chair

ROBERT MILLS:

EDUCATION AND

EARLY DRAWINGS

John M. Bryan

obert Mills (1781–1855) claimed to be "the first American who has passed through a regular course of study of architecture in his own country." He described himself as a "pioneer" and believed his training distinguished him from the gentlemen-amateurs who dominated American architecture before the Revolution and from the architect-builders who, in increasing numbers, emerged from the building trades at the outset of the nineteenth century.[1] Narrowly defined, Mills's claim has merit. A classical education, the grand tour, and a familiarity with architectural books provided the basis for the work of the gentlemen-amateurs; for them, architectural practice was the practical application of an essentially theoretical knowledge. Conversely, the carpenters, masons, and contractors who presented themselves as architect-builders employed historical form as a superficial insignia of erudition.

None of the gentlemen-amateurs—Gabriel Manigault (1758–1809) of Charleston, William Thornton (1759–1828) of Washington, D.C., Samuel Blodgett (1757–1814) of Philadelphia, or even Thomas Jefferson (1743–1826) of Virginia or Charles Bulfinch (1763–1844) of Boston—could match Robert Mills's knowledge of engineering, heating systems, vaulting, and fireproof construction. The training of most of the notable architect-builders had also been quite narrow: Samuel McIntire (1757–1811), the son, nephew, and brother of housewrights and wood carvers, learned his trade within the family circle; Solomon Willard (1783–1861) trained in Petersham, Massachusetts,

as a housewright; Asher Benjamin (1773–1845) worked as a carpenter in Connecticut before becoming a publisher, housewright, and finally an "Architect and Carpenter." Other native-born Americans who became successful as architects lacked Mills's educational foundation: Ithiel Town (1784–1844) trained as a carpenter in Thompson, Connecticut, and then studied with Asher Benjamin in Boston; Alexander Parris (1780–1852), who advertised himself as a "builder-architect," was apprenticed to a carpenter in Pembroke, Massachusetts. Isaiah Rogers (1800–1869) served an apprenticeship with Jesse Shaw, a Boston housewright. The father of William Strickland (1788–1854) was a carpenter; after several years as a pupil of Benjamin Henry Latrobe, William studied painting and worked as a set designer in New York.

Throughout Mills's youth in Charleston, South Carolina, in lieu of collegiate training and European travel, tradesmen who aspired to become architects attended evening classes that offered instruction in the five orders, descriptive geometry, and architectural drafting. In Boston, New York, Philadelphia, and Charleston the typical curriculum included the depiction of "Landschapes [sic.], Figures, Flowers" as well as "Architecture, with the theory and practice of perspective made easy."[2]

Robert Mills thought the amateurs and architect-builders were inadequately prepared. He wrote that "there is no other profession that embraces so wide a field of scientific research, and practical operation as that does of an architect." Further, he noted, "to be an accomplished architect is to be not only more than an accomplished scholar but an accomplished artist and mechanic."[3] He believed his training had unified, for the first time in America, the attributes of "these two sets of men" and had enabled him as "the Architect to get in between them," as Latrobe phrased it. Latrobe, writing to Mills, noted that public recognition of such a niche was a prerequisite for the socioeconomic definition of their profession.[4]

The amorphous status of the profession at the beginning of his career and the diverse components of his education imbue Mills's early work with a dynamic tension, an idiosyncratic quality born of seemingly incongruous allegiances. He professed a commitment to beauty but only in the context of utility: "Utility and economy will be found to have entered into most of the studies of the author & little was sacrificed to display; at the same time his endeavor was to produce as much harmony & beauty of arrangement in the whole as was practicable." He employed a traditional iconography but insisted on adapting historical forms to contemporaneous conditions: "I have always deprecated the servile copying of the buildings of antiquity; we have the same principles and materials to work upon that the ancients had, and we should adapt these materials to the habits and customs of our people as they did to theirs."[5] He was quick to point out that his emphasis on utility and local needs was quintessentially American, and from the outset of his training he was in close contact with building tradesmen. His interest in fireproof masonry vaulting and the Delorme dome quickly took him beyond vernacular American practices. Readings in acoustics and French and English works on penology and psychiatric care prompted him to propose buildings unlike anything that had been built in America.

Despite his use of European sources, Mills often emphasized that he was native born in order to appeal to the assertive nationalism of the period and to distance himself from immigrants who had some claim to expertise; this appeal to patriotism was an important aspect of his professional persona. Having been born in South Carolina and having never traveled abroad, he said he was "altogether American in his views" and thereby endowed with a perspective unavailable to a Maximilian Godefroy (1765–c. 1840), J. J. Ramée (1764–1842), or Benjamin Henry Latrobe (1764–1820).[6] These foreigners, like tradesmen and gentlemen-amateurs, were an identifiable source of competition. Immigrants such as Pierre Charles L'Enfant (1754–1825), James Hoban (1762–1831), John McComb (1763–1853), and Joseph Mangin (d. 1818) clearly dominated the quest for major commissions during the post-Revolutionary period. Also, the majority of the more obscure practitioners who advertised lessons in architectural drawing were foreign born and offered experience in London or Paris as their principal qualification.

Competing with Godefroy for the Baltimore Washington Monument, Mills wrote to the board of managers that "the education I have received being altogether American and unmixed with European habits, I can safely present the design submitted as American" and "for the honor of our country, my sincere wish is that it may not be said; To foreign genius and to foreign hands we are indebted for a monument to perpetuate the glory of our beloved Chief."[7] Mills was not alone in his chauvinism. Similar appeals for a native expression were voiced by other creators—John Trumbull, Horatio Greenough, and Ralph Waldo Emerson—as well as by patrons. In fact, the board of managers of the monument, in their advertisement, had noted their hope that an American might win in order that they need not "resort to any other country for a monument to the memory of their illustrious fellow-citizen."[8]

Robert Mills's emphasis on citizenship simultaneously tainted a segment of his competition, appealed to patrons, and was congruent with the symbolic intent of public works in the new republic. He believed that circumstances of birth and education distinguished him from his competitors. He was aware of educational, social, and political crosscurrents within his evolving profession, and he was optimistic, believing that in America liberty, education, and opportunity would "enlarge the mind and give the most exalted views on every subject of art & science."[9]

HABITS OF MIND

The prevailing impression of Mills's aesthetic development has been dominated by public monuments and buildings that have overshadowed the scope and nature of his accomplishments as an engineer, author, and cartographer, work that offers insight into his aptitudes and habits of mind. His emphasis on utility, economy, and education stems from a pragmatic bias, expected in an engineer but not necessarily anticipated or looked for as a formative influence in a young draftsman. Although some of his contemporaries established reputations in specialized aspects of engineering—Thomas Pope and Lewis Wernwag as bridge builders, William Weston in canal construction, and John Davis in waterworks management—Mills's mentor, Latrobe, practiced "both branches" of the profession, as did Mills and, to a lesser extent, his fellow apprentice William Strickland.[10]

Mills's initial experience with Latrobe involved making surveys for the Chesapeake and Delaware Canal in 1803; from then on he sought employment as an engineer as persistently as he pursued architectural commissions. During his residence in Baltimore, from 1815 to 1820, approximately one-third of his time was devoted to nonarchitectural projects—his service as the president and chief engineer of the Baltimore Water Company, a proposal for a flood-control system for Jones Falls, bridge construction, the design and installation of hot-air furnaces in residences, public buildings, and a factory, and his earliest publication on inland navigation, a scheme linking Baltimore via the Potomac and Susquehanna rivers to the hinterland west of the Allegheny Mountains.

Mills spent the following decade in South Carolina, serving first as acting commissioner of the Board of Public Works, from 1820 to 1822, and then as superintendent of public buildings, from 1822 to 1824. In these positions he participated in the design and construction of seventeen public buildings. He also worked on plans for canals connecting Charleston and Columbia and canals connecting the Savannah and Broad rivers, planned and published the route of canals to join the navigable waters of South Carolina with those of the Mississippi basin, participated in a proposal to dredge the Charleston harbor, and planned a municipal water system for that city. He compiled and published his *Atlas of the State of South Carolina* (1825), as well as a companion volume, *The Statistics of South Carolina* (1826). He also published a plan for a railroad between Washington, D.C., and New Orleans and prepared estimates for the South Carolina Railroad and Canal Company. During this period he wrote an essay on the development of a rotary steam engine and pamphlets on the drainage and reclamation of swampland throughout the state.

As support for internal improvements waned in South Carolina, he applied unsuccessfully for positions as principal engineer of Virginia and as an engineer with the federal Board of Internal Improvement.[11] Settling in Washington, D.C., in 1830, he continued to work as an engineer during the last two decades of his career; these final projects included surveys for a canal along the Susquehanna River, plans for the Washington Canal, and proposals for the Potomac River Bridge and an aqueduct bridge for the Alexandria canal. He also worked on improved water, heating, and lighting systems for the U.S. Capitol and continued to write about railroads. He published an essay concerning a telegraph route to the Pacific and compiled and published *The American Pharos* (1832), a guide to American lighthouses and aids to navigation, as well as several guides to the federal buildings in the capital city.

Except for rare responses to landscape in the *Statistics* and brief passages of sentiment in domestic correspondence, Mills's writing is relentlessly didactic. His books and essays address situations in which, he believes, education will promote con-structive public policy. The typical exposition consists of the division or classification of the subject into discrete units and, whenever possible, the presentation of these by the quantification of salient characteristics. In speaking of the reclamation of South Carolina swampland by a system of canals, for example, he suggests that the swamps bordering the Congaree, Wateree, and Pee Dee rivers average 4 miles in width; therefore, swampland adjacent to 25 miles of one side of these rivers would contain 100 square miles, or 6,400 acres. On average, a canal 33 miles long adjacent to the river bank would be required to drain 25 miles of swamp, and he computes that 3,484,800 cubic yards of earth must be moved to create the excavation and embankment for such a canal. He assumes that "the common daily task of the slave, in excavating earth or ditching, is equal to 500 cubic feet—nearly equivalent to 19 cubic yards," at a cost of "four or five cents per yard"; additional costs incurred by making the work massive enough to ensure its permanence would make the total cost per cubic yard twelve and one-half cents, or $13,200 per mile, bringing the total cost to $435,600, or "a little under 7 dollars" per acre. This penchant for enumeration is evident in his precise description of the composition and depth—335 feet, 6 inches—of thirty-eight strata encountered in boring for water in Charleston and in his list of 230 native plants, their common and scientific names, their uses and habits of growth.[12] The style and substance of his writing as well as his extensive practice as an engineer help explain the ideogramatic character of his architectural drawings.

BIOGRAPHICAL WRITINGS

Incomplete autobiographical essays in Mills's hand corroborate the account of his education that appears in *The Rise of the Arts of Design in the United States* (1834).[13] Similarities of fact, phrase, and sequence suggest that Mills composed the untitled manuscript, now in the collection of the South Carolina Historical Society, as a draft for a sketch subsequently submitted to William Dunlap.[14] According to the published account (but not noted in the surviving manuscripts), Mills attended the College of Charleston. All accounts state that his architectural training began in 1800, when he "was sent" to Washington "by his father" and "placed" in the office of James Hoban as a pupil or apprentice.[15]

Following the inauguration of Thomas Jefferson in 1801, Mills was befriended by the president and "given free access to his library." "About this period," the South Carolina manuscript says, "the

Author took the opportunity of Visiting the Eastern States, with the view to examine the progress and improvement there in Architecture and the fine Arts. He made drawings of all the principal buildings then erected, and, by means of letters, given to him by President Jefferson, he had access everywhere.'' Dunlap sums up the tour saying that Mills "made a professional visit to all the principal cities and towns in the United States.'' For this trip an introduction from Thomas Jefferson to Charles Bulfinch, dated July 1, 1802, survives, as does one written by Jedidiah Morse, the geographer, dated October 18, 1802; the latter is addressed to seventeen ministers, lawyers, and academicians in Norwich, New Haven, Hartford, and Middletown, Connecticut; Newport and Providence, Rhode Island; Salem and Newburyport, Massachusetts; Exeter, New Hampshire; and Portland, Maine.[16]

Another parallel between the manuscript and the published text concerns the basis of Mills's relationship with Thomas Jefferson. The South Carolina draft notes that "Mr Jefferson was peculiarly partial to Architecture, and possessed a good taste in this branch of the fine Arts. He appeared highly pleased, that an *American* Youth had engaged in the Study of this Science, and gave the Author every encouragement to persevere.'' The published text reads: "Mr. Jefferson was a great admirer of architecture, and was highly pleased to find an American directing his attention to the acquisition of this useful branch of science with a view to pursue it as a profession, and therefore gave Mr. Mills every encouragement to persevere.'' Both sources note that Jefferson's patronage included access to his library and the opportunity to "make . . . the general plan'' of Monticello; both also state that Jefferson introduced Mills to Latrobe and that Mills entered Latrobe's office as a student. Both narratives also cite the planning of the Chesapeake and Delaware Canal as Mills's first work for and with Latrobe.[17]

Unfortunately, beyond Dunlap's account and Mills's fragmentary sketches, little is known about his adolescence and early education. His father, William Mills (d. 1802), a tailor by trade, immigrated from Scotland around 1770 and established himself among Charleston's petite bourgeoise; he owned slaves and rental property and speculated on a modest scale in outlying farmland.[18] Mills's mother, Ann Taylor Mills, counted a South Carolina landgrave and governor among her ancestors, connections that assured a measure of gentility in a community conscious of pedigree.[19] Their social standing was threatened by the Revolution, for William Mills was a loyalist (albeit a rather inactive one); he signed two petitions welcoming the English but avoided prosecution after the war.[20]

When the war was over, Robert's older brothers, Henry and Thomas, were sent to Scotland, presumably to study, and Thomas returned with a copy of *The Modern Builder's Assistant*, by William and John Halfpenny, Robert Morris, and T. Lightoler. On the frontise page of this volume is this inscription: "To Thomas Mills from Robert his Uncle in London November 14th 1789 pr Mr James Spald.'' This book is the earliest evidence of an architectural interest in the family.[21]

Unlike his brothers, Robert did not go abroad, and the traditional view is that he attended the College of Charleston and may have participated in the "evening school, for the instruction of young men in Architecture'' advertised by James Hoban.[22] Hoban, however, left for Washington, D.C., when Robert Mills was only eleven years old. Given the competence of Mills's early drawings, it is probable that he received instruction similar to that offered by Hoban. Architectural lessons were available during his adolescence in Charleston. Thomas Walker, a stonecutter and mason from Edinburgh, "opened an evening school for teaching the rules of Architecture, from seven to nine in the evening (four nights in the week),'' and M. Depresseville "continues to keep his Drawing School, in different Parts of Landscapes, with Pencil or Washed, teaches Architecture, and to draw with method; also the necessary acknowledgments for the Plans.''[23] Blakeleay White's 1795 advertisement for instruction in the "principals of Modern Architecture, with drawing and designing, not only theoretically but practically'' is illuminating. He invites the public to inspect a "compleat frame of a double two story house in minature,'' at a scale of one inch to the foot, executed by a fourteen-year-old student. Teaching arithmetic, geometry, and drafting, as well as practical joinery, "from the hours of 6 to 9 in the Evening, five evenings in the Week,'' White promised to enable "almost any young man'' in one year to become "a compleat architect or master builder.''[24] A similar curriculum was advertised in 1795 by Thomas Mills, Robert's brother. At his Charleston Academy he offered instruction in every "branch of useful and polite literature,'' French, Latin, Greek, geometry, trigonometry, and "the principles of modern architecture, with drawing and designing.'' In his announcement Thomas Mills notes that he has hired an "ingenious teacher'' of architectural principles and that models, as well as "theoretical illustrations,'' will be employed:

At the commencement of this very useful undertaking the complete frame of a double three story house, in minature, will be raised, and lectures given explanatory of the subject by way of exhibiting to the friends of the young gentlemen a specimen of the manner in which this business will be conducted: by this method it will be evident, that a person may soon become a complete architect or masterbuilder. . . .''[25]

ARCHITECTURAL

DRAFTING

Robert Mills clearly had the opportunity to begin his architectural education close to home. As advertised, these lessons exposed the student to architectural pattern books, stressed a basic understanding of the classical orders, and required the drafting of plans and elevations. Thomas Walker, James Hoban, or Blakeleay White would have owned or had access to books such as James Gibbes's *Book of Architecture* (1728)—Hoban's elevations of the White House are based on plates from this volume—which students examined with care. Drafting implements included the compass and divider, the joint of which "must be firm, so that they will not easily be opened or twist" and "the points of them be not so sharp as to ordinarily peck the paper," a brass pen and a quill pen "which must not be too far split, for fear of too hastily shedding the ink."[26]

Students were instructed in the use of the square, india ink, a ruler with one square edge and one raked or angled edge, the latter for use with ink, and a pointed instrument to impress or score lines in the paper. The compass was used to pick up measurements, and lines were laid down in pencil; these might be pressed lightly into the paper with the scorer to control the flow of ink. Using ink was intimidating, for blotches were irremediable. After the ink dried, the draftsman or student began to develop an illusion of solidity by introducing translucent tonal washes to create areas of shade and shadow; these were followed by tinted washes, also of translucent watercolor, which gave life and color to the drawing. By tradition a salmon pink repre-

sented brickwork; ochres were used for timber framing, and blue-gray was used for stone or stucco. Voids were generally rendered in a dark gray or black. Perspectival devices, if any, were limited to the tentative use of cast shadow; small marionette-like figures were sometimes placed in the foreground to indicate scale.

These techniques, which Mills employed throughout his career, were part of the conservative eighteenth-century English tradition in vogue in Charleston during his adolescence. The earliest architectural drawings to survive in South Carolina —plans and elevations of the Exchange and Customs House (1766), designed by William Rigby Naylor (d. 1773) and based on a town hall (plates 48 and 49) in Isaac Ware's *Complete Body of Architecture* (1756)—contain the drafting methods and pictorial conventions that characterize much of Mills's work (figs. 1.1, 1.2).[27] As a graphic artist Mills was not adventurous; he consistently employed the order, predictability, and security of orthographic plans, sections, and elevations and rarely embellished his presentations with perspective or those incidents of weather and setting that often give an evocative quality to the drawings of Latrobe, Strickland, or Alexander J. Davis.

The limitations of Mills's draftsmanship reflect the nature of his talent rather than a lack of opportunity, for he spent five years with Latrobe, the greatest architectural draftsman of his day in America. Latrobe achieved illusion and unity of effect in sketches and finished drawings through the effective use of flora, fauna, genre, and landscape in the tradition of the English topographical watercolor drawing. Mills, with very few exceptions, eschewed these subjects and techniques.[28] His sketches in diaries and correspondence convey information

Figure 1.1
"A Building for a Town Hall," Isaac Ware. (Plate 49, A Complete Body of Architecture, *1768)*

rather than emotion; they inform rather than delight or seduce the viewer. The majority of his surviving sketches depict schematic plans for monuments and buildings or illustrate technical subjects (furnaces, railways, stairways, hoisting apparatuses, and formulas for determining the thickness of bridge piers and the radii of ionic volutes). These are notational drawings; they were intended solely as aids to memory and do not suggest that Mills aspired to the visual appeal and diversity of the subject matter found in the Latrobe sketchbooks.

A similar observation may be made concerning Mills's more polished drawings, for although he recognized the evocative potential of presentation drawings incorporating perspective and landscape, he rarely attempted such compositions; instead, he stayed within what he perceived to be the limits of his talent. He was satisfied as a draftsman to remain within the graphic conventions found in Owen Biddle's *Young Carpenter's Assistant* (1805), the first American handbook to devote attention specifically to drafting materials and techniques. Biddle's illustrations reflected the "strictly geometrical presentation of plans, sections, and elevations"

characteristic of early eighteenth-century English Palladian publications.[29] The meticulous clarity of Mills's drawings reflects the hatched engravings of books of this genre, illustrations that often incorporate the illusion of cast shadow and gradations of shade and reflected light. Mills, like a number of his contemporaries—Alexander Parris, John Melchior Ogden (1791–1882), and Hugh Smith (1782–1826)—maintained these conventions by consistently presenting images at right angles to the picture plane, juxtaposing plans and elevations, and omitting an environmental context or setting.

This conservatism is clearly at odds with the flexibility and capacity for growth evident in the stylistic and typological eclecticism of Mills's completed works. Perhaps precisely because he rarely seems to have viewed drawing as an end in itself, he never developed a facility for picturesque presentation, and his draftsmanship was cited as a contributing factor in the termination of his federal employment. In 1853, recommending against hiring him, Montgomery C. Meigs (1816–92), engineer of the U.S. Capitol, wrote Jefferson Davis, then secretary of war, that "as a draftsman Mr. Mills was tried in the Engineers office & not found qualified."[30]

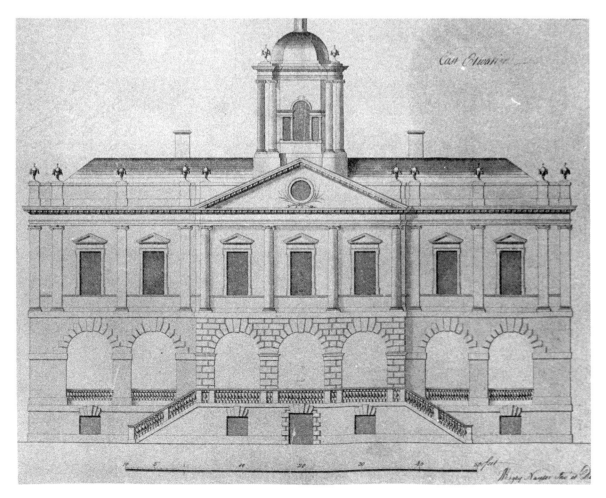

Figure 1.2
East elevation, Exchange
and Customs House
(1776), Charleston, South
Carolina, William Rigby
Naylor, 1766. (South
Carolina Department of
Archives and History)

MILLS'S FIRST

COMPETITION AND

COMPOSITE DRAWINGS

The earliest known signed and dated plans and elevations by Robert Mills were executed for the South Carolina College competition in 1802.[31] The drawings present front, rear, and end elevations; plans of the first and second floors; a section, front to rear, through the center of the proposed building; and a detailed cornice profile (figs. 1.3, 1.4). His submission brought him $150, half the prize, and his first architectural income; the remainder was awarded to Hugh Smith, an amateur and the only other South Carolinian known to have entered this competition. Mills's plan was *retardataire*, however, and had little influence on the buildings ultimately erected. It lacked rooms *en suite*, made no provision for storage or plumbing, and did little to address criteria stipulated by the trustees in their advertisement—that the plans should include apartments and offices for the faculty, classrooms, and student dormitories. Moreover, the massing was conservative: The plan called for a bilaterally symmetrical composition with a projecting, octagonal central block surmounted by a cupola and flanked by wings that terminated in projecting pavilions. Except for the Georgian cupola, the articulation was largely Adamesque and consisted of balustrades, Palladian windows, and fanlights.

The most notable aspect of this proposal was an open arcade at the base of the rear facade, which provided covered access to each of the ground-floor classrooms. At the time nothing of this sort existed in American academic architecture. Mills was familiar with the arcades of the English town and market halls, and, through prints, he was no doubt aware of arcaded academic quadrangles such as Sir Christopher Wren's Trinity College Library (1676–84), Cambridge, England. It is possible that he discussed the competition with Jefferson, for among Jefferson's papers was a proposal dated 1771–72 for an arcaded quadrangle at the College of William and Mary, Williamsburg, Virginia. Jefferson would use covered passages at the University of Virginia, in Charlottesville, and their appearance in the South Carolina College proposal is, at the very least, an indication of Mills's willingness to look beyond local precedent.

Design competitions were a major conduit for the transmission of ideas during the first quarter of the nineteenth century; they diminished the influence of local amateurs and builder-architects and fostered a growing recognition of the professional architect.[32] Coincidentally, regional and national competitions provided an incentive for attractive

and meaningful presentation drawings. The South Carolina College competition was advertised nationally, and surviving drawings present a cross section of architectural practice and draftsmanship as Mills began his career. Peter Banner (1794–c. 1828), "Architect and builder from London," sent two plans and elevations of the chapel and dormitories he was then working on at Yale; he also sent plans and elevations of the five buildings that he proposed for South Carolina (fig. 1.5). A rudimentary plan was submitted by Benjamin Silliman (1779–1864), a distinguished professor of chemistry and natural history at Yale. Hugh Smith submitted at least one elevation that survives. Other entries for which no drawings are known came from Asa Messer (1769–1836), "of Providence," a mathematician and third president of Brown University; S. Stanhope Smith (1750–1819), "President of the College of New Jersey"; and Edward Magrath, active as a builder-architect in Charleston between 1800 and 1810, and his partner, Joseph Nicholson, both of whom appear as carpenters in the 1803 city directories.

The plan by Benjamin Silliman is little more than a chart indicating the configuration and use of each room. It is conceived as a supporting element for the accompanying text rather than as an image in its own right. Its lines are of a uniform thickness; it presents neither structural nor decorative detail; it has no scale, elevation, or section—nothing to evoke a mental image of the proposed building. The drawings by Peter Banner, the builder-architect, rely less on labels and captions. Elevations accompany his plans, a scale specifies relative dimensions, bearing walls are boldly drawn, partitions are delicate, and an intelligible convention is used to depict windowsills, fireplaces, staircases, pews, and porches. But all of this information is conveyed without the use of shadow, texture, perspective, or material reference that would support the illusion of solidity; consequently, Banner's drawings remain two-dimensional, as lifeless as pressed flowers. The elevation by Hugh Smith has survived without supporting documents. Judged in isolation it is a more sophisticated rendering than those by Silliman and Banner, for he employs a raking light to emphasize projecting and receding elements and cast shadows and gradations of shade and reflected light to create an illusion of plasticity. But his failure to use perspective, create a setting, or juxtapose interior references limits one's ability to visualize the building in its entirety.

As drawings, those by Robert Mills are the most complex in conception and execution. Presenting a contiguous plan and elevation in the one drawing and grouping a transverse section, plan, two elevations, and a cornice profile in the other, he allows one to examine the building from different points

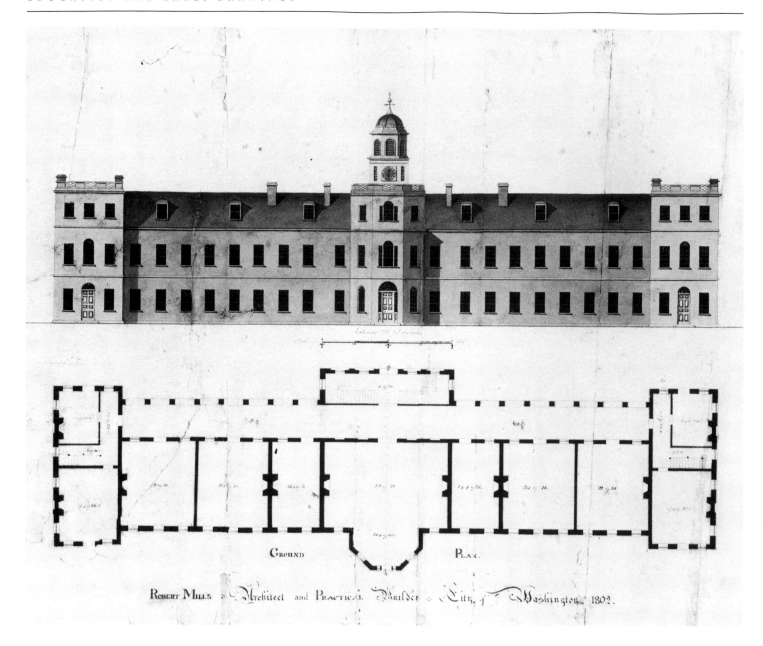

of view, as if one were turning and disassembling a model. The vertical alignment of a related plan and elevation on a single page was part of the pattern book tradition, but the fusion of five images into a meaningful whole was unusual in America in 1802 and may reflect Mills's awareness of the work of Latrobe, who often juxtaposed images within a single field. Latrobe's drawings for the proposed naval drydock, "No. I Section of Locks, Plan of Locks," "No. II" (plan, sections, and elevations of the drydock), and the Potomac Canal extension drawing ("No. I"), all executed in December 1802, exemplify this technique applied to projects with which Mills was familiar.[33]

In July or August 1803 Mills entered Latrobe's office and remained as a pupil and assistant for five years.[34] In composing drawings, Mills, like Latrobe, continued to use disparate views of the same object. In Mills's hands this composite method con-

veyed information but rarely produced a harmonious whole, for unlike Latrobe, Mills did not intentionally seek a visual unity through the manipulation of value, scale, and negative space. The various elements of Latrobe's composite drawings often coalesce into an image that assumes a life of its own independent of the referenced object. By contrast, Mills's drawings lack an effective organizing principle and therefore remain notational. The composite South Carolina College drawing exemplifies this shortcoming. It has no predictable baseline, it lacks scale, and the center of the composition is a void. Were it not for the fact that later drawings are equally discordant, this awkwardness might be dismissed as a sign of inexperience. Mills's continued use of composite imagery and disregard for compositional unity suggest that he concentrated on content and was somewhat insensitive to the drawings' aesthetic impact.

Figure 1.3
Principal elevation and plan, South Carolina College, 1802.
(Private collection)

Opposite: Figure 1.4
Rear elevation, second-floor plan, end elevation, transverse section, and cornice profile, South Carolina College, 1802.
(South Carolina Department of Archives and History)

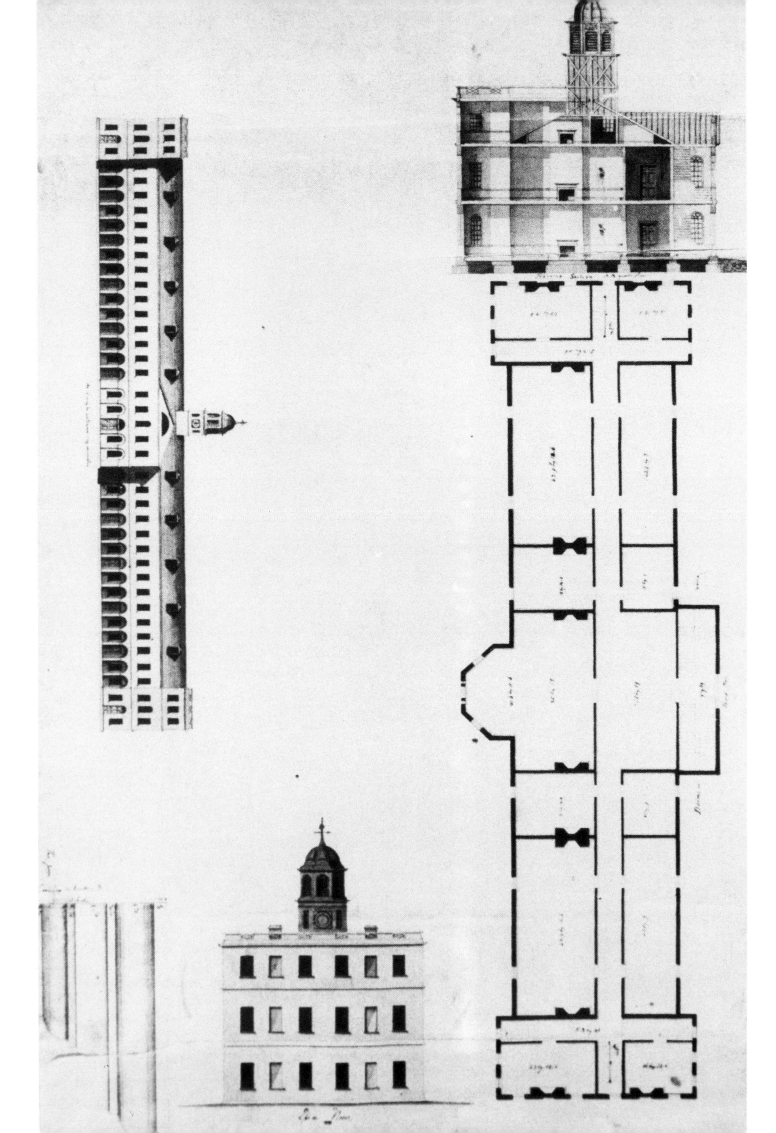

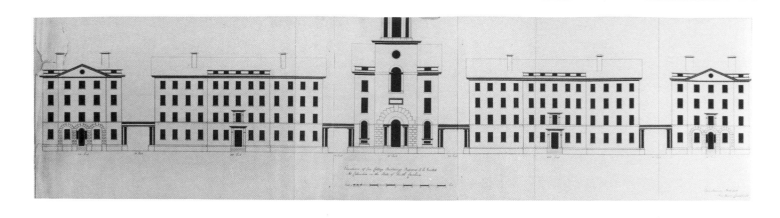

*Above: Figure 1.5
Principal elevation and
plan, South Carolina
College, Peter Banner,
1802. (South Carolina
Department of Archives
and History)*

*Below: Figure 1.6
West elevation,
Monticello (1768–1809,
Thomas Jefferson),
Charlottesville, Virginia, 1803.
(Massachusetts Historical
Society)*

Drawings "In Prospect"

From the outset Mills adopted an orthographic, multiview technique and presented both plans and elevations parallel to the picture plane. The principal appeal of this convention is that aspects of objects parallel to the picture plane are depicted in their actual shape; it is the most factual, or literal, of graphic conventions. In his early drawings when forced to present a diagonally receding plane, as in the elevation of the projecting central pavilion of the South Carolina College (see fig. 1.3) or the elevation of Monticello (fig. 1.6), Mills establishes apparent diminution in width by a vertical alignment with the plan, but he does not adjust the apparent height with illusionistic diagonal projections; consequently, belt courses, sills, lintels, and muntins remain solidly horizontal. His failure to adopt the axonometric and perspective techniques available to him in Latrobe's office provides an early indication that his sensibility was quite different from that of his mentor and his fellow student William Strickland. Both Latrobe and Strickland found the picturesque congenial and adopted compositional devices that resulted in vistas framed by foreground detail in the manner of Claude Lorrain.[35] They accepted the illusion inherent in perspective and used it in presentation drawings. Mills, on the other hand, rarely did so. He apparently preferred to hire a draftsman whenever he needed a drawing "in prospect," as is evident in the early published illustrations of his work.[36]

Mills appears to have been the first American architect to make a practice of using prints as a promotional device, and he usually hired an accomplished draftsman to produce drawings intended for public consumption. An early example is the 1812 engraving of the Monumental Church (1812–17), Richmond, Virginia, which he advertised as "a handsome picture, capable of ornamenting any room," offering "to bereaved relatives and friends an opportunity of possessing some domestic memento of the respect and sympathy mani-

Figure 1.7
Design proposal by Robert Mills for the Monumental Church, Richmond, Virginia, William Strickland (del.), 1812. (Virginia Historical Society)

*Opposite: Figure 1.8
"Elevation of the Principle
[sic] Fronts," Washington
Monument (1813–42),
Baltimore, Maryland,
1814. (Maryland
Historical Society)*

fested by a generous public for the loss of so much worth, talent, and beauty" (fig. 1.7).[37] As drawn by William Strickland, the image is an effective demonstration of two-point, oblique projection; it presents the building convincingly through the use of two axes at equal angles to the picture plane; a consistent shadow pattern enhances the illusion, and a bit of landscape—two couples, trees, a distant building, and dramatic sky—provides an evocative setting.

With few exceptions, Mills never attempted such a composition. When he desired a perspective of the Baltimore Washington Monument, for example, he turned to Hugh Bridport of Philadelphia; on the same trip he left drawings of the "B. Church [First Baptist Church (1816–18), Baltimore] with Wm Strickland to make a perspective." Mills may also have collaborated with George Strickland in the publication of the familiar image of Washington Hall (1814–16), Philadelphia.[38] Mills obviously recognized the aesthetic authority and consequent utility of such renderings, for in writing to the board of managers of the Baltimore Washington Monument he observed that his competition drawings were "projected upon geometrical principals, as

tal he wrote that monuments "isolated, or in the open air, should be *towering*," an attribute eminently suited to perspectival presentation.

Furthermore, as presentation or competition drawings, these elevations were executed expressly to elicit the client's interest. But here the viewpoint rises and remains perpendicular to the picture plane. As a result, the column appears static; it fails to soar away from the earthbound viewer. Mills admitted that his elevations, being without perspective, fell short in "exciting Interest," and his awareness of this shortcoming is evidenced by the fact that he submitted "a perspective view" shortly before the board was to make its selection.[40]

On at least one occasion he created his own "picturesque view" for publication. In 1827 J. Hill of Philadelphia published an engraving based on Mills's drawing of the Bethesda Presbyterian Church (1821–23) and the DeKalb Monument (1824–27), in Camden, South Carolina (fig. 1.9). The print features two of Mills's works and appeals to religious and patriotic sentiments. It also appeared at a time when he was actively seeking employment, for his position as superintendent of public buildings in South Carolina had been abolished in December 1823, and for the remainder of the decade much of his effort focused on publication as a means of supporting his family. Unable to procure the services of a Bridport or Strickland in the provincial village of Camden, he produced a perspective for the printer, and it is probable that some of the inconsistencies in this drawing are attributable to his tentative grasp of perspective.

*Figure 1.9
DeKalb Monument
(1824–27) and Bethesda
Presbyterian Church
(1821–23), Camden, South
Carolina, 1827. (South
Carolina Art Association)*

being best calculated to convey a correct view of the proportions and character of the mass," that this "mode of exhibiting a building" was not as exciting as a perspective rendering, and that he would send along a "picturesque view" if the "general principals meet your approbation."[39]

In the competition elevations the illusion of depth is grounded in the landscape. A diagonal projection is established by the edges of the boulevard and flanking trees. These rays converge on a focal point that coincides with the center of the radius of the triumphal arch, and this congruence visually anchors the monument within the composition. But within the monument itself, beyond the rudimentary use of cast shadow, there is little attempt to create an evocative illusion (fig. 1.8). This is somewhat surprising, for in his letter of transmit-

Here, in order to produce an angular, two-point perspective, Mills turned the principal subjects so that horizontal lines are at equal angles to the picture plane; the couple in the foreground establish the scale, and their heads coincide with the horizon line (fig. 1.9, A, A'). In checking the projection of the nave, it becomes apparent that he relied on one or more preliminary drawings to assure the convergence of diagonals at the lefthand vanishing point (B, B', C, C') and to establish the relative placement of things seen and unseen (E, E' and F, F'). But the steeple is not aligned on its proper vertical axis on the rear facade; it is shifted forward and upward in order to display its base above the roof line. Artistic license, however, cannot explain the failure of the righthand diagonals to converge upon a common point. Equally troubling is the break in B, B' and the failure of the portico steps to rise toward the righthand vanishing point. In short, although an angular, two-point perspective is intended, it is awkwardly executed.

St Paul's Church N. York

THE DRAWING

OF IDEAS

The early drawings and his reliance on others suggest that Mills did not consider himself a gifted draftsman. Latrobe, who knew him well, remarked that he "possesses that valuable substitute for genius—laborious precision—in a very high degree, and is therefore very useful to me, though his professional education has been hitherto much misdirected."[41] Precision is a hallmark of the early drawings, reflecting the experience denigrated by Latrobe. The elevations of St. Paul's Church, New York, and the Bank of Pennsylvania, Philadelphia, for example, apparently resulted from Mills's architectural tour during June and July 1803, only months before he joined Latrobe, and both present a palpable tension in the control of ink and wash

(figs. 1.10, 1.11). Cast shadows fail to break rationally across receding and projecting planes, but this flaw is a minor one. The primary impression is of crisp detail, distinctly modulated value contrasts, and linear clarity. These same stylistic characteristics dominate drawings done for Thomas Jefferson in 1802 or 1803, when, according to William Dunlap, "Mr. Mills resumed his studies, being furnished from Mr. Jefferson's library with such architectural works as he had (principally Palladio's)."[42] A copy of *I Quattro Libri dell' Architettura* was close at hand as Mills worked on the Rotunda House elevations and sections, for Jefferson owned the Leoni edition, published in London in 1715 (figs. 1.12, 1.13). Beneath the "Longitudinal Section" Mills signed "Thos. Jefferson Archt." and "Robt. Mills Del." to denote a collaboration that Fiske Kimball suggests was a study for the alteration of Shadwell.[43]

Opposite: Figure 1.10 Principal elevation, Saint Paul's Chapel (1766, Thomas McBean), c. 1803. (Thomas Jefferson Foundation)

Figure 1.11 Principal elevation, Bank of Pennsylvania (1798–1800, Benjamin Henry Latrobe), c. 1803. (Thomas Jefferson Foundation)

Bank of Pennsylvania

The Delorme Dome

These drawings exhibit the components of this phase of Mills's training: the legacy of the pattern books, the critical filter of Jefferson's intellect, and diligent execution. The elevation and longitudinal section display a confident delineation of minute detail and a penchant for stark value contrast; here the graphic conventions of shadow, shade, and reflected light are effectively demonstrated. On the curved interior surfaces of the rotunda, cupola, and cove (beneath the balcony), the shade gradually gathers intensity as the angle of tangency between the light and the wall surface increases; conversely, abrupt planes of shadow and specifically limited areas of shade pictorially define the architectonic composition of planar surfaces.

In the tradition of Palladio, Mills accentuates structural members—joists, partitions, and rafters —as a means of emphasizing, or framing, enclosed volumes. Analyzing this drawing, Douglas Harnsberger has shown that its minute details are meaningful, for the sequence of dots within the ribs of the dome and cove of the exterior walls represents a nailing schedule, a laminating technique found in Jefferson's copy of *Invention pur batir les couvertures courbes*, by Philibert Delorme (c. 1510– 70). Jefferson had used the Delorme system at Monticello. The appearance of Delorme fastenings in Mills's drawing reflects contact with Jefferson and is an early indication of his exposure to and interest in structural systems beyond the local vernacular.[44]

Shortly after joining Latrobe, Mills specified Delorme ribs in proposals for three South Carolina churches. The correspondence concerning his unrealized 1803 plans for the extension of St. Michael's Church, Charleston, the specifications of about 1804 for an "Episcopal Church to be erected on Johns Island," near Charleston, and his description of the dome of the Circular Congregational Church (1804–6), Charleston, all contain references to laminated ribs.[45] The principal advantage of this system was that it permitted the creation of large, open spans using short, easily managed lengths of timber. Mills also employed the Delorme system in Philadelphia at the Sansom Street Baptist Church (1811–12) and the First Unitarian (Octagon) Church (1812–13), in Richmond at the Monumental Church, the only extant example by Mills, and in Baltimore at the First Baptist Church (1816–18). These were "Auditorium Churches," which, as a building type, were the most notable achievement of his early career.

Only two of Mills's working drawings have survived, and one of these depicts the framing and sheathing of the dome of the Sansom Street Church (fig. 1.14). First and foremost, this drawing was intended to be intelligible: ribs, purlins, and framing of the monitor are all clearly legible. Having divided the sheet into quadrants and established relationships by juxtaposition, he presented four points of view concisely and simultaneously. The shadow and shape of the "principal ribs" in the section are the only indication that he was tempted by the spherical form to indulge in perspective illusion. The fusion of the quadrants into an imagined form must take place in the viewer's mind, and the impact of the drawing is primarily cerebral rather than sensual.

These characteristics are anticipated and appropriate in a working drawing; thus, it is not surprising that the drawing of the Sansom Street dome is comparable to plate 26, the illustration of the Delorme system, in *Young Carpenter's Assistant* (fig. 1.15). Mills's use of the dome antedates Biddle's publication, but the description of this technique in a popular handbook may have encouraged its adoption at Davidge Hall (1812), University of Maryland, by Robert Cary Long, Sr. (1770–1833), a Baltimore carpenter-builder, and by Alexander Parris at the Quincy Market (1823–26) in Boston. Maximilian Godefroy, who used a Delorme dome at the Unitarian Church (1817) in Baltimore and possibly at the city hall (1816) in Richmond, may have been familiar with Delorme's *Inventions* and the Halle au Bles, which, with its dramatic skylights, had sparked Jefferson's interest in promoting this system in America. Mills himself did not use the Delorme dome again after 1816, for it was flammable, and he had become increasingly concerned with fireproof construction.

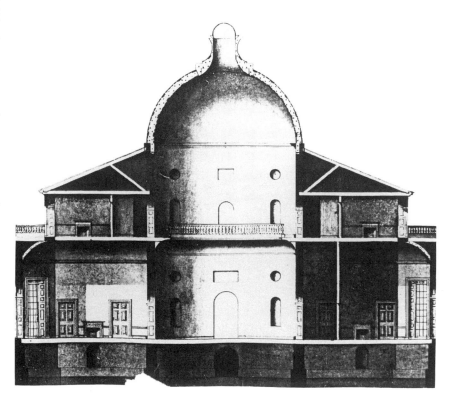

*Figure 1.12
Longitudinal section,
Rotunda House (Thomas
Jefferson), c. 1803.
(University of Virginia)*

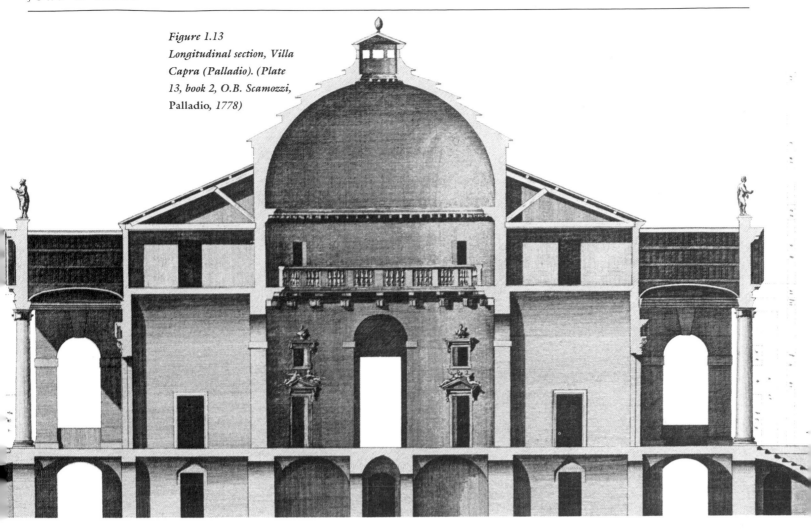

Figure 1.13
Longitudinal section, Villa
Capra (Palladio). (Plate
13, book 2, O.B. Scamozzi,
Palladio, 1778)

Fireproof Vaulted Masonry

Robert Mills took pride in his reputation for fire-proof construction. In institutional buildings throughout his career he employed barrel-vaulted corridors flanked by ranges of groin-vaulted rooms. The vertical load of the typical plan was conveyed to piers protruding into each corner of the rooms. Lateral thrust was countered by the opposing pressure of adjacent arches, by the use of hydraulic cement—which he believed made a single unit of each vault, thereby "relieving the lateral, and increasing the perpendicular press of the arches"—and, infrequently, by the use of metal tie rods in tension set into the masonry. Porticoes and antae played a secondary role in neutralizing lateral thrust. Mills maintained that exterior buttressing was unnecessary, that his integrated system of interior vaults served as relieving arches and permitted a reduction in the thickness of the walls.[46]

In his July 4, 1836, application to Andrew Jackson for appointment as "architect to the public buildings," he made "reference particularly" to his work "of a fire-proof character" and cited as his first experience the Bank of Philadelphia (1807–8). Throughout the construction of this Gothic Revival, vaulted bank, he had served as clerk of the works for Latrobe. Earlier, in 1805, as Latrobe's amanuensis he had conveyed instructions to John Lenth-

all, clerk of the works, during construction of the fireproof Treasury offices adjacent to the White House.[47] Late in his career, in rebuttal to the criticisms of Thomas U. Walter (1804–87) and Alexander Parris, Mills pointed to the stability of masonry vaulted buildings in South Carolina, Maryland, Connecticut, and Massachusetts, as well as to calculations of thrust by J. Rondelet and Hutton.[48]

Despite the importance of this aspect of his work, surviving drawings contain little evidence of his vaulting systems. A handful of longitudinal sections—of the Burlington County Jail (1808–10), Mount Holly, New Jersey; the powder magazine, Baltimore; and the Customs House (1833–35), New London, Connecticut—depict the vaulting with which, at great expense, he replaced the vernacular wood post and beam. Dashed lines on plans occasionally indicate groined vaulting, as in the plans for the South Carolina Asylum (1822–28) and South Caroliniana Library (1836–40), both in Columbia, South Carolina, and a jail (1839–41) and the U.S. Post Office (1839–42), both in Washington, D.C. However, no graphic evidence records his techniques for erecting and removing centering, his analysis of thrusts, or professional difficulties stemming from "the fact that these buildings are to be constructed upon an entire new plan which [only] a few of our mechanics are familiar with."[49]

Overleaf: Figure 1.14
Elevations, plans, and
sections of the framing
and exterior of the dome,
Sansom Street Baptist
Church (1811–12),
c. 1811. (American
Baptist Historical Society)

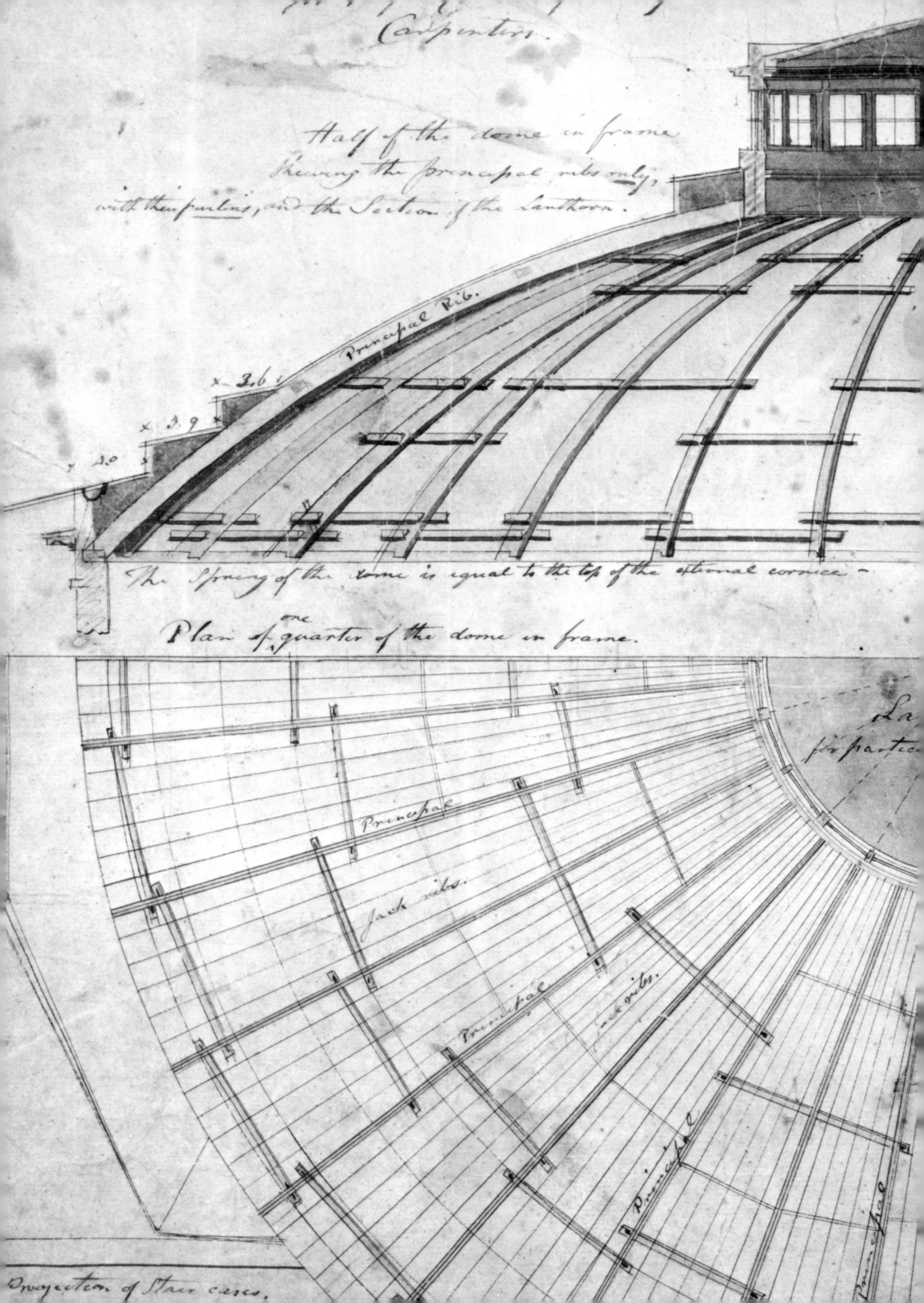

Half of the dome in frame
shewing the principal ribs only,
with their purlins, and the Section of the lanthorn.

Principal Rib.

x   3.6

x   3.9

x   3.0

The Spring of the dome is equal to the top of the external cornice —

Plan of one quarter of the dome in frame.

Principal

Jack ribs.

Principal

jack ribs.

La
for particu

Principal

Principal

Projection of Stair cases.

Half of the dome when
finished.

x 1/3 x

x ?? x

x 2.0 x

Plan of one quarter of the dome when finished.

ll.

tails No. 2.

3.0

3

Wall carried up ??

Acoustics

As the designer of public buildings, Mills often confronted the architectural implications of acoustics. His understanding of the nature of sound was based on Latrobe's writings and was the determining factor in his use of the Delorme dome and the development of the auditorium churches. Except for the working drawing of the Sansom Street Church dome, there are no plans by Mills of the auditorium churches, but six drawings for the John's Island proposal and seven for the St. Michael's extension do survive. These provide a measure of his draftsmanship as his education drew to a close and also reflect in part his concrete expression of acoustical theory (figs. 1.16, 1.17).

Chronologies can be established for the work on the Circular Church and St. Michael's, but the date of the John's Island proposal is a matter of conjecture. Its calligraphy is comparable to the signed and dated drawings of 1802–3, and an early date is suggested by the awkward admixture of federal and neoclassical design elements. In a reference that may encompass the John's Island plans, Latrobe wrote to Louis DeMun on November 12, 1805, that "Mills goes to Charleston to visit his churches & with a chance of remaining there."[50] All these plans were executed after he joined Latrobe, for in writing to the vestry of St. Michael's on October 15, 1804, Mills paraphrased an unpublished manuscript on acoustics by Latrobe, and the architectural implications of Latrobe's theory can be traced in each of the South Carolina proposals.[51]

Proposing to enlarge St. Michael's (1752–61) by adding a bay to the eastern end of the church, Mills attempted to replicate the existing elevations, but his proposal for the interior was radical and caused the building committee to seek other advice. Mills suggested moving the pulpit, lectern, and altar close against the wall of the new apse, thus gaining floor area for additional pews. He also reckoned that the concave ceiling of the new apse would function as an enlarged sounding board, deflecting the speaker's voice to all areas of the interior. Mills explained this unorthodox arrangement by saying that "the present situation of the pulpit is evidently very awkward. It is proposed to place it opposite the center aisle and in the altar niche. The advantage of this is that the speaker will not have his back to any of the congregation. . . . The crown of the niche it is placed in . . . is the receiver and augmenter of sound, as from its form it immediately disperses it to the cove which conveys it to the farthest end of the church."[52] This commitment to acoustics also prompted his startling proposal to remove the existing flat ceiling above the nave and replace it with a barrel vault that would be a continuation of the curve of the apse. This change necessitated cutting the girders, or cross ties, that

Figure 1.15
"Dome of Boards and Plank," Owen Biddle. *(Plate 26, Young Carpenter's Assistant, 1805)*

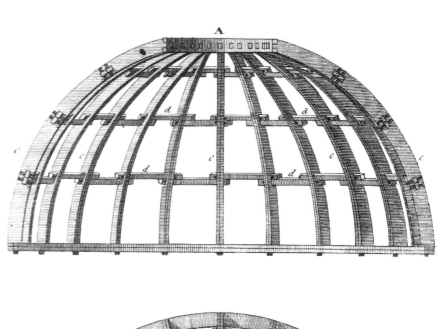

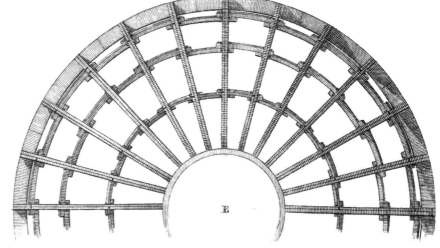

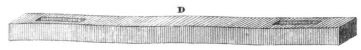

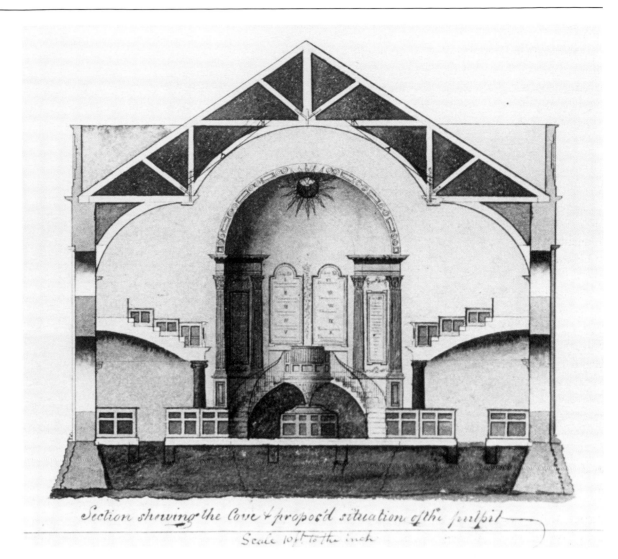

Figure 1.16
"Section showing the Cove
& Propos'd situation of
the pulpit," St. Michael's
Church (1752–61),
Charleston, South
Carolina, 1804.
(St. Michael's Church,
Charleston)

Section showing the Cove & propos'd situation of the pulpit

Scale 10ft. to the inch

Figure 1.17
Transverse section
of the revised proposal
accompanying the
"Doctrine of Sounds,"
St. Michael's Church,
1804. (St. Michael's
Church, Charleston)

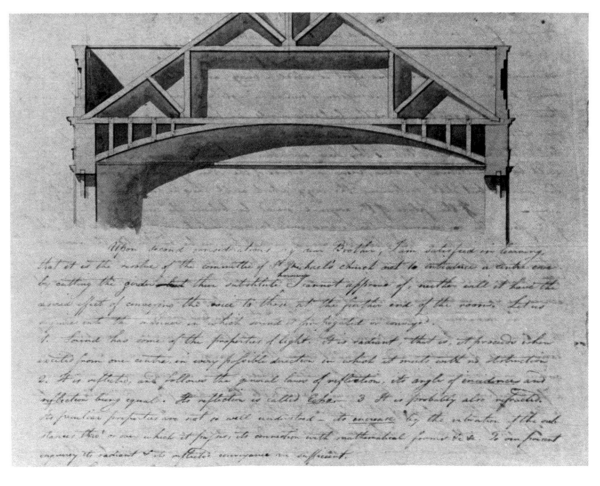

formed the base of the trusses supporting the roof, but this fact did not deter young Mills in the least, and in his specifications he noted summarily to the carpenter that "ere you cut the girder, dovetail stout braces into the collar beams and queen posts of the old rafters and strap them well with iron."[53] One of his sections clearly shows the new system of trusses and the proposed apse with its pulpit and memorial tablets in the place of the original Palladian window.

The building committee could not bring themselves to authorize such a potentially disastrous course of action. They sought the opinion of Thomas Bennett, a local builder of some reputation, and there was a delay. Mills, on learning of their concerns, sent via his brother Thomas an essay entitled "On the Subject of the Ceiling of St. Michael's Church and on the Doctrine of Sounds," a manuscript that demonstrates his reliance on Latrobe's writings. Around 1803 Latrobe had written an essay on acoustics; the draft remained among his papers and, much extended, was published in the *Edinburgh Encyclopedia*. To the Charleston vestry, Mills wrote:

Sound has some of the properties of light. It is radiant . . . and follows the general laws of reflection. . . . It is probably also refracted. Its peculiar properties are not so well understood . . . its increase by the vibration of the substances thro' or over which it passes, its connection with mathematical forms &c &c.[54]

Latrobe's manuscript draft notes:

[S]ound is also subject to the laws that govern the progress of light, being liable to reflection, perhaps also to refraction. Science I believe has made very little progress on this subject, compared with its extent, for sound has also I think a very intimate connexion with mathematical forms.[55]

They both considered the acoustically ideal interior to be a perfect sphere. On this point Latrobe had written:

[I]f it could be used when built the best possible room for speaking, and hearing, taking only the direct echo into view, would be a hollow globe. For let the situations of the speaker and hearer be where they will, a ring of first echo perfectly coincident will be produced.[56]

And Mills reiterated:

[I]f a hollow globe were constructed, a speaker placed in the center would receive echoes from every point of the surface at the same moment, that is, all the echoes would be consonant and primary; of course he would speak with the greatest ease.[57]

Unfortunately, such an interior would not be functional, and Latrobe had observed:

But as such a room is impracticable, that which most nearly approaches it must be next to it in perfection. Such a room is a cylinder covered with a half globe or semispherical dome. Such a room has all the advantages of the second with the additions of innumerable rings of first and secondary echoes produced by the dome.[58]

And once again Mills followed suit:

As globular rooms cannot however be constructed, the room consisting of part of a globe and of a cylinder will, of practicable rooms, be that in which the speaker will be most at his ease; for it will yield the greatest number of consonant echoes, as you will readily understand by forming a diagram.[59]

Mills, in short, applies the architectural implications of Latrobe's manuscript directly to his own proposal for the interior of Saint Michael's:

The most common room and in many respects the most convenient is the square or oblong quadrangle [like St. Michael's nave]. It is the cheapest in its construction and adapts itself best to all manner of communications with streets adjacent buildings and contiguous apartments. If such a room have a cylindrical ceiling being either a semicircle or a segment in its section, it will have a great advantage over the same form covered with a flat ceiling especially if the speaker be placed in its axis. In this situation his voice will be assisted by a line of primary consonant echoes, in the perpendicular section of the ceiling exactly over him.[60]

Finally Mills relates the purely functional argument concerning acoustics to an aesthetic maxim:

As simplicity in architecture generally produces beauty so is the simplest mode of producing an intended effect commonly the best. A cylindrical ceiling is of those that are not flat, the simplest and cheapest.[61]

And this statement also parallels one found in Latrobe's draft:

What is . . . inconsistent with the use of a building can never become ornamental. "Simplicity is one of the first of architectural ornaments, and the highest achievement of study and of taste."[62]

Like fireproof construction, acoustics remained of interest to Mills. His plans drawn in 1830 for improving acoustics within the U.S. House of Representatives helped establish the final phase of his career in Washington (fig. 1.18), but his explanation of these plans is merely a recapitulation of Latrobe's theory of consonant and disconsonant echoes.[63] The congruence of Latrobe's "Remarks on the best form of a room for hearing & speaking" and Mills's "Doctrine of Sounds" suggests that on occasion Mills was, as Latrobe later wrote to Godefroy, "a copyist, and is fit for nothing else."[64] In other respects, however, even these early proposals convey an originality that clearly separates Mills from his peers.

Opposite: Figure 1.18 Drawing No. 1, "Of the Plan of the Hall of Representatives." (Report no. 83, **Reports of Committees of the House of Representatives,** *21st Congress, 1st session, 1829–30)*

THE PRESENTATION

OF IDEAS

Mills bound the John's Island and St. Michael's presentation drawings as slender volumes and in both instances added a text of pragmatic specifications. A paragraph is addressed to each craftsman —laborer, bricklayer, carpenter, slater, coppersmith, joiner, plasterer, stucco plasterer, glazier, painter, paver, and stonecutter—in an order that reflects the sequence of work. These instructions, juxtaposed to the plans and elevations, allow the reader to visualize the construction process from beginning to end.[65] These booklike presentations may represent his attempt to conduct business at a distance, for the detailed instructions served as an-

notations, or captions, and explained the proposals in terms a patron could be expected to understand. The booklike format assured Mills that he had minimized the possibility of a misunderstanding—pertinent documents would be viewed sequentially and intact—and at the same time would convey his concepts to people hundreds of miles away he might never see. Unfortunately, these books did not secure the commissions, and neither project came to fruition. Mills did not attribute his disappointment to the nature of the presentation, however, for he subsequently used this format successfully in submissions for the First Presbyterian Church, Augusta, Georgia, the Burlington County Jail, Mount Holly, New Jersey, and the Baltimore Washington Monument. He also prepared a set of drawings and bound them with a "Descrip-

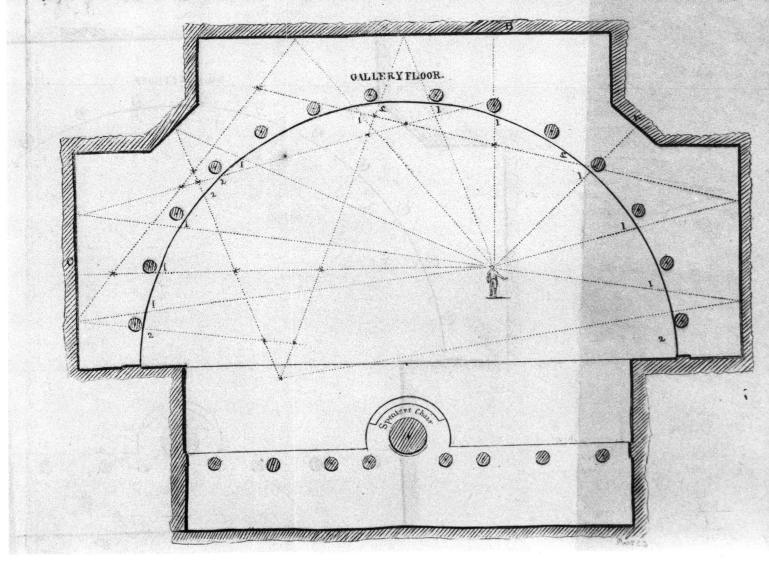

DRAWING No. 1.
OF THE PLAN OF THE HALL OF REPRESENTATIVES
AS IT NOW IS, WITH A DIAGRAM TO THE EXPLANATIONS.

REFERENCES.—The dotted lines 1.1, &c. emanating from the point or Speaker I. represent the *primary* or original rays of sound;—the dotted lines 2.2, &c. forming angles with the first lines at the point where they impinge against the walls, represent the *secondary* or reflected rays of sound:—the stars at certain points of intersection of the reflected rays, represent the number of *disconsonant* echoes, produced from the above number of primary rays.

GALLERY FLOOR.

Speakers Chair

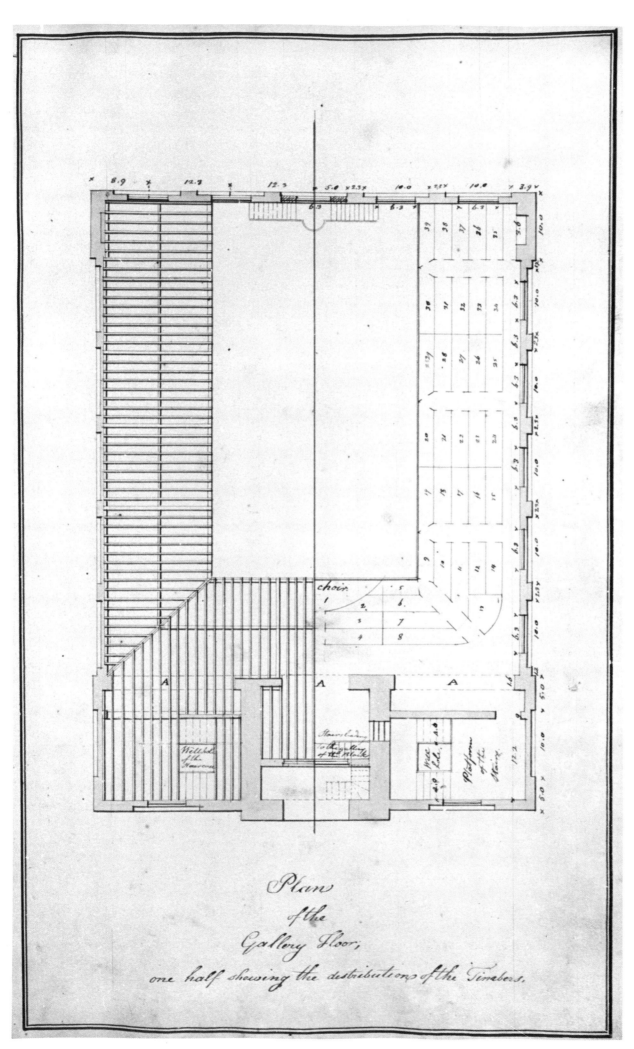

Figure 1.19
"Plan of the Gallery
Floor, one half shewing
the distribution of the
Timbers," First
Presbyterian Church
(1807–12), Augusta,
Georgia, 1807. (First
Presbyterian Church,
Augusta, Georgia)

tion of the manner of erecting and finishing" the New London Customs House.[66]

The existence of six examples produced over a span of thirty years suggests that the booklike presentation became part of Mills's method of operation. No comparable books by his peers are known. The physically similar "Plans of Houses" by Alexander Parris contains no prose; its forty-five leaves present plans and elevations of disparate projects; it lacks sections and perspectives; and, with the exception of one "Plan and Elevation of [octagonal timber framed] Roof," it contains no construction details. It was apparently bound for preservation as an album.[67]

In his earliest days with Latrobe, Mills had come into contact with handmade books, for at the outset of the survey of New Castle, Delaware, Latrobe ordered "a well bound book containing about three quires of the largest elephant paper" in which his assistants were "to record the survey in detail."[68] The New Castle work resulted in a report consisting of a map, elevations, and an explanatory essay presenting Latrobe's observations on the architectural implications of geography and climate.[69] The "References to the Plan and Sections of the Town of Newcastle" explains the desirability of orienting principal facades to the south and north, discusses the "unwholesome" character of northeast and northwest winds, and demonstrates the impact of these factors on the axes of the city plan. This essay is complex, closely reasoned, and addressed to the commissioners of New Castle; it has little in common with Mills's prosaic specifications. Nonetheless, the New Castle report may have provided a prototype for the simultaneous transmittal of drawings and an extended explanation.

Years before Mills entered the office, Latrobe had bound drawings for the Virginia Penitentiary (1797), in Richmond, for he had written to the governor and council that he wished to "retain the book of drawings . . . in order that I may complete my copy of them" and that he would "deliver the book" at the next council meeting.[70] His sketchbooks, always close at hand, were also suggestive. Fourteen of these survive; they vary in size from 7 3/16 by 10 7/16 inches to 8½ by 19¼ inches and in length from seven to seventy pages; they are bound in paper boards reinforced with leather and are physically akin to Mills's surviving bound plans.[71] Latrobe expressed on several occasions the desire to collect and publish his drawings, many of which bear evidence of having been bound.[72] The book was helpful to Mills in his attempt to establish a far-flung practice, and through his experience with Latrobe, bound drawings were comfortably familiar.

Mills felt that he began "the exercise of my profession, both as an Engineer & Architect" in 1804.[73] This claim notwithstanding, he remained an apprentice (albeit with increasing responsibilities) with Latrobe through the summer of 1808 and gained experience as pupil, as assistant, and as Latrobe's "professional child."[74] His only dated drawings that survive from this period are two bound sets, those for the First Presbyterian Church (1807–12), Augusta, Georgia, consisting of four plans, three sections, three elevations, and one "Detail of Framing of the Roof," and a similar set for the Burlington County Jail, Mount Holly, New Jersey, consisting of eight plans, four elevations, and one section.[75] In both cases the drawings are more fully developed than those for the earlier Charleston projects. In addition to general, descriptive plans and elevations, plans are also presented for the pilings and reversed arches of the foundation and for the joists, rafters, and reinforced plate of the First Presbyterian Church (fig. 1.19). The Burlington County Jail drawings delineate flues, ovens, and privies; dimensions are specified for virtually every surface and void, and the use of spaces is designated more fully than in any of his earlier work (fig. 1.20). The commentary that accompanies these drawings is notable for the articulation of an architectural program, a rationale reflecting theories of penology, the behavioral implications of design, and a specific moral bias. This text is addressed to "The building Committee of Burlington County Prison" and contains a descriptive tour cast in the present tense to engage the reader's imagination: "We enter the building (after ascending a flight of steps) thro' a strong door way into the Vestibule or waiting Hall. Before us is the keepers' office. . . ."[76] Walking through the building with the reader, Mills points out aspects of design and construction intended to promote health, safety, and efficient operation, and through these details his concept of the prison's mission is manifest.

The fervor of his prose conveys his belief in architecture as an agent of social reform; he expresses the relationship between form and import by discussing the "principles on which prisons should be instituted," the first of which is "strength and permanency," necessitating a mode of construction "distinct from a common house." "As little combustible material" as possible should be employed; rooms should be "vaulted or arched with Brick," corridors "paved with brick," and the stairs made of stone. "Humanity" and public interest are invoked as motives for making the building fireproof, and except for the roof system all structural components of the jail are fireproof. The corridors are spanned by longitudinal barrel vaults; springing perpendicular to the corridors are ranges of vaults forming the floors and ceilings of cells, offices, and communal rooms. This was Mills's first masonry vaulted building.

Overleaf: Figure 1.20 "General Section from East to West thro' the Debtors' & Keeper's apartments," Burlington County Jail (1808–10), Mount Holly, New Jersey, 1808. (Mount Holly Library)

General Section from East to West

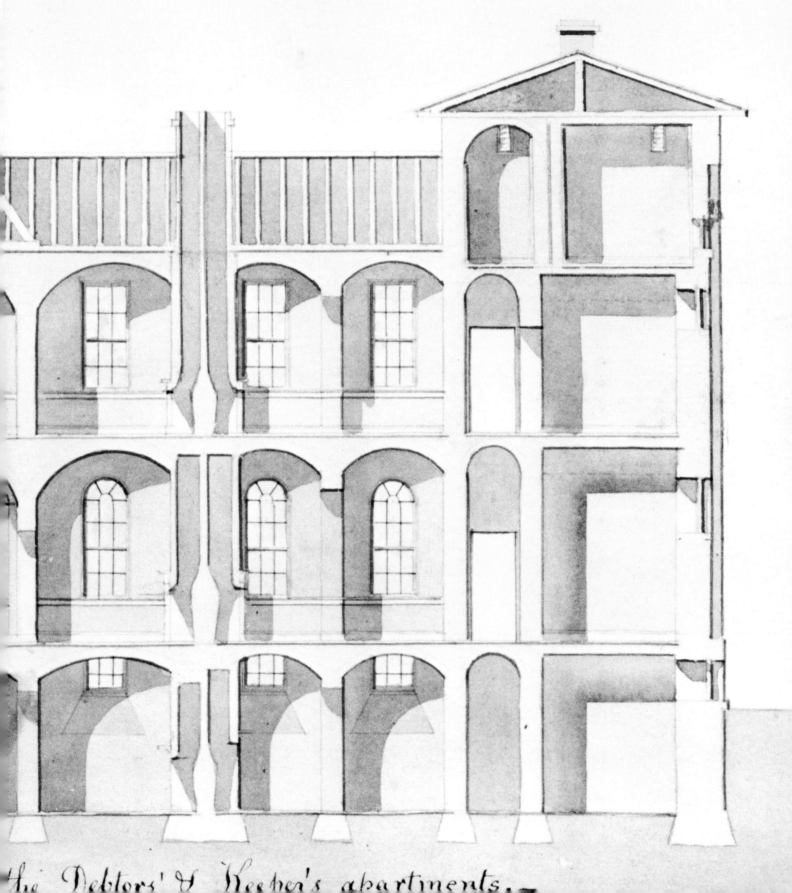

the Debtors' & Keeper's apartments.—

The Burlington County Jail reflects correspondence between Mills and Latrobe concerning the South Carolina Penitentiary (1806–8), which Mills designed. In developing this proposal Mills studied Latrobe's Virginia Penitentiary, and the ideological and iconographic linkage between these works is suggested by epigrams proposed for lintels and cornerstones. Latrobe directed that on the Virginia Penitentiary cornerstone this sentiment should appear: "The Monument of that Wisdom which should reform while it punishes the Criminal."[77] For the South Carolina cornerstone Mills suggested "Wisdom, Which while it punishes would reform the criminal" and for the Burlington County lintel "Justice Which, While Its Punishes, Would Endeavor to Reform the Offender."[78]

Less literal, but no less factual, were congruences of plan and detail. As originally proposed, the Burlington County Jail, like the Virginia Penitentiary, had multistory wings embracing an exercise yard; the courtyard elevations of both buildings consisted of loggias that gave access to cells ranged against the exterior walls. The arcades specified in the original Burlington County Jail plans, dated June 4, 1808, did not appear in the revised plan, dated January 1809; arcades, which might be appropriate in South Carolina, were not suitable in the New Jersey climate. Administrative functions were centralized in each plan (although only Latrobe's provided unobstructed sight lines for observation). Both used the blind arch as a major articulating device, and in both cases expressive fenestration consisted of lunettes compressed within the head of the arch; the unbroken plane below these lunettes was emphatically framed by the reveals of the arches and evoked an appropriate sense of closure. Latrobe had written that a penitentiary should present a "solemn character" and that the "only sort of beauty which is admisable, [is] simple & well proportioned solidity."[79] Mills knew that the blind arch was more than a decorative, Adam-style motif. In his essay to the building committee of the Augusta church he had written:

The utility of arches, both as regards strength and beauty, is generally admitted, and in public their introduction is peculiarly characteristic—. The expense attached to them is, on the whole not greater than a common wall of equal thickness, & for this obvious reason, because of their rendering unnecessary a large mass of materials, which would be requisite to fill up the reveals they make, not existing in a common wall.—The idea of expense is too often taken where arching is recommended, without just grounds, as experience fully evinces and a little reflection upon the preceding assertion.[80]

The elevations of the Augusta church were wholly dependent on the use of a blind arcade in which the arches served simultaneously to deflect superincumbent weight and to reduce economically the thickness of the wall. It was important that Mills explain the desirability of the blind arcade, for it was not part of the builders' vernacular. He had observed the use of relieving arches during the construction of the Roman Catholic Cathedral (1805–21), Baltimore, designed by Latrobe. Mills was involved in producing drawings of the cathedral when George Rohrback, clerk of the works, and John Hillen, a general contractor and member of the building committee, altered the plans without Latrobe's approval. They did not understand the import of Latrobe's system of relieving arches and prepared to thicken the foundation, claiming that it would not bear the weight of the walls. Latrobe wrote tactfully to Bishop John Carroll: "I expected such an objection. For who can think of a Cathedral and keep thick walls out of his head?"[81] And he made a distinction between his own work and that of amateurs, like Hillen, who dominated architecture in America:

The difference between a design made upon scientific principles, and one made by a happy fancy, and a knack of guessing improved by experience consists chiefly in this, that the former admits neither superfluity nor want either in its strength, or its extent, or in its decoration,— while the latter, whenever it is in doubt about a sufficiency of strength, or extent, or decoration runs into superfluity. . . . Nothing therefore is more common than to see mechanical builders, when a great weight is borne, or a great pressure resisted, take care that their Walls are big enough, well assured as they are, that too much strength does no harm.[82]

THE FLEXIBLE PRAGMATIST

In matters of form, structure, and rational planning, Mills drew heavily from Latrobe, but he rejected his mentor's insistence on total control as a contractual prerequisite. Autocratic and sensitive, Latrobe consistently sought to "establish my drawings as a code of unalterable law"; consequently, there was a contretemps with virtually every major patron during Mills's tenure in the office.[83] On the other hand, Mills, for better or for worse, was accommodating; for example, pragmatism prompted him to observe to Paul Hamilton, governor of South Carolina, that his prison could be erected in stages "without disturbing the whole" if funds were not available to undertake the entire work at once.[84]

A similar flexibility is evident in the alteration of the Burlington County Jail and the qualifying phrases that soften suggestions accompanying his drawings. To the board of the Augusta church he wrote, "If you have any kind of freestone in your neighborhood it would be advisable to make use of it for the sills of your doors and windows...."[85] And in Philadelphia he helped one of Latrobe's clients, Capt. John Meany, alter Latrobe's design, until the architect declared that "Captain Meany must do just as he pleases about his house, I care very little about its appearance. Please tell him that the design I made is I think the best thing he can make of it. But if anything else pleases him better, I hope he will adopt it." Or again, "I am a little sick of Captain Meany. I shall never get the least credit by his house, for the plan adopted by him forbids that, and therefore I am wholly indifferent about detail."[86] But Mills was far from indifferent and was soon in charge of the design and construction of Franklin Row (1809–10), Philadelphia, for Captain Meany.

Latrobe pointed out the danger of giving way to the wishes of ill-informed clients. Mills's first major commission, the Circular Congregational Church, Charleston, had been disastrously altered without his consent. In this, the first of his auditorium churches, the portico was changed from a stolid Doric to an attenuated Corinthian order, and only the principal facade was stuccoed, thus emphasizing the lack of integration between the portico and the rotunda and dissipating the formal drama of the latter in the diminutive scale of exposed brickwork. Latrobe observed, however, that the most lamentable alteration, the introduction of a gallery within the cupola, ruined the acoustical qualities of the interior and thereby effectively destroyed the rationale of the plan itself.[87] Despite these indignities, there is no evidence that Mills complained, and in decades to come his major works would evolve in response to external pressures. If Latrobe considered Mills's compliant demeanor unprofessional, then he also grudgingly recognized its efficacy. Writing to his friend Maximilian Godefroy, whom Mills had beaten in the competition for the Baltimore Washington Monument, Latrobe observed that "he wants that professional self respect which is the ruin of you and me, and therefore we shall go to the wall, while he will strut in the middle of the street."[88]

Latrobe was mistaken, for prosperity eluded Mills. Although rarely without work, he was unable to accumulate capital. The amorphous state of the profession, ill-advised investments, and severe economic cycles kept his finances in disarray until he obtained a measure of security in federal employment in 1830. The 1819 failure of the Baltimore banks, coupled with his commitment to Waterloo Row (1817–19), a speculative housing project, brought him to the brink of bankruptcy. Ten years later he was in the same position, for South Carolina cancelled internal improvement projects to

which he had committed his career. In trying times his flexibility served him well, for it gave great scope to his search for "professional emollument."[89] He emphasized, to a greater degree than has been recognized heretofore, his experience as an engineer; he wrote extensively on topics related to the development of a public infrastructure, worked as a supervising architect, cultivated a reputation for fireproof construction and the design and installation of hot-air furnaces, and, like his father, invested in rental property.[90] Mills's emphasis on utility and on large-scale, abstract form, along with a pragmatic, laissez-faire resignation in matters of detail, is expressed in an early letter to Thomas Jefferson:

Being the first american educated architect, I have flattered myself that with suitable recommendation, & by a general advertisement in form of an address, I may procure business from other parts of the Union. For the honor & benefit of my country I would desire to realize this, and would run the risk of trusting the execution of my designs to a stranger: for tho' some alterations or mistakes might be made in the detail, these would not be of such consequence as to destroy the general effect of the designs.[91]

Robert Mills never wholly lost this vision of a national clientele, of citizen-patrons to be reached through coordinated prose and imagery. This professional ideal crystalized early and was seminal in his subsequent writings, in the development of prototypical courthouses, jails, hospitals, and customs houses, and in the geographical and typological diversity of his oeuvre. The proletarian plainness of much of his provincial work may be attributable to his very willingness to entrust "the execution of my designs to a stranger." None of his peers attempted to reach as broad a public, and a disdain for public competitions, boards, and commissions, as expressed by Latrobe, was often voiced—although never by Mills—in this period when many believed democracy inimical to the arts. The competition for the First Presbyterian Church in Augusta, Georgia, for example, was the subject of a scathing essay in the *Baltimore Observer*, which questioned the feasibility of the basis on which Mills had determined to conduct his career. The anonymous writer, under the ironic pseudonym of "Democritus," said that the provinces should be left to "carpenters, masons, joiners and shinglers."[92] Robert Mills clearly disagreed.

1. Robert Mills to the board of managers of the Baltimore Washington Monument, January 12, 1814, Maryland Historical Society. Mills reiterates this belief in fragmentary manuscript autobiographies in which he claims to have been "the first native American who directed his studies to architecture as a profession" (Manuscript collection, Tulane University; for a transcription, see H. P. M. Gallagher, *Robert Mills, Architect of the Washington Monument, 1781–1855* [New York: Columbia University Press, 1935], 168–71). Also see the manuscript draft in Mills's hand, apparently the preface for a publication on his career: "The author of this work has the honor of being the first American citizen that entered upon the Study of Architecture as a profession. . . ." (*Papers of Robert Mills*, microfiche ed., 1980, Miscellaneous Papers, Part C, 11-518-1, A3, South Carolina Historical Society).

2. For notices of early American lessons in architectural drafting, see Rita S. Gottesman, comp., *The Arts and Crafts in New York, New York Historical Society Collection*, vols. 69 (1726–76), 81 (1777–79), and 82 (1800–1804) (New York: New York Historical Society, 1938, 1948, 1965, respectively). The typical quotation is from the advertisement of Alexander Gowan, *New-York Daily Advertiser*, January 22, 1798, in Gottesman, *The Arts and Crafts of New York* (1948), 81, 6. Also see Alfred Coxe Prime, *The Arts and Crafts in Philadelphia, Maryland, and South Carolina*, Part 1, 1721–85, and Part 2, 1786–1800 (New York: Da Capo, 1969).

3. Mills, "The Architectural Works of Robert Mills," Tulane University; see Gallagher, *Robert Mills*, 168.

4. Benjamin Henry Latrobe to Mills, July 12, 1806, in E. C. Carter and T. E. Jeffery, eds. *The Microfiche Edition of the Papers of Benjamin Henry Latrobe* (Clifton, New Jersey: James T. White and Company, 1979). Unless noted otherwise, all subsequent Latrobe correspondence cited hereafter is found in the *Microfiche Edition*. For a transcription of this letter, see Talbot Hamlin, *Benjamin Henry Latrobe* (New York: Oxford University Press, 1955), 585–91. Here Latrobe observes: "The profession of architecture has been hitherto in the hands of two sorts of men. The first,—of those, who from travelling or from books have acquired some knowledge of the theory of the art,—but know nothing of its practice:—the second—of those who know nothing but the practice,—and whose early life being spent in labor, & in the habits of a laborious life,—have had no opportunity of acquiring the theory. The complaisance of these two sets of men to each other, renders it difficult for the Architect to get in between them, for the Building mechanic find[s] his account in the ignorance of the Gentleman-architect; —as the latter does in the submissive deportment which interest dictates to the former."

5. Observations concerning utility and beauty are found in "Architectural Works of Robert Mills." Observations on adaptation versus copying are found in Mills, "Progress of Architecture in Virginia," Tulane University; this incomplete essay appears in Gallagher, *Robert Mills*, 155–58, and Don Gifford, *The Literature of Architecture* (New York: Dutton, 1966), 82–87.

6. "The Architectural Works of Robert Mills," see Gallagher, *Robert Mills*, 168.

7. Mills to the board of managers of the Baltimore Washington Monument, January 12, 1814, Maryland Historical Society.

8. *Maryland Gazette*, March 18, 1813.

9. "The Architectural Works of Robert Mills," see Gallagher, *Robert Mills*, 169–70.

10. Mills to Bernard Peyton, December 23, 1822, and January 15, 1823, Virginia State Library.

11. Robert Mills to George Tucker, January 8, 1823, Virginia State Library. Also see Mills to Thomas Jefferson, June 16, 1820, in which Mills, immediately prior to relocating in South Carolina, notes that "I have been engaged in various public works especially in the Engineering department. Being under the impression from the circumstance of the disposition of our people, and the local situation of our country that a better prospect opened for the encouragement of the Engineer than the architect. . . ." For his failure to obtain a position with the Federal Board of Engineers, see Alexander Macomb to Mills, September 16, 1826, War Department, Miscellaneous Letters Sent, vol. 3, 384–85, 1826, Record Group 77, National Archives.

12. Mills, *Statistics of South Carolina* (Charleston: Hurlbut and Lloyd, 1826), 311–13, 32–34, 66–93.

13. William Dunlap, *History of the Rise and Progress of the Arts of Design in the United States*, 2 (Boston: C. E. Goodspeed, 1918), 375; also see the *Papers of Robert Mills*, 1980, Miscellaneous Papers, Part C, 11-518-1, A3, South Carolina Historical Society.

14. William Dunlap, *Diary of William Dunlap, 1766–1839*, 3 (1832–34) (New York: New York Historical Society, 1930), 760, 774. On November 30, 1833, Dunlap wrote to Mills; Mills's response was received on February 17, 1834. The following day Dunlap noted: "Receive letter yesterday from Robt. Mills (Washington D.C.) Write on Hist. Art."

15. Hoban had an apprentice, Henry Munroe, on his staff; *Records of the District of Columbia and of the Offices Concerned with Public Buildings, 1791–1867*, April 16, 1799, M-371, reel 16, no. 1615, National Archives. As Mills's name does not appear in the official records, he must have served as a personal assistant or apprentice rather than as an employee. The nature of this arrangement is suggested in Latrobe to the president and directors of the Bank of Philadelphia, May 25, 1807, in which Latrobe notes that the young Mills "does not depend entirely for support on his industry, having a competence of his own" and will work cheaply to gain experience.

16. Thomas Jefferson to Charles Bulfinch, July 1, 1801, *The Presidential Papers Microfilm: Thomas Jefferson Papers*, series 3 (Washington, 1974). Jedidiah Morse to "Rev. Dr. Prince, Salem, Rev. Mr. Andrews and Dudley A. Tyng Esq., Newburyport, Rev. Mr. Kellogg, Portland, Mr. Benj. Abbot, Exeter, Rev. Mr. Patten and Jabez Denison Esq., Newport, Rev. Mr. Gans and William Wilkinson Esq., Providence, Dr. Joshua Lathrop and William Lammar Esq., Norwich, Rev. Henry Channing, New London, Theodore Dwight, Esq. and Mr. James Stedman, Hartford, The Honorable Saml W Danan [?] Esq., Middletown, Rev. Dr. Dana and President Dwight, New Haven," October 18, 1802, Yale University Library.

17. The canal was the major commission in the office when Mills joined Latrobe. Surveys to select a route began in July, just weeks before Mills's arrival; throughout the fall and into the winter, Latrobe, who was appointed chief engineer in February 1804, coordinated the work of the surveyors—Cornelius Howard of Baltimore, Daniel Blaney of Delaware, and John Thompson of Pennsylvania. See Ralph D. Gray, "The Early History of the Chesapeake and Delaware Canal," *Delaware History* 8, no. 3 (1958–59): 243–49.

18. For the marriage of William Mills, see *South Carolina Historical and Genealogical Magazine* 21 (1920): 27 and 23 (1922): 31. For his purchase of town lots, see Alexander Taylor to William Mills, November 9, 1777, *Charleston Deeds*, E-5, 113. For his management of rental property, see William Mills to Sarah Vincent Dewees, September 19, 1791, *Charleston Deeds*, G-6, 347. For his use of mortgages, see William Mills to William (Hasell) Gibbes, September 4, 1791, *Charleston Deeds*, G-6, 400. For speculation in farm land, see William Mills to William H. Gibbes, September 5, 1791, *Charleston Deeds*, K-6, 193, and William Mills to Charles Freer, October 30, 1793, *Charleston Deeds*, K-6, 194. Concerning the ownership of slaves, see William Mills's will, *Charleston Wills*, D, 269, probated on April 23, 1802.

19. For the genealogy of Ann Taylor Mills (born December 12, 1755, died June 9, 1790), see Laurens Tenney Mills et al., "A South Carolina Family: Mills-Smith," typescript, n.d., 28, South Caroliniana Library, University of South Carolina; also see the "Hackwood Register," a manuscript genealogy, Evans Collection, series 2, Box 1, 3, Georgetown University.

20. Although a captain in the militia, William Mills joined 200 of his fellow citizens in signing a petition urging the American general Benjamin Lincoln to surrender the city; he also signed a document rejoicing in the return of royal authority and a proclamation congratulating Cornwallis on his victories to the north. Those signing were recognized as loyalists by both sides and were deemed the "addressers." For a listing of the addressers, see *Year Book, City of Charleston, 1897* (Charleston: Walker, Evans, and Cogswell, 1897), 341–45; also see Richard Walsh, *Charleston's Sons of Liberty: A Study of the Artisans, 1763–1789* (Columbia: University of South Carolina Press, 1959), 92, n. 9.

21. William and John Halfpenny, Architects and Carpenters, Robert Morris, Surveyor, and T. Lightoler, Carver, *The Modern Builder's Assistant; or a Concise Epitome of the Whole System of Architecture* (London: Robert Sayer, n.d.); private collection. Gallagher, also citing an inscription, says that Thomas Mills, an architect living in Dundee, Scotland, was Robert Mills's uncle and may have provided the inspiration for his professional interests; see *Robert Mills*, 4, 7, 24, n. 2, 184. The records of the Royal Commission on the Ancient and Historical Monuments of Scotland, however, contain no reference to Thomas Mills (C. H. Cruft, curator, to the author, May 7, 1986). As the date of the Halfpenny inscription coincides with the trip noted in Ann Mills to Andrew Mills, November 20, 1787, Georgetown University, it would appear that the book was given to Thomas, brother of the American architect.

22. *Charleston City Gazette and Daily Advertiser*, May 4, 1790.

23. For Thomas Walker, see *Charleston City Gazette and Daily Advertiser*, October 31, 1793; for M. Depresseville, ibid., April 7, 1797.

24. *State Gazette*, November 12, 1795. This advertisement was brought to my attention by Dr. Woodrow Harris and appears in his dissertation, "The Education of the Southern Urban Adult: Charleston, South Carolina, and Savannah, Georgia, 1790-1812" (Athens, University of Georgia, 1979), 524–25.

25. *Charleston Gazette*, October 7, 1795.

26. R. T. Gunther, *The Architecture of Sir Roger Pratt* (Oxford University Press, 1928), 20–21, as quoted by F. Jenkins, *Architect and Patron* (Oxford University Press, 1961), 121.

27. "A Building for a Town Hall" (plate 49), in Isaac Ware, *A Complete Body of Architecture* (London: J. Rivington et al., 1768), is the probable source for the east elevation of the Charleston Exchange. The adjacent illustration, "Plans of a Town Hall at Oxford" (plate 48), may be the prototype for the plan.

28. For an analysis of Latrobe's technique and range of subject matter, see Charles E. Brownell, "An Introduction to the Art of Latrobe's Drawings," in Edward C. Carter II, John C. Van Horne, and Charles E. Brownell, eds., *Latrobe's View of America, 1795-1820* (New Haven: Yale University Press, 1985), 17–40. A collection of twenty-eight landscapes by Mills—sketches in pencil, pen and ink, and wash—record his travels in South Carolina and suggest a comparison with the Latrobe notebooks. Notations on Mills's drawings indicate that he intended to embellish them or use them as the basis for further work; these drawings are wholly topographical and contain no detail analogous to the flora, fauna, and genre scenes that enliven Latrobe's sketchbooks.

29. James Burford, "Historical Development of Architectural Drawing to the End of the Eighteenth Century," *Architectural Review* 54 (1923): 160; see also pp. 1–5, 59–65, 83–87, 141–45, 156–60, 222–27.

30. An addendum, signed "MC Meigs, Capit Engr," on the verso of Mills to Jefferson Davis, September 12, 1853, from a transcript in the Office of the Architect of the U.S. Capitol.

31. For a review of the competition, see John M. Bryan, *An Architectural History of the South Carolina College, 1801-1855* (Columbia: University of South Carolina Press, 1976), 3–25. In this, his first competition, Mills confronted an opinionated building committee and the need to practice his profession at a distance, problems that would be a leitmotif of his career.

32. For a concise review of the state of the profession, see James F. O'Gorman, "The Philadelphia Architectural Drawing in Its Historical Context: An Overview," and Jeffrey A. Cohen, "Early American Architectural Drawings and Philadelphia, 1730–1860," in *Drawing Toward Building: Philadelphia Architectural Graphics, 1732–1986* (Philadelphia: University of Pennsylvania Press, 1986); Cohen notes the impact of competitions, pp. 20–21.

33. Darwin H. Stapleton, ed., *The Engineering Drawings of Benjamin Henry Latrobe* (New Haven: Yale University Press, 1980), plates 3, 4, and 5, 119–21.

34. Latrobe to Thomas Jefferson, October 2, 1803.

35. Charles E. Brownell, "An Introduction to the Art of Latrobe's Drawings," 18ff; also see Lindsay Stainton, *British Landscape Watercolours, 1600–1860* (Cambridge: Cambridge

University Press, 1985), 10.

36. Mills, "Robert Mills Pocket Memorandum Book for 1816," June 5, 1816, Library of Congress. Here Mills notes "Drawings in prospect to be made: Washington Monument as altered, 1st Baptist Church Baltimore, Court House Richmond." Later diary entries note that he left drawings of the monument (November 18, 1816) with Hugh Bridport of Philadelphia and received drawings (December 28, 1816) of the First Baptist Church from his brother in Philadelphia.

37. George D. Fisher, *History and Reminiscences of the Monumental Church, Richmond, Virginia, 1814-1878* (Richmond: Whittet and Shepperson, 1880), 28. The engraving by W. Goodacre is based on a drawing by William Strickland and was published by W. Kneass of Philadelphia. See Margaret Pearson Mickler, "The Monumental Church" (M.A. thesis, University of Virginia, 1980), 44–45. Although she cites Strickland's relationship with Kneass, Agnes Gilchrist, *William Strickland, Architect and Engineer, 1788–1854* (New York: Da Capo, 1969), does not mention the illustration of the Monumental Church.

38. Mills, "Pocket Memorandum Book for 1816," November 18, 1816. Mills sent four drawings of the hall to Bridport on October 24, 1816. The diary entries concerning George Strickland appear on October 29, November 2, and December 11, 1816.

39. Mills to the board of managers of the Baltimore Washington Monument, January 12, 1814, Maryland Historical Society.

40. Mills to the board of managers of the Baltimore Washington Monument [January 1814], an introductory essay bound with the seven competition drawings, Maryland Historical Society. Mills to Robert Gilmor, April 6, 1814, Maryland Historical Society. The correspondence does not indicate whether the perspective drawing or drawings were executed by Mills.

41. Latrobe to Thomas Jefferson, October 2, 1803, *Thomas Jefferson Papers*, series 3, reel 57,

42. Dunlap, *A History of the Rise and Progress of the Arts of Design in the United States*, 2, 375.

43. Fiske Kimball, *Thomas Jefferson, Architect* (New York: Da Capo, 1968), 71; for a catalog of Jefferson's architectural library, see pp. 90–101.

44. Douglas J. Harnsberger, " 'In Delorme's Manner—': A Study of the Applications of Philibert Delorme's Dome Construction Method in Early 19th Century American Architecture" (M.A. thesis, University of Virginia, 1981), 28–29. Jefferson's use of the Delorme system at Monticello offered Mills the opportunity to examine the laminated ribs and no doubt greatly influenced his subsequent use of this technique to span his auditorium churches. It is hardly an exaggeration to say that the knowledge of the Delorme dome made the round and octagonal churches feasible.

45. The references to the proposed alteration of St. Michael's and the dome of the Circular Church, then under construction, are contained in "Communication recd from Mr. Robert Mills on the subject of the Ceiling of St. Michael's Church & on the Doctrine of Sounds," dated October 15, 1804, owned by the Vestry of St. Michael's, on loan to the South Carolina Historical Society; transcribed by George W. Williams, "Robert Mills' Contemplated Addition to St. Michael's Church, Charleston, and the Doctrine of Sounds," *Journal of the Society of Architectural Historians* 12, no. 1 (March 1953): 27–31. The Delorme reference in the John's Island proposal is found in the specifications for the carpenter: "Frame a Roof with Collar Beams in one Span, Rafters not more than Sixteen Inches apart, leaving an Aperture for Dome which is to be fram'd of pieces of Inch plank nail'd together in two thicknesses, at convenient distances apart, mortise the Ribs into Collar & strengthen them with proper Braces, leave a circular opening in Crown for Sky Light" (Library Society of Charleston). These specifications have been published by Rhodri Windsor Liscombe, *The Church Architecture of Robert Mills* (Easley, South Carolina: Southern Historical Press, 1985), 38–41.

46. Mills to the Committee on Public Buildings, February 21, 1838, S.D. no. 435, 25th Cong., 2d sess., 19–27.

47. Mills to John Lenthall, October 10, 1805, *Microfiche Edition of the Papers of Benjamin Henry Latrobe*.

48. For the criticism of Thomas U. Walter, see Thomas Walter to Levi Lincoln, chairman, Committee on Public Buildings,

House of Representatives, January 29, 1838, S.D., no. 435, 25th Cong., 2d sess., 11–19. For Alexander Parris's comments, see ibid., March 15, 1838, 31–34. For Mills's response, see ibid., 19–27, 31–34; his incomplete citations are to Jean Baptiste Rondelet (1734–1829), *Traite theorique et pratique de l'art de batir* (Paris: l'auteur, 1803) and Charles Hutton (1737–1823), *The Principles of Bridges: Containing the Mathematical Demonstrations of the Properties of Arches, the Thickness of Piers* (London: W. Glendinning, 1801).

49. Mills to Levi Woodbury, secretary of the Treasury, July 2, 1834, Personnel File, Miscellaneous Letters Received, 1834–36, Record Group 56, 116, National Archives.

50. Latrobe to Louis DeMun, November 12, 1805. For the context of this mention of Mills's travels, see Talbot Hamlin, *Benjamin Henry Latrobe* (New York: Oxford University Press, 1955), 214ff.

51. Latrobe, "Remarks on the best form of a room for hearing & speaking," manuscript collection of the American Philosophical Society, unpaginated. For the proposals by Mills, see n. 45. Latrobe noted to Mills that he had given advice "at an early period of your studies in my office" concerning "the designs of the churches you have given to the congregations at Charleston" (Latrobe to Mills, July 6, 1806, transcribed by Hamlin, *Latrobe*, 585–91).

52. Mills to the vestry of St. Michael's Church, March 1804, instructions to the paver; for a transcription, see George W. Williams, n. 45. Also see Liscombe, *Church Architecture*, for a survey of the churches and transcriptions of many of the relevant documents.

53. Mills to the vestry of St. Michael's, instructions to the carpenter and joiner.

54. Mills, "Communication Recd from Mr. Robert Mills on the subject of the Ceiling of St. Michael's Church & on the Doctrine of Sounds," October 15, 1804, owned by St. Michael's, on loan to the South Carolina Historical Society; for a transcription, see Liscombe, *Church Architecture*, 45–47.

55. Latrobe, "Remarks on the best form of a room," n.p.

56. Ibid.

57. Mills, "Doctrine of Sounds," n.p.

58. Latrobe, "Remarks on the best form of a room," n.p.

59. Mills, "Doctrine of Sounds," n.p.

60. Ibid.

61. Ibid.

62. Latrobe, "Remarks on the best form of a room," n.p.

63. *Memorial of Robert Mills, of South Carolina*, January 14, 1830, Reports of the Committees of the House of Representatives, 21st Cong., 1st sess., no. 83.

64. Latrobe to Maximilian Godefroy, October 10, 1814.

65. Mills, "Designs for an Episcopal Church to be erected on Johns Island near Charleston, S.C.," Library Society of Charleston; reproduced by Liscombe, *Church Architecture*, 38–41.

66. "Designs for Augusta Church, State of Georgia, by Robert Mills of South Carolina, Architect. Philadelphia—July 22d, 1807," eleven drawings and accompanying text, bound, 10 by 16 inches, collection of the First Presbyterian Church, Augusta, Georgia. "Designs for a Prison for Burlington County State of New Jersey comprising a Debtors' Goal, and Work-house for Felons by Robert Mills, Architect, Philadelphia, May, 1808," nine drawings and six manuscript pages, bound, 14⅛ by 10⅜ inches, Mount Holly Library, Mount Holly, New Jersey. "Designs for the Custom House Intended to be Erected in the City of New London State of Connecticut by Robert Mills, Engineer and Architect, Washington City, 1833" [signed "Robt. Mills, Archt. Augt. 28, 1834"], eight drawings and four pages of text, bound, New London Maritime Society, Custom House Maritime Museum.

67. "Plans of Houses, Notebook of Alexander Parris containing manuscript plans of house built in Boston, Mass. and Portland, Maine," unpaginated, 45 leaves, bound in stiff board covers, 9 by 11½ inches, Boston Atheneum.

68. Latrobe to John Bird, June 16, 1804.

69. Latrobe, "References to the Plan and Sections of the Town of Newcastle," Historical Society of Delaware; for a transcription, see Hamlin, *Latrobe*, 583–85.

70. Latrobe to the governor and council of Virginia, October 5, 1797.

71. For a description of the sketchbooks, see Edward C. Carter II, John C. Van Horne, and Charles E. Brownell, eds., *Latrobe's View of America, 1795–1820* (New Haven: Yale University Press, 1985), 43.

72. Latrobe to Christian Ignatius Latrobe, December 1, 1807: "When I publish the works, I shall inscribe the plan to you." Or again, Latrobe to Eric Bollman, May 11, 1816, requesting the recipient to discuss the possibility with A. & J. Taylor, the English publisher. See Hamlin, *Latrobe*, 97, n. 1.

73. Mills to Thomas Jefferson, June 16, 1820, credits Jefferson with having "first directed me in my professional pursuits" and notes that he has been active as a professional for sixteen years.

74. Latrobe to Bishop John Carroll, February 3, 1805, and Latrobe to the trustees of the Roman Catholic Cathedral at Baltimore, April 13, 1806. It is in a moment of distress, looking back at their relationship, that Latrobe refers to Mills as "my own professional child" (Latrobe to John Brockenborough, February 13, 1812).

75. George J. Giger, *A Model Jail of the Olden Time* (New York: Russell Sage, 1928), published an abstract of the Burlington County text and five of the drawings. The Augusta church specifications have been published by Liscombe, *Church Architecture*, 47–53.

76. Mills, "Designs for a Prison," n.p.

77. Hamlin, *Latrobe*, 123–24; also see John M. Bryan, "Robert Mills, Benjamin Henry Latrobe, Thomas Jefferson, and the South Carolina Penitentiary Project, 1806–1808," *South Carolina Historical Magazine* 85, no. 1 (January 1984): 1–21.

78. Mills to Paul Hamilton, governor of South Carolina, October 30, 1807, South Carolina Department of Archives and History.

79. Latrobe to the governor and council of the Commonwealth of Virginia, July 12, 1797.

80. Mills, "Designs for Augusta Church," n.p.

81. Latrobe to Bishop John Carroll, March 21, 1806. For Mills's participation in the production of drawings for the cathedral, see Latrobe to the trustees of the Roman Catholic Cathedral at Baltimore, April 13, 1806.

82. Latrobe to Bishop Carroll, March 21, 1806.

83. Latrobe to Bishop Carroll, March 26, 1806.

84. Mills to Governor Paul Hamilton, July 7, 1806, South Carolina Department of Archives and History.

85. Mills, "Designs for Augusta Church," n.p.

86. Latrobe to Mills, July 2, 1807. Latrobe to Mills, August 5, 1807.

87. Latrobe to Mills, July 12, 1806; transcribed in Hamlin, *Latrobe*, 585–91.

88. Latrobe to Maximilian Godefroy, October 10, 1814.

89. Mills to Eliza Barnwell Smith, March 9, 1808, South Carolina Historical Society.

90. Seeking employment at the midpoint of his career, Mills described himself primarily as an engineer (Mills to Bernard Peyton, secretary to the Board of Public Works, Richmond, Virginia, December 23, 1822, and ibid., January 15, 1823, Virginia State Library). Also see Mills's recapitulation of his architectural accomplishments in his rebuttal to Thomas U. Walter, n. 48. The only extant hot-air furnace by Mills is located in the South Carolina Asylum. Beginning with his supervision of the installation of the furnace in the Bank of Philadelphia, heating systems became a significant source of income for Mills; his 1816 *Diary* notes involvement in twenty-two installations or modifications. His expertise in this regard was noted in the *Federal Gazette and Baltimore Advertiser*, December 28, 1815, in a description of the Patapsco Factory furnace. Mills's furnaces were based on the work of Daniel Pettibone, who designed the furnace for the Bank of Philadelphia and had sold Mills "a license" to duplicate his system (Daniel Pettibone to Col. Samuel Lane, commissioner of public buildings, August 31, 1816, National Archives). Pettibone published the plans for several heating systems in *Economy of Fuel* (Philadelphia: A. Dickinson, 1812); see University Microfilms, American Culture Series, reel 419.3.

91. Mills to Thomas Jefferson, June 13, 1808.

92. *Baltimore Observer*, 24 (June 13, 1807), 391–93.

ors, of competent judg...

...ake it — But as my ...

...untry, and there are ...

...ferred to for decision ...

...rrect view can be that ...

...correct opinion, — ...

...erusal of these letters, ...

...ifficulty come to a mi... ...

...ith each other —

I salute ...

sentiments ...

...y. 2ᵈ 1810

could be found to w[?]

profession is novel in th[e]

no cases that can be [?]

it is impossible that [?]

[?] of the subject to fo[?]

I hope Sir that after [?]

[?] shall without fur[ther]

[?]tial good understand[ing]

[?] Sir with [?]

of respect

Rob[t] Mills

CHAPTER 2

THE YOUNG PROFESSIONAL

IN PHILADELPHIA

AND BALTIMORE, 1808–20

Robert L. Alexander

obert Mills began his own practice in Philadelphia in 1808, at age 27, following his assistantship to Benjamin Henry Latrobe. When he left Baltimore in December 1820, he had himself acquired mastery and maturity as an architect. He had designed numerous houses, churches, and public buildings, as well as several monuments. Not only did he supervise construction of many of these structures, but also he carried out several engineering projects. His activity was widespread, ranging from South Carolina to Virginia, Maryland, and Pennsylvania; elsewhere contemporaries knew of him through the publicity surrounding some of his works. Dependent at first on the modern English style of his mentor, he quickly developed an austere, economical manner that he undoubtedly considered American, later built some of the first works of the Greek Revival, and learned to tailor his advanced stylistic statements to the more conservative, even Georgian, tastes of some patrons.[1]

Mills's work developed through his residence in cities with varied architectural traditions. Philadelphia was an old city, established in the seventeenth century, while Baltimore was new, settled in 1729 but granted near self-rule by the state legislature in 1796. Both were major ports, deriving their wealth from shipping agricultural produce to foreign ports and importing necessities and luxury goods. In touch with Europe and concerned with being modern and safe places for doing business, their merchants desired substantial and up-to-date buildings. The building histories of the two cities were similar, with Philadelphia enjoying more of the out-

standing Georgian buildings amid the vast number of modest vernacular structures. Both supported builder-architects and the occasional gentleman-architect, whose designs in general were dated by a generation or more. Modern European ideas and styles were being adopted, and the term *architect* was slowly gaining acceptance.

Latrobe's Bank of Pennsylvania (1798–1800) and the pump house (1799–1801) for his waterworks gave Philadelphia two outstanding examples of modern English developments in the vein of Sir John Soane (1753–1837). His work in Washington—directing construction of the Capitol and the White House—increased his renown, and, although his accessibility was lessened, for several years he carried out commissions in Philadelphia. He also worked in Baltimore, where his Roman Catholic Cathedral (1805–21) held attention through its long period of construction.

Latrobe's influence in Baltimore was reinforced by that of Maximilian Godefroy, whose modern French manner provided his clients with some variations in taste. Both were based in neoclassicism, with minor ventures into such exoticisms as the Gothic Revival style, and their works demonstrated their belief that a building's purpose should be expressed through architectural forms with an occasional assist from sculpture. Perhaps their major contribution was a conception of public buildings—including ecclesiastical, financial, and other institutional structures—that differed radically from domestic buildings and from the predominant Adamesque and Georgian styles of the Federal period. Their compositions employed geometrical forms emphasized by bare wall planes with clean-cut openings and recesses. Their modern planning

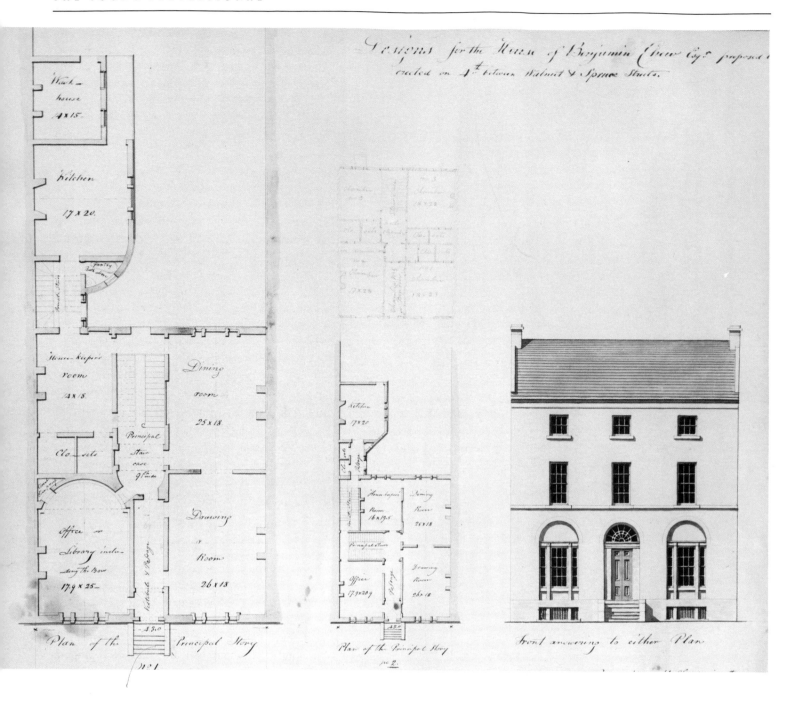

Figure 2.1
Drawing no. 1: elevation
and plans, Benjamin
Chew House (1810–12),
Philadelphia, Pennsyl-
vania; demolished.
(Historical Society of
Pennsylvania)

was directed toward increasing the building's use-fulness while retaining ceremonial elegance according to its nature. Preferring masonry or its imitation, stucco, they gave the public examples that stood out from the overwhelming number of brick buildings to show how material contributed to monumentality. From his five years of apprenticeship with Latrobe, Mills was imbued with these architectural ideas.[2]

As early as 1806 Mills took up residence in Philadelphia apart from Latrobe and in a small way began to practice on his own. In 1807 Latrobe assigned him to supervise construction of the Bank of Philadelphia, as well as the John Markoe House (1808) and other jobs that continued as late as 1811. Mills was already designing on his own account—for example, a penitentiary in his home state, South Carolina, and the First Presbyterian

Church in Augusta, Georgia—and he clearly considered himself a trained architect.

His personal life was developing as well. In 1806 he requested Paul Hamilton, governor of South Carolina, and President Jefferson to write character references to Gen. John Smith of Hackwood, near Winchester, Virginia. Mills had recently met the general's daughter, Eliza Barnwell Smith, and wished to court her actively. The prospect of their marriage, which took place on October 15, 1808, and future family responsibilities led Mills to consider his professional career seriously. In June 1808 he announced to Jefferson his intention to begin a practice and received from him a rather general letter of recommendation. Mills's assumption of professional status, like his separation from the direct influence of Latrobe, occurred over a period of several years.[3]

Opposite: Figure 2.2
Chew House. (Historical
Society of Pennsylvania)

EARLY RESIDENTIAL DESIGNS IN PHILADELPHIA

One of Mills's early house designs, the Benjamin Chew House (1810–12) in Philadelphia, is well documented by five drawings and several letters. In the first drawing its front had the tall shape of the developed Federal dwelling, but its openings were spread rather far apart to make three wide bays (fig. 2.1). The water table marking the top of the basement, the stringcourse incorporating the sills of the second-story windows, and the cornice drew horizontal lines across the façade, and the lines of the windows, from basement to cornice, produced a vertical movement. The arcade of the first story provided an undulating rhythm in an otherwise rather severe front. Window sizes changed in a hierarchic sequence; the largest lighted the significant public rooms on the main floor, and on the upper levels the different sizes of bedchamber windows reflected differences of authority in the household. Within the network of vertical and horizontal elements, then, changing proportional relationships provided an elegant intellectual order.[4]

Molded woodwork in the first-story openings stood out against the continuous brick texture. Large arches held a window on a shallow, recessed plane, blind above and below the window, the whole forming a Latrobean variation of the popular Adamesque Venetian window; its frieze bore square blocks simulating capitals above the posts. The entry arch, slightly smaller, was filled by a fanlight

and two heavy posts carrying an entablature. With a limited vocabulary of forms, this front simplified the modern English manner practiced by Sir John Soane as well as Mills's mentor, Latrobe.

Mills's design was followed fairly closely, as can be seen by comparing the drawing with the house itself (fig. 2.2). The major changes occurred in the basement windows, shown as tripartite in the drawing; in the increased ornamental wood, including an archivolt, at the entry; in the shortened window recesses; and in the omission of the stringcourse. Only the dormers do not appear in the drawing for the façade; Mills favored the segmental cornice in dormer windows and had already used them in the Richard H. Willcocks House (1810), which was nearly completed when the Chew House was being designed. The stoop in the photograph was a later replacement, for the railings and balusters are characteristic of ironwork of the 1840s.[5]

Because variant plans and different dates appear, the five drawings demand study to determine their sequence and to suggest the plan actually constructed.[6] The first drawing has an elevation and two plans, one at half the scale of the other. It shows the group of blocks that was standard for homes in Philadelphia: a large, broad front block for family living; a narrower back building to contain the kitchen and wash house, thus keeping the cooking fire out of the main block; and the narrow piazza, the name then given in Philadelphia to the connecting structure, with service stairs, pantry, and bath contained within the quadrant wall. Although the dimensions of the major rooms show little change, in the smaller plan the staircase has been turned 90 degrees, eliminating both the large curve of the office-library and the small one at the opening of the stair hall and thus cramping the service area.

The second drawing shows plans of the three stories (fig. 2.3). Here all rooms are strictly rectangular, but the principal staircase remains on the long axis, gaining some grandeur from the separate vestibule that broadens out the space from the entrance passage. Ten bedchambers are fitted into the second and third floors, two of them in the narrow areas above the main entrance hall, and large closets are conveniently arranged for all the larger rooms. Lighting is reduced to simple windows, with the only tripartite one in the chamber above the dining room. This drawing has been used so much, perhaps in construction, that it has torn along its major folds and the ends are frayed. Most of the dimensions have been altered, and most closets have been marked for elimination.

These two drawings are signed "Rob.ᵗ Mills," with the contraction of the first name that he employed for the rest of his career, and are dated April 5, 1810. The inscription at the top identifies these

as designs for the house of Benjamin Chew "proposed to be erected." In height they are identical; the first slightly exceeds the second in length, but the second clearly has lost some area at each end. Both have a frame composed of both a narrow and a broad inked line, but the second drawing lacks the framing lines at the ends of the sheet of paper.

The third drawing, "Plan of the Principal Story of the house of Benjamin Chew" (fig. 2.4), is very close to the large plan in the first drawing. There are differences in dimensions, small changes in the closets, a separate vestibule at the entry, and an octagonal rather than circular end for the office and library. The width of the house front is established at 44 feet, and the side walls are incomplete, suggesting that these could be party walls. (Mills employed a common abbreviation for indicating dimensions; e.g., the notation "9.10" below the

right portion of the façade means 9 feet and 10 inches.)

The fourth drawing is entitled "Designs for the Coach house and Stables of Benjamin Chew" and shows two different arrangements of the interior. This drawing is dated April 26, 1810, and its paper, like that of the third, is gray.

The fifth drawing, with three plans, lacks identification beyond being labeled the three stories of a narrow city house. The paper of this drawing has yellowed with age, and, although colored washes appear in all five drawings, only this one has a brown wash. The technique is far less skillful than that of Mills, and the drawing lacks backlining (the use of a heavy line for the right and lower sides of walls), which Mills regularly employed. Conventional representations, such as windows, door jambs, and fireplaces, are not in the forms used by

Figure 2.3
Drawing no. 2: plans of
three stories, Chew House.
(Historical Society of
Pennsylvania)

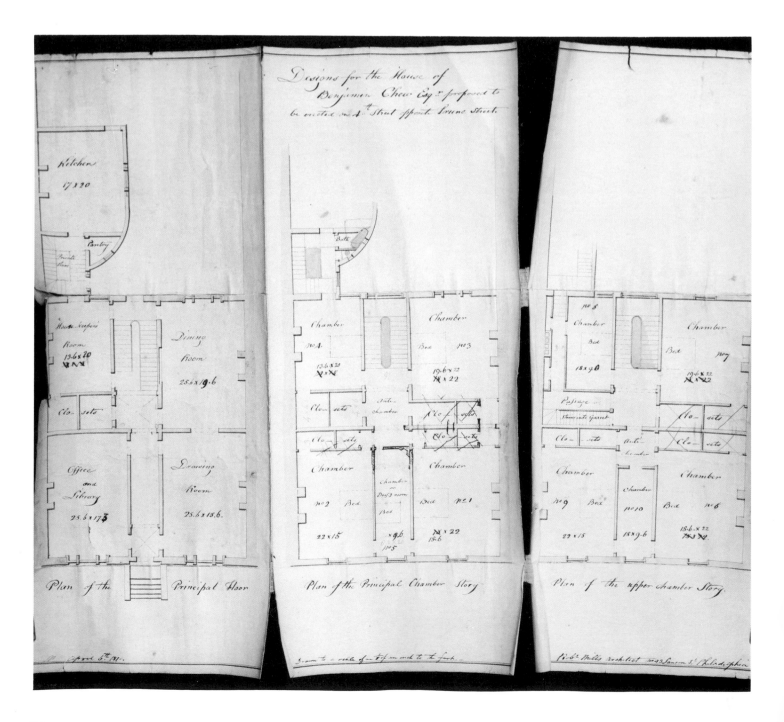

Mills. Although the handwriting is of the period, it differs in several respects from that of Mills. Dimensions are not given in the form customary for Mills. Clearly, this drawing was not by Mills.

The differences and similarities between these drawings have been noted here in order to unravel the sequence of and some of the reasons for their making. The first two, dated April 5, bear the original design and probably served as the basis for a conference between the client and the architect. The sheets have the same vertical dimension and the same frame. Chew apparently liked the large plan on the first drawing but decided against having so many closets on the upper stories and increased the width of the front to 44 feet. Mills then reworked the principal floor plan as the third drawing and submitted it along with the plan for the stables, both on gray paper with the latter dated April 26,

1810. The third drawing shows further changes made for the client. The office received an octagonal end; the china closet in the housekeeper's room was enlarged; and the smaller closet was turned to open into the vestibule of the principal staircase. All the dimensions of the main block differ from those of the first plan, but they correspond to the changed dimensions of the second drawing. At the back, too, a change appears in the more precise articulation of the pantry quadrant wall at the corner of the kitchen. Because the titles of these two plans no longer have the conditional phrase "proposed to be erected," Mills may have considered that they embodied all the client's decisions and choices. Indeed, the plan as constructed was probably close to this design.

The fifth drawing, showing a narrow row house plan, was perhaps made by Chew's builder. Some photographs of the house show an adjacent, smaller house on the right (south) and another slightly removed on the left (north). Chew may have built the smaller houses for the income they would provide and for the economies arising from construction of several in one campaign.

Still supervising the Markoe House, Mills showed in the Chew House a continuing dependence on his mentor. Wide enough for five bays, the façade has been simplified into three, reducing the amount of articulation and expanding the bare wall surfaces. Latrobean details include the tripartite window and arched recess, but the latter is filled to the edges by the window. Mills was able to adapt to such local preferences as the use of the piazza and back building, while Latrobe preferred to place the kitchen in the basement. The old-fashioned central hall and four-room plan has undergone sophisticated alteration, partially through the influence of Latrobe, as seen in the rooms with circular and octagonal ends and in the dining room niche to receive a sideboard. The semicircular vestibule and staircase recall the same parts in the Markoe House.

Mills has carried further an aspect insisted on by Latrobe but also traditional, especially in southern mansions—the separation of private and public elements. Just inside the entrance vestibule, the visitor might turn to enter the office or the drawing room, for these two rooms and the passage itself constituted the public area. Doors closed off the farther half of the house, so that the dining room and the stairway to the family chambers were insulated from the professional and business world and the occasional caller. For greatest privacy, Mills installed a bathtub in the upper level of the back building; in the Markoe House at this time he was also installing a tub, a relatively unusual and modern convenience, guided by very specific directions mailed by Latrobe.

Supercilious though Latrobe might be about

Figure 2.4
Drawing no. 3: revised plan for first story, Chew House. (Historical Society of Pennsylvania)

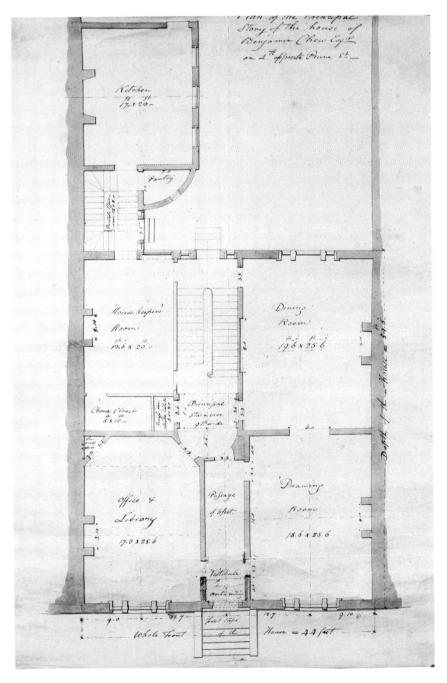

Mills's other qualities—he referred to him as a "wretched designer"—still he recognized his former assistant as "a very snug contriver of domestic conveniences."[7] Measures to protect family privacy were but one aspect of these arrangements. Several other devices appear in the plans: the fireproof closet in the corner of the office; the closet for outer garments by the staircase; the housekeeper's easy control of and passage to the china closet, pantry, kitchen, and dining room; and the clever use of space under staircases to allow passage from the kitchen to dining room. For an age accustomed to wardrobes for storage of linens and clothing, closets were an innovation and for Chew too much so, for he deleted most of the closets Mills had attached to the bedchambers in the second drawing.

A modification in design practices that lay behind a number of these conveniences—the designation of specific functions for the rooms—Mills owed to Latrobe. Although such functions were probably often intended, American architectural drawings had rarely named a room by use, yet the use had to be specific in order to have details designed to promote the function. This practice was compatible with Mills's personal interests. His early and repeated concern for utility reinforced Latrobe's instruction regarding the path of movement that allowed easy yet controlled passage from the kitchen and pantry, through the housekeeper's room, and to the dining room, traversing the three parts of the house via open passages and rooms and under two staircases. Such a collocation of structure, planning, and organization of spaces for use and flow of traffic would characterize the larger, more complex buildings that Mills later designed for government and institutional use.[8]

Another of Mills's lifelong practices was to give the client some choice. In the first two drawings, for example, he offered Chew three different plans for the principal story, and the fourth drawing offered two choices for the layout of the stables. What Mills may have recommended in conferences is not known, but he surely did prefer one or another, here probably the larger plan in the first drawing. In this case it is interesting to note that Chew wanted the grander plan, although the circular end for his office gave way to the octagonal shape that was probably easier for his carpenters to build. Providing alternatives was more than an exercise of Mills's ingenuity, for it involved the client more fully in the planning process and led to a greater degree of agreement between client and architect before construction, a desideratum stressed by Latrobe.

Like other architects of the day, Mills was treading new ground in exploring relationships with the client. Along with fellow students he received from Latrobe a grounding in professionalism, and much

of his career was devoted to the advancement of architecture as a profession. Latrobe, as a result of his own experience, put much emphasis on appropriate payment for professional services. Nothing brought out public ignorance of the nature of the profession better than the submission of a bill, and, as Mills learned in his relations with Chew, Latrobe's instruction seemed more like prophecy. On June 4, 1810, Mills sent a bill for $160, which Chew found most unreasonable. Although Mills used Latrobe's argument that an architect required an education as expensive as that of a lawyer, Chew's profession, the latter still was not satisfied. To Chew's suggestion that they submit the question to arbitration, Mills responded that he would not hesitate if competent judges could be found; his profession, Mills stated, was novel in this country and no previous cases could be offered as precedents on which to arrive at a correct opinion. In one letter Chew disingenuously protested that all he wanted of the architect was a drawing with colors showing lots of ground he wished to sell, yet he had been collecting lumber for two years, engaged in the planning process, and began construction almost immediately. Mills settled for $100, partially on the grounds that he would not supervise the construction.[9]

Thomas W. Francis, an acquaintance of Chew and perhaps the purchaser of one of the lots, wrote to Chew on receiving a bill from Mills. Francis was bemused and incensed by the sum demanded by this "soi-disant Artihect," and although the outcome of his protest is unknown, in 1811–12 he built a house virtually identical to Chew's.[10] Mills encountered this lack of understanding of his profession over the next several decades, and he repeatedly defined the nature and duties of the architect and defended his actions and decisions in many private, government, and even congressional inquiries.

Chew at least paid homage to his architect by carrying out the design with but few changes, so that it acquired grandeur and monumentality from the dominance of the large arches against the expanse of bare surfaces, stripped of virtually all ornament and restricted in vocabulary. It stood out from the customary small-scaled fronts crowded with numerous openings, decorative arches and lintels, and rusticated masonry.

A composition of such mastery certainly was grounded in several previous works. Few are known, none of them large mansions like the Chew House. Among the earliest was a pair of identical houses on Chestnut Street—the Gideon Fairman House and the Richard H. Willcocks House (fig. 2.5), the latter essentially completed in the spring of 1810. Each was three stories above a high basement. Three stringcourses carried windows, decreasing in size as they rose, with a semicircular

Opposite: Figure 2.5 Richard H. Willcocks House (1810), Philadelphia, Pennsylvania; demolished. (Bryan's Illustrated Business Directory of Philadelphia, 1856.)

portico at the entry and a dormer with the segmental cornice. The three arched windows of the tall second story resembled a triumphal arch, the center one higher and wider, with a tripartite window in the center. The basement story was designed for "offices"—meaning the kitchen, laundry room, and rooms for other necessary services—as well as commercial space, including shops. Although Latrobe was in great part responsible for introducing the high basement, Mills intended a further development. He set the buildings back a few feet in order to front the basement with a covered walk, an experiment that was not carried to completion. Here, with a limited vocabulary, Mills sought stability in providing support for all the openings, but the block achieved unity only by virtue of identical repetition in the two houses, and the basement was not fully coordinated with the upper front.[11]

The drawing of Franklin Row (1809–10) on Ninth Street, made for its builder, Capt. John Meany, and his partner, John Savage, contains one of Mills's rare statements on architectural ideas and theory (fig. 2.6). Dated May 1, 1809, and labeled "Design No. 2," it shows two designs for a range of eleven houses. A distinctive treatment at the end to close the composition indicates that Mills was thinking in terms of the whole block rather than the simple repetition of one house. Between the two elevations Mills wrote, "Another arrangement of the Front on 9th Street, which places each door *separate* or distinct from each other, but which does not possess the same advantages in producing that symmetry in the disposition of the Windows (as well above as below) that the finished design underneath gives." In using the word *symmetry*, he was referring not to mirror images around an axis but rather to the Vitruvian concept of symmetry as the appropriate and necessary proportional relationships of all parts to one another and to the whole. The upper design provides each house with a separate doorway, requiring a large number of arches for the doors and wide windows on the first story, but they are crowded together while the upper windows are spread too far apart for their small size. In the lower elevation two doors are placed within a single arch, so that the number of first-story openings is smaller and their spacing greater; the smaller windows above are doubled in number, and their reduced spacing is appropriate for their size. Openings set too close provoke a staccato rhythm, while those too far apart make a ponderous rhythm. Probably the need to keep each element of the organism in place dictated the insistent water table and stringcourses.[12]

As executed—some houses were ready for sale by October 1810—the row followed still a different design, perhaps a putative "Design No. 1" by Mills (fig. 2.7). Its alternating large and small openings

on each floor solved the problem of proportionate spacing. On the ground floor, however, the alternating arches differed not only in size—wide for tripartite windows, small for individual doors—but also in their levels, the variations disrupting the horizontal rhythm. Most of the openings floated uncertainly in the wall because of the lack of stringcourses. Although Mills usually provided visual support for these elements, Captain Meany may have simplified the construction for the sake of economy. The dormers, one for each house, had semicircular cornices, an unusual and attractive feature carrying the arch motif to the roof.

Mills thus had some experience with varied combinations of rectangular and circular elements before he designed the Chew House. He employed the stabilizing effect of the horizontal support for windows and spaced the openings for rhythms appropriate to their size and to the overall surface. His brief statement on the drawing indicated Vitruvius as the source for some of his architectural theory.

In addition to designing for clients, Mills by 1812 had accumulated enough capital to engage in speculative building. Several deeds record the exchange of plots during the next few years, each one large enough for two to four houses. These structures

provided further opportunities to design variants of his basic vocabulary and patterns. Because of difficulties in interpreting the documents and because the buildings have not survived, only one of these structures can be understood well. A 38-foot lot at the northwest corner of South Eighth and Locust streets was transferred to Mills on May 1, 1812, for a ground rent of $114 per year. A year and a half later, on December 17, 1814, when Mills sold it for $7,000, it held two tenements with a high basement and three residential stories (fig. 2.8). The building apparently had a single entrance and stair hall in the center of the three bays. Single openings marked the center and the top story, and tripartite windows were set in the outer bays of the principal and second stories. No stringcourses were made, but perhaps the basement cornice carried the openings of the main story. Nevertheless, the massive sills and lintels for the large windows and the substitution for the usual cornice of a series of battlements over the center and corners gave the front the appearance of enormous strength. Especially unusual were the triangular lintels on the principal story, which were designed about the same time as those of the Monumental Church in Richmond, Virginia.[13]

Figure 2.6
Alternative elevations and plan, Franklin Row (1809–10), Philadelphia, Pennsylvania; demolished. (Private collection)

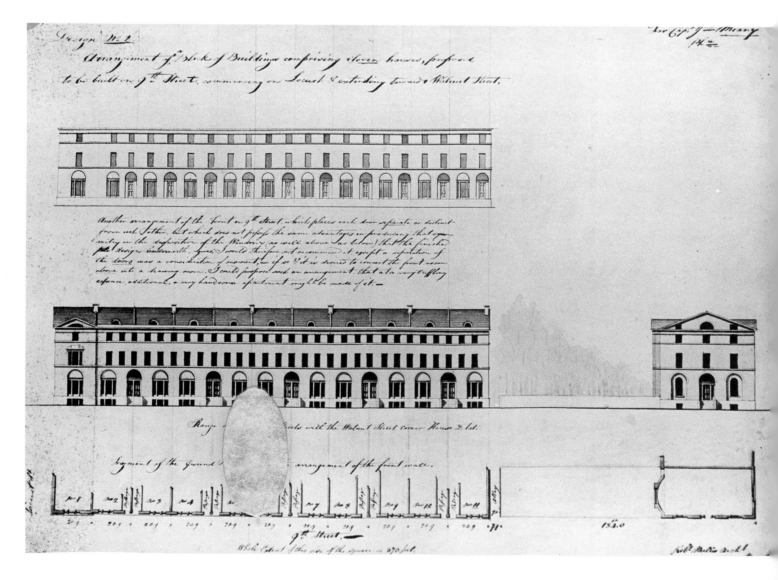

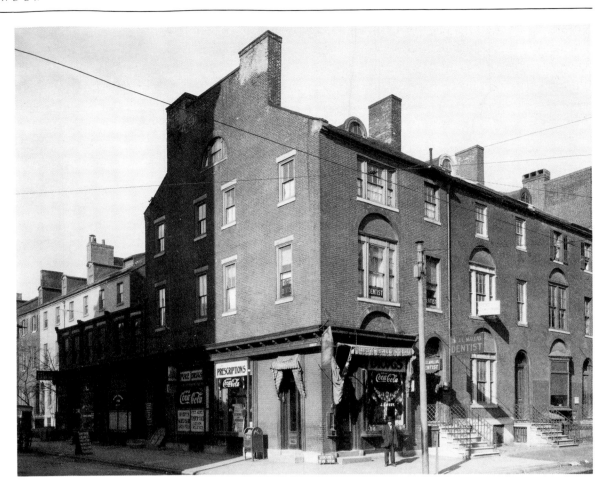

Figure 2.7
Franklin Row, 1917.
(Philadelphia City
Archives)

Figure 2.8
Eighth Street Houses
(1812–14), Philadelphia,
Pennsylvania, 1915;
demolished. (Philadelphia
City Archives)

WATERLOO ROW

Mills turned away from the dramatic expression of strength to develop the linear and rhythmic aspects of design in Waterloo Row (1817–19) in Baltimore, where he relocated in April 1815 to direct construction of the Baltimore Washington Monument. The directors of the Baltimore Water Company appointed him their president on August 2, 1816, an engineer's position (Mills, like Latrobe, considered himself an engineer). Within six weeks of his appointment he began to lay out Calvert Street through company property. From December 12 to 20, he designed the block of twelve houses later named Waterloo Row (fig. 2.9). Construction began in the spring of 1817 and was completed two years later. The timing suggests that Mills's mandate as president included development of the low, irregular grounds acquired by the company. Thus, although he had to obtain approval from the directors, still he was essentially his own client, and the buildings represented what he most desired in a row house.[14]

Mills employed the vocabulary and methods familiar from Philadelphia, including the arched recesses containing windows and doors, single and tripartite forms (the latter containing cornices and pilasters with block capitals), sills merging with stringcourses, and dormers with the segmental cornice (fig. 2.10). A network of horizontal and vertical lines organized the block-long front. Against the red wall plane, white freestone stringcourses at the first- and second-story levels and white wood cornices unified the length of the block, serving as horizontals that held the arches and windows in place. The vertical lines of the first-story Venetian windows and doors continued upward through the upper windows and downward into the basement windows and marble stoops. To gain a proper Vitruvian symmetry, Mills designated much of the spacing of Franklin Row as built. Large arcades on the main floor established a regular rhythm while, above, alternating single and tripartite windows provided a counterrhythm. The design was neither

Figure 2.9
Elevation and plan,
Waterloo Row (1817–19),
226 North Calvert Street,
Baltimore, Maryland;
demolished. (G.P. Schott,
Historic American
Buildings Survey)

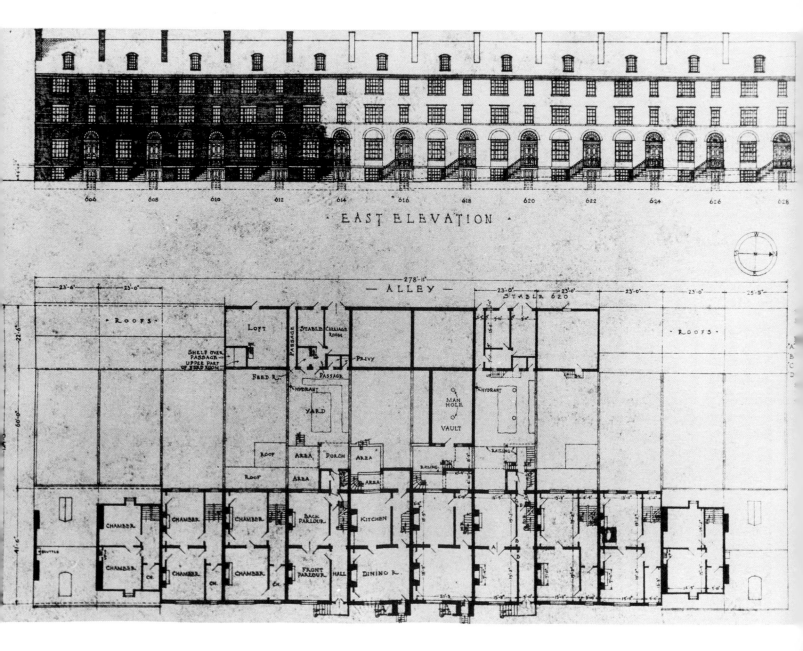

rigidly repetitive nor irresolute in relating large and small, arched and rectangular shapes.

In Waterloo Row Mills perfected his method of controlling the long front and introducing sufficient variety to avoid monotony. Fluidity and interest arose from the coordinated rhythms along the whole row, stressing his concern for largeness of effect in the urban block. One small detail showed Mills's willingness to sacrifice even utility to abstract design; the fanlight rose so high that its upper part was blocked by the hall ceiling. He rarely emphasized design with the same strictness, but its effect appeared in numerous later works; for example, the rhythm of the enormous colonnade of the Treasury Building (1836–42) is contained and quickened by the tall basement and entablature that sweep through the length of the block.

The townhouse plan adopted for many rows in Philadelphia and Baltimore permitted two large rooms on each floor and allowed them direct natural light. Mills used this plan for the expensive houses forming Waterloo Row. The front door opened onto a hall with a dividing arch at its midpoint and a stairway at the back, and two doors from the hall led to front and back drawing rooms. Upper stories essentially repeated this layout. On most floors fireplaces warmed the large rooms, and usually their projection into the room facilitated the inclusion of closets. Waterloo Row is unusual, however, in that it lacks back buildings; the kitchen and dining room were located in the basement, an arrangement not only preferred by Latrobe but also perhaps considered more modern. Access to the basement was by the stairway in the hall or by a short staircase at the back of the house. By avoiding back buildings Mills increased the free flow of light and air, the lack of which was often a significant problem for occupants of row houses.[15]

During the row's demolition in 1967, enough parts were salvaged to permit reconstruction of a typical first story at the Baltimore Museum of Art. The taste reflected on the house's exterior is continued inside, for the rectangular rooms are articulated with the same austerity and precision. Broad surfaces are defined by simple baseboards that separate floor and wall, shallow cornices that stretch out with apparent muscularity as though supporting the ceiling, and the enframement of doors and windows running almost the full height of the room. Frames are composed of simply paneled posts supporting a tall entablature with a prominent cornice. Mantlepieces of clouded black marble work with the window frames to make prominent visual focal points that emphasize the three-dimensionality and spaciousness of the two drawing rooms joined by a wide opening (fig. 2.11). Central medallions enhance the expanse of the ceilings. Exceptions to the general austerity, they are formed of a few large details applied to the surface—acanthus leaves radiating from the center, alternating anthemion and palmette in the outer ring, and bell flowers (the only Adamesque element) within concentric circles of square section.

The same character appears in the front entry, its woodwork similar to that of the drawing rooms and its fan- and sidelights composed of leading in straight lines and circles; the pattern of the fanlight is one that Mills employed in several other buildings. The emphasis is not on the small-scaled parts, oval forms, and looping arches and swags of the Adamesque Federal style but rather on the bald presentation of regular geometrical shapes. Not only does the vocabulary of forms differ from that of the Federal period, but also the broader scale and precise definition of mass and void show a change in taste. This taste, called masculine in its time, sought a largeness of effect inside to equal that gained outside. Waterloo Row represents the beginning of the Greek Revival interior.

In these city and row houses Mills worked with

Figure 2.10
Waterloo Row, 1917.
(Lawrence Hall Fowler,
Evergreen Library,
The Johns Hopkins
University Library)

brick, white stone, or wood, materials that had been used for several generations, from colonial times into the Federal period; yet, he achieved a monumentality and expressed a new authority through his forms and design. The restricted vocabulary can be interpreted as Mills's reaction against the elegances of the Federal style as well as a statement of his preference for an American architecture.

RICHMOND HOUSES

Several houses in Richmond, Virginia, long attributed to Mills, were constructed during his Philadelphia and Baltimore years. During the period 1812–17 he was in the city several times to supervise construction of the Monumental Church. Some writings and the building style itself can be used to strengthen these traditional attributions. These houses share some elements with the works already studied and also reflect some differences from the style developed in Philadelphia and Baltimore.

The Brander House (1816–17) and the smaller Joseph Marx House (1816–17) are closest to works by Mills. The first is a two-story, gabled house on a corner lot, the second two stories over a high basement; in both cases the kitchen and other service areas probably were located in the basement. Both had the typical arched recesses containing windows and doors on the main or first floor, entries had the tripartite form with the entablature cut off abruptly at the edge of the recess, and upper windows sat on sills that merged with a stringcourse. Dormers on both houses had segmental cornices. Disposed across the brick walls, these elements had the strongest relationship with contemporary works in Philadelphia and Baltimore. A few new elements were incorporated: A stringcourse ran over the tops of the uppermost windows, rectangular panels recessed above the main-floor windows alleviated the expanse of brick necessary for high-ceilinged rooms inside, and the white stone (possibly marble) lintels of the windows had end blocks

Figure 2.11
Drawing room during
installation at the
Baltimore Museum
of Art, Waterloo Row.
(Baltimore Museum
of Art, gift of the City of
Baltimore; installation
and renovation made
possible by bequest of Mrs.
John D. Wing, in memory
of her son Hanson
Rawlings Duval, Jr.)

Opposite: Figure 2.12
Brander House
(1816–17), Richmond,
Virginia; demolished.
(The Valentine Museum,
Richmond, Virginia)

with a hemispherical boss. The elevation of the Brander House was unusual in having a high gable, or pediment, over its long dimension, the three-bay front with the portal (fig. 2.12). [16]

The Joseph Marx House was built by Joseph Marx for his mother and insured on October 20, 1817, when it was probably virtually completed. His son-in-law, Samuel Myers, Jr., built the Brander House about the same time. A note by Mills in his 1816 journal records ordering glass for Mr. Myers on March 30, an indication that construction had begun, and Myers insured the house on January 1, 1818. Both were designed probably in 1814 or 1815, when Mills was visiting Richmond. He had known the client earlier, for he wrote to his wife on September 3, 1813, that he was to dine with Mr. Marx that day. Perhaps the question of house designs was an important topic of that dinner conversation, a not unusual approach for Mills. A note in his 1816 journal indicates that he purchased mantlepieces and other work in marble for Mr. Marx to the value of $554.25, sufficient to supply both the Marx House and the Hanover House, and mantlepieces for Mr. Myers at $150. [17]

For Joseph Marx himself Mills built the much larger Hanover House (1815–17), one of the most expensive of the day, insured for $23,000 on October 20, 1817. Its construction began probably in 1815, for on about March 20, 1816, while Mills was in Richmond, he sketched the roof, noting a place there for a central platform of 14 by 16 feet. Two stories high and approximately square, the structure had entrance porches on the west and north and a two-story porch across the south, or garden,

side. The elements of the three-bay faces were disposed quite widely so that much wall surface was exposed. Simple and tripartite windows, each with a rectangular recess below to the level of the water table or stringcourse, had stone lintels and corner blocks with the circular motif. No arched elements were employed, perhaps because the client preferred the prominent stone lintels in the stuccoed, or "rough cast," walls. [18]

Latrobe and others had made stucco finish popular in Richmond and elsewhere around the turn of the century, and with the addition of incised lines it usually simulated masonry. In Richmond Mills used it in the renovation (1815) of the John Ambler House, where he brought two discrete buildings together into one form with the south side stuccoed, as the insurance policy reads, "plaistered in imitation of free Stone." In response to a letter from Ambler, Mills wrote on February 2, 1816, "It gives me much pleasure to hear that the finish of the exterior of your house gives so much satisfaction to yourself & others. I was aware that when finished the house would have a very imposing effect." Other houses attributed to Mills in Richmond, as well as the Monumental Church, were stuccoed and lined in a similar manner. [19]

Perhaps the first of Mills's Richmond houses was the stuccoed Cunningham-Archer House (1814–15). Only a note in the 1816 journal, recording the purchase of marble mantlepieces for Mr. Cunningham at $470, documents a link between this house and Mills. A pedimented portico with a full Ionic entablature supported by four Roman Ionic columns almost nine diameters high—good Palladian

proportions—fronted the middle of three bays. An unusual aspect was the recessed field of both lateral bays. Openings on the first story were single windows in an arched recess and, for the entrance, a Palladian motif. The water table and stringcourse provided strong horizontal elements supporting the arched recesses and the second-story windows, and the cornice and balustrade closed the design at the top. The horizontality of the front, a three-story block, was maintained by reducing the uppermost windows to low rectangles. While window frames in other cities were almost nonexistent to promote resistance to fire, these all have broad wood members, topped by a stone lintel with a raised band on all four of its edges. No plan of the house is known, but photographs suggest a central hall with four rooms, although one of the back corner rooms may have been subdivided for services. The wide hall had a screen divider to separate the entrance from the stairway, thus resembling the division in the Chew House between private and public areas. [20]

Mr. Cunningham built a similar house, Howard's Neck (c. 1815) in Goochland County, Virginia, about forty miles west of Richmond, to which he removed permanently in 1825. The similarities with the city house are close enough to suggest Mills as the designer, but the execution by local carpenters resulted in a drastic simplification of moldings and decorative parts. Again the block is preceded by a four-columned, pedimented porch, here in a full Tuscan order, perhaps based on a model offered by Sir William Chambers (1723–96), but with the columns attenuated to nine diameters. The main front, the south front, has three bays, the lateral two in large rectangular recesses as in the city house. All windows are simple rectangles, with white stone lintels set into the Flemish bond brick fabric. No stringcourses are used, and a recessed, stuccoed panel appears between the lower and upper windows all around the structure. The tripartite entry deserves notice for the unusual lintel shaped as a long, low, triangular pediment, flanked by end blocks with circular ornament above the side posts. This lintel recalls the contemporary triangular lintels in the Eighth Street house in Philadelphia, a relationship that suggests that Mills may have made designs for Cunningham as early as 1813. [21]

In the plan, perhaps a repetition of the city house, two large rooms and a broad central hall occupy slightly more than half the house, with the stair hall slightly off axis; under its curving run opens the back door, a Millsian use of this kind of space. Three clouded marble mantlepieces are further signs of Mills, for they have the basic design he employed, with plain brackets supporting the shelf and a simple recessed panel in the frieze. Although some of the city house mantles were more elabo-

rate, having small columns like those of Waterloo Row, still the $470 recorded in the 1816 journal could easily have included the three at Howard's Neck.

In three Richmond houses attributed to Mills, the porch stretched across the entire garden front, an element derived from the city's geography. Overlooking the falling hillside and river valley, the porch allowed the residents a magnificent view and also made their mansions visible to the rest of the community. In addition to the Hanover House, Mills designed two in which giant columns supported the two-story porch—the Page-Anderson House (1815–16) and the John Brockenbrough House (1817–18). The first, designed for Carter B. Page and the subject of several entries in Mills's 1816 journal, had four great columns arranged in a curve to support the back porch on two levels. On the street front the two-story block had a one-room addition on either side, so that it had five bays on the first story and three bays on the second. Of its plan, little is certain. Old photographs suggest that the entrance hall and stair extended half the depth of the house, so that three rooms stretched across the back of the main block. This organization is known from Mills's Brockenbrough House as well as the Wickham House (1812), designed by Alexander Parris. Perhaps Latrobe established the three-room suite on the garden front, for it appeared in his Harvie-Gamble House (1798–99), in Richmond. Mills may have designed the Page-Anderson House in May–June 1814, when he spent several weeks in Richmond; it was essentially completed when insured on February 13, 1816, for $14,000. A little later, on May 5, Mills shipped wallpaper and in July ordered three clouded marble mantlepieces from Moore and Herkness in Philadelphia; they were shipped in December, but none appears in photographs of the interior. Until its demolition about twenty years ago, this great house retained its original two-story porch despite the addition of a third story and a complete exterior renovation to make it conform to the Italian villa taste of the later nineteenth century. [22]

Of Mills's houses in Richmond, only the John Brockenbrough House remains standing. A third story was added in the mid-nineteenth century, and changes in the end walls accompanied extensive interior alterations. Five bays are spread across the 67-foot front, but the back wall is treated as three bays, with tripartite windows on each level (fig. 2.13). The rear windows are placed on the intercolumniations of the back porch, and the columns are paired so that they dominate rather than are diminished by the wide spaces of the back wall —perhaps another instance where the Vitruvian concept of symmetry played a role in design. In addition to the great columns, all the tripartite win-

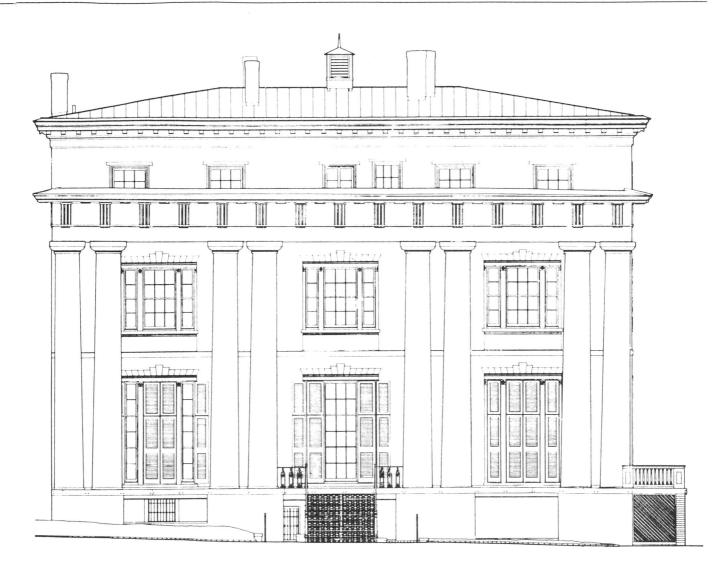

*Figure 2.13
South (garden) front,
John Brockenbrough House
(1817–18), Richmond,
Virginia; altered.
(John Shirley, Historic
American Buildings
Survey)*

*Figure 2.14
Restored plan,
Brockenbrough House,
Glave Newman Anderson
and Associates.
(Glave Newman Anderson
and Associates)*

dows create vertical lines; the podium and entablature run without interruption across the building, while a stringcourse appears and reappears between the columns. As in the earlier row houses, recesses tie the upper windows to the stringcourse. The garden front has a network of lines as carefully designed as those of Waterloo Row. The vocabulary of forms and their anchoring in place support the attribution to Mills, and the fairly strict use of his linear composition dates this house close to the time of Waterloo Row. [23]

Despite many signs of the architect's modern manner, other stylistic suggestions appear in the

separate parts. Doric columns, unfluted and without a base, occurred in modern English revivals of the ancient Doric. Yet, the proportions here (the columns were eight diameters high) and the introduction of two and three metopes over the intercolumniations refer to more conservative English practice, such as the Palladianism taught by Chambers. This conservatism is pointed up by the flat arches over the windows, composed of rusticated voussoirs with exaggerated keystones. On the front, too, the windows, with their broad frames with cornices repeating the cornice of the small porch, recall eighteenth-century practice more than that of Mills. Such differences in taste probably have to be laid to the demands of the client.

A number of Latrobean elements appear in the plan and in the interior as well (fig. 2.14). The original disposition of the rooms, which has been studied carefully in preparation for restoration, shows an unequal division into front and back sections. The oval entry with niches and the adjacent semicircular, niched stair hall—motifs known to Mills through Latrobe—evoke eighteenth-century England. On the other side of the entry were service stairs and a pantry, close to the dining room. The suite of three large rooms across the back followed the current fashion, probably introduced to Richmond by Latrobe. In fact, the plan seems to be a simplified, reversed version of that of Latrobe's John Peter Van Ness House (1813) in Washington, D.C., and the stairway with niches virtually duplicates that of the Markoe House. So much alteration has occurred that little can be said of the decorative treatment. Some woodwork by Mills perhaps survives in occasional doors with simple moldings and corner blocks with the circular motif. On the second floor is a dark clouded marble mantlepiece that certainly was ordered from Moore and Herkness in Philadelphia, for it is identical with others obtained by Mills. [24]

These Richmond houses shared with Mills's Philadelphia and Baltimore houses a number of elements of his vocabulary and his approach to design. Significant aspects of planning and the stuccoed exteriors derived from fashions established by Latrobe. Late eighteenth-century English styles appear also—the Palladian as well as the elongation of proportions derived from Robert Adam and common in the Federal style.

STYLISTIC

ADAPTATIONS

Two more houses begun in 1817 demonstrate that Mills employed different styles consciously to meet the tastes of his clients or of the region. The Richard Potts House (1817–19), in Frederick, Maryland, built of brick with white stone sills and woodwork for the openings, exemplifies the Baltimore city house. The elevation drawing shows it two stories and two bays wide with a tripartite entry and window on the first story; on the drawing two similar windows on the upper story, hanging from the cornice, have been replaced by small windows. All openings lack frames, having just a narrow strip of wood to hold the parts inside the brickwork; concern for fire safety promoted this type of window and door frame in Baltimore. As a whole, the walls have been simplified; they are devoid of even a water table or stringcourse. The vocabulary and linear pattern used by Mills at this time are evident, and control of the parts is recognized by the manner in which the upper windows hang from the cornice. [25]

Richard Potts, Jr., of Frederick, was distantly related to Mills by marriage, and the latter passed through that city several times a year on visits to the home of his wife's parents in Winchester, Virginia. In 1819 Potts occupied his new house, the first notice of which appeared on July 23, 1817, when Mills mailed a set of plans with a bill of materials. After a conference with his client, Mills provided a new set of drawings, with a new list of materials, for

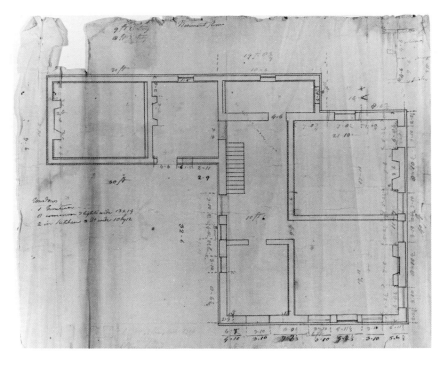

a larger house. Five drawings have survived, one with the smaller dimensions (first-story plan) and four with the larger (front and side elevations and basement and chamber-story plans). The front elevation shows that Mills himself changed the large windows to simple rectangular ones, for the erased lines can still be seen on the drawing. The plan is developed from the townhouse type, having a wide hall and two adjacent, almost square rooms; as the lot is a corner one, the back building juts out at a right angle.

The basement plan, frayed from much use during construction, has a number of interesting notations (fig. 2.15). It was intended as a working drawing with dimensions carefully indicated to guide the mason. But with ink of another shade, certainly after another conference, Mills changed the positions of the basement windows to correspond with those actually built—three openings on each floor —and at the same time changed the dimensions at these places. Finally, in the upper right corner he sketched in pencil the one-story office wing built for the lawyer Potts at the left of the main entrance. He may also have changed the entry to a more Federal door with sidelights and a broad elliptical fanlight, perhaps more in keeping with the setting on Court Square.

Mills's interior finish is quite plain, with relatively simple woodwork. The greatest amount of ornament, in fact, is the series of panels with raised

Figure 2.15
Plan of basement,
Richard Potts House
(1817–19), Frederick,
Maryland; altered.
(Henry Francis du Pont
Winterthur Museum and
Library, Joseph Downs
Manuscript Collection)

ovals on the entry doors; this oval motif reappears below the windows inside the house. For this house also Mills acquired clouded gray marble mantlepieces in the basic design, flat posts and lintel, and blunt consoles to support the shelf (fig. 2.16). Sometimes he employed recessed panels on the

Figure 2.16
Marble mantlepiece,
Potts House.

larger surfaces, but the grooving used here is identical with that on the mantle in the John Brockenbrough House.

The Hampton-Preston House (1817–18) in Columbia, South Carolina, has even more Georgian elements than the Brockenbrough House. The drawing shows a five-bay front, the walls stuccoed and lined to represent masonry but with heavier blocks and rustication for the foundation and corner quoins (fig. 2.17). A long balustrade rises directly above the cornice, and the first-story windows have their own large cornices. These massive elements surround an elaborate centerpiece in which the lines of four Roman Doric columns on the porch rise through the blocks of the deck balustrade to pilasters against the upper wall and into the piers of the octagonal drum carrying a dome above the inner staircase. This rise is accompanied by a series of setbacks from the rail-lined steps to the porch, the deck, the upper wall and balustrade, and the dome, thus emphasizing late baroque massing. James Hoban and others had kept this fashion alive in South Carolina. At the same time, Mills's precise linear design controls the disposition of the parts. [26]

The Hampton-Preston House was designed for the merchant Ainsley Hall, perhaps during February–March 1817, while Mills was in Charleston, and Hall occupied it in 1818. The front of the house differs greatly from the drawing, and because Mills was so little in South Carolina during its construc-

tion, his participation in the changes seems unlikely. The alterations—for example, in the projecting central three bays under a broad pediment and the emphasized corner quoins and voussoirs of flat and segmental arches—increase the building's conservative appearance. A porch with Ionic columns, resembling the one in the drawing, appears at the back of the house. The interior seems to have had small change since its construction. A screen once separated the entrance area of the broad hall from the inner end with the staircase, as was done in the Cunningham-Archer House in Richmond; a similar screen still stands in the upper hall. One back corner has been divided into service areas, but the other three rooms preserve most of their original treatment. Although mantlepieces have been replaced, the ornamental plaster seems original; broad cornices stretch out in support across the ceiling, and in the center are medallions composed of circular moldings. Wainscoting with small-scale, old-fashioned decorative details throughout the house, however, suggests changes made for local taste. Thus, the conservative aspects increased in construction, perhaps owing to Mills's absence.

These contemporary house designs show a stylistic range of which Mills certainly was conscious. The modern manner he developed in Philadelphia and Baltimore appears in the Richard Potts House in rural Maryland. The John Brockenbrough House, built in the region where Jefferson was still living, exhibits English Palladianism along with the modern English style of Latrobe. Farther south and inland, Georgian tastes were satisfied by the Hampton-Preston House. Mills's own contribution—the design system and vocabulary—endowed even the most conservative house with an austerity and monumentality.

These works in other cities, moreover, had an impact on Mills's last house in Baltimore. Shortly before leaving in December 1820, he designed a house (1820–22) for the merchant John Hoffman, to be built at the corner of Franklin and Cathedral streets (fig. 2.18). In April 1821 Hoffman applied for establishment of the street limits and a month later requested grading, as he had begun the house in the meantime. Completed in 1822, it survived remarkably well until its razing in 1908. Only three bays wide, it showed a close relationship with Mills's recent houses. A high basement of smooth rusticated ashlar blocks supported the stuccoed and lined rubble walls. A tripartite door and flanking tripartite windows rested on the basement; all were composed of pilasters with blocks for bases and capitals (like those of Waterloo Row) and had a raised oval worked in the panels below the sidelights of the windows. The windows, like those in the John Brockenbrough and Hampton-Preston

houses, were taller than those Mills had customarily employed. Although no stringcourse marked the upper story, the otherwise unframed windows had stone lintels. Two dormers, in line with the lower windows, had segmental cornices and a smaller version of the pilasters. [27]

Against this plain, sober façade Mills set a massive porch. Two modern (that is, with angular scrolls) Palladian Ionic columns with plain shafts supported full entablatures running back to pilasters against the wall. From the broad cornices rose a vault fronted by an arch with the same entablature moldings, which gave the form an impressive strength. The vault continued with the rising steps into a vestibule that opened within the body of the house, an uncommon motif reappearing almost a decade later a few blocks away in the Archbishopric (1829) on North Charles Street, designed by William F. Small. Mills himself employed another version on the side of the Hoffman House, hollowing out the mass of the block for an apsidal vestibule framed by a molded archivolt borne on pilasters. Of the interior little is known. The principal stairway rose from a circular room near the center, as in the Benjamin Chew House ten years earlier. The garden front of the second Ainsley Hall House (1823–25) in Columbia, South Carolina, has an apsidal entry opening into the adjoining circular ends of

two large rooms; a similar disposition probably appeared by the side entry of the Hoffman House. Both of these elements came from Latrobe, but whereas he placed the entrances on the basement level, Mills led from arched entries directly to the principal story and the curvilinear elements. [28]

The John Hoffman House was a solid, stable block with a deceptive simplicity that concealed the precision of organization and control over the parts. Its stuccoed and lined surface did away with the small scale of a brick wall, achieving monumentality in the manner of Latrobe. At the Richard Potts House the door complex is located at the back of the thickness of the wall, and the Hoffman House entries carried this recession further, a new development in Mills's residential works. Following the forced return to eighteenth-century practices in the southern cities, Mills's domestic designs became more three-dimensional. The masses had long been precisely marked through their surfaces, and now the incorporation of clearly delimited voids pointed up change that had been developing slowly and was more visible in Mills's public buildings.

Whereas Mills's residential style grew fairly directly out of his teacher's work and he remained in Latrobe's debt through 1820, significant changes appeared in his work during this period. During an early experimental stage, culminating around

Figure 2.17 Elevation, Hampton-Preston House (1817–18), Columbia, South Carolina; changed in construction. (South Carolina Historical Society)

Opposite: Figure 2.18 John Hoffman House (1820–22), Baltimore, Maryland; demolished 1908. (Robert L. Harris, The Peale Museum)

1815, he focused on the development of his linear system. This activity was aided by his restricted vocabulary of forms. Required to employ other stylistic treatments from 1815 to 1820, he moved in the direction of three-dimensional composition, enriching the mass by means of voids. Yet, his own manner shone through these stylistic devices, and these exercises proved fruitful in requiring a flexibility that would serve him well in succeeding decades.

For most of this time Mills's clientele was the middle class. Virtually none of the Philadelphia and Baltimore housing was intended for low-income groups. In both cities he worked within the traditional materials and types and developed a distinctive style. From 1815 to 1820, especially with commissions in Richmond and Columbia, he found the wealthy and upper-middle class, clients whose distinct personal preferences forced him to accept their tastes and thus affected his style. The new stage in his architectural and professional development served as preparation for the 1820s, when he worked in South Carolina and dealt with a different regional taste. It encouraged his return to Palladio.

EARLY CHURCH

DESIGNS

Parallel with the residential works carried out during this period, Mills was engaged in many works of a more public nature. Churches constituted the largest number of a single type, and during this period he designed six, all of which were built. As early as 1803–4 he designed ecclesiastical works, such as the Circular Congregational Church in Charleston, South Carolina. His book of designs for the First Presbyterian Church in Augusta, Georgia, was completed in 1807, after he had settled in Philadelphia. Four of his churches during the Philadelphia and Baltimore period were centralized buildings, having a circular or octagonal form, thus resembling the Circular Church. Two churches were rectilinear, resembling the Augusta building. Like the houses of this period, they exhibited a wide range of stylistic qualities.[29]

Much has been made, and rightly so, of the fact that Mills designed and built more central-type churches than any other architect of the day, European or American. Yet, others also employed the simple, regular geometrical shapes, sometimes enclosing them within larger blocks. The type can be understood as an extreme development of the Age of Reason, going beyond the meetinghouse in establishing close contact between the preacher and the audience. Mills not only pointed out that with the centralized design the whole congregation could see and hear the preacher from close up but

also fortified his arguments with references to his own acoustical experiments that grew out of Latrobe's study of this science. His churches exhibited the open, spacious interiors preferred in the previous century, usually painted in a high key and well lighted by windows and broad, glazed monitors in the dome.[30]

In addition, the central-type design can be seen as having a special attraction for Mills, who was an enthusiast of the theoretical, a characteristic he showed as early as his 1802 essay on the Tuscan order, and of the geometrical, as shown by his experiments in geometry undertaken in row houses. With the churches, however, the design was not simply for a façade but for the whole building. The prototype, especially for circular buildings, was the Roman Pantheon, popular in the eighteenth century and especially favored by Thomas Jefferson, for whom Mills drafted rotundas about 1803. And although Mills did not press the point with his clients, his use of the Delorme system for dome construction permitted a broad interior without piers and columns obstructing the view. He probably learned of this system from Jefferson, who favored it so much that he forced Latrobe to use it in the national Capitol. No doubt Mills used this kind of structure for his Circular Church in Charleston, and he extended the concept to cover large rectangular halls.[31]

In 1811–12 Mills designed three centralized churches, the Sansom Street Baptist Church (1811–12) and the First Unitarian, or Octagon, Church (1812–13), both in Philadelphia, and the Monumental (Episcopal) Church (1812–17), in Richmond, Virginia. The first was his largest, capable of seating 2,500 to 4,000 persons under its 90-foot dome. Its construction must have occupied much of 1811, its plastering was completed before December 16, 1812, and it probably was first used about a month later. The smaller Octagon Church seated only 300. Planned sometime after August 1811, the work was begun in March 1812 and was unusually rapid, requiring only eleven months; plastering was completed by January 8, 1813, and the building opened for use just after February 12, 1813. Cornerstone ceremonies for the Monumental Church, with its 70-foot dome, took place on August 1, 1812, and it was dedicated on May 4, 1814. About two years was a typical time for construction of a building this size.[32]

The Sansom Street Baptist Church had a massive entrance structure almost as wide as its cylindrical auditorium. Two square blocks flanked the cavernous central entrance screened by two Ionic columns in antis bearing a full entablature. The blocks had tall, arched recesses on the front and side, and each block carried a small belfry echoing the shape of the large dome. Mills went to ancient and modern sources in selecting the parts. The Ionic columns were derived from those of the ancient Erechtheum in Athens, but the entablature owed its two-band architrave to the eighteenth century and its fanciful cornice, decorated with small, recessed panels, to Mills. Except for the panels, the cornice continued across the stair blocks and around the body of the building. The motif of the two-column screen in the entry echoed modern European ideas, but for Mills it came directly from Latrobe's pump house for the Philadelphia waterworks.[33]

Behind the porch, the circular structure broadened out on either side and its dome rose higher. A remarkable drawing for this building shows in detail just how such a dome was built on the Delorme system (see fig. 1.14, pages 18–19). The drawing is quartered to show an exterior and a view from above, a plan, and a section, the latter two showing in detail how the planks were joined, strengthened by purlins, to follow the desired curve. The whole structure sat on top of the walls without exerting any outward pressure. Large beams, often difficult to acquire and always expensive, were unnecessary, and this system has proved strong enough that several contemporary domes of this type survive today. The profile drawing shows also the monitor that supplied light and steplike rings that can be traced back to the Pantheon. In the Roman temple they served a structural function in containing some of the thrust of the brick and concrete, especially during construction, but in the Philadelphia church their function was aesthetic and cultural in certifying the ancient lineage of the domical form. Although other architects continued to build these rings at the lower curve of the dome, Mills eliminated them, perhaps for economy.[34]

The Delorme dome satisfied a need of the age when many domes were raised as signs of urbanization and modernity. It suited the capabilities of craftsmen who lacked the skills to make domes of brick or stone, the needs of congregations whose funds usually were limited, and the needs of architects who wanted the form for its grandeur and its symbolism of modernity. It served for octagonal as well as circular buildings, and the central shape might also be contained within a rectangular form topped by the dome. Its light and quickly and cheaply built structure made it especially suitable for American use.

The interior showed Mills using the circular form symbolically for the Baptists. The pulpit stood at the head of the aisle opposite the entrance, elevated to make the preacher more accessible to the large audience in the horseshoe-shaped galleries. Two lesser aisles paralleled the main one, and another crossed the floor between the side entrances (although it may have been eliminated). The basin was placed at the crossing of the aisles, under the center of the dome, allowing the ritual of baptism to be a focal point.

For the two octagonal churches Mills employed domes of similar form; that at Richmond is still standing. Carpenters easily fabricated something like a squinch to provide continuous support at the wall angles. Both structures had a portico appended to one of the eight sides. In the Octagon Church the apse and pulpit presumably were situated opposite the entrance, and to either side of the building projecting blocks provided additional entries; perhaps this small church had no galleries. Arched recesses filled the intermediate sides, and elements of the portico cornice reappeared in recesses and on the side blocks. A drawing made about 1828 shows lunette windows, over the doors and in recesses, composed of a series of semicircular and radial muntins or cames with an outer border of small circles, the pattern used in many of Mills's buildings. Cast shadows in the drawing underscore the three-dimensionality of the masses and spaces. The glazed monitor, approximately a third of the dome's diameter, and numerous windows allowed a flood of light to illuminate the religious discussions, which were as rationalist as the geometrical form of the building. This church, like the one in Richmond, was stuccoed and lined to achieve the effect of masonry.[35]

Following a disastrous theater fire in Richmond in which seventy-one citizens died, a committee was formed to raise money to build a monument on the site of the fire. Designs were sought from several architects—Latrobe and Henry Hiort are known to have submitted some—and Mills sent in two by February 25, 1812. His link with the committee was through his father-in-law, Gen. John Smith, a member of Congress, who wrote on this date that the committee now wished a place of worship adjacent to the monument. By March 5 Mills sent a new design that was adopted by the end of April, and he was soon named to supervise construction of the Monumental Church.[36]

In its disposition the building is similar to the Octagon Church, with some variations that help make it appear monumental in a figurative sense (see fig. 1.7, page 11). The octagon, of stuccoed brick, supports a 70-foot dome and a 22-foot lantern. The main porch fills the street side, a broad block at the back around the sanctuary would carry the intended tower, and at the intermediate sides are blocks with a portico and gallery stairs. The actual monument—the victims' ashes were buried under the church—is the 33-foot-square porch, built of masonry. Its screen of two columns in antis bearing an entablature repeats the form of entry used for the Sansom Street Church, now on all three sides of the porch to provide an easy flow of traffic. The grand effect of the block with three open sides contrasts with the small scale of the side porches with two free-standing but smaller columns. All the parts are fused by the lines of water table and cornices, the upper lines continuing as stringcourses. Tripartite windows and recessed panels in the stair wings enhance the sense of mass, and curvilinear elements are limited to the tower base and windows above the side porches. The prominent window lintels seem to be flat abstractions of the gable and flanking acroteria of a Roman alter; their massiveness resembles heavy lintels in several other buildings designed by Mills about this time.[37]

An early engraving, noted in a newspaper advertisement as endorsed by Mills, shows two significant changes made during construction. The tower was never completed, as a later engraving by W. Goodacre suggests by showing it in shadow. In the engravings a high attic rising above the main entrance bears a large stone block with the allegorical figure of Richmond mourning, seated among broken columns and other signs of ruin. When construction of this part continued in 1815–16, financial limitations led to reduction of the block to a pediment and the sculpture to an Egyptoid sar-

cophagus within the porch. The porch now was blocked by the large sarcophagus; its doors were closed, and all entrance is through the small cramped side entries that were intended to serve the galleries only. Mills retained the acroteria flanking the pediment to invoke the image of a Roman altar and increased the signs of mourning by incorporating lachrymal urns in the frieze. The triangular lintels over the triple windows make another reference to ancient Roman altars.[38]

The order used for the Monumental Church is unusual not only for the omission of the metopes and triglyphs of the Doric frieze but also for the treatment of the column. Its capital has a wide, flaring curve derived from archaic Greek architecture—in particular, a temple at Paestum; use of this form by English architects in the late eighteenth century and by Latrobe represented an interest in the origins of architecture. One ancient example, at Delos, showed a narrow band of fluting at top and bottom as a guide for workmen who were to complete the flutes, an intention not understood in Mills's day. Robert Adam (1728–92) and George Dance, Jr. (1741–1825), first introduced and then lengthened this strip of fluting below the capital as

Figure 2.19
First Baptist Church (1816–18), Baltimore, Maryland; demolished. (Historic American Buildings Survey)

a means of modernizing the Ionic order. Mills combined the two developments in several works between 1813 and 1817, separating the elements of base, shaft, capital, and elongated necking in order to combine them in a variety of ways. In keeping with well-established theory of the day, he employed this form of Doric for the Baltimore Washington Monument and the Monumental Church, emphasizing their serious purpose, and a parallel form of Ionic largely in private houses, recognizing the owners' social status. This method of varying columns and the concern for expression through the orders, it may be noted, occurred while Mills was developing his pattern of vertical and horizontal elements as well as the varying rhythms of arched and rectangular openings, both large and small, in his rows and individual houses. At the same time, freedom in handling the entablature was possible, as all three of these churches demonstrated.[39]

Mills organized the interior of the Monumental Church in a manner recalling the Sansom Street Church; it has a wide aisle from the main portal to the sanctuary, paralleled by two lesser aisles, and another crosses the auditorium between the side entries. The latter are broad, shallow spaces occupied largely by two curving staircases to the galleries. Because of the late change in the monument, the doors of the main entry have remained closed, so the worshiper does not see first the apsidal niche with the altar and raised pulpit (all remodeled now), screened by two tall Ionic columns of the Erectheum type. From the original entry the viewer's eye followed the sequence of pews, the curved rows of Doric columns, and the broad curving face of the galleries, all leading to the prime religious focal point in the sanctuary. Moving forward, the eye then followed rising lines into the well-lighted dome and glazed monitor. At various points the eye rested upon Mills's commemorative ornament—acroteria on blocks above the Doric capitals (making references to Roman funerary altars) and, instead of classical palmettes on the necking of the Ionic columns, alternating stars and downturned torches, symbolic of eternity and mortality. Stained glass now fills the tripartite windows, darkening the interior in keeping with the later taste that eclipsed the bright lighting preferred in the Age of Reason. Yet, the austere discipline of the interior witnesses to the nascent Greek Revival as much as does the exterior.

Designed within a short period, these three churches show the rapid development of Mills's style. Similarities were great in several respects: the overall form of a centralized building with a dome; the location of entries, aisles, and pulpit; the placement of windows; the tendency toward a simplified stylistic treatment that became more personal and severe. In some respects these churches resemble his residential work of the same time, specifically, for example, in the window forms and more generally in that they form a series of varied treatments rising from a basic idea. They demonstrate a stylistic progression, a move from the late Federal toward the Greek Revival, not as great contrast but as gradual change.

After several years Mills again designed three churches within a short period, from 1816 to 1817, but instead of reflecting similarities they represent three different approaches in form and style, similar to the contrasts exhibited in his later residential works. The earliest and best documented was his First Baptist Church (1816–18) in Baltimore (fig. 2.19). Planning and initial stages of its construction are recorded in brief entries in Mills's 1816 journal, thus providing valuable information on the pace of work on such a structure. Mills was occupied from February 3 to February 12 with drawings, which were accepted, as was his offer to supervise construction. On March 17 advertisements requested bids. On April 2 excavation began, and on April 22 Mills laid out the circle of the church. On May 3 he laid out the porch and on October 8 the founda-

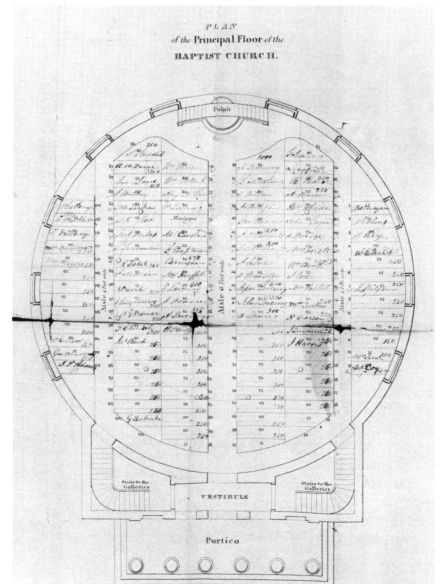

Figure 2.20
Pew plan, First Baptist Church, engraving based on drawing by Robert Mills, c. 1817. (Maryland Historical Society)

tions for the columns. Meanwhile, he made working drawings on February 20, June 6, August 20, and November 14, and before the end of the year he sketched the trusses for the vestibule roof. On February 20, 1817, detailed drawings for the dome were needed, and eleven months later, in March 1818, the church was dedicated. Construction thus occupied almost two years. On December 14, 1816, he arranged to have Antonio Capellano carve the capitals, for which the sculptor was paid on August 11, 1817. Mills drew pew plans from December 4 to December 10, 1816, and one set of engravings after these drawings has survived (fig. 2.20). On November 18, 1816, he commissioned William Strickland in Philadelphia to make a perspective drawing of the church, but neither the drawing nor any engraving made after it seems to have survived.[40]

The building was composed of three parts—a six-columned portico, a broader vestibule block, and the cylindrical, domed auditorium—all bound together by the tall, continuous frieze and cornice. Barren surface planes of stuccoed brick emphasized the hard corners and angles where parts met. Of the five arched recesses under the portico, three were openings, with fanlights separated by a tall cornice from the doorways below. A similar doorway opened at the side of the vestibule block under the gallery staircase, and large rectangular windows continued on this level around the auditorium wall. Small windows on the upper level circled the whole building, and although as broad as the windows below, the upper ones appeared squashed against the frieze. In the colonnade each burly, unfluted shaft seemed to compress its base and flatten the spare, modern Ionic capital against the entablature. The tensions, compressions, and oppositions gave rise to the appearance of muscularity as a complement to the increasing hardness, discipline, and precise articulation of forms that characterized Mills's Greek Revival style.

The entrance block housed a vestibule and two staircases to the galleries, shaped like those of the Monumental Church. The dome, Mills recorded, had a clear span of 76 feet 4 inches; with a radius of 53 feet, it was less than hemispherical, kept low to improve hearing and speaking according to Mills's understanding of acoustics. This was his fifth centralized church, and each one, he felt, demonstrated the correctness of his science of acoustics and the superiority of the shape for an auditorium. A main and two lateral aisles led through the auditorium; the baptismal basin stood opposite the entrance, flanked by two flights of steps rising to the pulpit overhead. Basin and pulpit, well lighted by the broad, low monitor atop the dome and numerous windows, formed a single focal point. From early in his career, Mills insisted that utility must precede ornament. Internally and externally this building exemplified his belief. Virtually nothing of Georgian or Federal taste survived here.[41]

On March 5, 1817, Mills wrote to his wife that his departure from Charleston was delayed, so he would attend to one or two churches in prospect. No record of intervening negotiations survives, but a finished elevation, dated Baltimore, January 2[2], 1818, is still owned by the First Baptist Church (1818–22) of Charleston (fig. 2.21). Newspapers carried an advertisement for bids on April 20, 1819, as well as notices of the cornerstone ceremony on September 16 and the dedication on January 17, 1822. A few years later Mills published a description and evaluation of the building:

The baptist church exhibits the best specimen of correct taste in architecture of the modern buildings in this city. It is purely Greek in its style, simply grand in its proportions, and beautiful in its detail. The plan is of the temple form, divided into four parts; the portico, vestibule, nave, and vestry rooms. The whole length of the building is 110 feet, and breadth 60.

The facade presents a portico of four massy columns of the lightest proportions of the Doric, surmounted by a pediment. Behind this portico (on the main walls) rises an attic story squared up to the height of the roof, and crowned by a cupola or belfry. The side walls of the building are opened by the requisite apertures for windows and doors, and a full cornice runs round the whole.

You enter the vestibule by three doors, on each side of which the gallery stairs ascend; by three opposite doors you pass into the aisles, dividing the pews into blocks; at the extreme end of the nave of the church are the baptismal font and pulpit, lighted by a large vaulted window.

Around three sides of the nave a double colonnade extends, rises up to the roof, and supports the galleries. The lower order of the columns is Doric, the upper Ionic; each with their regular entablatures; the whole finished in a rich chaste style, and producing from the unity of the design, a very pleasing effect. This building is situated on Church, below Tradd, street.[42]

The building gains a classical quality from the fusing of the vestibule and auditorium into one rectangular, templelike body and the binding of the portico and vestibule by the continuation of the full Doric entablature across and around to the sides of the block. These elements point to the tradition of the English architect James Gibbs (1682–1754), whose St. Martin-in-the-Fields (1720–26), in London, also has a vestibule-auditorium block behind a monumental portico. As at St. Martin's, the Baptist Church retains a distinction between the vestibule and auditorium by architectural decoration, here by the short run of the entablature and attic wall. In Charleston stands one of the major Gibbsian churches in America, St. Michael's (1752–61); the Second Presbyterian Church (1809–c. 1816) and

St. Paul's Church (1811–16) demonstrate the continuing strength of this tradition in the city.[43]

Mills, then, developed a design to conform with local taste. Even the two rows of arched windows along the sides of the Baptist Church follow the Gibbsian pattern, and the small domed belfry gave it a nodding recognition. In his description, however, Mills emphasized the correctness of his Greek style, using terms such as "grand," "beautiful," and, for the portico columns, "massy." Nevertheless, some significant Georgian details lingered, such as the Doric column with a base and two metopes over the intercolumniation; such details, already old-fashioned in Europe, were promoted by Sir William Chambers. On the whole, however, ornament has been reduced to little more than the essentials of the orders. Moldings, such as those of imposts and arched entries, have been drastically simplified. Decorative window muntins are straight and circular lines, not ovals and ellipses, and the fanlights over the doors show Mills's favored pattern.[44]

Architectural use of line underlies the general horizontality of the building, especially through the dominance of the Doric entablature and the attic. This line functions in small elements—for example, in one change between the drawing and the completed building affecting the treatment of the entrances. The cornice of the doorway lintels has been eliminated and impost moldings introduced, so that the horizontal line continues across the front, disappearing behind the pilasters, stepping back in the arched ways, but unifying the separate parts by its continuity. Line, then, is a significant element in this design. The bold juxtaposition of the portico against the block and the compression of the Doric capitals recall the Baptist church in Baltimore, as do the plain wall surfaces and lack of moldings along the sides. Overall, the building shows Mills responding to his patrons' conservatism yet leading them toward the Greek Revival.

Little is known about Mills's second church in Baltimore, St. John's Episcopal Church (1817–18), on Liberty Street, consecrated in 1818, sold to a Methodist group in 1828, and destroyed in the fire of 1904. A single block, it was approximately 84 feet deep, with a front about 64 feet wide, dimensions that suggest a meetinghouse rather than a basilican building. The front was subdivided with a three-bay center and a single bay on each side. A short flight of steps, an attic rising above the cornice, and a slight projection emphasized the center, and a tall, arched door flanked by lower ones gave it the appearance of a triumphal arch; the lateral bays had blind recesses. All the arches contained fanlights above the broad frieze customarily em-

Figure 2.21
First Baptist Church
(1818–22), Charleston,
South Carolina.

ployed by Mills. These arched forms were prominent elements of the modern English style passed to Mills through Latrobe. Another feature of European neoclassicism appeared in the rectangular paneled recesses in the attic and above the small arches. The interweaving of these two contrasting shapes, arched and rectangular, gave this modest structure a modern appearance. Small though it was, St. John's belonged stylistically to the family of Latrobe's Baltimore cathedral.[45]

Congregations in Baltimore, in contrast with the Baptists in Charleston, evidently were able to accept more advanced architectural treatment. Mills was able and willing to adapt his architectural style to his client's taste, all the time retaining many aspects of his transitional late Federal–early Greek Revival manner. The same pattern in his development that appeared through his residential work occurred in his churches as well. The intense self-centering of the period 1810–15 gave way to more openness in his willingness to expand his stylistic repertory.

PUBLIC BUILDINGS

Mills's public buildings of the period exemplified great variety of both stylistic treatment and function. All had in common the acceptance of an institution, group, or public body as a client and the need to provide spaces for varied activities and usually for large numbers of people. The earliest works during the Philadelphia years included a design for a state capitol for Pennsylvania and one to provide fireproof wings for Independence Hall.

Following action by the legislature to establish a new seat in Harrisburg, plans for a new building, or complex, were sought. A drawing by Mills, dated April 16, 1810, presents the front of the capitol overlooking the Susquehanna River from a small hilltop in Harrisburg (fig. 2.22). An elevation and plan for a complex more than 700 feet long show a careful siting of the buildings among several straight and curved avenues and large plots of grass. The five-part complex has the largest structure as the culminating center, with two-story structures at the ends and intermediate one-story offices, all connected by covered colonnades. Although they are rectangular, some conceal circular elements within their bulk. The central structure has two large legislative halls, one a Latrobean ellipse composed of two semicircles connected by straight lines and the other having a semicircular end. The intermediate buildings and the larger office building at the south contain two circular fireproof rooms. The governor's house, at the north end, contains only rectilinear elements.[46]

The design's remarkable aspect is the bent axis centered in the legislative building, creating a V-shape with broadly spread arms. Buildings follow the diagonals in plan, but in elevation the effect is rather like a Palladian country villa with colonnades curving forward from the central block to the outer buildings. As the plan shows, the other side of the complex is designed as the major approach to the capitol and the setting for ceremonial activities. In the center is a six-columned entrance portico, and at the ends the colonnades continue across the outer structures.

At this time Mills was not far removed from Jefferson and his love for Palladio, and the choice of this arrangement for a large complex is understandable. The architectural vocabulary also shows much debt to this source in the extensive use of columns, especially around entrances, disposed in the wall plane as well as in small two-column porticoes and a tall four-column screen before the angle in the central structure. Several uses of the arched forms, however, derived from Latrobe: Tall, arched windows light the legislative halls, and the tripartite form of the rectangle continued into the upper semicircle, making it a Roman bath, or thermal, window. Small arched recesses face closets rather than rooms of some importance, a clear sign of Mills's still immature design facility. Although a horizontal line links all the outer structures, it breaks abruptly at the taller central building.

Following the departure of the state legislature, the city of Philadelphia gained use of the old State House, Independence Hall, and in 1812 city officials received permission from state authorities to replace the old wings with fireproof structures. Mills had begun working on these as early as October 1809 at the urging of Charles Willson Peale, who wanted better quarters for his museum. The finished drawing, dated April 1812, presents two alternative designs for the wings, both dependent on the existing three buildings of the complex (fig. 2.23). The stringcourses of the central structure determined the height of the stories and the horizontal lines of the wings; keystones were repeated; and small bays among large bays echoed the size of those in the old buildings. Despite these concessions to the earlier style, the design shows clearly the familiar vocabulary of Mills's early houses and less of the diversity apparent in the capitol design. On one side the wing shows tripartite recessed arches and on the other rectangular recesses with panels overhead; on both the lines of the tripartite windows continue into low windows on the upper story. Although the bays differ in size, changes between large and small sizes occurred in the houses also, as in the Benjamin Chew and Richard Willcocks houses. These wings (1812–14) were built with rectangular openings and lasted until 1896.[47]

Between the two designs for these public buildings Mills refined his personal vocabulary. They lack the strength of design he developed over the next few years; perhaps it was the experience of working with the two large complexes that awakened him to the need for control over the building's length and the possibility of developing a system for maintaining such control. Mills's next design for a public building, Washington Hall (1814–16), in Philadelphia, offered implicit criticism of these two works. Despite the search for monumentality through colonnades and the large size of the central structure, irresolution in the variety of motifs and a residential conception still appeared in the capitol design. The design of the wings of the State House, on the other hand, was constrained by the older style of the existing buildings.

For Washington Hall Mills submitted ten or more designs, but only the one followed in construction is known (fig. 2.24). After the Washington Benevolent Society purchased an old mansion for its meeting place, the building proved insufficient, and in 1813–14 it was converted by Mills into a hotel (it later was connected with the hall on the adjacent lot). The society decided on September 19, 1813, to build Washington Hall. Its building committee selected one of Mills's designs,

which he then revised according to their suggestions for presentation to the membership on May 18, 1814. Excavation began on July 14, and the cornerstone was laid on August 16. More than two years later, on October 1, 1816, the dedication took place with a crowd of 5,000 persons in the auditorium. On the upper level, 120 feet long and 70 feet wide, the auditorium was notable for its expanse, unobstructed by interior supports except those for galleries on two levels, a suggestion that the Delorme roofing system had been adapted for use here. On the ground floor were numerous rooms of various sizes for meetings and card, dancing, and supper parties, the kind of activities for which assembly rooms were built in England. Although Mills did not attend the opening, he wrote a description that was published the following year along with an aquatint made after a drawing by George Strickland.[48]

Perhaps the greatest importance of this short-lived building (it burned in 1823) was its modern motif of a circular, domed recess fronted by a two-column screen, which Mills had employed as the entrance (without the dome) for the Sansom Street Church. In Washington Hall, raised above the en-

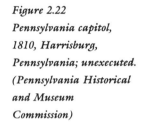

Figure 2.22
Pennsylvania capitol,
1810, Harrisburg,
Pennsylvania; unexecuted.
(Pennsylvania Historical
and Museum
Commission)

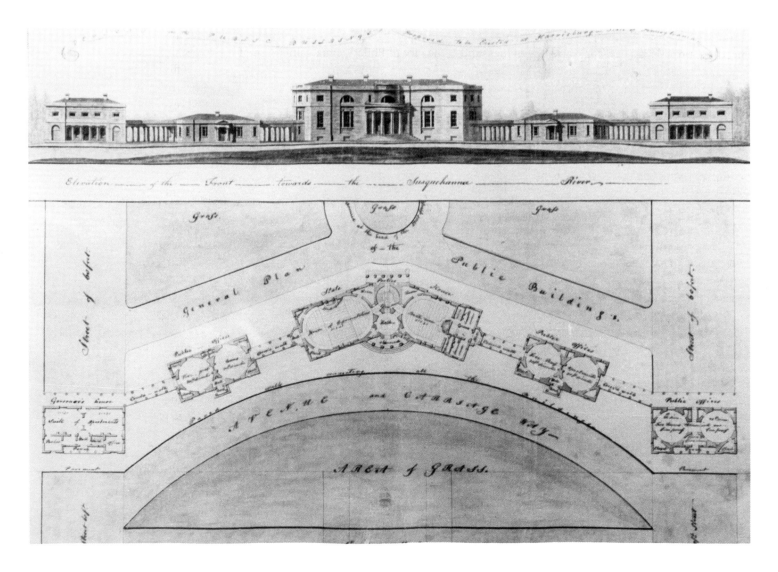

Elevation, on Chesnut Street, of the Court Houses, State State House, agreeably to an act of the...

Robert M...

trance on the level of the auditorium, it was diminished by enclosure in a thin, stepped attic story. Although the columns were of the Erechtheum type, the front included elements popular in modern Europe. Exaggerated horizontal masonry joints (all of scored stucco) in the basement, recessed panels and niches with busts, military trophies, and wreaths—these details abounded in the late eighteenth century, when the domed recess and screen motif appeared; in combination they suggest a source in France, where they were more common than in England. In developing his ten or twelve designs for this building, Mills certainly sought ideas in architectural publications, including some recent French books.[49]

While Mills was engaged in designing the hall, he enjoyed a more prestigious success in winning the competition for the Baltimore Washington Monument (1813–42), and with these two commissions he became involved in more than the politics of architecture. When the state legislature of Maryland authorized the monument in 1810, it delegated all responsibilities for financing through public lotteries and for design and construction to a board of managers composed of wealthy Baltimore merchants. These managers were, if not members of the Washington Benevolent Society, sympathetic

to an anti-Jeffersonian political movement whose leader was Robert Goodloe Harper. Thus, the monument, like Washington Hall, was a political statement by the revived Federalist party. Mills, according to an early history of the hall in Philadelphia, was "a member of the Society." When notice of his victory in the monument competition reached Philadelphia, the selection of his design for the hall a few weeks later was undoubtedly assured. Similarly, during his residence in Baltimore this political affiliation served him well, for he received commissions from many of the managers of the monument as well as other Federalists, including Harper. During his later years in Washington, Mills's political leanings aided him in gaining support, but toward the end of his life they probably led to his dismissal from government work.[50]

The question of the relationship between architecture and politics in this period is not always clear. Latrobe, for example, could work for both Jefferson and Harper at almost the same time. Mills, on the other hand, could not enlist any Jeffersonian as a client during his years in Baltimore. And in 1820, after Mills recommended a builder to Jefferson, the former president would not aid Mills in his search for employment. Latrobe, a foreigner, seems to have been above political considerations,

Figure 2.23
Alternative designs for wings for Independence Hall (1812–14), Philadelphia, Pennsylvania; demolished 1896. (The Athenaeum of Philadelphia)

and] *Fire-proof Offices contemplated to be erected as Wings to the*

1812.

Ph April 1812.

attracting clients by his ability. For the native architect, Mills, political affiliation could be an important consideration.[51]

Whether Mills's Federalist standing affected his employment by clients in Richmond is not known. While in Richmond he provided designs for the city hall and courthouse, and the foundations were begun. Overall, the design was Latrobean in its massing of a central block flanked by smaller side blocks, and the six-columned portico resembled the one for the Baptist Church then under construction in Baltimore. On the grounds that the building provided too little office space, a design by Maximilian Godefroy was accepted and followed. At the same time, other work by Godefroy in Richmond provoked objections. Perhaps both architectural conflicts concealed political struggles.[52]

Two projects of 1818, neither constructed, again show different stylistic treatments. In 1817 the city of Baltimore acquired land for a House of Industry, a place where the poor of all ages could be housed, where they would work and learn trades in order to become self-sufficient. Mills submitted a set of drawings and covering letter, all dated February 26, 1818. Only one of the drawings has survived, distinguished primarily by the wide range of colored washes (fig. 2.25). On the lower part, identified as

"Design No. 3," is the half-plan of a U-shaped building, a central block with a projecting six-columned portico and two long wings, each with a small tripartite entry. Administrative offices occupy the center, and workrooms for the preparation of cloth and manufacture of clothing flank a long hall in the wing. The elevation, larger than the plan and perhaps corresponding to a plan on a lost sheet of drawings, shows the backs of all three blocks and the expanse of the open court. The whole is three stories over a raised basement, with many windows filling the walls, most supported by the two stringcourses and cornice.

In his letter Mills emphasized the need for light and air in the workrooms. He also commented:

I would observe, that in all the designs simplicity and economy have been studied. If any liberty has been taken in deviating from this ground rule it will only be found upon the Elevation of the principal front; There I have endeavoured to do away with the idea of exhibiting this institution in the gloom of a prison. Cheerfulness and an air of freedom should be strongly marked on the face of this building, and I have studied to give it this character.[53]

The many doors would permit freedom of passage, no doubt, but simplicity and economy dominate the long walls and processions of rectangular

Overleaf: Figure 2.24 Washington Hall (1814–16), Philadelphia, Pennsylvania; burned 1823. (The Port Folio, ser. v, 1817)

windows. Only in the center of each part does the tripartite motif appear, as a door on the basement level and in the next two stories as Palladian windows in an arched recess. These few Latrobean contributions to cheerfulness, along with the entrance portico, occur in a design as stark as the rotunda of the Baptist Church just being completed in Baltimore. Mills's reference to the "character" of the building was related to the modern belief that the style should express the purpose of the structure, an idea perhaps gained from Latrobe or from architectural books.[54]

A few months later, on July 31 and August 31, Mills submitted three or more plans (now lost) for the Second Bank of the United States, in Philadelphia. While a Millsian austerity with a slightly modern European accent marks the House of Industry design, it was succeeded by alternatives in the Greek Revival style dictated in the notice issued by the bank's board of directors. William Strickland won the competition for this building (1818–24), which is frequently recognized as the first monument of the Greek Revival.[55]

Figure 2.25
Elevation and half-plan,
House of Industry,
Baltimore, Maryland;
unexecuted. (Historical
Society of Pennsylvania)

TOWARD AN AMERICAN ARCHITECTURE

Throughout the residential, ecclesiastical, and public buildings of this early period, Mills's methods revealed an experimental quality. To submit as many as ten designs for some projects, he tried, as in the Benjamin Chew House, various ways of correlating the demands of use, movement of people, budgetary limitations, and symbolic expression. In his use of lines to unify house and row house façades, he employed a device long known to architects, and through experiment he converted it into a system of design. Again, variations in the architectural orders had been fashionable since the later eighteenth century, but Mills built more examples of variant combinations than others did. Serious concern with the theory and practice of architectural design is shown by the simultaneous pursuit of these several ideas.

Experimentation and the hope of improving his chances of gaining a commission may have been

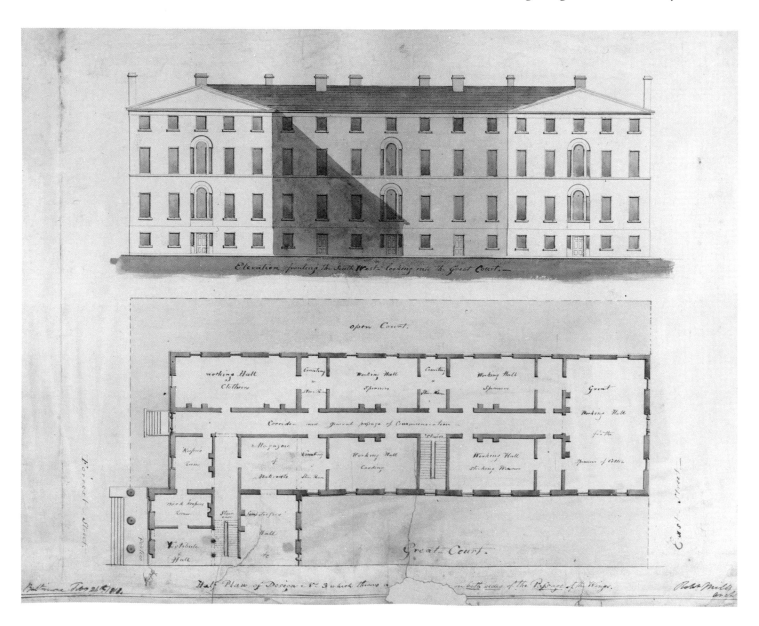

among the reasons for Mills's alternative designs, but he may have had additional reasons. When other architects followed this practice, they often stressed a choice in style; Latrobe or Godefroy, for example, might offer both neoclassical and neo-gothic designs for a project. Mills often pointed out the grounds for a choice—for example, economy or budgetary limits, as in the case of the multiple plans for the House of Industry; utility, as in the separate doors for each house; or the beauty of Vitruvian symmetry, as in the elevations of Franklin Row. By providing alternatives Mills ensured further discussions with the client, where not only the choice but other questions might arise. As shown by the drawings for the Benjamin Chew and Richard Potts houses, a variety of changes might arise from such conferences, and Mills apparently was willing and able to meet the client's desires. When later changes were made, as for the commemorative monument of the Monumental Church, Mills again provided alternatives; and he did so at several stages in the long building history of the Baltimore Washington Monument. Clearly Mills considered drawings and the provision of choices as important means for reaching agreement with clients before construction.

Two further observations can be made on Mills's activities following acceptance of a design. When he had to continue making drawings for details, he produced these during the construction period, as in the case of the Baptist Church in Baltimore. In the pattern of his mentor, Latrobe, he kept just ahead of the workmen. As construction moved along, he hired a better draftsman to make a perspectival drawing, especially if it might be published as an engraving, in order to exploit the publicity of a new building. In this respect he differed from others, including Latrobe, who employed drawings of this type to persuade a client to accept a design.

Once his design was accepted, Mills sought the further employment of supervising construction. This work was desirable because it paid better than design alone and might continue for some years. One letter requesting such employment, written to the building committee of the Baptist Church in Baltimore, has survived. Mills described his services: "I will undertake to form all your contracts and see them executed, and regulate the description of work to be done in such a manner as to realize your wishes in economising in the cost of the whole." As a result of his experience, he continued, "I will be able to distinguish between what is really necessary to the strength and durability of the building without resorting to useless expense which is often lavished upon buildings of this nature either from a want of this experience or a want of a knowledge of design."[56] Of his knowledge of his business,

all evidence suggests that he could direct any kind of construction, from a brick house to monumental masonry public buildings. His competence in contracting as well as supervision of the stages and quality of work was to play an important role in his government employment.

Following the difficulty with Benjamin Chew over his bill for professional services, Mills obviously learned how better to deal with and work with clients. Personal friendships arose, and when in Richmond he stayed with John Brockenbrough or John Ambler. He helped them in personal ways —for example, by buying a hat for Mrs. Ambler. On the professional side, he showed all willingness to rework a design to meet criticisms and preferences. He learned how to direct a client toward selecting one from a limited number of choices. And he clearly learned to meet his client's stylistic tastes.[57]

In Mills's few statements of his architectural philosophy, economy and utility usually predominate. Explaining his plans to the House of Industry committee, for example, he wrote, "I have always considered the *Plan*, as the most important for consideration, should either of these, which I have the pleasure of laying before you, meet your approbation, I have little doubt but I should be able to provide the elevations corresponding with your ideas of what may be suitable to the funds of the institution." Yet, he did not ignore the visual nature of his works, as witness the reference to symmetry on the Franklin Row drawing and his comments on the appearance of the John Ambler House. To this end Mills refined his domestic style by experimenting with the geometry of his designs and by limiting the vocabulary of forms to achieve a character of austere monumentality. Later in life he summed up his method of balancing the several criteria: "Utility and economy will be found to have entered into most of the studies of the author, and little sacrificed to display; at the same time his endeavors were to produce as much harmony and beauty of arrangement as practicable. The principle assumed and acted upon was that beauty is founded upon order, and that convenience and utility were constituent parts."[58]

For Mills, a child of his age, meaning was a part of beauty, not simply as allegorical decoration but inherent in the nature of the forms. His early essay on the Tuscan order concluded with emphasis on the characteristic appearance of "Solidity and Simplicity" that dictated where the order should be used; that is, the expressive character of a building should be consistent with its purpose and use. For Mills the great Doric column forming the Baltimore Washington Monument possessed the "solidity and simplicity of character emblematic of the illustrious *personage* to whose memory it is dedicated."[59] This idea lay behind his development of special American orders for use on the Monumental Church and mansions.

Mills was very much aware of his nationality. Indeed, he was not averse to using it in his efforts to gain a commission. In the letter accompanying his designs for the Baltimore Washington Monument he wrote:

Being an American by Birth and having also the honor of being the first American who has passed through a regular course of Study of Architecture in his own Country, it is natural for me to feel much Solicitude to aspire to the honor of raising a Monument to the memory of *our illustrious Country*man. . . . For the honor of our Country my sincere wish is that it may not be said: To foreign Genius and to foreign hands we are indebted for a Monument to perpetuate the Glory of our beloved Chief." [60]

Yet, there is no doubt that throughout his career Mills's goal was to develop an architecture appropriate for his country, to show foreign visitors, as he wrote to Jefferson, "that the *American* talent for architecture is not a whit inferior to the European." [61] Despite his beginnings in a Georgian mode with Hoban and his absorption of the modern European manner of Latrobe, his peripatetic practice put him in touch with political sentiments as well as artistic activities in several parts of the country. Imbued early on with the ideas of Jefferson and Peale, he lived and worked in an atmosphere that underscored the need for American forms. Mills was a transitional as well as a national architect, and the two aspects were inseparable.

Mills is seen as an architect of the Greek Revival despite his loose definition of the style. He emphasized the "purely Greek" aspects of his Baptist Church in Charleston in part as homage to Latrobe, whose Bank of Pennsylvania in Philadelphia was a model of the "purely Greek" style, and in part because he considered it appropriate for America. He later wrote, "It was fortunate that this style was so early introduced into our country, both on the ground of economy and of correct taste, as it exactly suited the character of our political institutions and pecuniary means." [62] He employed Greek elements, such as the orders; expressive forms, such as the heavy triangular lintels and severely plain wall surfaces; and symbolic ornament, such as the decoration of the Monumental Church. His was not an archaeologically correct revival but a free adaptation in buildings designed for modern, American uses. It was not a subtle or florid architecture, but in the overall plan and precise details it was as pragmatic as its author, who, in correspondence with associates and clients, usually got to the point in his first sentence. Far from being a copyist, he developed from the mix of ancient and modern forms an architecture that served his country in the whole range of human activities.

1. Much of the information in this essay comes from the basic work H. M. Pierce Gallagher, *Robert Mills, Architect of the Washington Monument, 1781–1855* (New York: Columbia University Press, 1935), which considers many of the buildings discussed here. Documents and other contemporary sources of information will be included in the microfilm edition of The Papers of Robert Mills, housed at the National Museum of American History, Smithsonian Institution, Washington, D.C. This essay will not touch on Mills's nonarchitectural work, such as engineering projects and improvements in heating; these will be the subject of future studies. The commemorative monuments of this period are included in the essay by Pamela Scott.

Part of my work was done as a National Endowment of the Humanities Fellow at Winterthur Museum and Library in 1981–82, and the University of Iowa has been consistently supportive. I am indebted also to the National Historical Records and Publications Commission and the National Endowment for the Humanities for their support of The Papers of Robert Mills. My colleagues on this project in documentary history have contributed much to my work by their helpful conversations and efforts. Among numerous individuals I single out for special thanks Jeffrey A. Cohen, who has been an unfailing source of information and aid on the Philadelphia scene and Mills's work there.

For their courteous assistance I wish to thank Linda Stanley and the staff of the Historical Society of Pennsylvania; the director and staff of the Valentine Museum, Richmond, Virginia; Elizabeth McKemie, Patricia Loughridge, and Tucker Hill, the Museum of the Confederacy, Richmond, Virginia; Karen Stuart and Donna Ellis, Maryland Historical Society; and Richard Richardson, Hall of Records, Annapolis, Maryland. For their kind hospitality I wish to thank Arthur and Audrey Potts and John Cheatham, Frederick, Maryland.

2. On the architecture of Philadelphia, see Theo H. White, ed., *Philadelphia Architecture in the Nineteenth Century* (Philadelphia: University of Pennsylvania Press, 1953); Luther P. Eisenhart, ed., *Historic Philadelphia from the Founding until the Early Nineteenth Century, Transactions of the American Philosophical Society* (1953; reprint ed., Philadelphia, 1980), 43, part 1; and George B. Tatum, *Penn's Great Town* (Philadelphia: University of Pennsylvania Press, 1961). For the architecture of Baltimore, see Richard Hubbard Howland and Eleanor Patterson Spencer, *The Architecture of Baltimore* (Baltimore: The Johns Hopkins University Press, 1953). These books discuss and illustrate many of the buildings considered in this essay. For Latrobe and his works, see Talbot Hamlin, *Benjamin Henry Latrobe* (New York: Oxford University Press, 1955). For Godefroy and his work, see Robert L. Alexander, *The Architecture of Maximilian Godefroy* (Baltimore and London: The Johns Hopkins University Press, 1974).

3. For the penitentiary, see John M. Bryan, "Robert Mills, Benjamin Henry Latrobe, Thomas Jefferson, and the South Carolina Penitentiary Project, 1806–1808," *South Carolina Historical Magazine* 85 (1984): 1–21. For the Presbyterian Church, see John M. Bryan, *Robert Mills, Architect, 1781–1855* (Columbia: The Columbia Museum of Art, 1976), 15–16. Rhodri Windsor Liscombe, *The Church Architecture of Robert Mills* (Easley, South Carolina: Southern Historical Press, 1985), 7–9. Mills to Thomas Jefferson, June 13, 1808, and Jefferson to Mills, June 23, 1808, *Thomas Jefferson Papers,* microfilm ed. (Washington, D.C.: Library of Congress, 1974).

For the Bank of Philadelphia, see Hamlin, *Latrobe,* 345–47. For the Markoe House, see Hamlin, *Latrobe,* 340–44. Jeffrey A. Cohen, in James F. O'Gorman, *Drawing toward Building: Philadelphia Architectural Graphics, 1732–1986* (Philadelphia: University of Pennsylvania Press, 1986), 54–57. Mills's great dependence on Latrobe at this time is evident in his drawing (c. 1808) for a villa (not built) for Joseph Hand of Bristol, Pennsylvania (Liscombe, *Church Architecture,* 7). It includes three plans, three elevations, a section, numerous details of the cornice, windows, and sash construction, and a list of panes of glass of different sizes. Latrobe, too, included lists of dimensions and crowded on a single sheet both large and very small elements (cf. drawings for the Markoe House in Cohen, in O'Gorman, *Drawing,* 55, 56).

4. The Chew Family Papers, Box 85, Historical Society of Pennsylvania, Philadelphia; bills and receipts in this collection indicate that Chew began construction of this house by the autumn of 1810 and that he probably occupied it about two years later. Cohen, in O'Gorman, *Drawing,* 58–59, discusses the house and in particular the drawing for the stables. I thank John M. Bryan for generously allowing me to use this material, which he called to my attention.

5. This photograph, identified by Jeffrey A. Cohen, was pasted on a blank page at the back of J. Randolph, *Memoir of the Life and Character of Philip Syng Physick, M.D.* (Philadelphia: Ferdinand J. Dreer, 1870), at the Historical Society of Pennsylvania. The smaller houses beside the main one, for there were two, appear in stereoscopic views in the Boise Penrose Pictorial Philadelphia Collection, Historical Society of Pennsylvania.

6. The Chew House drawings are all in black ink; dimensions are in inches, height preceding width: No. 1—white paper, 15⅝ by 19⅞ inches, pink, yellow, blue, and gray washes; No. 2—white paper, 15 ⅝ by 19¾ inches, gray and yellow washes; No. 3—gray paper, 24¾ by 19⅜ inches, pink and yellow washes; No. 4—gray paper, 12¾ by 19 ⅛ inches, pink, yellow, gray, and black washes; No. 5—yellowed white paper, 14⅞ by 12⅝ inches, pink and brown washes. Plan types are discussed in William John Murtagh, "The Philadelphia Row House," *Journal of the Society of Architectural Historians* 16, no. 4 (December 1957): 8–13.

7. Latrobe wrote: "Mills is a wretched designer. He came to me too late to acquire principals of taste. He is a copyist, and is fit for nothing else. . . . But he also has his merit. He is an excellent man of detail, and a very snug contriver of domestic conveniences . . . " (Latrobe to Maximilian Godefroy, October 10, 1814, Pittsburgh, in John C. Van Horne et al., eds., *The Correspondence and Miscellaneous Papers of Benjamin Henry Latrobe,* 3 vols. (New Haven: Yale University Press, 1984–88), 3:579–81.

8. On Latrobe's teaching of professionalism, see his letter of July 12, 1806, to Mills in Van Horne et al., *Correspondence,* 2:239–44.

9. Chew Family Papers.

10. For an 1839 view of the Francis House, see John T. Faris, *Old Churches and Meeting Houses in and around Philadelphia* (Philadelphia: J. B. Lippincott Company, 1926), opp. 48, left edge.

11. Mills is named as designer of these two houses, 700–702 Chestnut Street, at the southwest corner with Seventh Street, in James Mease, "Observations on the Present Style of American Architecture, with a Plan for Improvement," *Archive of Useful Knowledge* (Philadelphia, 1811–13), 3, 1 (July 1812): 84. Both are represented in J. H. Rae, *Rae's Panorama of Chestnut Street* (Philadelphia, 1831), plate 11. Their history and occupants are discussed in Casper Souder, Jr., *The History of Chestnut Street, Philadelphia; from the Founding of the City to the Year 1859. With Illustrations* (Philadelphia, 1860), 331, at the Historical Society of Pennsylvania; this was the site of the Morris House, designed by L'Enfant. Fire insurance survey no. 3411, May 21, 1810, for Richard H. Willcocks [702 Chestnut Street], Philadelphia Contributionship, Philadelphia. Mease mentions also four houses with the high basement on Locust Street, designed by Mills and built just after the Fairman and Willcocks houses, that were set back about 18 to 20 feet from the property line with the intention of being fronted by broad, covered, colonnaded walks. In his letter of March 26, 1805, to William Waln, Latrobe described and argued for the elimination of the old-fashioned back buildings and the location of services in the basement (Van Horne et al., *Correspondence,* 2:35–41).

12. Kenneth Ames, "Robert Mills and the Philadelphia Row House," *Journal of the Society of Architectural Historians* 27 (1967): 140–42; the author offers another interpretation of the word *symmetry,* along with a possible source of design in Soane, and also considers the problem of half-windows in the lower elevation. Explanations of symmetry appear in Vitruvius, Book 1, chapter 2, and Book 3, chapter 1 (e.g., Vitruvius, *The Ten Books on Architecture,* trans. M. H. Morgan [Cambridge, Massachusetts: Harvard University Press, 1926], 14:72–75). Vitruvius considered symmetry of central importance in design, and many architectural writers from the Renaissance to Mills's day reiterated and explicated the concept; see, for example, the definition by John James, English translator of Perrault's treatise, quoted in William Bainter O'Neal, *Jefferson's Fine Arts Library* (Charlottesville: University Press of Virginia, 1976), 284. For the surviving house of this row, see Edward Teitelman and Richard W. Longstreth, *Architecture in Philadelphia: A Guide* (Cambridge, Massachusetts: The MIT Press, 1974), 65.

13. For the deeds, see Palmer to Mills, May 1, 1812, IC-23-234; Mills to R. Ware, December 17, 1814, MR-22-389, Recorder of Deeds, City Hall, Philadelphia. I am indebted to Lee Nelson for supplying a list of deeds recorded by Mills. Mills installed a large number of marble elements, including mantlepieces, in these houses, according to his 1816 journal (Robert Mills, "A Pocket Memorandum Book, or Daily Journal for the Year 1816," fol. 68v, Mills Papers, Manuscript Division, Library of Congress).

Ames ("Robert Mills and the Philadelphia Row House," 144–45) brings Carolina Row (1812–15) into the Mills literature. This row, 923–933 Spruce Street, suggests a regression, for it lacks all horizontal supports and centers one large arched tripartite window in the second story, with three openings on the first and two on the third story. Variety in the sizes and rhythms of openings is matched only by their antistructural disposition over the surface, so that no vertical lines rise up the face of the building, and, except at the edges, no part of the supporting wall is continuous from ground to cornice. Compared with the emphasis on solidity and strength in the contemporary Eighth Street houses, Carolina Row seems not so much experimental as antiarchitectural and perhaps an imitation of Mills's style.

14. William Voss Elder III, *Robert Mills' Waterloo Row—Baltimore 1816* (Baltimore: Baltimore Museum of Art, 1971); the author earns my thanks for his continuing helpfulness. Robert L. Alexander, "Baltimore Row Houses of the Early Nineteenth Century," *American Studies* 16 (1975): 65–76. Details of Mills's relations with the Water Company appear in his 1816 journal (Mills, "Memorandum Book"). Construction of Waterloo Row began after his requests of March 19 and April 24, 1817, for laying out and grading Calvert Street (*Records of the City of Baltimore: Eastern Precincts Commissioners, 1812–1817; Western Precincts Commissioners, 1810–1817* [Baltimore, 1909], 251, 256). Completion, about May 25, 1819, is dated by the insurance surveys, which state the values of the houses at $10,500 to $12,000 ("Record of Surveys," E, 230–32, Baltimore Equitable Society, Baltimore). Stephen Bernhardt, president of the Baltimore Equitable Society, generously made these archives available for my research.

Waterloo Row was built by the Calvert Street Building Company, an association of contractors and suppliers of materials, for which Mills served as agent and treasurer. Each member received a house or portion of one according to his contribution of materials, labor, time, and money, but these very expensive houses were difficult to sell because of the financial depression of 1819. Mills received one house, which remained in his name until 1823, when it was sold by court order to satisfy debts of the building company (Chancery Court [Record], 118 [1821], 512–55 and 123 [1823], 372–410, Maryland Hall of Records, Annapolis).

15. For the town house plan, see Murtagh, "Philadelphia Row House," 12.

16. Mary Wingfield Scott, *Houses of Old Richmond* (Richmond, Virginia: Valentine Museum, 1941), 131. Policy no. 1016, January 1, 1818, Mutual Assurance Society, Virginia State Library, Richmond. Mills, "Memorandum Book," fol. 68v. Mills's 1816 journal records the design of a house (not built) for Captain Thorndick Chase of Baltimore with quickly sketched plans and elevations, the latter closely resembling the Brander House (ibid., November 11 and 13 and fol. 55).

17. Scott, *Houses,* 129. Policy no. 917, October 20, 1817, Mutual Assurance Society. Mills to E. B. Mills, September 3, 1813, Richmond, Mills Papers, South Carolina Historical Society. Mills, "Memorandum Book," fol. 68v.

18. Scott, *Houses,* 112–14. Policy no. 916, October 20, 1817, Mutual Assurance Society. Mills, "Memorandum Book," fols. 21, 68v. Robert L. Alexander, "The Special Orders of Rob-

ert Mills," in *The Documented Image: Visions in Art History,* ed. G. P. Weisberg, L. S. Dixon, and A. B. Lemke (Syracuse, New York: Syracuse University Press, 1987), 252–53.

19. Policy no. 1730, November 28, 1815, Mutual Assurance Society. Mills to John Ambler, February 2, 1816, Baltimore, Virginia Historical Society, Richmond. Mills purchased $150 worth of marble mantlepieces for Ambler (Mills, "Memorandum Book," fol. 68v).

20. Scott, *Houses,* 119–21. Policy no. 1133, November 7, 1815, Mutual Assurance Society. Alexander, "Special Orders," 251, 252–53. The Valentine Museum, Richmond, has an excellent collection of interior photographs of this house and others in the city.

21. Robert A. Lancaster, *Historic Virginia Homes and Churches* (Philadelphia: J. B. Lippincott, 1915), 181. Scott, *Houses,* 252. Elie Weeks, "Howard's Neck," *Goochland County Historical Society Magazine* 2, no. 2 (Autumn 1970). Sir William Chambers, *A Treatise on the Decorative Part of Civil Architecture,* 3rd ed. (London, 1791), was very influential for a generation and more after its publication. While reinforcing the authority of Palladio, Chambers was permissive in choosing and altering parts as necessary (e.g., ibid., 42–43).

The Hayes-McCance House also has been connected with Mills. It was under construction by 1816 and was much altered about 1834 (see Scott, *Houses,* 138–41). The triple entrance on the garden side after alteration still had a triangular lintel between corner blocks, similar to that of Howard's Neck and the Eighth Street houses, evidence that strengthens the attribution.

22. Policy no. 545, February 13, 1816, Mutual Assurance Society. Mills, "Memorandum Book," May 3, June 2, and fols. 25, 29, 36, 38, 62, 76v. Mary Wingfield Scott, *Old Richmond Neighborhoods* (1950; reprint ed., Richmond, Virginia: The Valentine Museum, 1975), 152, 153, 243. Edward F. Zimmer and Pamela J. Scott, "Alexander Parris, B. Henry Latrobe, and the John Wickham House in Richmond, Virginia," *Journal of the Society of Architectural Historians* 41 (1982): 202–11. Hamlin, *Latrobe,* 99–101.

23. Scott, *Houses,* 146–51. Policy no. 1023, January 1, 1818 (not finished); policy no. 2580, August 19, 1818; policy no. 4598, November 15, 1822, Mutual Assurance Society. Although the 1818 date for the columns has been questioned, I believe they were part of the original design. The porch columns are not mentioned before the 1822 policy, but the value of the house, $20,000, is the same as that in the previous policy of August 19, 1818. The columns are not mentioned in the Page-Anderson House policy either. In both cases the porch does appear in the plan drawn on the policy.

A third design related to the Brockenbrough House and Waterloo Row by the extreme to which the lines have been pushed is the house designed early in 1817 (not built) for Henry Didier, Jr., of Baltimore (Alexander, "Special Orders," 248). For the date of the drawing, called the Dedian House, see Gene Waddell, "Robert Mills's Fireproof Building," *South Carolina Historical Magazine* 80 (1979): 116n.

24. For the restoration report, see Glave Newman Anderson and Associates, Inc., *White House of the Confederacy* (Richmond, 1976). For a plan of the Van Ness House, see Hamlin, *Latrobe,* 466. This building served as home and headquarters for Jefferson Davis and is now part of the Museum of the Confederacy.

25. Charles McC. Mathias, "Court Square, Frederick," *Maryland Historical Magazine* 47 (1952): 119–20. Robert L. Alexander, "The Potts House Drawings by Robert Mills," *Winterthur Newsletter* 29, no. 1 (Spring 1983): 9–10. The drawings and specifications for the Potts House are in the Winterthur Museum and Library. The Potts House still stands, with a third floor added in 1894 and other alterations of about 1946.

26. Charles C. Wilson, "Robert Mills, Architect," *Bulletin of the University of South Carolina* 77 (February 1919): 29; Wilson commented, "It is rather Colonial in spirit, and not like Mills' usual work." Waddell, "Fireproof Building," 117n. The merchant Ainsley Hall sold this house to Gen. Wade Hampton in 1822.

27. J. Hoffman to the Commissioners, April 23 and May 19, 1821, 1821–39, 40, RG 3, S1, Box 27, Baltimore City Archives, Baltimore. Anonymous to Mills, [Decem]ber 29, 1821, Balti-

more, South Carolina Historical Society. Thomas W. Griffith, *Annals of Baltimore* (Baltimore: W. Wooddy, 1824[–29]), 251. Clayton Coleman Hall, ed., *Baltimore, Its History and its People,* (New York and Chicago: Lewis Historical Publishing Company, 1912), 1:133. Elder, *Waterloo Row,* 16, 20. For additional illustrations, see Robert L. Alexander, "Neoclassical Wrought Iron in Baltimore," *Winterthur Portfolio* 18 (1983):158–59.

28. For Small's Archbishopric, see Robert L. Alexander, "William F. Small, 'Architect of the City,' " *Journal of the Society of Architectural Historians* 20 (1961): 70. For the second Ainsley Hall House, see James C. Massey, "Robert Mills Documents, 1823: A House for Ainsley Hall in Columbia, South Carolina," *Journal of the Society of Architectural Historians* 22 (1963): 228–32. For an example of the plan with circular elements by Latrobe, see the Pope House (1811) in Hamlin, *Latrobe,* 107.

29. For the Circular and the First Presbyterian churches, see Liscombe, *Church Architecture,* 5–9.

30. For Latrobe's essay on acoustics, see Van Horne et al., *Correspondence,* 1:401–7. For Mills's first essay on acoustics, October 15, 1804, see "Communication recd. from Mr. Robert Mills on the Subject of the Ceiling of St. Michael's Church & on the Doctrine of Sounds," *Journal of the Society of Architectural Historians* 12 (1953): 27–31.

31. For Mills's essay on the Tuscan order, see Gallagher, *Robert Mills,* 153–54. For the Delorme system, see Douglas James Harnsberger, " 'In Delorme's Manner': A Study of the Applications of Philibert Delorme's Dome Construction Method in Early 19th Century American Architecture" (Master's thesis, University of Virginia, 1981). For Mills's drawings for Jefferson see William Howard Adams, ed., *The Eye of Thomas Jefferson* (Washington, D.C.: National Gallery of Art, 1976), 222, 241, 242–43, 272.

32. For the Sansom Street Baptist Church, see Liscombe, *Church Architecture,* 9–11; and "Plasterer's Daybook, 1812," December 16, 1812, 40, Historical Society of Pennsylvania (the anonymous author of this valuable manuscript frequently recorded gauging the work of his fellow plasterers in Philadelphia). For the Octagon Unitarian Church, see Liscombe, *Church Architecture,* 11; "Plasterer's Daybook," January 8, 1813, 43; and Cohen, in O'Gorman, *Drawing,* 62. For the Monumental Church, see *Richmond Enquirer,* August 4, 1812; Margaret Pearson Mickler, "The Monumental Church" (Master's thesis, University of Virginia, 1980); Liscombe, *Church Architecture,* 11–13; and Alexander, "Special Orders," 243–47.

33. Hamlin, *Latrobe,* 157–67. Rich Borneman, "Some Ledoux-Inspired Buildings in America," *Journal of the Society of Architectural Historians* 13 (1954): 15–17. Darwin Stapleton, ed., *The Engineering Drawings of Benjamin Henry Latrobe* (New Haven: Yale University Press, 1980), 28–36, 144–98.

34. This drawing, now at the American Baptist Historical Society, Rochester, New York, was identified by George Thomas, architect, of Philadelphia. Thanks to the generosity of Dell Upton of the University of California, Berkeley, I know of the following critical comment by Thomas U. Walter, an architect of the next generation after Mills and soon to be a rival of Mills: "Rode by the Unitarian Church, was struck with the insulated appearance of the Portico, I dont admire a portico which does not embrace the whole width of the house, but oftentimes we are obliged to resort to this measure or else loose a portico altogether— the antae of the Church in question are too small— . . . . I think the effect produced in the front of the Unitarian Church by the antae is extremely bad and should always be avoided— I have always admired the Portico in itself, but think the cornice inapplicable to a Pediment it is taken from the Choragic monument of Thrasellus, as is the entablature— the guttae appear too small, perhaps it is because the wreaths are omitted—" (Diary 1834–36, Thomas U. Walter Papers, The Athenaeum, Philadelphia).

35. This building is known only through the drawing (now at the South Carolina Historical Society) made by Mills about 1827–28 (Waddell, "Fireproof Building," 116n). Although Mills's memory played tricks in later years, this drawing is congruent with his 1811–12 style and may have been based on his own copy of the original design.

36. A series of five letters from Mills's father-in-law, Gen.

John Smith, reveals details of the history and selection of Mills's design and preparation for construction: Smith to Mills, February 25, 1812, Washington, D.C., Alderman Library, University of Virginia (Liscombe, *Church Architecture,* n.31); Smith to Mills, March 5, [March–April], April 30, and June 6, 1812, Washington, D.C., Richard X. Evans Papers, Georgetown University Library, Washington, D.C.

37. The concept of a domed centralized structure with an attached cubical block with tripartite openings in three sides appeared in the Medical Hall of the University of Pennsylvania (Hamlin, *Latrobe,* 194–96, plate 16; Cohen, in O'Gorman, *Drawing,* 51). When Latrobe designed this structure in 1805, Mills was still closely connected with him, and thus it may have served as source for the Monumental Church.

Construction of the monumental porch reached the vault when it was stopped and the porch covered for protection (Brockenbrough to Mills, Richmond, May 20, 1813, South Carolina Historical Society). It was taken up again in 1815–16, when Mills altered the design. More stone had to be quarried, and its color in the pediment differs from that of the rest of the porch. The 1816 journal has drawings for the flaming urn and notes that Mills hired Baughman and Hore, stonemasons of Baltimore, to make the sarcophagus (Mills, "Memorandum Book," inside front cover, August 8). It is probable that William Steuart and Thomas Towson, stonemasons of Baltimore, completed the sarcophagus and built the vaulted roof of the porch (bill of Steuart and Towson to Mills, December 31, 1817, Georgetown University Library). Antonio Capellano carved the urn and completed the cornices with lachrymal urns (Liscombe, *Church Architecture,* n. 31). Daniel Raynerd covered the interior surface of the vault with fine and well-preserved decorative plaster, following one of his designs in Asher Benjamin, *The American Builder's Companion,* 6th ed. (1827; reprint ed., New York, 1969), plate 36. See also Jack Quinan, "Daniel Raynerd, Stucco Worker," *Old-Time New England* 65, nos. 3–4 (Winter-Spring 1975): 1–21.

38. No copy of the early engraving is known, but the photographic negative of a very early one is in the Valentine Museum, Richmond, Virginia (W. Strickland and the engraver W. Kneass have been suggested as the authors). One drawing, a newspaper notes, Mills "has taken the liberty to recommend for publication" (*Richmond Enquirer,* December 5, 1812). The Goodacre engraving (fig. 1.7) probably depended on this early one.

The lintels link the Monumental Church with several houses designed by Mills about the same time (1812–14)—the Eighth Street houses in Philadelphia, Howard's Neck in Goochland County, Virginia, and perhaps the original Hayes-McCance House in Richmond. This motif seems to be Latrobe's, as drawings of 1812 for a marine hospital in Washington show massive lintels, both flat and triangular (Edward C. Carter, ed., *The Papers of Benjamin Henry Latrobe,* microfiche ed. (Clifton, New Jersey: James T. White and Company, 1976), 277. The Millsian house (c. 1813–15) of James S. Cox, next to that of his son-in-law, John Markoe, had large lintels over tripartite windows and for the door a massive lintel decorated with a raking gable and wreath (for illustration, see Cohen, in O'Gorman, *Drawing,* 55). A date of completion is suggested by the measuring of plaster on September 19, 1815, thus putting the house in the period of Mills's activity as a designer ("Plasterer's Daybook," 149).

39. Mills's development of the orders is studied in Alexander, "Special Orders," 243–56.

40. Liscombe, *Church Architecture,* 13–14. Mills, "Memorandum Book," passim. Letter of E. B. Mills to Mills, February 20, 1817, Baltimore, South Carolina Historical Society. For the receipt of Capellano, Library of Congress. For the engraving of pew plan, see the Wilson Family Papers, Maryland Historical Society. *The First Baptist Church* (souvenir pamphlet published in 1935 for the 150th anniversary), Maryland Historical Society.

A letter of July 19, 1817, and two drawings for the Baltimore Library (not built) preserve another circular design related to this church building (letter and drawings at the Maryland Historical Society). The cylinder is encased in a two-story block with narrower wings and a dome rising above. The basement is rental area, the upper story devoted to library functions, with

much care for adequate lighting. The entrance employs the motif of the Sansom Street Church, two giant columns in antis, creating the usual oddly shaped vestibule with irregular corners and passages and with stairs, like those of the Baptist Church, in the corners. It looks like a compressed version of Mills's design for the city hall and court house in Richmond.

41. W. M. Williams, in his *Reminiscences of a Pastorate of Thirty-Three Years in the First Baptist Church of Baltimore, Md.* (Baltimore, 1836), 24, reports: "[The church] was an imposing structure, but a perfect failure as an audience room. The acoustics were horrible. For twenty-odd years I was like one preaching to an audience on the other side of the Blue Ridge mountains, for I knew that all in the centre of the house beyond the fourth line of pews could not hear unless the voice was pitched very high. That line of pews was like a mountain range. Frequently when strangers preached, those on the other side of that mountain never heard a sentence. Fortunately, I was blessed with good lungs and had the ability to throw my voice over it."

Mills employed the raised pulpit and flanking stairs earlier, for example, in his 1804 plan for extending St. Michael's in Charleston, with the reading desk rather than the basin below (Liscombe, *Church Architecture,* fig. 22). There, the pulpit hovers in free space as the stairs rise twelve steps in a near semicircle. At the Baptist Church the stairs rise eight steps, clinging to the shallow curve of the wall, a clear change from the Georgian aspects of the earlier design.

Latrobe was sufficiently impressed with this building to inform Mills, "Your portico of the Baptist Church is a beautiful thing" (Latrobe to Mills, November 20, 1817, Washington, D.C., in Carter, *Papers . . . Latrobe,* 139/A8).

42. Liscombe, *Church Architecture,* 14–15. Beatrice St. Julien Ravenel, *Architects of Charleston* (Charleston, South Carolina: Carolina Art Association, 1945), 119–21. For the description see Robert Mills, *Statistics of South Carolina* (Charleston, 1826), 411.

43. For St. Martin's, see James Gibbs, *A Book of Architecture* (1728; reprint ed., New York: Benjamin Blom, 1968), plates 1–7. For St. Michael's and the Second Presbyterian and St. Paul's churches, see Ravenel, *Architects,* 27–33, 96–98.

44. For Chambers's Doric order, see Chambers, *Civil Architecture,* 49–52 and plates.

45. Liscombe, *Church Architecture,* 14.

46. Liscombe, *Church Architecture,* 9. Mills to John Dorsey, April 23, 1810, Horace Wells Sellers Collection, Independence National Historic Park, Philadelphia. In 1819 Mills wrote to a member of the building committee as though responding to a request to develop or expand the capitol design and inquiring about material and labor costs, probably in preparation for a new design and estimate (Mills to George Bryan, Baltimore, February 22, 1819, Maryland Historical Society). On April 24 he received $200 as prize for second place in the competition for the building (*The Inquirer and Cincinnati Advertiser,* May 18, 1819). See also Agnes Addison Gilchrist, *William Strickland, Architect and Engineer, 1788–1854* (Philadelphia: University of Pennsylvania Press, 1950), 49–50; and Henry-Russell Hitchcock and William Seale, *Temples of Democracy: The State Capitols of the U.S.A.* (New York and London: Harcourt Brace Jovanovich, 1976), 59–63.

47. Cohen, in O'Gorman, *Drawing,* 60–62 with bibliography. These wings were completed probably in 1814, not long after the plaster was measured ("Plasterer's Daybook," July 22 and August 16, 1814, 104, 108); a small amount of additional finishing or repair occurred in 1816 (ibid., April 3, 1816, 169).

48. For the old Bingham mansion, see Van Horne et al., *Correspondence,* 2:256–57n. For Washington Hall, see *Plan of a Loan Proposed to be Received by the Washington Benevolent Society of Pennsylvania* (Philadelphia, 1814), at the Historical Society of Pennsylvania. *A Summary Statement of the Origin, Progress, and Present State of the Washington Benevolent Society of Pennsylvania* (Philadelphia, 1816), in the American Philosophical Society Library. David Hackett Fischer, *The Revolution of American Conservatism: The Federalist Party in the Era of Jeffersonian Democracy* (New York: Harper and Row, 1965), 125. Liscombe, *Church Architecture,* 11. For the bill of August 23, 1816, for plaster cast-

ings at Washington Hall to the amount of $121.56, see the "Plasterer's Daybook," 189. For Mills's description, see "Washington Benevolent Society," *The Port Folio,* series 5 (1817), 164–66, 222–28.

49. Mills used this motif twice in 1816. In January he employed it as the entrance in the central pavilion of one of his nine designs for the Merchants Exchange in Baltimore ("Memorandum Book," fol. 13). For the history of the competition for this building, see Hamlin, *Latrobe,* 486–89. That summer he used the Sansom Street Church variant (i.e., without the semidome) for the new front he added to Tusculum, the William Gwynn house in Baltimore (Alexander, "Special Orders," 249). In both it appeared more architectonic than at Washington Hall.

50. For the Washington Monument, see J. Jefferson Miller II, "The Designs for the Washington Monument in Baltimore," *Journal of the Society of Architectural Historians* 23 (1964): 19–28. For the Washington Benevolent Society, see Fischer, *American Conservatism,* 110–28; for Mills's membership, see *Summary Statement,* 24. While diverting water from property owned by Harper, Mills proposed and later carried out a row of seven houses on the west side of Courtland Street, below Franklin Street in Baltimore (Mills to Harper, February 12, 1818, Maryland Historical Society). The land belonged to Harper, who received five of the houses. Mills may have sold one house, but he surrendered the other to its mortgage holder, Robert Oliver ("Land Book of Robert and John Oliver," April 15, 1820, 168, Oliver Papers, Maryland Historical Society). The large debt he incurred in this construction led to his bankruptcy. The court records of his bankruptcy proceedings are missing.

51. In 1816–17 Latrobe made designs for both Jefferson and Harper (Hamlin, *Latrobe,* 468–70, 498). In 1819 Mills recommended the carpenter-builder Richard Ware to Jefferson (Mills to Jefferson, Baltimore, March 20, 1819, The Papers of Thomas Jefferson, Alderman Library, University of Virginia). In 1820 Mills requested that Jefferson help him get an appointment as engineer for the state of Virginia, a request Jefferson sidestepped by saying that he was not involved in this state activity (Mills to Jefferson, June 16 and Jefferson to Mills, June 22, 1820, ibid.). Perhaps Jefferson simply was adhering to a long-held rule that he would not use his political position to render such services.

52. Liscombe, *Church Architecture,* 13. Alexander, *Godefroy,* 120–21, 126–29.

53. Liscombe, *Church Architecture,* 14. The drawing for the House of Industry is at the Historical Society of Pennsylvania; the letter is at the South Carolina Historical Society.

54. For the best treatment of character in architecture during this period, see Jacques Francois Blondel, *Cours d'architecture enseigné dans l'Académie Royale d'Architecture,* 9 vols. (Paris, 1771–77), 1:373–447. See also Robin Middleton, "Jacques François Blondel and the *Cours d'architecture," Journal of the Society of Architectural Historians* 18 (1959): 140–48.

55. Mills's letters are in the Library of Congress.

56. Mills to the building committee of the Baptist Church, Baltimore, February 8, 1816, South Carolina Historical Society.

57. One further instance of a question over Mills's salary is known, but he was saved from difficulty by a considerate client. Dr. Brockenbrough, chairman of the committee of the Monumental Church, wrote, "It is our wish to have a distinct understanding on the score of your remuneration, as much on your account as ours" (J. Brockenbrough to Mills, Richmond, May 20, 1813, South Carolina Historical Society).

58. Mills to the Committee of the House of Industry, Baltimore, February 26, 1816, South Carolina Historical Society. Gallagher, *Robert Mills,* 170.

59. For the essay on the Tuscan order, see Gallagher, *Robert Mills,* 153–54. For the essay on the Washington Monument, see William D. Hoyt, Jr., "Robert Mills and the Washington Monument in Baltimore," *Maryland Historical Magazine* 34 (1939): 154–57.

60. Mills to the board of managers of the [Baltimore] Washington Monument, January 12, 1814, Philadelphia, Maryland Historical Society.

61. Mills to Jefferson, June 13, 1808, Philadelphia, *Thomas Jefferson Papers.* Lillian B. Miller, *Patrons and Patriotism; The Encouragement of the Fine Arts in the U. S., 1790–1860* (Chicago: University of Chicago Press, 1966).

62. Gallagher, *Robert Mills,* 169. Recent structural investigations in connection with the restoration of the John Brockenbrough House have revealed that in the late 1820s or early 1830s the original fanlight doorway in front was removed, the entrance hall changed from rectangular to oval, and the stair replaced by a spiral stairway. Other interior changes occurred at the same time, made by a local builder rather than Mills. I am indebted to Richard C. Cote, curator, White House of the Confederacy, for this information.

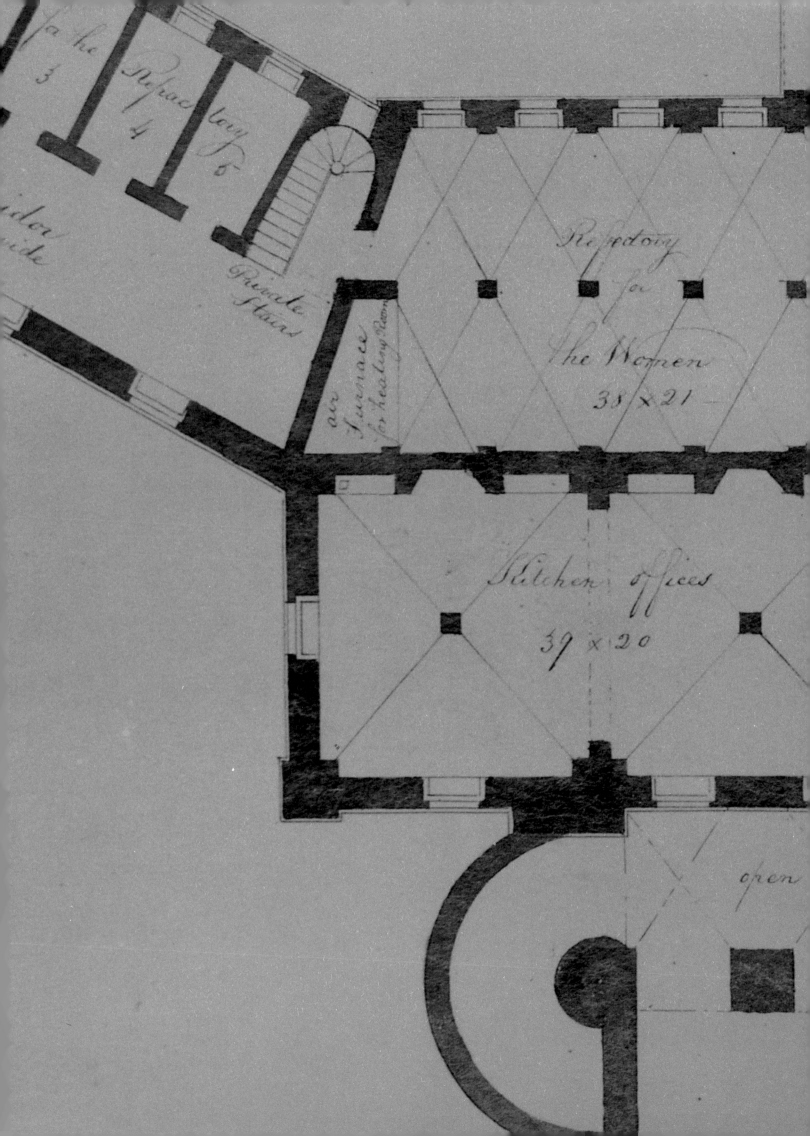

a the Refractory
3 4

Refractory fo

idon
side

Private
Stairs

an Furnace
for heating Room

Refectory for

The Women
38 x 21

Kitchen offices
39 x 20

open

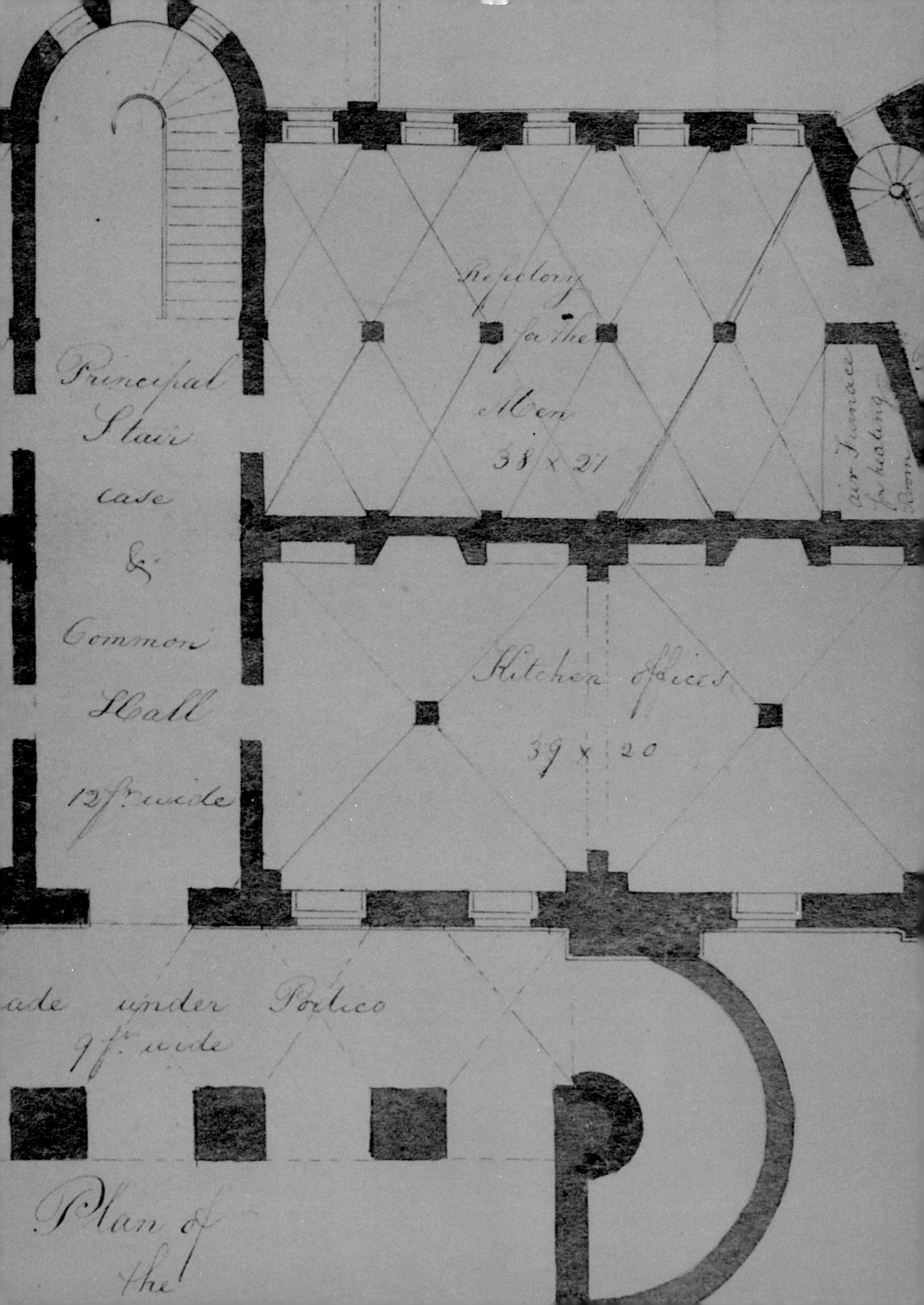

Principal

Stair

case

&

Common

Hall

12 ft wide

Refectory

for the

Men

38 × 21

air furnace

for heating from

Kitchen offices

39 × 20

ade under Portico

9 ft wide

Plan of

the

CHAPTER 3

ROBERT MILLS:

PUBLIC ARCHITECTURE

IN SOUTH CAROLINA,

1820–30

John M. Bryan

John M. Bryan

n February 21, 1817, Robert Mills wrote to his wife telling her of his safe arrival in Charleston, South Carolina, and of the changes he found after an absence of twelve years; three weeks later he wrote from Petersburg, Virginia, recounting the first stages of his return trip to Baltimore.[1] This trip is notable primarily because it occurred at a time when he was seeking employment and South Carolina was embarking upon an extensive program of internal improvements. The War of 1812 and the growing importance of inland markets prompted South Carolina and other seaboard states to promote transportation in an effort to strengthen their ties with the hinterland. Nationally, Jeffersonian democrats supported internal improvements as a means of binding regions together, and, until states' rights clouded the issue, South Carolina was a leading proponent of roads and canals. Her most prominent spokesman, John C. Calhoun, justified public investment in transportation, saying that "whatever impedes the intercourse of the extremes . . . weakens the union. . . . Let us bind the republic together with a perfect system of roads and canals. Let us conquer space."[2]

Calhoun's fervor was based on the belief that improved navigation would channel commerce to Charleston and stem the westward flow of capital. In 1817, at the urging of the governor, Andrew Pickens, the legislature agreed to retain an engineer to survey all rivers in the state, submit a report on potential canals and roads, superintend construction of public buildings, and "recommend repairs and alterations."[3] The engineer was to be paid

$4,000 per year and was to be chosen by the legislature. The following year $1 million was appropriated to carry out this work. John L. Wilson (1789–1832) was appointed civil and military engineer but found it impossible to manage the forty-odd projects dispersed across the state. He was dismissed and was replaced in December 1819 by a Board of Public Works with five members. Abram Blanding (1776–1839) served as the salaried acting commissioner for roads, rivers, and canals, and, by virtue of his industry, as de facto head of the public works programs. Thomas Baker, a contractor, was acting commissioner for public buildings. Other members included Joel R. Poinsett, politician and an influential proponent of internal improvements, as president of the board; William Jay (1794–1837), an English-trained architect from whom the board purchased prototypical designs for courthouses and jails; and Robert G. Mills, a contractor (no kin to the architect).

The Board of Public Works held its organizational meeting on January 24, 1820; the board members carried on the work begun by John Wilson, but by the end of the year their efforts were called into question, and on December 20, 1820, Robert Mills, who was living in Baltimore, was appointed as a salaried acting commissioner for public buildings. He replaced Thomas Baker and was thus in a position to modify or replace the plans by William Jay, whose seat on the board was taken by Nicholas Herbemont (d. 1836), tutor of French at the South Carolina College.[4] Led by Blanding and Mills, its two salaried acting commissioners, the board was to direct the creation of a network of canals and erect courthouses and jails throughout the state.

Robert Mills served as acting commissioner of the Board of Public Works from December 20, 1820, to December 31, 1822, as superintendent of public buildings from January 1, 1823, to December 31, 1823, and finally as a consultant to the state, from 1824 to 1829. In each capacity he was responsible for the design and construction of public buildings; here he refined ideas of functional planning and techniques of masonry vaulting that characterized the federal buildings of his later career. During these years he had few professional peers in South Carolina, and his public buildings—fourteen courthouses, thirteen jails, the asylum for the insane in Columbia, and the County Records Office and powder magazine complex in Charleston—reflect his growing self-confidence in their rejection of traditional programs and ornament. His work in South Carolina marked the beginning of the public practice for which he is remembered, but this was not a period of unalloyed success. Tax revenues fell steadily throughout the decade as cot-

ton moved westward; the cost of canals and fire-proof construction exceeded estimates, and public support dissipated quickly, for the scope of the work precluded the realization of immediate benefits. Mills was identified with the most expensive projects through his work and writings, and in December 1823 the legislature removed him from office. Roderick Evander McIver, a clerk of court and sometime contractor, was appointed in his place. For the rest of the decade whatever work Mills did for the state as an architect was on a building-by-building basis.

Athough often unemployed, Mills was seldom idle, for in addition to sporadic public work he obtained private commissions for buildings and monuments, prepared estimates for the South Carolina Railroad Company, lobbied for the dredging of the Charleston harbor, and worked to establish a municipal water system for the city. None of his proposals for public works came to fruition. He was unable to eke out a satisfactory living and began, as

Figure 3.1
"Geographical, Statistical and Historical Map of the State," **Atlas of the State of South Carolina** *(1825). (South Caroliniana Library)*

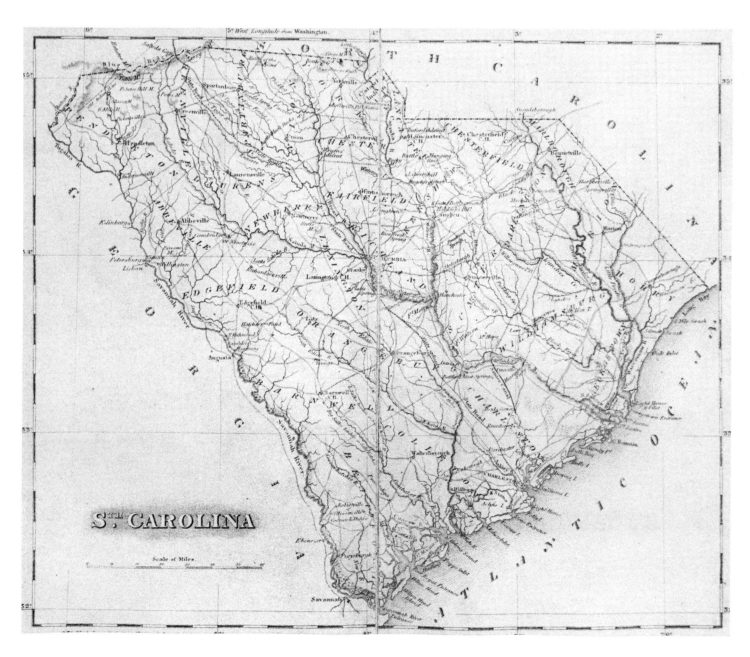

early as 1822, to seek employment elsewhere. Writing increasingly occupied a major portion of his time, and he said that from 1822 to 1826 he had "devoted all his time, talents and means" to the preparation, publication, and distribution of his *Atlas* and *Statistics of South Carolina*.[5] For the former he compiled, redrew, and corrected twenty-eight county maps created by nineteen surveyors; the resulting *Atlas* (1825) was the earliest systematic statewide map in the United States (fig. 3.1). The 829-page companion volume, the *Statistics* (1826), recounted the social and natural history of each district and emphasized the potential for economic development based on an intelligent use of natural resources. Other writings of this period include a manuscript (unpublished) proposing a rotary engine, an essay advocating a monorail from Washington, D.C., to New Orleans, and a partial draft for "The Architecture of Robert Mills."[6]

Insofar as he turned to writing as an alternative to architectural and engineering projects, Mills's literary and cartographic work reflects a determination not to become a general contractor or accept the "meanest mechanical employment" where he might readily have found work.[7] His prose is largely analytical and didactic: Whatever the immediate subject, he tends to consider a broad spectrum of ramifications and to buttress arguments with mathematical demonstrations and appeals to authority. Now and then throughout his writing, personal statements offer glimpses of the values that motivated his public work.

INTERNAL

IMPROVEMENT —

IDEALS AND IDEAS

In Baltimore, immediately before moving to South Carolina, Mills published *A Treatise on Inland Navigation* (1820), a pamphlet proposing a canal uniting the waters of the Susquehanna and Potomac rivers and linking Baltimore to "the country west of the Allegany mountains." He claimed that with "a perfect navigation of the Susquehanna to Baltimore, a preference would be given to this river, rather than to the canal of New York." Having noted that the Potomac at Shepherdstown, West Virginia, was 310 feet above sea level and that the Susquehanna at Middleton, Pennsylvania, near the falls of the Conewago, was 160 feet above the tide, he proposed a canal flowing northeastward along the eastern face of the mountains from the former to the latter. A spur from this canal, near Emmitsburg, Maryland, would descend to Baltimore along the ridge dividing the Gunpowder and Patapsco rivers.[8] To bolster this proposal he cited canals in

New York, Pennsylvania, Virginia, and South Carolina, as well as examples in China, Russia, Egypt, Europe, and England; he reviewed construction and transportation costs, ancillary social effects, and the possibility of transcontinental communications based on railroads and canals. Much of the *Treatise* was drawn from Albert Gallatin's *Report on Public Roads and Canals* and on letters by Robert Fulton and Benjamin Henry Latrobe that appeared as appendices in Gallatin's *Report*.[9] Mills observed in his preface that his own travels across the mountains had piqued his interest in canals. He also wrote of his training under Latrobe during the construction of the feeder canal (1803) in Elkton, Maryland, for the aborted Chesapeake and Delaware Canal.[10]

Mills's reading, early experience, and the Baltimore *Treatise* are apparent in the essay *Inland Navigation: A Plan for a Great Canal between Charleston and Columbia* (1821), which he published during his brief tenure as acting commissioner of the Board of Public Works for South Carolina. For South Carolina he proposed a canal 110 miles long, to begin in Columbia on the north bank of the Congaree River and to be carried by an aqueduct across the river (to avoid swamps downstream), proceeding to Charleston along the ridge between the Congaree and Santee and Cooper rivers to the north and the Edisto and Ashley rivers to the south. He intended this to be the principal link in a chain of canals stretching from the Charleston harbor to the foot of the Appalachian Mountains in the northwestern corner of the state, where, he said, one could stand at the crest of a narrow ridge and "pitch a stone with ease" into streams that flowed east (into the Green River) and west (into the Mud River, which joined the French Broad, which in turn flowed into the Ohio River). He envisioned connecting the canals of South Carolina to the Ohio, Mississippi, and Missouri rivers, opening "2000 square miles of trade" and making Columbia the "great thoroughfare from the west to the seaboard." Charleston, he wrote, "is better situated than New York for a commercial intercourse" with the "western country." At the height of his optimism he imagined that his canal would "constitute part of this grand rout" via the Columbia River to the Pacific through which would flow the East India trade of the New World.[11]

Such hopes for inland navigation in the South Carolina piedmont proved a costly delusion, but in assessing Mills's hyperbole as well as his responsibility it must be remembered that the state was committed to canals before his arrival. None of the routes he suggested was realized, and, although he argued for canals, by the time they came under attack in South Carolina in 1823 his responsibilities had shifted to the construction of public buildings, the other facet of the internal improvements program. Although he took part in little canal construction, he did undertake preliminary surveys for a canal to connect the Savannah and Broad rivers; he directed work on the Columbia Canal and participated in the certification of work executed on the Landsford Canal. His writing on canals is important primarily as a chapter in his efforts to develop the "engineering department" of his professional life.

Gallatin's *Report,* the foundation of Mills's writings on canals, concentrates on costs and anticipated revenues, noting that transportation is vital to the internal unification and the external defense of the Republic.[12] But with the whole nation as his canvas, Gallatin never illustrates in detail the effects of canals and turnpikes on daily life. The appendix by Latrobe goes into some detail concerning matters of civil and military engineering, but it does not attempt to evoke an image of canals in service. On the other hand, Robert Fulton, whose letter is the final element of the Gallatin *Report,* seeks to convince by example rather than by force of argument; although he presents calculations based on the transportation cost of staples—salt, molasses, and coffee—and compares labor costs per mile of men, boys, and horses on canals and turnpikes, his examples all concern money.

Mills's presentation differs from these essays in the addition of passages concerning the impact of canals on patterns of life. Having lived in both Philadelphia and Baltimore, cities that then had the major municipal water systems in the United States, and having served as president of the Baltimore Water Company, Mills observed that his canal might serve as the source of supply for similar systems in South Carolina. The canal would provide for fire protection, pure drinking water, cleaner streets, urban fountains, and irrigated gardens and would promote bathing and hygiene. By providing both drainage and irrigation, canals would increase the value of agricultural lands through which they passed. The labor force would be freed from the demands of overland transportation and would therefore become more productive. Finally, 1,280,000 acres of reclaimed swampland would become an agricultural "goldmine" instead of a source of disease.[13]

Mills was consistently more effusive in his assessment of benefits than Gallatin, Fulton, or Latrobe, and when South Carolinians turned against canals he remained steadfast. Projections that appear in his earlier essays are reiterated in the last of his South Carolina publications, the *Statistics of South Carolina.* The descriptive breadth of his writing conveys an empathy for the public and a broad, Vitruvian approach to planning.

Mills's first publication on public works, "Report on the Survey of Jones Falls" (1817), concerned an immediate, well-defined goal and presented in a concise format many of the interrelated benefits that were more diffusely presented throughout the later South Carolina writings.[14] On August 9, 1817, torrential rains had caused a flash flood in Baltimore. Jones Falls, a stream closely lined by houses and streets, usually flowed through the city at an average depth of three feet, but in the course of the afternoon it rose ten, and in some places twenty, feet above its banks. Houses were flooded, bridges and mills were destroyed, and a number of people were drowned. The city council sought flood-control recommendations, and Mills's plan was one of eleven submitted. The council members complimented his proposal as being "that which is most suitable to their view," but their sense of urgency evaporated as the waters receded. Nothing was done.[15]

The council did, however, publish Mills's plan, which seized flood control as a starting point for addressing a series of issues. Dredging the channel would make the waterway navigable as high as Madison Street, allowing wharves to be developed, and the income from these would defray the expense of the work recommended. The low wharves were to serve as a contained floodplain in times of high water, but under normal conditions their usefulness as landing areas would encourage the development of property abutting the stream, then largely lined with privies and outbuildings. Along either embankment Mills suggested "a promenade" and "a recess here and there . . . planted with trees and provided with seats" to take advantage of "the romantic scenery." He also specified that new bridges should span the stream with a single arch, thus avoiding the damming effect of debris against piers, which had exacerbated the 1817 flood. He cited bridges over the Seine and D'Oise rivers but did not mention the Colossus, designed by Lewis Wernwag in Philadelphia. Pits were to be dug into the streambed at intervals, and sand and gravel would be mined periodically from these; thus, sediment, previously a nuisance, was to become a resource. Tolls would be collected from water-borne commerce; mill sites would be leased along the banks. Mills calculated that revenues would exceed construction costs in less than four years. When the committee, declining to recommend adoption, cited the "infinite extent and magnitude" of the plan, it might have been describing the sweeping vision that characterized Mills's proposals for South Carolina, where, for example, he linked flood control with the abolition of slavery.[16]

Mills's pamphlet, *Internal Improvements of South Carolina* (1822), introduced him to the citizens of South Carolina and presented his argument for the embankment of rivers throughout the low country. As the reader of his day would have anticipated, he noted that levees improved navigation, increased land values, and promoted public health (through the draining of swamps), but his emphasis on moral and political benefits was unexpected. He stated unequivocably that "slavery is an evil" and that "the day *will come* when we must part with our black population." He rationalized the existence of slavery by arguing that a wise and inscrutable Providence may have intended that blacks, who seemed resistant to diseases of the lowlands, should serve as "pioneers" to make the "low lands in a state fit for the residence and labor of a white population" and that the resulting agricultural improvement would fund repatriation, perhaps to Sierra Leone under the auspices of the Colonization Society. To achieve this, he reasoned that the state could buy 6,000 slaves, whose labor would improve 2,000 square miles of swampland in ten years. Proceeds from the sale of this land would fund the repatriation of 120,000 slaves (at a cost of $400 each), and the state would still realize a profit of $42,624,000. Urging abolition he wrote, "If the evil be of fearful magnitude now, what will it be fifty years hence?"[17] The more commonplace—and complacent—viewpoint in South Carolina was that voiced by John Drayton: "If it [slavery] is an evil, it will sooner, or later, effect its own cure."[18]

Mills's moral argument is colored but not wholly obscured by his ownership of slaves and the racism inherent in the advocacy of repatriation.[19] Nonetheless, his recurring use of a moral justification for public works distinguishes his internal improvements writings from those of his peers. In this particular instance the focus on abolition proved ironic: Abolitionist agitation hastened the rejection of these internal improvements in South Carolina, for these entailed regional and federal cooperation, which threatened states rights.[20]

Invoking morality to justify his proposals, Mills often reveals that the sweep of his vision reflects his understanding of a divine plan. He suggests that public works are but the fulfillment of a Christian obligation to improve the lot of mankind: "Wherever a kind Providence has pointed out the habitation of man, the natural condition of the country admits of its improvement, to any extent commensurate with his wants, comforts and prosperity." Or again, the "divine sentiment of charity" justifies "legislative consideration" concerning the eradication of pauperism.[21] This piety was not merely a public gesture. Latrobe, who knew him well, considered him excessively religious, and Mills's own domestic correspondence assumes an active, interventionist God.[22] The concentration on public works promoting the general welfare—fireproof, well-planned prisons, hospitals, and offices—stems from his training with Latrobe, circumstances of professional opportunity, and his religious convictions.

Patriotism and a sense of place also played a formative role in Mills's public work. These emotions, he wrote, were "implanted in the human breast for wise purposes." Extensive colonial anecdotes contained in the *Statistics* record his historical interests, while elaborate iconographies for public monuments describe his visualization of patriotic acts. But on a deeper, more general level he said that "love of country" was "like a talisman upon the heart, riveting its partiality to places, which often in themselves possess nothing worthy of regard." He also observed that nurturing this attachment through promoting the general welfare was "the wisest policy the State can pursue."[23] His primary role as an architect in South Carolina was to place throughout the state buildings that would promote this end.

THE COURTHOUSES

Mills modified two courthouses that had been designed by William Jay, designed fourteen others, and strongly influenced seven more for which others were responsible. Before Mills's arrival, judging from county petitions, courthouses were typically of vernacular frame construction and were erected without any consideration for the court's dignity or security. The standard plans that the Board of Public Works purchased from Jay in 1820 were intended to be an improvement. A published description of these plans does not fully match drawings attributed to Jay, but in both instances the courtroom is on the first floor and interior stairs provide the only access to the second floor.[24]

The Marlborough County Courthouse (1822–24), in Bennettsville, the first of those designed by Mills, was a departure from Jay's plan and from the earlier vernacular buildings. As he had done with his auditorium churches, Mills developed a prototype to meet a specific set of needs and, satisfied with this solution, he applied it with minor variations at least twelve times over the next two decades (fig. 3.2). For protection against fire his courthouses were constructed of masonry bearing walls. Whenever he had control, the courtroom was on the principal floor, above a raised basement containing vaulted rooms (for offices and storage) flanking a barrel-vaulted central corridor. Lacking studded walls and joists, this lower level was intended to be fireproof. With four exceptions his courthouses were rectangular in plan with gabled roofs and attached tetrastyle Tuscan porticoes; typically, the portico was raised upon an arcade and framed by lateral stairs, which provided a ceremonial entry to the principal floor. A central entry at grade below the portico gave access to the lower level.

Of the several exceptions, the Georgetown County Courthouse (1822–24), in Georgetown, and the Williamsburg County Courthouse (1821–25), in Kingstree, had hexastyle porticoes that spanned the full width of their facades, and in both cases the lateral stairways were compressed within the portico itself and screened from view by the raised basement. The Kershaw County Courthouse (1825–30), in Camden, the only fully developed temple plan, was without a raised basement and originally had a giant Ionic portico; its entry opened into a vestibule that contained the staircase to the courtroom on the principal floor. The Chesterfield County Courthouse (1825–27), in Cheraw, was an anomaly; its interior reflected the basic elements of the Millsian pattern, but its attached portico, which was also typical in its order, stairs, and entries, was located on one of the long sides of the building and was thus perpendicular to the axis of the gable roof. The courthouses were without applied ornament: The lateral stairs, porticoes, belt courses, and recessed panels that articulated the "flank" elevations constituted the austere vocabulary of this set of buildings.

Functionally, Mills's courthouses offered fire protection and segregated uses in a manner that ensured quiet for the court. Symbolically, the Palladian raised basement was identified with architectural dignity in South Carolina, as exemplified by Drayton Hall (1738); the Charleston Exchange and Customs House (1766), designed by William Rigby Naylor; and the Charleston City Hall (1800), attributed to Gabriel Manigault. Waddell and Liscomb have suggested the Villa Arsiero as a prototype for Mills's courthouses—he owned a copy of Scamozzi's *Palladio*—and have noted that the Worcester County Courthouse (1801–3), in Worcester, designed by Charles Bulfinch, may have provided a precedent.[25] Similarities between Mills's program and Asher Benjamin's "Plan and Elevation of a Courthouse" have been pointed out by Pamela Scott; she has also noted that Mills's tendency to develop typical plans based upon repetitive cellular modules (in this case, the groin-vaulted offices) may reflect the influence of J. N. L. Durand's *Precis et lecons d'architecture* (1802–9).[26] Her conclusions are bolstered by the fact that in the Benjamin plan the lower offices are 16 by 16 feet and 16 by 21 feet; Mills consistently used similar dimensions for his courthouses—16 by 16 feet for Kershaw County; 15 by 20 feet and 20 by 20 feet for Alexandria; 19 by 19 feet for Lancaster County; and 18 by 18 feet for the proposed South Caroliniana Library.

To this list of possible prototypes should be added Latrobe's work on the south wing of the U.S. Capitol, the planning for which began at the time Mills entered the office. This revision of Thornton's

Figure 3.2
Horry County Courthouse (1823–25), Conway, South Carolina. (Robin Smith)

plan included vaulted fireproof areas for offices and record storage below an elevated meeting hall. A description from Latrobe's "Report," dated February 1804, is applicable to Mills's formula for the courthouses: "The great feature of this alteration is to raise up the floor of the legislative hall . . . and to use the whole lower story as the situation for committee rooms and offices."[27]

The masonry vaulting that was an essential characteristic of Mills's courthouses stemmed from his years of training in Latrobe's office. In Charleston as a youth he had known the vaulted basement of Naylor's Exchange, but it was a familiarity with the fireproof Treasury wings at the White House,

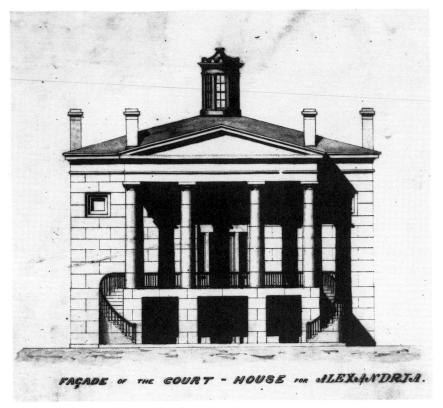

FAÇADE OF THE COURT - HOUSE FOR ALEXANDRIA.

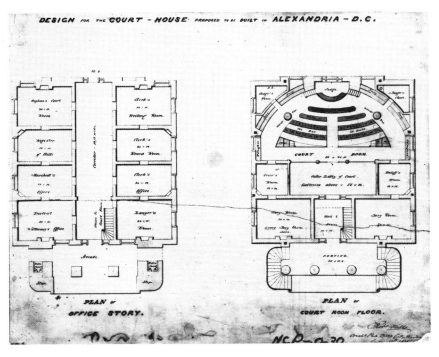

DESIGN FOR THE COURT - HOUSE PROPOSED TO BE BUILT IN ALEXANDRIA - D.C.

PLAN OF OFFICE STORY.

PLAN OF COURT ROOM FLOOR.

Figure 3.3
Plan and elevation,
Alexandria Courthouse
(1838-39), Alexandria,
Virginia. (National
Archives)

the South Carolina Asylum was largely responsible for the escalation of building costs from an initial budget of $37,281 to a final cost of more than $91,000. [28]

Cost overruns damaged Mills's reputation within the state; nonetheless, when reviewed nationally his system of vaults, countered thrusts, and thin walls was said to be cheaper than vaulting designed by Latrobe, Thomas U. Walter, Ammi B. Young, or Ithiel Town. In 1853, writing in Mills's defense, Representative R. W. Thompson claimed that the U.S. Capitol by Latrobe had cost $48 per square foot, the New York Customs House by Town had cost $94.07 per square foot, Girard College by Walter had cost $118.98 per square foot, and the Boston Customs House by Young had cost $91.75 per square foot. By contrast, Mills's U.S. Treasury had cost only $16.83 per square foot; his marble east wing of the same building only $24.44 per square foot, his Patent Office $19.24 per square foot, and his Post Office $24.18 per square foot—comparisons that give meaning to his repeated assertion that he worked to achieve economy without sacrificing permanence. The insecurity of contractors and masons, due to imperfect knowlege and an occasional vaulting failure, must have also impeded the more widespread use of fireproof construction. The only documented failure of a vault by Mills occurred at the Newberry County Courthouse (1821–24), in Newberry, and was attributed to freezing weather during construction. Nonetheless, reports to Congress in 1838 by Walter and Alexander Parris charged that Mills's work at the U.S. Treasury and the Patent Office was unstable, a criticism that still echoed through the controversy that led to his dismissal from government service—this despite the fact that the vaulting of neither building had "sprung or become dislodged to the width of a single hair." [29]

Masonry vaulting and the vertical separation of functions are related to the use of lateral stairs within or flanking prominently elevated, projecting porches. These stairs are a third leitmotif of Mills's South Carolina public buildings. In at least nine instances these were "winding" spiral stairs as described for interior use by Palladio. [30] Mills's lateral stairs framed his porches like those on the river facade of the Villa Foscari (1570), where the danger of flooding had prompted Palladio to employ a raised basement within which service facilities were located. The lateral stairs of the Horry County Courthouse (1823–25), in Conway, most nearly resemble those of the Villa Foscari; others resemble the curving, lateral stairs designed by the English Palladians—those by Isaac Ware for Wrotham Park (1754), in Middlesex; those by Sir William Chambers for Roehampton (1758), in Surrey; or those by Robert Adam for Kedleston Hall (1761), in Derby-

the foundations of the Roman Catholic Cathedral, Baltimore, and Latrobe's instructions for the centering for the vaults at the Bank of Philadelphia that allowed him to use vaulting in the Burlington County Jail, the fireproof wings at Independence Hall, and subsequent work. Despite Mills's consistent advocacy, fireproof construction never became commonplace in South Carolina during the nineteenth century, primarily because it was a good deal more expensive than traditional timber framing. Mills estimated in his diary that the South Caroliniana Library would cost $34,800 using timber framing and $64,000 if fireproof (the appropriation had been $15,000). The masonry vaulting of

shire, and the west front of Osterley Park (1765–75), in Middlesex. Lateral staircases were an important element in the facades of the courthouses for Horry, Greenville, Orangeburg, Union, Lancaster, Williamsburg, Georgetown, and Sumter counties as well as at the Fireproof Building, the asylum, and the later Alexandria Courthouse (1838–39), in Alexandria, Virginia (fig. 3.3).

Inasmuch as lateral stairs allowed the lower entry to be framed within the basement arcade, they expressed the functional separation of the floors. The use of exterior stairs also maintained the firebreak between floors, buffered the court from noise and traffic, and conserved interior square footage. The United States Bank (1800), later the Charleston City Hall, attributed to Gabriel Manigault, may have introduced this Palladian motif to South Carolina.[31] In New York Mills had seen a similar pair of staircases at the Government House (c. 1800); he was also familiar with Latrobe's specifications for the circular stair within the proposed Mississippi lighthouse (1805) and had himself considered a similar stair for the Baltimore Washington Monument in 1816.

Palladio described both solid- and hollow-core "winding stairs"; Mills used both types. The ascending spiral twisted around a solid core on the facades of the courthouses of Georgetown, Williamsburg, and perhaps Greenville and Union counties, as well as at the Fireproof Building and the Alexandria Courthouse. The service stairs of the asylum, located in the angle between the central block and the wings, were also designed with a solid core, the inner end of each tread serving as a drum of the central column. The solid-core spiral also appears in his design for the South Caroliniana Library (1836–40), in Columbia. The cylindrical space defined by the staircase, which Palladio spoke of as the "column in the middle," was open, and the treads cantilevered from the wall in the central staircase within the Fireproof Building. The porticoes of the Orangeburg County Courthouse (1826–28), in Orangeburg, and the asylum were flanked by hollow-core spiral stairs. Only three of the exterior lateral stairways have survived intact—those at the asylum and at the Horry and Georgetown County courthouses); among them, only the asylum steps are the exposed, curving form Mills had used most frequently (figs. 3.4, 3.5).

The South Carolina Asylum plans and elevations differ from the stairs as built, for the drawings indicate projections from either end of the portico that would have served simultaneously as footings for the outermost columns and as a cylindrical solid

Figure 3.4
Plan, South Carolina
Asylum. (South Carolina
Department of Archives
and History)

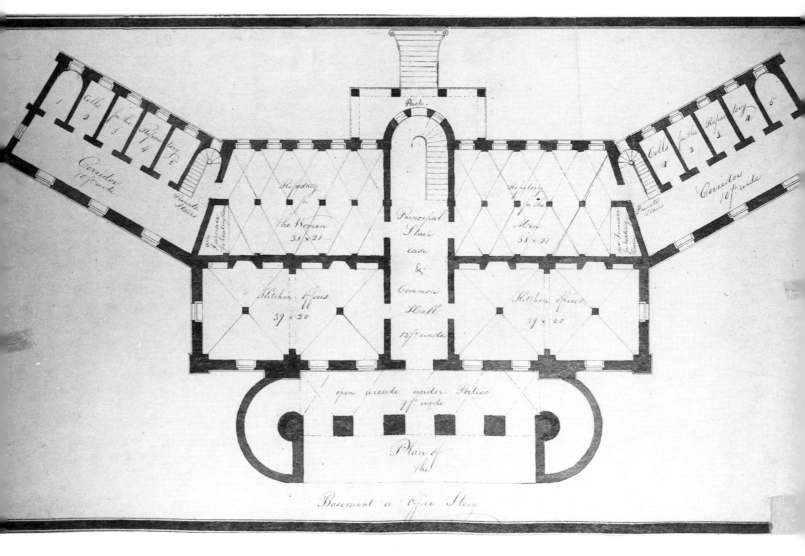

Figure 3.5
Stairway, north facade,
South Carolina Asylum
(1822–28), Columbia,
South Carolina.
(John M. Bryan)

core around which the staircases would have turned. As drawn, the staircases were to have been visually integrated into the portico: The face of each tread was to have been a radius originating at the center of the column and common to the concentric circles formed by the base of the column and the inner and outer arcs of the staircase. Although the projections were deleted (perhaps during the final stages of construction when landscaping, plumbing, and the fireproofing of the upper floors were sacrificed to save money), the treads were constructed as radii, but the impact of this integration was lost, for the corner of the portico, the channeling of the basement, and the void between the portico and the stairs effectively disassociated the staircase from the body of the portico. This alteration had the unfortunate effect of isolating the stairs as a disharmonious appendage.

PROFESSIONAL

PRACTICE

The modification of plans during construction was not unusual; contractors and commissioners on site played an influential role in the administrative structure that Mills did much to create. During the

1820s in South Carolina, the creation of courthouses and jails began with a petition to the legislature. An appropriation, typically $10,000 for a courthouse and $5,000 to $8,000 for a jail, initiated Mills's involvement. He provided "plans, specifications, and estimates, of the quantities and quality, of both materials and work to be furnished" and advertised for bids. He received proposals and participated in drafting contracts for constuction that often cited "plans and specifications signed by Robert Mills." Surviving documents do not suggest that he, or anyone else, considered siting except insofar as the sale of an obsolete courthouse might make way for or defray the cost of new buildings. As work got underway, he corresponded with contractors concerning alterations of plans and the quality of materials and workmanship. Because of the use of substandard brick, the walls of the Greenville County Courthouse (1821–24) had to be taken down twice during construction; a similar problem caused him to direct that the Union County Jail (1822–23) be faced with stone.[32] He also reviewed invoices; payment was usually made in three installments—one-third on execution of the contract, one-third on completion of the walls, and a final payment upon acceptance of the work. Cost was a function of quantity as determined by measurement of the finished building or enumeration within the original specifications.

Each judicial district had a Commission of Public Buildings that reported to the legislature; these commissioners were Mills's primary clients. His immediate superior, the president of the Board of Public Works, submitted annual reports to the legislature, and the report for 1821, Mills's first full year of service, reflects his critique of "the usual course of contracting for public building" and changes he instigated to conform with the "practice prevailing in Europe and in several of our Northern cities." In South Carolina contracts had been let to general contractors, who might or might not be skilled "mechaniks" and whose profit was a percentage of the cost of labor and materials. Mills proposed that "the Board be authorized to engage a fit person, a mechanic, who has no interest in the contracts, to superintend personally the faithful execution of such contracts as might be made for materials or work, with the several persons employed about the buildings."[33] This latter system was adopted and reflected Mills's own experience when he worked for Latrobe in Philadelphia. Correspondence between Latrobe and his clerks of the works—Mills in Philadelphia and John Lenthall in Washington—expresses the frustration Mills experienced in directing widely separated projects. At the same time superintendents and commissioners often lamented Mills's absence when a decision needed to be made or work certified for payment.

THE JAILS

The procedure adopted for the courthouses was used in the construction of district jails, the other building type for which Mills developed a prototypical plan. Of thirteen jails that can be attributed to him, only those in Union and Lancaster counties survive. His interior plan for jails was in many respects like that of the courthouses: The lower floor consisted of a central corridor that contained the staircase and was flanked by rooms used as lodging for the keeper and confinement for debtors; the upper floor contained cells for felons. Judging from the Union County Jail (1822–23) and Lancaster County Jail (1821–22) and documents concerning the jail at Pendleton, it is probable that the upper floor was typically constructed as an open span (analogous to the courtrooms) and then subdivided into cells through the use of nonbearing, wood partitions (fig. 3.6). If this was the case, then the South Carolina district jails differed from Mills's Burlington County Jail in Mount Holly, New Jersey, which was vaulted throughout, and from his initial proposal for the Marlborough County Jail (1822–24), in Bennettsville, South Carolina, for which he recommended fireproof construction. Cost, no doubt, was the determining factor. Only the Lancaster County Jail is known to have been vaulted on its lower level; its second-floor cell partitions have been removed, making the relationship between its plan and that of the courthouses self-evident.

The elevations of the jails lacked projecting elements that might have diminished the impression of enclosed volume. Mills further emphasized closure through the liberal use of rough-hammered granite sills and lintels, by reducing the size of window openings on the second floor (to 2 feet 4 inches by 3 feet 8 inches at Lancaster), and, at Union and Spartanburg, recessing the entry behind three arches carried by monolithic granite piers (18 inches wide, 14 inches deep, and 7 feet 2 inches high at Union). Latrobe had noted the apt and "solemn character" of stone in describing the Virginia Penitentiary (1797), in Richmond. Mills was also familiar with the Massachusetts State Prison (1802–5), Charlestown, Massachusetts, designed by Charles Bulfinch, the most notable feature of which was its introduction of the use of massive units of Chelmsford granite 6 to 14 feet long.[34] Although the jails varied in detail, it appears that the basic plan was often repeated with little modification, for the Union County Jail is said to have been based on the Marlborough County Jail, and the specifications for the Edgefield County Jail (1825–26), in Edgefield, call for it to be "in every particular and after the model of the Union jail"; the Newberry County Jail, in turn, was to be "in all respects similar to the present gaol at Edgefield."[35]

Mills's standard plans for the courthouses and jails were developed while he was acting commissioner of the Board of Public Works or superintendent of public buildings. During this period, from January 1820 through December 1823, his salary was paid by the treasurer of the upper or lower division of the state as a line item in the "Internal Improvement" budget; there is nothing in the records to indicate that he maintained an office. After being replaced in January 1824 by McIver, he worked as a contract employee and was paid from specific project budgets under the control of the various district commissioners of public buildings (the one exception being his work in Charleston, where he both served on and was paid by two commissions). But during the remainder of the decade these payments were irregular; consequently, debt and financial insecurity became prominent themes in his domestic correspondence. In 1825 he was paid $25 for "drafts" of the Chesterfield County Courthouse; in 1826 he was paid $500 for supervising the construction of the Fireproof Building in Charleston and another $500 as superintendent of the asylum, for "as he was no longer the architect of the state, he did not consider himself under obligations to render his service." The last of these miscellaneous appropriations came after he left the state—$2,000 paid in September 1839 to redeem plates of the county maps from Henry S. Tanner, a printer in Philadelphia.[36] Without a regular salary, he found life difficult, and from 1822 to 1829 he sought employment in Virginia, Maryland, and Washington, D.C.

Figure 3.6
Lancaster County Jail
(1821-22), Lancaster,
South Carolina.
(John M. Bryan)

PRINCIPAL FRONT of the LUNATIC ASYLUM COLUMBIA SOUTH CAROLINA.

Figure 3.7
Elevation, South Carolina
Asylum (1822-28),
Columbia, South Carolina.
(South Carolina Department
of Archives and History)

THE SOUTH CAROLINA

ASYLUM

The cornerstone of the South Carolina Asylum (1822–28) was laid on July 22, 1822. Those present basked in "sentiments of sociability, humanity and benevolence," cognizant that it was to be the largest building in the state and based on avant-garde theories of psychiatric care.[37] Mills's design, which replaced an earlier plan by John L. Wilson, was intended to be fireproof and to further therapeutic practices advocated by William Tuke (1732–1822) and his grandson Samuel Tuke (1784–1857), English Quakers who were instrumental in psychiatric reform.[38] Knowledge of the Tukes' theories had already influenced psychiatric hospitals in America. The Friends' Asylum (1817), in Frankfort, Pennsylvania; the Asylum for the Insane (1818), later called the McLean Asylum, in Charlestown, Massachusetts, designed by Charles Bulfinch; the Bloomingdale Asylum (1816–21), in New York City, designed by Thomas C. Taylor; and the Retreat (1821–24), in Hartford, Connecticut— all reflected English precedents described in the Tukes' writings, which were republished in Philadelphia from 1813 to 1815.

The South Carolina Asylum differs from its

American predecessors in the degree to which its plan, structural detail, and landscaping realize ideals articulated by the Tukes. Nothing is known concerning the asylum plan by Wilson except that it had been intended to serve both as a lunatic asylum and a school for the deaf and dumb. Mills's involvement coincided with the decisions to create an institution specifically to serve the insane, to make the building fireproof, and to incorporate gardens within the plan—all of which increased the initial estimates from $28,932 to $46,500.[39] During Mills's participation as supervising architect, from 1822 to 1824, the exterior of the central block and the first segments of the obliquely angled flanking wings were enclosed; costs escalated to $91,000, and the legislative committee was quick to note that it had been "directed in the plans, calculations, and production, by Mr. Mills who was the Architect of the State when the work was commenced."[40] The institution received its first patient on December 12, 1828, but had long before lost public support, and the legislature had decided to fund neither plumbing nor grounds in an effort to contain the cost of construction.

Mills's initial plans called for a central block, 40 by 80 feet and five stories high, having a raised basement and fronted on the north by a hexastyle Doric portico on an arcade (figs. 3.7, 3.8). As with the courthouses, access to the service areas—kitchens, laundry, storerooms, furnaces, and refectories) was through the arcade beneath the portico. At either end of the portico, winding lateral stairs provided access to the main floor. The upper floors of the central block flanked the central hall, which contained the principal staircase and opened onto corridors leading into the flanking wings. Mills planned for the wings, each composed of a series of wards, to sweep back to the south and enclose a semicircular garden 500 feet in diameter; this garden in turn would be subdivided into segments accessible to the various wards. Samuel Tuke had noted that large activity rooms were needed to accommodate groups of patients (Mills located these in the asylum's central block); private bedrooms were to be provided (Mills placed these on the south side of the flanking wings); the sexes were to be visually as well as physically separated (Mills angled the corridors, thus cutting off visual contact and minimizing the need for physical restraint); wide corridors were to serve as "exercise galleries during inclement weather" (each of Mills's bedrooms opened into such a corridor); and metal sash and concealed hinges should provide security unobtrusively (these were installed at the asylum, where "security is agreeably deguised under appearances familiar to the eye in every private house"). Further, the building was heated by hot-air furnaces, as recommended by the Tukes.

Samuel Tuke also stressed the salutary effects of orientation and landscape; in these respects the asylum is the most notable of Mills's works in South Carolina. He was criticized for facing the building away from the town but did so in order that the dormitory cells might have a southern exposure. The grounds to the north were to be "laid off in walks, with trees, shrubbery, and seats" for "the respectable class of patients." To the south, within the semicircular embrace of the wings, the grounds were to be "divided into sections for the several classes, and for the requisite domestic accommodations of the Institution." The roof of the central block was used as a "walk . . . which is surrounded by a parapet wall, [and] is appropriated exclusively to visitors. It overlooks those [on the flanking wings] of the patients, as well as all the courts of the Institution."[41] These early American roof gardens and walled courtyards were Mills's response to the need for controlled access to nature in an urban setting.

Technologically, the most exceptional aspects of the plan were the heating and ventilating systems. A system of underground drains connected with ducts in the corridor floors to cool the building by convection. Jefferson had used an underground ventilating tunnel at Monticello, but insofar as is known, the asylum was the first instance of its use

in South Carolina. The heating system can be reconstructed from Mills's plans and writings, contemporary accounts, and fragments that survive in situ.[42] Two separate furnaces were used to heat the building, each consisting of three distinct elements—a firebox, a heat chamber, or reservoir, and a system of flues and dampers, or registers, which distributed the heated air throughout the building. The fireboxes were located at one end of the refectories, long and narrow rooms (21 feet by 38 feet) that occupied the southern side of the central-block basement. To facilitate fuel delivery and removal of ashes, each of the fireboxes was located near an exterior entry.

The furnaces, which shared a common wall and flues with the fireplaces used for cooking, were approximately 4 feet wide, 4 feet high, and 6 feet deep and were made "mostly of brick." They had one or more hinged metal doors through which wood was loaded, fires were stoked, and ashes were removed. They also had at least two adjustable metal dampers, one of which controlled the flow of air into the fire chamber to regulate the rate of combustion. The other dampers controlled the flow of air into flues (probably cast iron), which passed through the fire chamber. Air heated in these flues passed by convection into a heat chamber, or reservoir, a sealed, vaulted brick chamber (5 feet 7 inches wide, 6 feet 10 inches deep, and 6 feet 7 inches high) resembling a kiln, which contained a series of interconnected flues. Here it was thought that the heated air, like water flowing within a constricted course, would gather momentum. The flues within the reservoir opened into a network of flues, or channels, within the walls, through which the air rose to dampers or registers located in each corridor throughout the building.

Although notable as the oldest extant architecturally integrated hot-air system in America and the only one by Mills to have survived, this was not his first furnace nor, beyond its apparent primacy in South Carolina, was it noteworthy in the evolution of heating technology. As employed by Mills, the central hot-air furnace had been used by William Strutt in the Belper Mills (1792) near Derby, England; similar systems were installed in the Quaker asylums at Derby and Wakefield. In America the hot-air furnace was popularized by Oliver Evans, who advocated its use in factories.[43] The most fully described early use of a central air system by Mills is in an industrial setting, the Patapsco Factory (1816), in Baltimore. The *Niles Weekly Register*, under the heading "Economy of Fuel," published a full account of this project in order that "the public may be benefited, and . . . the merits of this most deserving and modest individual may be more generally known."[44] The factory was large—100 feet long, 40 feet wide, and several stories (60 feet)

Opposite: Figure 3.8 North facade, South Carolina Asylum. (Robin Smith)

high, or "240,000 cubic feet" (the portion of the asylum built by Mills contained 237,000 cubic feet)—and the furnace was composed of similar elements and worked on the same principles. By regulating the rate of combustion and adjusting the registers, it was said, the factory maintained "the mild temperature of May" and did so economically. The article concludes with a comparative cost analysis of Mills's furnace and an alternative steam system and notes that the furnace required less than a cord of wood per week, or less than one seventh of that formerly consumed.

The emphasis on economy is taken directly from Daniel Pettibone's *Economy of Fuel*, the source of Mills's Patapsco plan.[45] Pettibone appears in Mills's 1816 *Diary*, but the architect was aware of the inventor before coming to Baltimore, for Pettibone's work was published in Philadelphia in 1812 and carried an endorsement by both Latrobe and George Clymer, president of the Bank of Philadelphia. On January 31, 1812, the latter wrote that a Pettibone furnace heated the lobby of the bank that had been constructed to Latrobe's design under Mills's supervision. From Pettibone, Mills obtained a license to build more furnaces, and no less than twenty-two furnace installations are noted in his 1816 *Diary;* most of these were residential, but on July 9, 1816, he noted that he had "made plans of furnaces for St. Pauls Church and the Asylum House [illegible words] near Pha."[46] Beyond economy and efficiency, a central hot-air system offered many advantages in an institutional setting. As opposed to the open fireplace and the radiating stove, the furnace permitted the firebox to be located away from the area to be heated and thereby promoted safety, cleanliness, and ease of service.

THE FIREPROOF BUILDING

Perhaps the best known of Mills's public buildings in South Carolina is the County Records Office (1822–27), Charleston. Commonly known as the Fireproof Building, it was a project that, like the asylum, spanned his work as a state employee and a "Superintendent" (figs. 3.9, 3.10). In 1819, before his return to South Carolina, the legislature had noted the need for fireproof repositories in both Columbia and Charleston,[47] and Mills acted while the project was in its formative stage. He corresponded with the Charleston city council concerning such a facility in October 1821, but not until two months later did the legislature appropriate $25,000—$10,000 for the purchase of a site and $15,000 for the construction of fireproof offices.[48] On May 20, 1822, the city council voted to pay him $200 for plans concerning the improvement of the square adjacent to the city hall.

Mills's plan entailed siting the new state office within an open space that would serve simultaneously as a firebreak and as a linkage between the city hall, the state offices, and a proposed federal courthouse and academy of fine arts; it would also be Charleston's first city park. Walkways within the park were cross-axial and divided the lot into quadrants. One pair, perpendicular to Meeting Street, formed the east-west axis and separated the new building from the existing city hall. The other pair, which extended through the park from Chalmers to Broad Street, formed the north-south axis and was intended to set off the proposed courthouse and academy. The prominent site and the fact that the building was to be occupied by ten state offices induced Mills to design the most complex of his South Carolina buildings.

Plans were completed during the spring of 1822, for Mills advertised for bids from April 21 to May 13, 1822.[49] Although removed from his post as superintendent of public buildings in December 1823, he was appointed, together with Simon Magwood, Thomas Blackwood, and Thomas Johnson, as "Commissioner for completing the fire Proof Buildings" on December 13 of that year. The following week he was also appointed a commissioner of public buildings for the Charleston district, a group that had "full Power & Authority to design, construct & finish the Public Buildings authorized by law in the same manner as the Superintendant of Public Buildings." Their authority included all public buildings in the district "Except the fire Proof Buildings & the Court House."[50]

Insofar as work in Charleston was concerned, these appointments mitigated Mills's loss of office, especially since his fellow commissioners "found it requisite to have some skilful architect to superintend the work & inspect the contracts and appointed Mr. Robert Mills for that purpose."[51] He was also retained by the commissioners of the fireproof offices and for $500 took bids, drafted contracts, checked construction (but was not continually on site), and measured and certified completed work for payment.[52] The pace of application for payment and certification of work suggests that construction progressed smoothly.

As Mills was living in Columbia (120 miles away) and traveling throughout the state in conjunction with his *Atlas*, courthouses, and jails, the commissioners hired an on-site supervising architect, John Spidle, to direct construction. Together on May 5, 1825, they approved the work of the principal brickmason, John Gordon, including the interior plastering of walls and ceilings and the exterior stuccoing of eaves and cornices. The work of the stonemasons James Rowe and John White—cutting and installing the cantilevered interior stair

Figure 3.9 Elevation, County Records Office (Fireproof Building) (1822–27), Charleston, South Carolina. (South Carolina Historical Society)

Figure 3.10 Plans of the ground and main floors, County Records Office. (Stephen Thomas, Historic American Buildings Survey)

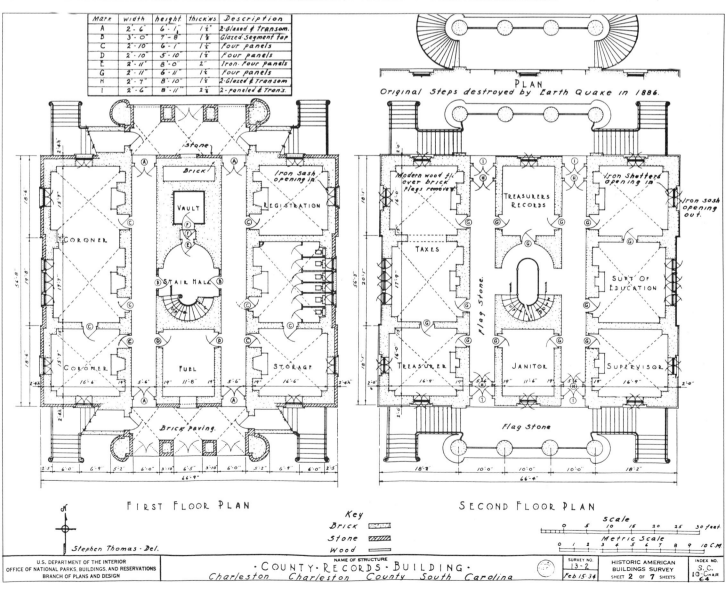

Mark	width	height	thick'ns	Description
A	2'-6"	6'-1"	1⅛"	2-Glazed & transom.
B	3'-0"	7'-8"	1⅜"	Glazed Segment top
C	2'-10"	6'-1"	1⅜"	Four panels
D	2'-10"	5'-10"	1⅜"	Four panels
E	2'-11"	8'-0"	2"	Iron-Four panels
G	2'-11"	6'-11"	1⅜"	Four panels
H	2'-7"	8'-10"	1⅜"	2-Glazed & Transom
I	2'-6"	8'-11"	2⅜"	2-paneled & Trans.

PLAN

Original Steps destroyed by Earth Quake in 1886.

FIRST FLOOR PLAN

SECOND FLOOR PLAN

Stephen Thomas - Del.

Key
Brick
Stone
Wood

Scale
0   5   10   15   20   25   30 feet

Metric Scale
0 1 2 3 4 5 6 7 8 9 10 CM

U.S. DEPARTMENT OF THE INTERIOR
OFFICE OF NATIONAL PARKS, BUILDINGS, AND RESERVATIONS
BRANCH OF PLANS AND DESIGN

NAME OF STRUCTURE
·COUNTY·RECORDS·BUILDING·
Charleston Charleston County South Carolina

SURVEY NO.
13-2
Feb 15 34

HISTORIC AMERICAN
BUILDINGS SURVEY
SHEET 2 OF 7 SHEETS

INDEX NO.
S.C.
10-CHAR
64

treads as the brick walls rose, facing the basement with brownstone, and setting the flagstone flooring and brownstone sills, thresholds, capitals, and parapet—was measured periodically from November 23, 1823, through February 16, 1826. A blacksmith, John Johnson, was paid for fabricating and installing metal balusters and other trim on October 4, 1826, and at the year's end Robert Downie was paid for "souldring conducting pipe" on the roof. The commissioners of the fireproof offices reported on December 11, 1826, that the interior was ready for occupancy (Benjamin Hunt, commissioner in equity, had been for "some time" in rooms assigned "by Mr R. Mills the Architect"); they expressed the belief that the exterior was within days of being completed and observed that they had exceeded their budget because "there had been two Architects one counteracting the other." The final cost for the building and lot was $53,803.81.[53]

The elevations did not conform in several respects to Mills's drawing and descriptions, and some of these alterations are attributable to Spidle. Mills envisioned a Palladian block five bays wide on a raised basement, its principal facades (north and south) fronted by projecting Doric porticoes elevated on arcades with winding lateral stairs similar to those planned for the asylum. Mills's surviving elevation indicates that the brownstone columns were to be fluted, a supposition bolstered by the fact that the base of the capitals is channeled to accept fluting; instead, the columns were left plain and covered with roughcast stucco. Other changes for which Spidle may have been responsible affected both the proportions and horizontality inherent in Mills's elevation. The use of quoins in lieu of continuous horizontal channeling diminished the visual effectiveness of the basement as a podium; the nature of Mills's intention in this regard is evident in the channeling of the asylum and the Georgetown County Courthouse, as well as in the Fireproof Building elevation. Equally significant was the deletion of the belt course between the second and third floors and the lengthening of the third-floor windows, changes that erased the illusion of an attic story and the closure this had provided in Mills's elevation. This latter alteration adversely affected the east and west facades, which, Gene Waddell has observed, were to resemble triumphal arches. These elevations consist of three bays, the central bay being recessed and vertically integrated through the use of a Latrobean triple window on the main floor and a thermal window above. Despite the alteration of proportion and emphasis, the intended effect is perceptible and may derive from the end elevations of Latrobe's proposal for the New York City Hall (1802).

These exterior changes did not affect the interior plan, which, arguably, is the most notable feature of the Fireproof Building. The plan had to satisfy three primary criteria: the secure storage of government records, accessibility to diverse offices without the disruption of other tenants, and adequate lighting and ventilation. Meeting these goals Mills adapted the concept he used repeatedly in the lower floors of his courthouses and jails by inserting a central bay flanked on either side by hallways extending through the building from north to south. This wholly fireproof central bay contained a vault at grade secured by two wrought-iron doors, three rooms without fireplaces or combustible materials of any kind, and, its principal feature, an oval stairwell with cantilevered brownstone stairs and balconies. The stairwell was crowned by a skylight, which provided circulation of light and air as well as vertical access throughout the building. Mills had incorporated a fireproof vault in the Benjamin Chew House, in Philadelphia, but there is no direct precedent in his ouvre for the double hall and central stairwell. The latter, which recalls a Palladian rotunda reduced to a utilitarian scale, represents a creative solution to problems inherent in the design criteria. Eight exterior entries provided flexible access to the hallways, and of all the building's elements the off-center disposition of these entries best signifies the license with which he adapted classical precedent.

THE POWDER MAGAZINE COMPLEX

During construction of the Fireproof Building, as a commissioner of public buildings for the Charleston district, Mills also designed an addition (1822–24) to the Charleston County Jail and a complex of nine powder magazines, barracks, and a gatehouse (1822–27). The advertisement soliciting bids for the jail, dated March 20, 1822, noted that his plans and specifications would be "in the hands of the commissioners" the following week. This jail (demolished c. 1855) was a rectangular addition to the existing jail and was described by Mills in the *Statistics* as being four stories high, "divided into solitary cells" and "the whole made fireproof." His description suggests that, like other jails throughout the state, it reflected criteria he first considered in 1806 for the South Carolina Penitentiary project and first realized with the construction of the Burlington County Jail, in Mount Holly, New Jersey.[54]

The powder magazines, too, represented ideas expressed earlier in his career; these he described as being "brick, rough cast, and made fire-proof," "all of a circular form, with conical roofs, and disposed in three ranges, 130 feet apart." He noted that the central magazine was the largest and was reserved for the storage of publicly owned gunpowder and that its "roof is made bomb-proof."[55] In 1809 Latrobe had designed a magazine for the Navy Yard at Gosport, Virginia, which was to be "an octagon externally and a circle internally"; a masonry vault beneath its roof was intended to render it "bomb proof." On the French principle of "three very strong walls" and one "light wall . . . placed opposite to an open part of the country or toward a river," he had also proposed "a small square powder house" for the Washington Navy Yard on the eastern branch of the Potomac.[56]

These plans would have been known to Mills when, on October 4, 1817, an explosion of the Levering Gunpowder Works in Baltimore led him to propose a complex of vaulted, circular magazines to the Baltimore City Council.[57] He recounted the potential danger of collecting gunpowder within one large, centrally located magazine. He

The island was located in the salt marsh and "a bold navigation extends up to the spot, and affords every convenience to the importers of powder." By the end of the year the board reported that contracts had been let and that the buildings "are in a state of forwardness."[60] Additional appropriations included $17,380 in 1825 and $2,000 in 1827. In 1824 Mills solicited bids for the construction of a palmetto log embankment "not to exceed 340 feet" along the margin of the creek, but this aspect of the work was deemed too expensive and was abandoned.[61]

Judging from rubble on the site, the eight smaller magazines were 16½ feet in diameter and the larger public magazine was approximately 20 feet in diameter (fig. 3.11). Their walls of Charleston gray brick were covered with roughcast and were 2 feet thick; lintels, thresholds, and door jambs were made of brownstone, and all had slate roofs. The most architecturally notable component of the

Figure 3.11
Powder magazines and barracks (1822–27), Charleston, South Carolina, c. 1909. (Nora M. Davis, "Public Powder Magazines at Charleston," 1944)

observed that the "form generally adopted is a square or parallelogram" and went on to recommend a cluster of magazines "on a circular plan" to be sited on the banks of the Patapsco River as "the transportation of powder by water is much less liable to accident than by land." The only surviving drawing from his Baltimore proposal depicts a vaulted "square or parallelogram" magazine adapted from plate 6 of Lewis Lochee's Elements of Fortification (1780), a source that, like his description of the "fosse and embankment" at Charleston, indicates a familiarity with the literature of military engineering.[58]

The plans for the Charleston magazine have not survived, but they are cited in the Board of Public Works's Report for 1821 and resulted in an initial appropriation of $8,000. From this appropriation in September 1822 Mills paid Mrs. Anne Langstaff $1,000 in partial payment for Laurel Island, a five-acre site adjacent to the Charleston Neck and New Market Creek, a tributary of the Cooper River.[59]

magazine complex was the gatehouse, about which little is known. Mills said it was a barracks "two stories high, and covering the grand gateway leading into the magazine court";[62] it was apparently a triumphal arch incorporating a residential interior in the manner of Claude Nicolas Ledoux (1736–1806). Shortly before its demolition, around 1940, it was described as "a most picturesque ruin of a building distinguished from all other structures around Charleston by two Roman arches through the center and an up and a down stairs room in each wing. Obviously a gate yet the parapet gables and absence of battlements gave it the appearance of a home rather than a military structure."[63] In American architecture such a form was idiosyncratic but not wholly unique. In 1852 Mills himself proposed lock-keepers' quarters within the superstructure of the Potomac River Bridge, and the same year, two miles from the magazine complex, Edward Brickell White used a triumphal arch as a porter's lodge for the College of Charleston.

THE *ATLAS*,

STATISTICS, AND

OTHER WRITINGS

The winter legislature of 1823 did not reappoint Mills as superintendent of public buildings. Instead, he was placed on the two commissions then directing state construction in the Charleston district. On December 19, 1823, the legislators also "sanctioned" or ratified a provisional contract that Mills had made with Abram Blanding, superintendent of public works, for the publication and sale of maps of each of the twenty-eight counties.[64] This agreement authorized Mills to use state-owned district surveys as a data base; he was to provide twelve atlases to the state free of charge, and the superintendent of public works was to purchase another fifty copies for $600. With this subscription to defray publication costs, Mills hoped to sell single maps and bound atlases at a profit.

Beyond his search for work, several factors reinforced Mills's interest in producing an atlas. For three years he had crisscrossed the state, and he knew the collection of surveys that John L. Wilson, as state civil and military engineer, had used to publish a state map in 1822. Five of these district maps—those of Fairfield, Lexington, Newberry, Union, and York—had been published but were on a scale of one mile to the inch, too large to be useful in the field. Finally, Mills's concern for canals entailed cartography. Two of his South Carolina proposals, the Columbia to Charleston canal and the Savannah River to Broad River canal, had involved the presentation of a detailed geographical knowledge. His maps for these proposals have not survived, but his manuscript "Report" (1821) concerning the potential Savannah River canal, written as a preface for maps that were attached, describes trekking through the Great Swamp and along Bees Creek between the Savannah and Broad rivers in the Beaufort District to establish the feasibility of a canal.[65] High water "prevented a survey to be made in a direct line," but through "circuitous examinations" he obtained a series of levels and discovered a potential route along what he deduced to be the prehistoric bed of the Savannah River. In addition to outlining alternative routes, the report conveys a sense of history and geology, an awareness of the social implications of canals, and a first-hand topographical knowledge. In short, his earlier involvement with South Carolina canals, before his responsibilities focused on architectural projects, laid the groundwork for the *Atlas* and its explication, *The Statistics*.

The *Atlas* and *Statistics* occupied much of Mills's time and attention from 1823 through 1826. The *Atlas* contains twenty-eight district maps, on a scale of two miles to the inch, and is "Prefaced with a Geographical, Statistical and Historical Map of the State," the margins of which contain an extensive text on topography, settlements, commerce, and civil and military history, text that foreshadows the *Statistics*.[66] Mills considered these works a set portraying the nature of the state. The district maps he used were the result of an 1816 appropriation to create a state map. George Blackburn, professor of astronomy at the South Carolina College, initiated this project and made observations of latitude, but his contract was not renewed in 1817. Instead, the legislature decided to commission surveys of each county as a more efficient approach. Nineteen surveyors were hired to produce county maps, which were then reduced and consolidated by Wilson, and the resulting state map was published by Henry S. Tanner of Philadelphia in two printings in 1821–22. As there proved to be little demand for Wilson's map or the printed county maps, the legislature declined to fund the publication of an atlas in 1821 and again in 1822 but allowed Mills to undertake it as a speculative venture.

Eighteen of the original county surveys survive, and the scope of Mills's contribution and his use of other sources can be determined by a comparison of these base maps with those published in his *Atlas*. The *Atlas* maps differ from earlier surveys in format and often in scale and detail. Notations in Mills's hand on the original surveys indicate additions and corrections; the standardization of cartographic conventions and typography in the published work may represent his collaboration with Tanner or Tanner's editorial contribution, for the plates from which the *Atlas* was printed were engraved in Philadelphia by "H. S. Tanner & Assistants." The legend of each map bears the surveyor's name and notes that the map was "improved for Mills' Atlas, 1825." "Improvement" entailed redrawing surveys that were not on a scale of two miles to the inch; adding a legend to each map denoting "geological position," the bearing and distance of the courthouse from Columbia, and the latitude and longitude of the county seat; and, on occasion, adding, deleting, or otherwise altering place-names and topographical features that appeared on the original district surveys. To the manuscript survey of the Richland District, which is signed by Marmaduke Coate, Mills added, "[Columbia] Canal 30 foot fall" and "Saluda Canal fall 31 feet"; on the published map his notation concerning the fall of the Saluda Canal does not appear, but his addition of "or Brisbane's" as an alternative designation for "Garner's Ferry" was retained.

Revisions no doubt continued through publication. On the Richland map, as on other surveys, he deleted mileposts, substituted his own legend for the surveyor's, and supplied a standard scale. On the Fairfield manuscript survey he added shoals and islands in the Broad River, supplied the names of "the Old York Road" and "Grubs Road," converted roads from faintly dotted to perceptible solid lines, and added a conventional grid to indicate the town of Winnsboro; the latter two changes may have been made by the engraver. Throughout the state he added details to existing surveys. In Pendleton, the westernmost district, he added the home of "Gen Earle" and the "Big Esatoe Creek," and on the Darlington survey, to the east, he supplied the names of land owners and topographical features that had not appeared on earlier maps and altered others that he believed to have been incorrectly designated.

Presented to the South Carolina Senate on September 29, 1826, the *Atlas* was commended by the Senate as a "fine specimen of American Science and Art." It was the first systematic atlas of any state in the union, and the *American Farmer* touted it as being significantly better than comparable European publications.[67] But acclaim did not bring financial success. Mills had hoped to sell the atlases for sixteen dollars and single maps from two to three dollars; however, the lack of subscriptions and the need to pay the printer induced Mills to petition the legislature to subsidize the distribution of the maps in order to "dissiminate correct geographical information of its territory among the people." He offered to cut the retail price in half, "provided your honorable body would make your petitioner a compensation in some measure commensurate to the sacrifice of interest he would have to make, which may not exceed the sum of one thousand dollars."[68] His request was denied—somewhat ironically, for it was made on the same day that the senate congratulated him on his achievement. Periodically for the next twenty-two years he sought help from the state in disposing of maps, atlases, and finally the plates themselves.[69]

The detailed knowledge of the state presented visually in the maps is fully articulated in the encyclopedic *Statistics,* which Mills called "an appendix to the Atlas."[70] Here he meant to recount the natural history of the state, including flora, fauna, and all aspects of topography, with an emphasis on minerals, timber, and navigable waters. He dwelt on the social and military history of European settlers and the folklore and way of life of the Indian population. He also described economic development and opportunities for internal improvement and discussed the relationship between health and topography as he understood it. To gather material on each county and major settlement, he sent a questionnaire throughout the state and compiled the information under some fifty headings: "History of settlement, origin of its name, situation, boundaries, soil adaptation to particular products," and so forth, and two-thirds of the book consists of the recitation of these characteristics.

The *Statistics,* unlike Jefferson's *Notes on Virginia,* is primarily descriptive rather than analytical; nonetheless, within this restrictive format his interests are evident. Despite his removal from office there is no trace of bitterness in his repeated support for internal improvements projects. The benefits of canals and reclamation of swampland are leitmotives throughout the work, as is his support for scientific farming. The *Statistics* integrates and often paraphrases his earlier writing on these topics. He also emphasizes the American Revolution as having conferred meaning on scenes of action; detailed accounts of numerous engagements, taken largely from David Ramsay's *History of the Revolution in South Carolina* (1785), illuminate his abiding interest in public monuments.

Mills's response to picturesque or sublime aspects of landscape is romantic, especially marked in passages describing the up-country: the "wildness of the steep and rugged rocks—the gloomy horrors of the cliffs—the water falls" and the "magnificent prospects of ocean" which "nothing can exceed for grandeur." Except for his domestic correspondence, descriptions of landscape contain his most openly emotional writing. Passages concerning geology often convey an attempt to reconcile biblical and scientific literature; he accepts both as potential sources of proof. In his discussion of marine fossils, for example, he cites "Genesis i, 2, 9; which clearly proves the Neptunian origin of this globe." His theology—an acceptance of the fallibility of man and redemption through grace—is manifest in discussions of socially funded programs for the poor, the infirm, or the criminal.

Other recurring themes in which he takes delight include anecdotes presenting the Indian as a noble savage in terms familiar to readers of James Fenimore Cooper. He also dwells on local customs that define a sense of place and provide "an evidence that the primitive simplicity of former days is not entirely passed away," such as the "general turn out of all the villagers on a whortleberry expedition once or twice a year" in Edgefield. But his expression of emotion, bias, and opinion is the exception, for the *Statistics* is aptly named. The bulk of the text is a prosaic recapitulation of facts—the names of Indian towns, a listing of native flora, their habits of growth and potential uses, a survey of mineral resources. It is, as he intended, a verbal equivalent to the factual landscape presented in the *Atlas.*

A week after the South Carolina Senate accepted the *Atlas,* Mills mailed his first essay on railroads, "A Plan of a Rail-Road," to John McLean, U. S.

Postmaster General, proposing a mail route via an elevated, horse-drawn monorail from Washington to New Orleans (fig. 3.12).[71] As he had done earlier with canals, Mills presented the cost of construction, calculated operating costs, and concluded that savings resulting from the advantages of his suggestion over the then-current relay stagecoaches would pay for the entire project in fourteen years. Here he rejects canals and embraces railroads. The essay breathes enthusiasm, as if its author, having finished the dry *Statistics,* found the new technology vivifying: "Happy is it for our country that this system of improvement has been so early substituted for that of canals. What an honour will redound to that city which shall first accomplish the great work of throwing a chain of connection like this, between the east and west!"

The railroad Mills proposed "differs entirely from those commonly used." It was to be a single rail supported a minimum of three feet above the ground on posts every nine to fifteen feet. The cars were to consist of two boxes suspended on either side of the rail, like saddlebags, connected by a frame attached to wheels running upon the top of the rail. Theoretically, the concave rims of the wheels, the convex surface of the rail, and the equilibrium established by the low center of gravity of the cars would keep the cars level. The elevated track virtually removed the need for grading during construction and minimized maintenance during use, for debris and damp would not be in constant contact with the rail. Elevating the track also re-

Top: Figure 3.12
Elevated horse-drawn
monorail, 1826.
(Baltimore Gazette and
Daily Advertiser, July 7,
1827)

Bottom: 3.13
Elevated railroad, 1824.
(Frontispiece to Henry R.
Palmer, Description
of a Railway on a New
Principle, *1824)*

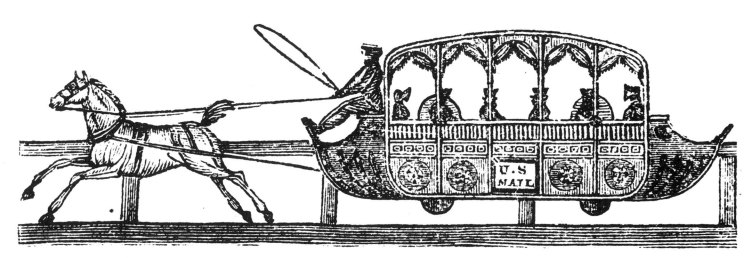

duced the risk of accident and, by reducing friction, would "diminish the quantity of animal torture." Mills wrote that it took twenty-six days to deliver the mail from Washington, D.C., to New Orleans, but using his system "if the case was urgent, it would be possible to accomplish the rout in four days, (the nights inclusive)." When Mills wrote, there were no operative steam-driven railroads in America, and he did not consider steam a power source; he did, however, note that similar railroads were in use in England, and it is probable that his plan is based on the work of Henry R. Palmer, whose published specifications match Mills's proposal (fig. 3.13). In discussing friction Palmer notes the problem of "extraneous substances lying upon" the rails and the "resistance occasioned by dust

thereby strengthening the mass, will give them the effect of a continuous arcade." This technique would also "furnish the means of providing a series of dwellings below, for the operatives and others on the roads, especially in the crossings of ravines and sinkings in the country. . . ."[73]

The idea of an elevated railroad spurred no practical interest, so Mills sought employment with what was to become the Baltimore and Ohio Railroad Company. In the spring of 1827, he requested a recommendation from Robert Gilmor, telling him that he had submitted a manuscript on railroads to Fielding Lucas for publication; that summer from Baltimore he wrote to Eliza that he hoped to find railroad work and to settle the family in Baltimore again.[74] Prospects did not materialize, and later in

lying upon the rails." On the same subject Mills said that an elevated rail is not liable "to be covered with dust, or any extraneous matter." In discussing the optimal harness Palmer says that the "horse is connected by a towing . . . length of rope which will enable him to vary his height without much altering the angle of draught," and Mills says "a track rope is required, which enables them to draw without material alteration of the angle of draught. . . ."[72]

The "Plan of a Rail-Road" was used by Mills in his attempt to find work as an engineer, and although he never participated in a major railroad project, he did continue to circulate his writings and develop his ideas. In 1853, at the end of his career, a refined version of the 1826 plan appeared in Scientific American. Here Mills proposed an elevated, suspended, steam-driven train capable of speeds of 100 miles per hour for the "New Pacific Railroad Line" (fig. 3.14). He noted that if "it is wished to combine architectural effect with this construction, the space between the posts or pillars, under the rail, may be arched, and while

the year he described his "Manual on Rail Roads" to Maj. Gen. Alexander Macomb, chief engineer of the Department of War; he asked Macomb's advice, offered to dedicate the manual to him, and requested not to be forgotten "should any professional business" become available.[75]

The only "professional business" Mills did with railroads during the 1820s appears to have been the preparation of estimates in 1828 for the South Carolina Canal and Railroad Company, the corporation whose "Best Friend of Charleston" was the first American-built steam locomotive to operate in the United States, in December 1830, and whose 136-mile track from Charleston to Hamburg, South Carolina, was the longest in the world when it opened in 1833.[76] Mills is not known to have participated in the development of the Charleston to Hamburg line, nor was he successful in his application to Joel R. Poinsett for a position with the new Charleston to Cincinnati Railroad in 1836.[77] Nonetheless, he continued to write and suggest improvements to those who were busy in the field. In 1834 he suggested that "steam carriages on common

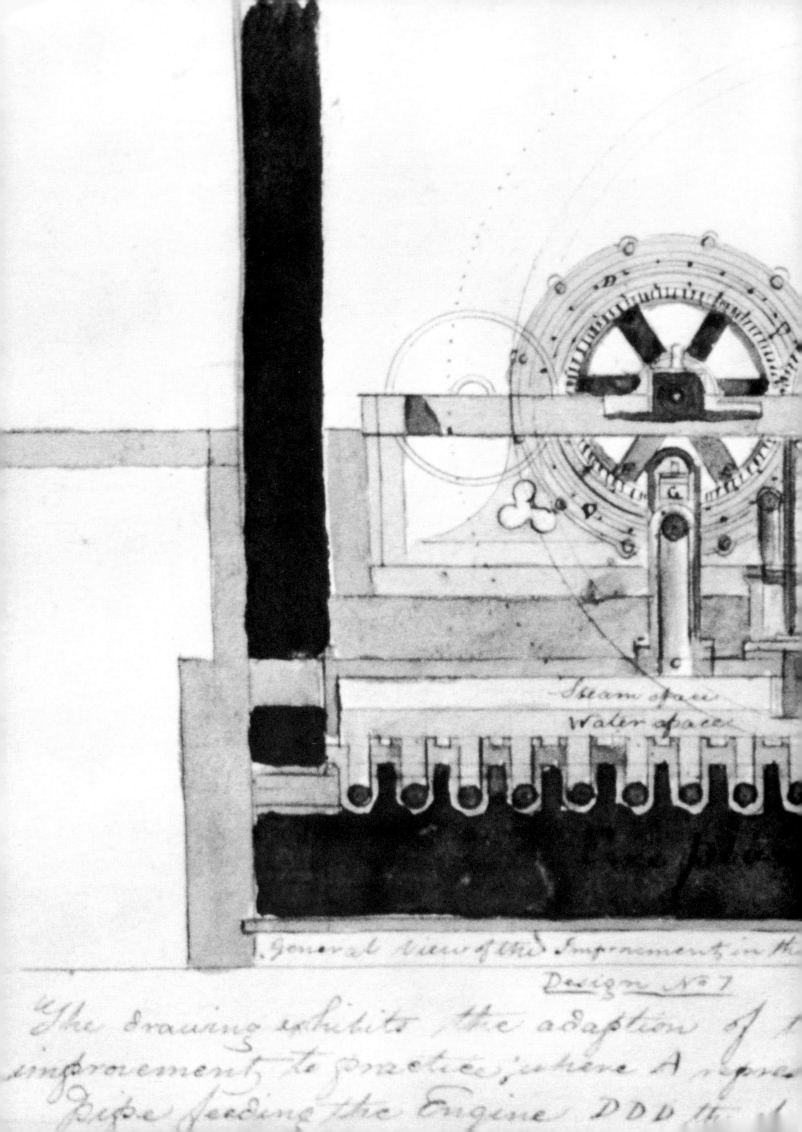

Steam space.
Water space.

General View of the Improvement in the

Design Nº 7

The drawing exhibits the adaption of t
improvement to practice, where A repre
pipe feeding the Engine D D D t

Fig IV

Plan of the Nature & Intent of the Steam Boat

safety valve

ser

ler B

Steam Engine

eral modifications of the proposed

the fire place B the boiler C the steam

wheel E E & arms of the moveable whee

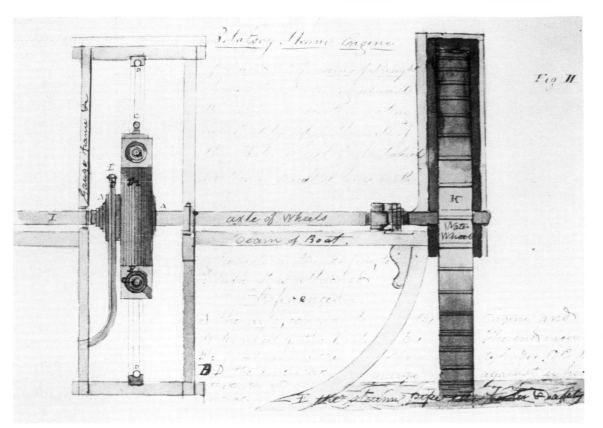

Figure 3.16
"End view of the Rotatory
Steam Engine," 1824.
(Franklin Institute)

roads" would replace canals and railroads. Addressing the telegraph, another innovation, he wrote Congress in 1852 concerning a route to the Pacific and noted that the telegraphic cable ought to be sheathed in rubber and laid inside the hollow of a rail line.[78]

Although no steam locomotives were in operation in America in 1826, it is surprising that Mills did not consider steam in the monorail essay, for in 1824 he had prepared a manuscript for publication entitled "Improvements in the Rotatory Engine" (fig. 3.15). This manuscript consisted of plans to replace the reciprocating piston with a rotary piston. Mills suggests several ways this might be accomplished and argues that the rotary engine would be a great improvement since the traditional reciprocating engine expends three-fourths of its power in reversing the stroke of its pistons and in transforming the rectilinear energy of the piston stroke into the circular motion of the drive shaft. This energy savings would mean that a "Rotatory Engine upon either plan stated before, if only 8 horse power (so called) will be equal in effect to a Reciprocating Engine of 20 horsepower." He cites numerous advantages, including the elimination of vibration, an increased efficiency in fuel consumption, and smaller, lighter engines. This last advantage would mean that the rotary engine could advantageously be adapted "in navigating and propelling wheel carriages."[79]

Ten drawings, plans, sections, and elevations illustrate the engine and are the most complex extant set of mechanical or engineering drawings by

Mills. The illustration "End View of the Rotatory Steam Engine," for example, depicts an engine "in operation acting immediately upon the axle of the Water wheel of a boat" (fig. 3.16). The frame, beam, and engine housing of the boat are shown in section; beyond the hull, water is indicated to establish a context. The exterior of the engine housing is stripped away to provide a view of the cylinders and piston rods, and the mechanical apparatus is drawn of straight lines to emphasize the parallel action of the rotary engine and the water wheel.

Mills's lucid, confident presentation suggests he was accustomed to this type of subject matter. No comparable drawings by Mills exist, but he often tinkered with machines and instruments. During one of his trips to Baltimore he wrote to Eliza that he was experimenting with a model steam engine and a surveying instrument, both invented by "a gentleman from the Western country."[80] His optimistic interest in mechanical engineering was similar in many respects to that of Latrobe. Latrobe used a horse-drawn railroad during the construction of the Chesapeake and Delaware Feeder Canal (1805), and, although involved in the manufacture of steam engines, he never considered their application to railroads. Like Mills, Latrobe failed in his attempts to profit from the new transportation technologies. On the other hand, William Strickland, so unpromising as a student with Mills in Latrobe's office, was actively engaged in the development of railroads in Pennsylvania during the very years that Mills was struggling in South Carolina.

THE MAXCY AND

DEKALB MONUMENTS

In a manuscript draft urging South Carolinians to erect a monument to heroes of the Revolution, Mills wrote that "monuments have always served as beacons of safety to public virtue and beacons of warning to the vicious."[81] Intentionally didactic, commemorative monuments constitute a final category of his work in South Carolina and evoke themes evident in his writings, buildings, and internal improvements projects—a sense of history, his unremitting search for work, a commitment to permanent construction, and a belief in the utility of symbolic form.

During the late 1820s Mills wrote often to Robert Gilmor and the managers of the Baltimore Washington Monument concerning the completion of the monument, its inscriptions, decorative detailing, and possibilities of employment. In one of these letters he observed that the "great outline" of

his proposal for the Bunker Hill Monument, for Charlestown, Massachusetts, had been accepted, that he had thought about "the decoration of the *Tympanum* of the Grand *Portico* of the *Capitol* at Washington," monuments to "DeKalb and Kosciusko," the Maxcy Monument, and "a Monument to commemorate the worthies of the Revolution belonging to this state. . . ."[82] His monument to revolutionary "worthies" was never executed, but the DeKalb Monument (1824–27), in Camden, and the Maxcy Monument (1824–27), in Columbia, were and relate to his earlier monuments—the Aquilla Randall Monument in Baltimore and the Baltimore Washington Monument. The South Carolina monuments also foreshadow aspects of his later proposal for the Bunker Hill Monument, his plan for the Washington National Monument (adopted in 1845), and his use of literary sources.

The Aquilla Randall, or North Point, Monument (1816–17) marked the spot where the First Mechanical Volunteers turned back the British assault on Baltimore (fig. 3.17). Mills's proposal for this

Figure 3.17
Plan and elevation,
Aquilla Randall
(North Point) Monument,
Baltimore, Maryland,
c. 1817. (Peale Museum)

monument consisted of an Egyptian Revival obelisk on a cubic base with recessed bas relief panels; the obelisk itself was to be crowned by a Greek tripod supporting a globe or spherical covered bowl. As constructed, it was shorn of its tripod and bas relief, but the proposal, with appropriate changes in iconography, served a decade later as the basis for the Maxcy Monument. Among the earliest American obelisks, the North Point plan was Mills's initial use of Egyptian Revival forms. A description attributable to him of the similar Maxcy Monument noted that winged globes beneath the cavetto molding were "sarcophagic symbols of immortality" and that this was "perhaps the second instance of a monument being crowned by a tripod, the first being that of Lysicrates, or as it is better known, the Lanthern of Demosthenes."[83]

In a similar vein, describing the obelisk submitted for the Bunker Hill Monument, Mills wrote that its balconies were to be supported by "winged globes symbols of immortality peculiarly of a monumental Character" and that its crowning tripod "is the classic emblem of immortality." Establishing a pedigree for this proposal, he referred the Bunker Hill selection committee to "Kercher" concerning "obelisk[s] that were celebrated above the rest, namely that of Alexandria; that of the Barberins; those of Constantinople; of the Mons Esquilinus; of the Campus Flaminius; of Florence; of Heliopolis; of Ludorisco; of St. Makut, of the Medici of the vatican; of M. Coelius, and that of Pamphila. The highest on record mentioned, is that erected by Ptolemy Philadelphus in memory of Arsinoe."[84] Here Mills meant Athanasius Kircher (1601–80), whose works contain text and illustrations on the origins and ornament of obelisks.[85] The tripod was similarly available through literary sources, Comte de Caylus having observed that "on est quelquefois surpris de la prodigieuse quantite de Trepieds qu'on voyoit dans la Grece."[86] When Mills used the tripod again, in 1838—in pairs, flanking each entry—as a prominent feature of his program of ornamental iron work for the base of the Baltimore Washington Monument, he wrote to Robert Gilmor that he had recently examined M. F. Dandre-Bardon's *Costume des anciens peuples* in search of an appropriate design for "fascial pillars."[87] He also juxtaposed the tripod and fasces on the roof of the temple base of the Washington National Monument in 1845. In this instance, on the "grand terrace" he planned "four massive zocles 25 feet high, supporting so many colossal symbolic tripods of victory 20 feet high, surmounted by fascial columns with their symbols of authority."[88]

Pamela Scott has demonstrated that this monument is derived from the Bastille Monument proposal by J. Molinos and J. LeGrand, perhaps as illustrated in A. G. Kersaint's *Discours sur les*

monumens publics, a copy of which was sold by Thomas Jefferson to the Library of Congress in 1815. Scott has also established Comte de Caylus's reconstruction of the Mausoleum of Halicarnassus as the prototype relied upon by Molinos and LeGrand and noted Caylus's "ecclectic mixture of 'les formes Egyptiennes & l'elegance des ornemans Grecs.'"[89] This eclecticism was a salient characteristic of the abstract, architectonic memorials of revolutionary France that influenced Mills. The base of the Maxcy obelisk is given the form of a Roman cippus by its cavetto cornice, pediments, and antae (fig. 3.18), and both the obelisk and cippus base may be a free adaption of the widely published monument to Massena, Prince d'Essling, which, like the Maxcy Monument, was surmounted by an obelisk and was 21 feet high, the height of the Maxcy Monument discounting the tripod.[90]

On the other hand, Mills need not have searched through foreign publications. Latrobe, in a perspective for the congressional cenotaphs (1816), had presented a fully developed cippus in the sunlit foreground and, as an alternative, a cubic, unorna-

Figure 3.18
Maxcy Monument (1824–27),
Columbia, South Carolina.
(Robin Smith)

mented base with inset tablets of contrasting stone in the distance (fig. 3.19). The latter design was adopted and closely resembles the Maxcy Monument pedestal. Years earlier, in 1812, Latrobe had questioned Mills's use of marble tablets framed by freestone in the memorial for the Monumental Church competition, for he felt that Mills's design was remarkably close to his own. The DeKalb obelisk, lacking the pedestal base and the crowning tripod, is simple but is similar to the Maxcy Monument in its sparing use of text and bas relief. Both are simply ornamented with an initial and star; the Maxcy Monument also carries the emblem of the Clariosophic Society, which sponsored it, as well as the winged globe and tripod.

These monuments recall themes that characterize Mills's public work in South Carolina—diverse sources of influence, a sense of history, permanent construction, and a penchant for spare forms and terse statements. Promoting a South Carolina monument to heroes of the Revolution, he observed that monuments and brief inscriptions speak "more than Volumes written on the page of history." [91]

Figure 3.19
Cenotaphs (post-1799),
Congressional Cemetery,
designed by Benjamin
Henry Latrobe.
(Library of Congress)

1. Robert Mills to Eliza Mills, February 21, 1817, South Carolina Historical Society, and Robert Mills to Eliza Mills, March 10, 1817, Georgetown University.

2. *Annals of the Congress, Debates and Proceedings,* 14th Cong., 1st sess., 854, quoted by N.G. Raiford, "South Carolina and the Issue of Internal Improvement, 1775–1860" (Ph.D. diss., University of Virginia, 1974), 7.

3. Thomas Cooper, *South Carolina Statutes at Large* (Columbia: A.S. Johnston, 1836), vi, 58–60, 91–92; for Governor Pickens see Governors' Messages, November 25, 1817, South Carolina Department of Archives and History.

4. *Charleston Courier,* February 5, 1820, 2–3; *Camden Gazette,* February 3, 1820, 2–2.

5. Mills to the president and members of the Senate of the State of South Carolina, [1826], South Caroliniana Library; also see General Assembly Petitions, 1826, no. 116, South Carolina Department of Archives and History.

6. Mills, "Improvements in the Rotatory Engine," 32 pp., signed "Engineer and Architect, Columbia, State of South Carolina, 1824," Franklin Institute. Mills's proposal for a monorail was published in the *Baltimore Gazette and Daily Advertiser,* July 7, 1827, vol. 68; his specifications emulate those found in Henry R. Palmer, *Description of a Railway on a New Principal* (London: J. Taylor, 1824). The manuscript "Architectural Works of Robert Mills" is in the collection of Tulane University; for another draft manuscript, also in Mills's hand, see *Microfiche Papers of Robert Mills,* 1980, Part C, Miscellaneous, 11-518-1-A3, South Carolina Historical Society.

7. Mills to Benjamin Chew, August 2, 1810, Chew Papers, Historical Society of Pennsylvania.

8. Mills, *A Treatise on Inland Navigation* (Baltimore: F. Lucas, 1820), iii, 35, 74–77.

9. Albert Gallatin, *Report of the Secretary of the Treasury on the Subject of Public Roads and Canals* (Washington, D.C.: R.C. Weightman, 1808), 104–23.

10. In 1806, during his courtship, he began frequent visits to Winchester, Virginia, in the Shenandoah Valley; see Mills to Thomas Jefferson, October 3, 1806. Following his marriage in 1808, he made the trip to Winchester from Philadelphia or Baltimore several times each year until he moved to South Carolina. In applying for a position as an engineer in Virginia, he stressed his training under Latrobe on the Chesapeake and Delaware Canal; see Mills to Bernard Peyton, December 23, 1822.

11. Mills, *Inland Navigation: Plan for a Great Canal between Charleston and Columbia and for Connecting Our Waters with Those of the Western Country* (Columbia: Telescope Press, 1821), 11–12, 69n., 9, 21, 57.

12. Gallatin, *Report of the Secretary,* 71.

13. Mills, *Inland Navigation: Plan for a Great Canal,* 7.

14. Mills, "Report on the Survey of Jones' Falls," *Baltimore American,* October 3, 1817, 2; addressed to the mayor and city council of Baltimore, September 25, 1817.

15. "Report & Resolution on the petition of B.H. Latrobe," March 24, 1830, Doc. no. 801, Baltimore City Archives. Latrobe, Thomas Poppleton, mapmaker, and Lewis Wernwag, engineer, were among the contestants. Latrobe proposed to enclose the watercourse in a tunnel; Wernwag suggested straightening the channel and increasing the height of the embankments. Wernwag later accused Mills of having copied a report that he claimed to have entrusted to Mills to transmit to the council; see Lewis Wernwag to S. Smith, July 15, 1837, Baltimore City Archives. Mills had earlier designed the cladding, exterior detailing, and tollhouse of the Lancaster-Schuylkill Bridge (1811) and had taken credit for the 330-foot span that had been designed by Wernwag; the bridge company's records are in the collection of the Historical Society of Pennsylvania. Lee H. Nelson, "The Colossus of Philadelphia," in *Material Culture of the Wooden Age,* ed. Brooke Hindle (Tarrytown: Sleepy Hollow, 1981), 163 ff., corrects this attribution and defines Mills's role. They worked together on the Belvidere Bridge, Baltimore, 1817. Wernwag, in a letter that intimates blackmail, pressed Mills to hire him in South Carolina. He speaks of paying sawyers and says, "I done this & left you in peace, but it is now your time, & it is now in your power to do something for me remember I have kept it quiet our connection with the falls Bridge, this could be done in future, you know me . . ." (Lewis Wernwag to Mills, January 13, 1821, Smithsonian Institution).

16. Mills, *Internal Improvements of South Carolina* (Columbia: State Gazette, 1822), 28 pp.

17. Ibid., 12, 16.

18. John Drayton, *View of South Carolina* (Charleston: W.P. Young, 1802), 145.

19. He inherited two slaves in 1802 from his father (*Charleston Wills,* vol. D, 1800–1807, 269). When he married Eliza Barnwell Smith in 1808, she brought slaves with her as household servants, one of whom they sold when leaving Abbeville in 1829.

20. For the political context of Mills's work see Norman G. Raiford, "South Carolina and the Issue of Internal Improvement."

21. Robert Mills, *Statistics of South Carolina* (Charleston: Hurlbut and Lloyd, 1826), 301, 433.

22. Robert Mills to Eliza Mills, April 20, 1821, Georgetown University, is typical: "I have just set the public works here into operation again. . . . I wait however on circumstances to regulate my movements, as I humbly trust in the superabundant care & direction of our heavenly Father. Nothing I believe is too insignificant to escape the notice of his eye, and he has promised direction to all that put their trust in him. The philosophy of the world would laugh at the confidence of the christian in believing that the great God condescends to notice the little wants in the private walks of life."

23. Mills, *Statistics,* 294–95.

24. "I understand that the Board of Public Works have adopted a general plan for Court-Houses in the State, varying a little in size, in proportion to the difference of the Districts in which they are erected. In this plan durability, strength, convenience, neatness and economy have been consulted. Having had an opportunity of looking at this plan I have no hesitation in saying, that the erection of this building may be considered a strong evidence of public improvement. The size will be convenient and the arrangement of the interior will be far superior to that of any within the State; it will be in height two stories, and its first floor will contain a large lobby for the stairs, through which you enter the Court room, a spacious Court room and two offices. The arrangement of the court room is remarkable for its convenience, affording accommodation to the Judges and other officers, the Lawyers. . . . In the Court room there is also a gallery of considerable width, ornamented with neat columns, extending the whole length of the building, in front of the judges bench, which adds much to the appearance and convenience of the spectators. On the second floor there will be five offices with a large passage, into which they will open" (*Camden Gazette,* October 19, 1820, 3-1).

25. Gene Waddell and Rhodri Liscombe, *Robert Mills's Courthouses and Jails* (Easley, South Carolina: Southern Historical Press, 1981), 11, nn. 54, 55, fig. 19A.

26. Pamela Scott, review of Gene Waddell and Rhodri Liscombe, *Robert Mills's Courthouses and Jails, Winterthur Portfolio* 20 (Winter 1985): 299–301.

27. Benjamin Henry Latrobe, "Letter . . . to the Chairman of the Committee of the House of Representatives . . . Report of the Surveyor of the Public buildings," February 28, 1804.

28. "Report of the Commissioners of the Lunatic Asylum," May 8 and December 3, 1824, South Carolina Department of Archives and History.

29. R.W. Thompson to Millard Fillmore, February 7, 1853.

30. O.B. Scamozzi, *Palladio,* 2 (Vicenza: Francesco Modena, 1776), plate 3.

31. For an illustration see Beatrice St. Julien Ravenel, *Architects of Charleston* (Charleston: Carolina Art Association, 1964), 63.

32. For the Fireproof Building, see the *Charleston Courier,* April 25, 1822; for the Williamsburg, Newberry, York, and Greenville courthouses and the Union, Spartanburg, Lancaster, and York jails, see the *Courier,* February 21, 1822; the issue of March 20, 1822 contains the announcement of the Charleston jail. For the Laurens courthouse and jail, a typical proposal, see Timothy D. Williams to Robert Mills, May 18, 1822; also see the Lancaster jail contract signed by Willis W. Alsobrook, Robert

Mills, and John Buling [?], July 4, 1822, South Carolina Department of Archives and History. Report of the Commissioners of Public Buildings for Greenville [Jeremiah Cleveland, Richard Thruston, Alex Sloan] to the Legislature of South Carolina, November 17, 1824. For the Union jail see Mills to the president of the Board of Public Works, November 30, 1822, South Carolina Department of Archives and History.

33. "Report of the Board of Public Works, 1821," in *Internal Improvement in South Carolina, 1817–1828,* by David Kohn and Bess Glenn (Washington, D.C.: privately printed, 1938), 109.

34. Ibid., chapter 1, n. 84. For the state prison by Bulfinch see Kirker and Kirker, *Architecture of Charles Bulfinch* (Cambridge: Harvard University Press, 1969), 211–15. The state prison did much to promote the subsequent use of New England granite; see John M. Bryan, "Boston's Granite Architecture, c. 1810–1860" (Ph.D. diss., Boston University, 1972).

35. Waddell and Liscombe, *Courthouses and Jails,* 12, 34, 38.

36. Records concerning payment are found in the manuscript "Treasury Ledgers, Journals and Vouchers," South Carolina Department of Archives and History. For the Chesterfield plans see Chesterfield Courthouse Specifications, March 7, 1825, reprinted by Waddell and Liscombe, *Courthouses and Jails,* 38–39; for the Fireproof Building see Report of the Commissioners of the Fire Proof Offices, December 11, 1826, no. 1826-172-05; also see Gene Waddell, "Robert Mills's Fireproof Building," *South Carolina Historical Magazine* 80, no. 2 (1979): 110–11, n. 12. For the asylum see Report of the Commissioners of the Lunatic Asylum, December 2, 1923, no. 1823-16-01, and for the payment to redeem the plates see Treasury Ledgers, Charleston, 1827–1842, 169, South Carolina Department of Archives and History.

37. *Charleston Courier,* August 3, 1822.

38. William Tuke established the Retreat in York, England, in 1792; his grandson, Samuel Tuke, published influential tracts on the architecture of asylums, notably *Practical Hints on the Construction and Economy of Pauper Lunatic Asylums* (York: William Alexander, 1815), containing the criteria and plans for the Wakefield Asylum by William Stark.

39. Report of the Committee on the Lunatic Asylum, South Carolina Senate, December 16, 1822, South Carolina Department of Archives and History.

40. Report of the Commissioners of the Lunatic Asylum, n.d. [December 1824], South Carolina Department of Archives and History.

41. *The Pioneer,* March 20, 1824, Yorkville, South Carolina.

42. The first evidence of the furnace system was discovered when a laborer accidentally broke through a wall into the heat chamber or reservoir in March 1986. Phelps Bultman, architect in charge of the restoration, and Steven Olawson, graduate student, were most helpful in the investigation of the furnaces. For a review of early heating systems in America, see Samuel Y. Edgerton, "Heat and Style: Eighteenth-Century House Warming by Stoves," *Journal of the Society of Architectural Historians* 20 (March 1961): 20–26; also see Eugene S. Ferguson, "An Historical Sketch of Central Heating: 1800–1860," in *Building Early America,* ed. Charles E. Peterson (Radnor, Pennsylvania: Chilton, 1976), 165–85.

43. Oliver Evans, *Young Mill-wright and Miller's Guide* (Philadelphia: privately printed, 1795).

44. *Federal Gazette and Baltimore Advertiser,* December 28, 1815; reprinted in the *Supplement to Niles' Register-Scraps,* 183.

45. Daniel Pettibone, *Economy of Fuel, or, Description of his improvements of the rarefying air-stoves . . . for warming and ventilating hospitals, churches . . .* (Philadelphia: A. Dickinson, 1812); see University Microfilms, American Culture Series, Reel 419.3.

46. Daniel Pettibone to Col. Samuel Lane, commissioner of public buildings, Washington, D.C., August 31, 1816, National Archives. Seeking work on federal buildings, Pettibone recounts his experience in the design and construction of heating systems; in the course of this presentation he notes that Mills "received from me a license to build such Machines"; Pettibone specifically states that the Patapsco Factory furnace was of his design. Mills, *Diary,* July 9, 1816, Library of Congress.

47. Committee on Public Buildings, General Assembly Papers, Report no. 86, 1819, South Carolina Department of

Archives and History.

48. Waddell, "Robert Mills's Fireproof Building," 105–35, is a complete account of the construction. The asylum absorbed funding that might otherwise have been allocated for a similar building in Columbia; a rivalry between Columbia, the new state capital, and Charleston, the old state capital, is reflected in these appropriations.

49. *Charleston Courier,* April 25, 1822.

50. Resolution Appointing Commissioners of Fire Proof Buildings, General Assembly, 1823, no. 50. Resolution Appointing Commissioners [of] Public Buildings for Charleston, General Assembly, 1823, no. 34, South Carolina Department of Archives and History.

51. Report of the Commissioners of Public Buildings for Charleston District, n.d., no. 59-1, South Carolina Department of Archives and History.

52. Report of the Commissioners of the Fire Proof Offices, General Assembly, December 11, 1826, no. 172-05, South Carolina Department of Archives and History.

53. For a summary of accounts see Waddell, "Robert Mills's Fireproof Building," 110 ff. For the complaint concerning the conflict between Mills and Spidle, see Report of the Commissioners, December 11, 1826, and for changes attributable to Spidle see Waddell, 115–20. Alterations of the stairs, pediments, and parapet are the result of repairs made after the 1886 earthquake.

54. *Charleston Courier,* March 20, 1822; Mills, *Statistics,* 420. The octagonal wing is usually attributed to Mills (see Ravenel, *Architects of Charleston,* 126), but it was a wholly new building by Louis J. Barbot and John H. Seyle. The plan of the rectangular wing (18 by 51 feet) by Mills appears in the Robert Allen manuscript "Survey Book," 1851, South Carolina Historical Society. For the South Carolina Penitentiary and the Burlington County Jail, see chapter 1, nn. 75, 77, 78.

55. Mills, *Statistics,* 421.

56. Latrobe to Paul Hamilton, Secretary of the Navy, July 14, 19, and 20, 1809.

57. Mills to the mayor and city council of Baltimore, October 12, 1817, Baltimore City Archives, A484.

58. Lewis Lochee, *Elements of Fortification* (London: privately printed, 1780), plate 6; see also pages 19–20 for a brief discussion of magazines by M. Vauban. J.N.L. Durand, *Precis de lecons D'architecture,* 1 (Paris, 1802), plate 3, for a similarly vaulted roof. For vaulted magazines within tower bastions by M. Vauban see Ian Hogg, *History of Fortification* (New York: St. Martin's Press, 1981).

59. Mills, *Statistics,* 422; Kohn and Glenn, *Internal Improvement,* 105, 156.

60. Kohn and Glenn, 150.

61. Nora M. Davis, "Public Powder Magazines at Charleston," in *Year Book of the City of Charleston, 1942* (Charleston, 1944), 208; the photograph showing six of the magazines and the gatehouse appears in the pamphlet, A.K. Gregorie, "Notes of the Bedstead Tomb at St. Michael's" and N.M. Davis, "Public Powder Magazines" (Charleston: Historical Commission, 1944).

62. Mills, *Statistics,* 422.

63. *Charleston News and Courier,* May 5, 1929.

64. Report of the Joint Committee on the Report of the Superintendent of Public Works on the Map of the State, December 19, 1823, and Report of the Superintendent of Public Works on the Map of the State, December 19, 1823, General Assembly Miscellaneous, 1823, no. 6, South Carolina Department of Archives and History.

65. Mills to the president and members of the Board of Public Works, December 13, 1821, Legislative Papers, Committee Reports, no. 104; also see N. Herbemont to the president and members of the Senate, December 12, 1821, Legislative Papers, Miscellaneous Communications, 1821, no. 9, South Carolina Department of Archives and History.

66. Mills, *Atlas of the State of South Carolina* (Baltimore: F. Lucas, 1825); see the introduction by Gene Waddell in the facsimile *Mills' Atlas* (Easley: Southern Historical Press, 1980) for a thorough review of the district surveys and Mills's role in the preparation of the *Atlas.*

67. For Mills's presentation see General Assembly Papers, 1826, no. 23; for acceptance and commendation by the Senate see Acts and Resolutions of the General Assembly, Senate, December 1, 1826-14-01, South Carolina Department of Archives and History; for the national context see *American Farmer* 8 (1826): 231–32, and Walter W. Ristow, "Robert Mills' *Atlas of the State of South Carolina, 1825*, the First American State Atlas," *Quarterly Journal of the Library of Congress* 34, no. 1 (January 1977): 52–66.

68. General Assembly Petitions, 1826, no. 117, South Carolina Department of Archives and History.

69. Unable to pay Henry Tanner, Mills unsuccessfully sought a loan of $1,500 from the legislature in 1827 (General Assembly Petitions, November 30, 1827-93-01); in 1837 he received $2,000 "for the Redemption of the Plates of the Survey," which he was to repay either in cash or by "delivery to the State of one hundred Atlases of the Districts of the State, or more" (Manuscript Acts, 1837, no. 2742, Appropriation Act of 1837, and Reports and Resolutions, 1837, 13–14; also see Vouchers of the Lower Division, January 1839). He must have provided the atlases, for the state paid $122.15 for "Freight from Philadelphia, & c. maps of the State" (Receipts and Payments, Treasury of the Lower Division, September 1837–October 1838). The plates are not known to have survived, but Mills had them in his possession in 1852, for at that time he offered to sell them to the state (Mills to Governor Means, August 18, 1852).

70. Mills to Thomas Jefferson, February 15, 1826. In his reply, Jefferson speaks of "the Statistical adjunct you propose" (Thomas Jefferson to Mills, March 3, 1826).

71. Dated "Columbia, S.C., December 16, 1826," published in the *National Intelligencer,* republished in the *Baltimore Gazette and Daily Advertiser* 68, no. 10323 (July 7, 1827).

72. Henry R. Palmer, *Description of a Railway on a New Principle* (London: J. Taylor, 1824), 16–17, 40–41.

73. *Scientific American* 8, no. 47 (August 6, 1853). The *Charleston Courier* (September 8, 1853) republished a review of Mills's plan from the *Baltimore American Times:* "to us it appears better calculated to amuse the fancy, than for practical use."

74. For a history of the development of the B & O, see Alfred R. James, "Sidelights on the Founding of the Baltimore and Ohio Railroad," *Maryland Historical Magazine* 48, no. 4 (December 1953): 267–309. Mills to Robert Gilmor, April 22, 1827, and Robert Mills to Eliza Mills, August 4, 1827, South Carolina Historical Society.

75. Mills to Alexander Macomb, November 8, 1827, National Archives.

76. For Mills's estimate see *First Semi-Annual Report, South-Carolina Canal and Rail-Road Company* (Charleston: A.E. Miller, 1828), 18–19.

77. Mills to Joel R. Poinsett, March 17, 1836, Historical Society of Pennsylvania.

78. Mills, *Substitute for Railroads and Canals* (Washington, D.C.: James C. Dunn, 1834), 12 pp. *Senate Reports,* 32d Cong., 1st sess., August 18, 1852, no. 344, 13.

79. Mills, "Improvements in the Rotatory Engine; or several modes by which a Direct Circular Motion may be obtained, using either as an Agent, Steam Air Water Gunpowder or any other Propelling Power" (1824), 21. In the collection of the Franklin Institute, Philadelphia.

80. Robert Mills to Eliza Mills, August 4, 1827, South Carolina Historical Society.

81. Mills, n.d., Georgetown University.

82. Mills to Robert Gilmor, March 1, 1828, Maryland Historical Society.

83. *Columbia Telescope and South Carolina State Journal* 13, no. 56 (December 28, 1827).

84. Mills to the Monument Commission, March 20, 1825, Bunker Hill Monument Association, transcribed in Gallagher, 204–7.

85. Athanasius Kircher, *Ad Alexandrum VII. Pont. Max. Obelisci Aegyptiaci* (Romae, ex typographia Varesii, 1666), *Obeliscus pamphilius hoc est Interpretatio nova* (Romae, typis Ludovici Grignani, 1650), 57–58, 213, and *Romani Collegii Societatis Jesu Musaeum Celeberrimum* (Amstelodami Ex Officina Janssonio Waesbergiana, 1678), 10–13 and frontispiece. Each contains passages similar to Mills's historical recitation. *Romani Collegii,* which illustrates more than twenty examples, opens with a vista of obelisks crowded by Christian symbols in the Jesuit museum.

86. Comte de Caylus, *Recueil D'Antiquites Egyptiennes, Etrusques, Grecques et Romaines* (Paris: Chez Duchesne, Libraire ru S. Jacques, au bas de la Fontaine Saint Benoit, au Temple du Gout, 1756), 2:161, plate 53.

87. Mills to Robert Gilmor, March 12, 1838. Michel Francois Dandre-Bardon, *Costume des anciens peuples* (Paris: C.A. Jombert, 1784), 1:9, plate 27, for a tripod with a cauldron similar to those used by Mills; I owe this observation to Pamela Scott. For the definitive treatment of the Washington Monument, Washington, D.C., see Pamela Scott, "Robert Mills's Washington National Monument" (Master's thesis, University of Delaware, 1983).

88. [Mills], *Description of the Design of the Washington National Monument* (New York: Oliver Brothers, 1848), transcribed by Scott, "Robert Mills's Washington National Monument," appendix 2, 87.

89. Comte de Caylus, "Dissertation sur le Tombeau de Mausole," *Memoires de litterature, tires des registres de l'Academie Royale des Inscriptions et Belles-Lettres,* 26 (1759): 331–32, quoted by Scott, "Robert Mills's Washington National Monument," 36.

90. Illustrated in F.G.T. de Jolimont, *Les Mausolees Francais* (Paris: de L'Imprimerie de Firmin Didot, 1821). Although the date of acquisition cannot be established, a copy of de Jolimont was owned by the South Carolina College Library. For an illustration see Richard A. Etlin, *The Architecture of Death* (Cambridge, Massachusetts: MIT Press, 1984), plate 258.

91. Robert Mills, n.d. Georgetown University.

CHAPTER 4

THE WASHINGTON YEARS:

THE U.S. PATENT OFFICE

Douglas E. Evelyn

hen Robert Mills moved his practice to Washington, D.C., in 1830, he filled a void in a city becoming a national capital in physical form as well as in name. Its early shapers—James Hoban, George Hadfield, Benjamin Henry Latrobe, and William Thornton—had died. Charles Bulfinch had finished his work on the Capitol and returned to Boston. Mills alone among the major architects of the era chose to reside there, and for a quarter century he participated in building and engineering projects that altered the face of the city and the character of federal architecture. Chief among these were fireproof buildings for the Patent Office, Treasury Department, and Post Office, constituting a new generation of monumental federal offices. Mills designed and supervised the construction of the original wings for the Treasury Building (1836–42) and Post Office (1839–42) and oversaw construction of the initial wing of the U.S. Patent Office (1836–40) (figs. 4.1, 4.2, 4.3). This effort represented an unprecedented American building program in scope, speed, and technical and administrative demands.

Although other architects completed the Treasury Building and Post Office, Mills sustained his involvement with the Patent Office through numerous proposals for extensions in the 1840s and eventual supervision of initial construction of additional wings between 1849 and 1851. This essay will concentrate on his experience with the Patent Office, for his direct association with the building extended over most of his Washington career and provides a useful lens for viewing individuals, systems, and prevailing conditions that influenced his work and the practice of public architecture in Washington at that time. In addition, the Patent Office posed special challenges, as it involved both exhibition and office spaces and was partially designed by others but executed by Mills. How Mills confronted the tensions created by mixed authorship and building functions deserves particular attention.

A NEW BEGINNING

Mills relocated for economic reasons as well as to give full range to his talents. He had five children to support and needed a professional and residential base. Although prospects were dim in South Carolina, the administration of John Quincy Adams had called for a program of internal improvements and improved public buildings. In 1826 Mills wrote fellow South Carolinian John C. Calhoun, then secretary of war, that his six-year engagement with the state of South Carolina's Board of Public Works was about to end and suggested that his "professional services may be useful to the U. Sts. Board of Internal Improvement in carrying any of its plans into execution." He reminded Calhoun of his past affiliations with Benjamin Henry Latrobe and Thomas Jefferson, his atlas and statistical compilation of South Carolina, and his practical application of "many points of design which were new in our Country. . . ."[1]

The following spring Mills wrote his wife's cousin Charles Nourse, the chief clerk in the War Department. Noting that Nourse's position made him "aware of every vacancy that occurs in the Engineer department," Mills complained that he was

Opposite:
Detail of longitudinal
section, U.S. Patent Office
(1836–40). (Machen
Collection, Columbia
Historical Society)

"tired of wandering about from state to state dependent upon the precarious business created by the act of Legislative bodies." He opted for "the service of the general government even at a moderate salary . . . as . . . there would be more stability" than from state assignments. In addition to a reliable income, Mills also sought continued professional development. He claimed that there was no opportunity in South Carolina "for the exercise of my profession" and asked consideration for any government position "requiring the aid of my professional services, either in the Engineering or architectural department." At a pivotal point in his career, his eyes turned north.[2]

The following May Mills wrote Calhoun from Baltimore, where for many years he had been supervising the construction of the city's Washington Monument. This time Mills reminded Calhoun of his knowledge of railroads, in case the government's rumored interests in surveying the area between Baltimore and the Ohio River might require additional federal positions. That fall he sent the War Department's chief engineer, Gen. Alexander Macomb, a letter describing his manuscript entitled "A Manual on Rail Roads," suggesting his willingness to dedicate a published version to Macomb and asking if the engineers or West Point would be interested in copies. These ploys were unsuccessful, but Mills persisted after Andrew Jackson became president in 1829, both by mail and personal visits as he passed through the capital en route to and from Baltimore, where he supervised the hoisting of the 20-ton statue of George Washington in November. It was an ironic commentary on Mills's career and the conditions for his practice that this culminating moment of one of his most notable projects coincided with a period of extreme financial difficulty for his family in his native state.[3]

By January 1830 Mills was committed to moving north, planning to decide by April between Washington and Baltimore. While he explored opportunities in both cities, his wife prepared to move from Abbeville, South Carolina. Eliza was demoralized by seeing students withdrawn from the school she had established, converting their household goods into cash, and dickering with creditors. She wrote her husband in February that she "had no idea that we owed so much in this place as I found we did,

Figure 4.1
Treasury Building (1836–42), Washington, D.C. Mills called his colonnaded wing of the Treasury "the most extensive of modern times." Like the Patent Office, it was occupied in 1840 while work continued on exterior details. Its monumental scale contrasted sharply with the abutting State Department, of an earlier generation of executive buildings. (Stereoview, c. 1860)

upon speaking of a removal. . . ." They were barely solvent and concerned that debts against their property in South Carolina would leave insufficient funds to purchase a house in the north. Eliza pledged to run a boarding establishment "for her share of business" when they relocated. By May she had sold the coach, horse, piano, and "Nanny," an elderly slave. Friends gave her eighty dollars, which she felt obliged to consider a loan and which was sufficient to get the family to Charleston. There she would wait with relatives until her husband sent funds for the trip north. Meanwhile, in Baltimore Mills was awaiting word from the monument's board of managers to proceed with additional ornamental and landscaping work, which he had estimated at $21,500. He was also surveying the nearby Susquehanna Canal, another prospect for further employment. But developments in Washington showed greater promise. With the help of George McDuffie, a congressman from South Carolina, Mills's plans for improving the acoustics of the Hall of Representatives had been favorably reviewed by the House and ordered to be printed and engraved for distribution. Pleasantly surprised,

Mills reported to his wife that "he had no idea they would take this course" and prepared to make further presentations in the weeks ahead.[4]

The possibility of work at the Capitol was a new element in Mills's choice between the two cities. It was the most potentially significant project of many options he had been exploring, especially as Charles Bulfinch's position as architect of the Capitol had been terminated as of June 30, 1829. Bulfinch had earlier opposed Mills's plans for correcting the acoustics, without offering satisfactory alternatives.[5] Mills confidently predicted that the project would lead to other assignments, and he advanced proposals in March to improve the water supply to the Capitol and alter the Capitol dome.[6] In April he provided Gulian C. Verplanck, chairman of the House Committee on Public Buildings, with an estimate of $7,000 to improve the acoustics. Verplanck's proposed appropriations for public buildings included that amount "for altering the hall of the House of Representatives, according to the plan of Robert Mills," as well as a request to pay Charles Bulfinch $1,100 for "extra services" on various buildings besides the Capitol and "for al-

lowance for returning with his family to Boston."[7] Although Congress failed to act on the appropriation before adjourning, Mills was sufficiently encouraged to decide in favor of Washington, especially as Verplanck had promised to reintroduce the measure in the next session.

Writing from Washington on June 3, 1830, Mills informed Robert Gilmor, president of the Baltimore Washington Monument Society, "I have located myself & family here, and as there is no architect now to the public buildings, I shall hope to succeed in getting the general government business." Bulfinch's departure was clearly a factor. In addition to the chances for a variety of federal and local engineering assignments, Mills hoped to improve on public buildings that were inadequate to house the rapidly growing functions of government. But his optimism was guarded. He asked Gilmor to inform him of any relevant work "in Baltimore or . . . elsewhere than in this City" and urged action by the Maryland legislature to fund his proposed work to complete the monument.[8] And, in Washington, he turned to a variety of smaller projects while awaiting the return of Congress in the fall.

Baltimore, with four times the population, was further developed and more commercially dynamic than Washington. But the nation's capital would have attracted Mills at this moment precisely because of its lack of definition. Its plan was still an outline, awaiting a blend of local and federal funding, talent, and will to produce a workable municipality and a suitable showcase for the nation. English writer Frances Trollope's 1830 account was more kindly than most: "Washington may be scorned as a metropolis, where such cities as Philadelphia and New York exist; but I considered it as the growing metropolis of the growing population of the Union, and it already possesses features noble enough to sustain its dignity. . . ."[9] Mills would have sensed its potential and recognized the need for municipal systems and public buildings comparable to those he had developed from Charleston to Philadelphia during the previous three decades. Work in Washington would permit use of his professional talents in shaping the capital city of the nation as well as the public architecture of an expanding national government.

Despite his enthusiasm about possibilities in Washington, the period was actually one of continued insecurity for Mills and his family. His odd jobs included supervising construction of an engine house and privies between the Treasury and State departments, for $100; preparing the Senate chambers to accommodate the full Congress during the impeachment trial of Judge Peck, for $20; and providing designs, specifications, estimates, and drawings for a customs house in Mobile, Alabama, for $300. He was also dismayed by Maryland's in-

ability to pay contractors who had gone into arrears during the hoisting of the Baltimore Washington Monument the previous fall. His friend Robert Gilmor had been unable to get the state legislature to compensate them and Mills for their extra costs. In his search for work, Mills even asked Gilmor in November to let him be in charge of the monument, "with the privilege of fixing some small tax on visitors." Characteristically, however, during this period of extreme difficulty he continued to publish and promote his ideas, to lay the ground for future work. He prepared a publication on American lighthouses and joined the Columbian Institute for the Promotion of Arts and Sciences, a local intellectual society that included city and national officials who were concerned with scientific matters and who would figure in decisions about public projects. Finally, as Congress returned for the winter session, Mills announced his architectural services in the *Daily National Intelligencer*. He was prepared for what the new year would bring.[10]

PROPOSING A NEW PATENT OFFICE

The Patent Office was one of several executive agencies seeking improved facilities in the early 1830s. It had been established in 1790 within the Department of State in response to the Constitution's provision for promoting "the progress of science and useful arts." The patent system encouraged inventors by allowing them a patent—a grant of protection from competition—for a limited time. Applications customarily included specifications, drawings, and a model illustrating the claimed invention, along with a fee that was deposited in an account to defray the office's expenses. For most of its first three decades, the office was supervised by William Thornton, the designer of the Capitol, and located in a brick and wood building called Blodgett's Hotel, midway between the White House and the Capitol.

Following the War of 1812, as the nation sought economic self-sufficiency, the rapidly increasing business of the Patent Office became a symbol of the nation's potential. But the office was both understaffed and overcrowded. Between 1816 and 1825 Thornton's staff consisted of one clerk, William Elliot, and a messenger, plus various draftsmen working on a piecemeal basis, including Elliot's son, William Parker Elliot, who would later figure prominently in Mills's experience with the new Patent Office. The quarters were shared with the city and federal post offices, each of which had its own increasing needs for space. In 1827 Congress gave the Patent Office temporary relief after a special committee found that deficiencies in recordkeeping and preservation of models amounted to a "deranged condition" and prevented the office from meeting its obligations to inventors. Over the next three years, the patent fund—then with a balance of about $60,000—was used to add two more clerks and to extend the building by a third.[11]

In 1832 John D. Craig, patent superintendent, convinced the secretary of state, Edward Livingston, that, with the office's business increasing "in a greater ratio than the population of the country," it needed more space. The postmaster general, William T. Barry, added his plea, and on April 4 a message from President Jackson asked Congress to consider purchasing a spacious building known as the "brick Capitol," which had been temporarily used by Congress following the British attack on the Capitol in 1814 and was being offered by William Brent. The House Committee on Public Buildings rejected the notion of purchasing and renovating Brent's building for a total of $31,000 in favor of erecting for $40,000 a new one near the White House that might also serve the needs of the Treasury Department. Although Congress funded neither proposal at the time, the issue of new public buildings had been placed on its agenda to stay.[12]

The prospect of new federal construction attracted Mills's rivals. Ithiel Town, a prominent New York architect and engineer then successfully promoting his popular truss bridge, sent his young partner, Alexander J. Davis, to Washington in 1831 and 1832. Davis was guided about the city by Town's close friend William Elliot, met Robert Mills and other Washingtonians, and sketched views of the Capitol, the city hall, the "Hall of Representatives," and at least three alternative designs for a new patent office building. Davis referred to one project as "*making plans of the capitol,*

*Figure 4.3
Original wing,
Patent Office (1836–40),
Washington, D.C.;
occupied in 1840.
(Daguerreotype attributed
to John Plumbe, Jr.,
c. 1846, Prints and
Photographs Division,
Library of Congress)*

interior views, &c. for publication in concert with Mr. Town." It was a competitive environment. In one letter to Davis, Town urged him to discuss the publication with Gulian Verplanck, congressman from New York, but warned him not to mention the project to "Mr. Mills ye Architect, nor to any of ye Washington citizens. . . . Should you talk with Mills about the plan of such a Book, he would be very likely to anticipate the plan & say he had intended it himself—." Coincidentally, Mills had written Verplanck two months earlier suggesting the need for a book of reference drawings on the Capitol, including the plan, section, and elevations, to help inform strangers as well as to assist those working on the building.[13]

As a result of these visits, Town and Davis's firm assembled various proposed designs for a patent office building and engaged William Parker Elliot to be its representative in Washington. Elliot (1807–54) had been raised in the orbit of the Patent Office, performing piecemeal drafting and copying work. He claimed five years' architectural training from George Hadfield (1763–1826), a close friend of his father's. His subsequent study in London and Paris was curtailed when Thornton's death and the election of Democrat Andrew Jackson as president in 1828 irrevocably changed the Elliots' relationship to the office.[14]

The transition was contentious. The outgoing secretary of state, Henry Clay, named Dr. Thomas P. Jones of the Franklin Institute to succeed William Thornton. The senior Elliot bitterly contested being passed over "for party purposes" and within months charged Jones with malfeasance and conflict of interest. Jackson's incoming secretary of state, Martin Van Buren, decided that both Jones and Elliot should leave the office but agreed to assign William P. Elliot a table where he could receive piecemeal assignments recording inventions and making copies of patent documents. This arrangement soured when the new superintendent, John D. Craig, decided to economize by assigning Elliot's duties to one of the salaried clerks in the office. On his objections that Craig's action breached the promise Van Buren had made to his father in 1829, the son was allowed to keep his table as a private business, making drawings for inventors seeking patents. When this privilege was withdrawn in December 1833, Elliot set himself up as a patent agent across the street and proceeded to lambaste Craig's administration of the Patent Office, eventually helping drive him from office in 1835. The Elliots' intense loyalty to the patent system and their bitterness over their treatment by the Jackson administration would be reflected in the son's actions in the years ahead.[15]

This transitional episode represented more than a succession of federal administrations: It represented a clash of cultures. Thornton and the Elliots were part of the local establishment; they had grown with the city and for thirty years had helped shape its life and institutions, including the early Patent Office. New people were now in charge, and the Patent Office would never again be dominated by local figures. To Washingtonians of this period, Mills, arriving with the wave of Jacksonian appointees, would inevitably be an intruder. Mills was not one to proclaim his politics; he was discreet in maintaining business and social relationships on a nonpartisan basis. But in the early 1830s, Mills was in and the Elliots were out. The Elliots' interests in the Patent Office would be sustained in the years ahead by the son's work as a patent agent and his vigilant attention to Mills's erection of the new Patent Office.

As the Elliots were being ousted from the Patent Office, Mills had secured a position as a draftsman at the General Land Office, a bureau of the Treasury Department. Here he could receive a steady salary while trying to develop his architectural practice. During this period he made designs and oversaw the contracting and construction of fireproof federal customs houses in several ports, including Newburyport and New Bedford, Massachusetts, and New London and Middletown, Connecticut. These projects were performed outside his salaried position and were paid for by the local collector of customs. In this work Mills demonstrated the principles of his fireproof construction on federal projects and began, in effect, to act as the federal architect. He also began to train northern mechanics in principles of masonry vaulted construction that he had used widely in the Mid-Atlantic and the South. In Washington he finally received funding in 1833 to improve the acoustics of the House of Representatives, and he made recommendations for paving Pennsylvania Avenue and improving the water supply to the Capitol and other public buildings. Although he still was not making full use of his professional talents, the focus of his architectural work had shifted sharply from Baltimore and other localities to federal buildings and the building and engineering requirements of the emerging capital city.[16]

By 1834 physical conditions at the Patent Office had worsened, and the destruction of the Treasury Building by fire the year before had pointed up the vulnerability of the similar brick and wood buildings used by other departments. On April 2 Congress requested "an estimate of the cost of erecting a fire proof building for the Patent Office such as will answer all the wants of that Department for fifty years to come. . . ." Mills and Patent Superintendent Craig responded. Craig's proposal was for a three-story building 120 feet by 50 feet, with brick walls, wood floors, and iron ceiling supports, joists, and stays. The first floor was divided by a central hall into six offices and two large rooms for exhibition of the "most splendid and valuable models. . . ." The upper floors were each single large rooms for the "reception and exhibition of models." Not being an architect, Craig left the estimates to others but assumed the costs could adequately be covered by the patent fund.[17]

Mills made a significantly different and more thorough proposal. His building would be "a parallelogram 150 feet long by 60 feet wide, exclusive of the wing projection on each front, one of which is filled up by a colonnade." It featured "a basement story *entirely above the ground* which will be useful for *sub-offices*," repair shops, and "heavy or cumbrous models." The principal story above would contain offices for the superintendent and clerks along the building's street side and model rooms opposite. Mills stated that "a roomy staircase at each end of the central corridor leads to the grand model Saloon above, covering the entire area of the second story, 146 feet by 52 feet, besides the wings." If needed in the future, another room of like dimensions could be added above, "lighted and aired from the roof by means of the lanterns represented in the drawing of the front." The drawing has not been found, but presumably this added room would have extended above the window area of the walls and required the lighting from above. To meet the requirement for a fireproof structure, Mills recommended the exterior walls be of "cut free stone," giving an estimate of from $60,000 to $75,000, depending on the extent of fireproofing.[18]

A week later Mills wrote to William Noland, commissioner of public buildings, that his figures contemplated "Tyle floors" supported by "Arches of Brick" and presented a variety of cost options for a smaller building of 120 by 50 feet, presumably to allow comparability with Craig's proposal, for which estimates of about $47,000 and $67,000 had been submitted. Mills's options started with a basic brick building at $36,160, adding respectively wing buildings, a Doric portico, and cut stone exterior walls, for a maximum possible cost of $59,316. He pointed out that costs could be calculated for a larger building in proportion to the extent of ground covered and concluded that all costs were "predicated upon the plan of *arching* all the rooms with *brick*, the cheapest as well as the most secure from fire, compared with Cast iron. . . ."[19]

Mills typically laid out a range of options for his federal clients—allowing for various dimensions, configurations, and materials. Just as typically he would recommend unflinchingly the strongest and most fireproof construction, stressing his preference for masonry over iron. His estimating was thorough, in keeping with the competition and the resources available in the patent fund, and respon-

sive to the needs for offices, workshops, various exhibit areas, and possible future expansion. His most important contribution at this time, however, was to name the building's eventual location. He proposed that "a very beautiful situation . . . presents itself on the *Public Square* lying immediately North of the *General Post Office.* . . ." This square, located on a ridge midway between the Capitol and the White House, had been reserved by the city's planner, Pierre Charles L'Enfant, in 1791 for a nondenominational church to honor the nation's heroes. Mills helped determine its use as what came to be called a "Temple of Invention."[20]

The firm of Town and Davis had been actively seeking various architectural projects in the nation's capital that spring but appears not to have responded to the Patent Office competition until William P. Elliot urged Davis in May to send designs for an "*altogether* fire proof" building "of free stone & cast iron, with as little wood as possible . . . with six apartments for clerks and machinists and a larger room for the coarser models" on the ground floor and an upper story "to consist of *one* large and grand exhibition room for the fine models:—the roof to be supported by columns." Elliot wrote that although other building projects had stalled, "all the talk is about the proposed new Patent Office," with the appropriation bill about to pass and Mills having "submitted two or three plans. . . ." Over the next three weeks, Elliot opened an office associating himself with Town and Davis. He reported to Davis on June 5 that he had received Patent Office drawings from Davis, presented them to members of Congress, and intended to approach the president and cabinet. He promised Davis to keep the plans "out of view of Pirates." Congress again failed to appropriate funds for the new building, but Mills and the Town, Elliot, and Davis combination were now primed for competitions ahead for the Patent Office and other projects required in the national capital.[21]

The contest came in 1836 when Congress finally appropriated funds for both new Treasury and Patent Office buildings. A new patent superintendent, Henry Ellsworth, had vigorously reorganized the Patent Office on his arrival in August 1835 and persuasively argued for improved quarters. His initial reports to the secretary of state described disarray in the office, burdensome procedures required by the current patent law, and "the *absolute necessity* of some provision for the *accommodation of models*," several hundred of which were jammed into the garret, their weight endangering the building. In response, Congress established a select committee to study the needs of the patent office. Simultaneously, other committees revived discussions of needed fireproof public buildings following a devastating fire that razed fifty-two blocks of New

York City in December 1835. Congress was ready to act.[22]

In April the select committee on the Patent Office, chaired by John Ruggles, senator from Maine, called for a total overhaul of the patent law to end rampant abuses in the system and encourage American inventors to continue their unprecedented record of productivity. Its report claimed that in a short time America had "achieved what would have taken Europe a century to accomplish" and had "become all at once a manufacturing, as well as an agricultural nation." But contemporary practice, which allowed patent protections without examination of the invention for novelty, cheated inventors and led to fraud and litigation. The committee called for a strict examination system, requiring each application to be accompanied by models, drawings, and specifications and thoroughly screened by experts. Finally, it urged space for the systematic arrangement of models for exhibition and examination, arguing that the existing flammable quarters exhibited the "improvidence of the Government" instead of "facilitating the study of the useful arts." The solution was to use the $152,000 surplus in the patent fund to build a new fireproof building for the Patent Office.[23]

The committee emphasized the importance of exhibitions both to prospective inventors and the general public: "The halls of the Patent Office should present a national museum of the arts, and be a general repository of all the inventions and improvements in machinery and manufactures, of which our country can claim the honor. . . ." Displays of models and manufactures would be augmented by other government collections, samples of natural resources, and "Indian curiosities and antiquities." Together these exhibitions would surpass any in the world and present evidence of American accomplishment and resources that would stimulate creativity and pride, impress foreign visitors, and "elevate our national character."[24] The report reflected a national mood. It was time to place America on exhibit in a building that would last, itself a symbol that the nation would endure. Proposals for the Treasury and Patent Office buildings from both Mills and the team of Town and Elliot (Davis had left the firm in 1835) competed in various congressional committees during the spring, culminating in action in the closing days of the congressional session.

Congress approved construction of the buildings on July 2, 1836, but left final choice of plan and architectural supervision to President Jackson. In a letter to Jackson on July 4, Mills asked to be named "architect of the public buildings," pointing to his thirty-year record of constructing complex buildings "of a *fire-proof character*" in Philadelphia, Baltimore, South Carolina, and Louisiana, and the five customs houses and marine hospital he had designed since his arrival in Washington. He also cited success in securing cost-saving bids, as he had recently done for the Charleston, South Carolina, marine hospital, by pitting lower District of Columbia labor rates against higher local rates—resulting in "a difference of $7,900 below the Southern bid, and $900 less than the estimate." Mills further claimed that the "general designs" for the proposed public buildings were "originally and essentially mine" and asserted that "another" (presumably Elliot) had made "trivial modifications" in plans that Mills had publicly exhibited. He closed by reminding Jackson of his improvements to the public grounds and his earlier plan for the "New patent office," which could be found in the commissioner of public buildings' office.[25]

Mills was supported by the chairman of the House Committee on Public Buildings, Leonard Jarvis of Maine, and while other members favored Elliot, the president opted for Mills's superior experience. Jackson appointed Mills on July 6, 1836,

as architect to aid in forming the plans, making proper changes therein from time to time, and seeing to the erection of said buildings *in substantial conformity to the plans hereby adopted, which are, in their general outlines, to be, as to the Treasury building, that plan annexed by said Mills; and, as to the Patent Office, that annexed by Mr. Elliot:* The former building to be erected on the old site, and the latter one on the square north of the Post Office.

After six years Robert Mills finally had gained a salaried federal position exercising his professional talents. He immediately left his clerkship at the Patent Office, where he had worked since February 1835, adopted the title "Architect of Public Buildings," and went to work, as Elliot played a vocal role on the sidelines.[26]

Mills's association with the new Patent Office over the next fifteen years occurred in two phases. The first lasted from 1836 to about 1842, resulting in a building that combined office and exhibition spaces. This phase was briefly interrupted in the spring of 1838 when a congressional investigation into the adequacy of his work halted construction on the Treasury and Patent Office buildings. Then, during the 1840s, he advanced various proposals for extending the building, although it was the establishment of the Department of the Interior in 1849 that provided the needed impetus for the second phase of the work. New conditions prevailing at that time, as well as the continuing criticism by William P. Elliot and others about aspects of Mills's performance, led to his dismissal from his federal position in 1851 and a bitter end to his half-century career. He died in Washington at age 73 in 1855.

C O N S T R U C T I N G
T H E   N E W   P A T E N T
O F F I C E: 1 8 3 6 – 4 0

Launching this federal building program required new systems and authorities. President Jackson's statement of July 6, 1836, named the site for the Patent Office, identified general plans to follow, and authorized two key positions. The commissioner of public buildings would supervise contracting, oversee accounts and payments, and "superintend generally the detailed modifications of plans." The implication was that the plans were general in nature, which would support Mills's later contention that they were outlines only and that he was never in possession of detailed plans by Town and Elliot. As architect he was "to aid in forming the plans, making proper changes therein from time to time" and keeping within "substantial conformity" to the "general outlines" annexed to Jackson's statement.[27] His task was to erect fireproof offices and exhibition space for the Patent Office according to a rival's designs and within guidelines of authority, funding, and materials stipulated by Congress and the president. Although Jackson gave Mills architectural authority, Congress controlled the purse and quickly demonstrated its incapacity to exercise informed oversight of federal construction.

The first issues to be resolved concerned materials and funding. Congress had required that the building be fireproof and of freestone (sandstone) from the same quarries in nearby Aquia, Virginia, that had been used for the Capitol and the White House unless a "cheaper and more suitable material" could be found, leaving the ultimate decision to the president. But Congress based its appropriation of $108,000 on Town and Elliot's estimate for a brick building with wood floors, which Mills considered combustible. President Jackson was in Tennessee for the summer, and Congress would not return until winter. Mills wrote Jackson in August that even "with the utmost economy, and omitting the Portico," he needed at least $150,000 or would be forced to reduce the size of the building to smaller than that needed by the Patent Office. Mills had to take advantage of the building season, make the building fireproof, and meet the clients' needs, as well as stay within the appropriation. He also wanted to use granite instead of the more porous sandstone, if at all possible.

Mills's approach was to lay the foundations to the full dimensions in granite but to delay "operations on the expensive details of the plan" and wait to ask Congress for additional funds. But when Mills urged Jackson's successor, Martin Van Buren,

to continue the building in granite, "in preference to free stone, the difference in expense being small," Van Buren decided that since the "cut granite, though more suitable would not be cheaper or as cheap, the direction given by the late President in regard to the material must be that followed out." Economy was the order of the day. Although the additional funds were granted, Mills was forced to proceed with the sandstone, resulting in increased maintenance costs in the years ahead. But it was probably the last use of sandstone for a federal building, for Congress would soon demand that only granite or marble be used for public edifices.[28]

While Mills resolved issues of materials and constructed the foundations, Elliot carped on the sidelines, accusing Mills in a letter to Alexander J. Davis in November of "murdering the plans of the Treasury Building and the Patent Office" and failing to make working drawings. A month later he wrote the editors of the *Daily National Intelligencer*, taking issue with Mills's comments about the combustibility of the building that he and Town had proposed. He also claimed that Mills was injuring the "exterior . . . as may be seen in the deformity of the windows and the circular projection on the north side," which were contrary to the "Grecian style" and would "destroy the simplicity and harmony of the building. . . ."[29] He attached congressional letters endorsing the Town and Elliot design and threatened to take up his differences with Mills on another day.

By late 1837 Mills was predicting occupancy of the Treasury Building the following winter and expected to roof the Patent Office in early 1839. He had overcome difficulties with deliveries of materials and finding and training a workforce, especially masons. Pressures for fireproof office space had worsened when Blodgett's Hotel burned down in December 1836, destroying the quarters and records of both the Patent Office and the Post Office. Mills was alert to these pressures, ordering materials ahead and using the winter months to prepare the stone and complete sashes and window frames needed for the next year's work.

The new Patent Office building had a hybrid plan, with the east portion of the lower two floors devoted to offices and the west portion and entire upper floor intended for exhibitions. This plan was well served by Mills's preferred approach to fireproof construction, involving a modular system of brick groin vaults, which permitted him to create large exhibition spaces without relying on partitions or the use of iron cross beams to support the ceiling. In the Patent Office Mills planned to erect these vaults in three ranges, one forming a center corridor the length of the wing, the others set between the corridor and each wall. The vaults for the most part had common dimensions, whether intended for an exhibition or office space, and would be supported by pilasters at the walls and two rows of columns in the center. The approach was efficient and yielded reinforcing vaults of great visual grace (figs. 4.4, 4.5). This scheme may have been based on designs by J. N. L. Durand (1760–1834) for galleries or exhibition halls.[30]

Mills also preferred to use a fast-binding hydraulic cement because of its hardening speed and strength, as well as its waterproofing quality. As vaults were completed on the lower floors, Mills would coat the exposed outer surfaces with hydraulic cement, which, he maintained, "becoming dry and hard in a short time, prevents the rainwater from penetrating them; thus keeping the underworks dry," permitting the rooms beneath to be finished quickly and occupied soon after the roof was in place. As the year ended the walls of the Treasury Building had reached "the springing line" of the third-floor arches. At the Patent Office, arches had been completed in the entire basement and the eastern, or office, wing of the principal floor (fig. 4.6); the western wing would be vaulted the following spring and the outside walls readied to receive the entablature by the following winter.[31]

Although Mills was optimistic, external forces converged to impede construction. Levi Lincoln,

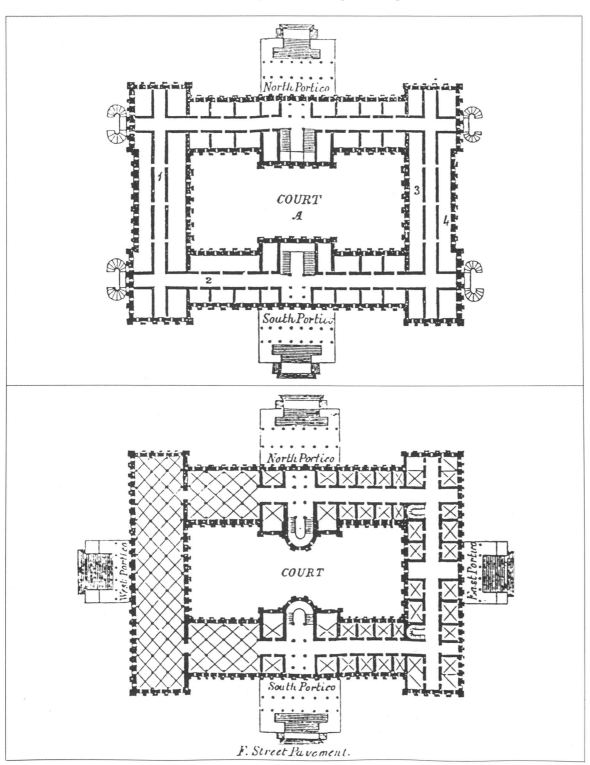

Figure 4.4
Mills's comparison of the Town and Elliot version with his own version of the 1836 plans for the second floor of the Patent Office. Lower plan shows Mills's intended vaulting scheme. (Scientific American, August 23, 1851)

Opposite: Figure 4.5 Vaulting in second-floor vestibule, Patent Office. Mills outlined the vaults with moldings converging in rosettes. His semicircular stairway conserved exhibit space on the floor above. (Stereoview, c. 1870, National Portrait Gallery)

Massachusetts Whig congressman and chairman of the House Committee on Public Buildings and Grounds, held an investigation in early 1838, which threatened to stop the work on both buildings and cost Mills his job. The country was undergoing an economic crisis blamed on Jacksonian policies and accompanied by the ascendancy of the Whigs in Washington, who gained a congressional majority for the first time. The Post Office, bereft of quarters since Blodgett's Hotel had burned, urgently required new accommodations. Some officials charged that Mills's Treasury Building would require the removal of the older State Department building and would block the view of the White House from the Capitol, a revered feature of L'Enfant's plan for the city. (Mills was asked to furnish estimates for removing the Treasury and using the materials to erect a post office on the site, the Treasury to be combined in a consolidated executive complex to be massed on Lafayette Square, across from the White House.) Mills's techniques of vaulted masonry construction were unfamiliar to most members of Congress, and the buildings were of great scale and expense, highly visible symbols of the administration in power. All these local, national, and partisan concerns contributed to the ensuing investigation by consulting architects Thomas U. Walter and Alexander Parris.

Mills suspected personal rivalry as well, charging to Lincoln that the "professional defamation" caused by the investigation "mortified" him and could have been brought on by only one person, an individual who had "resorted to every means to injure my professional standing" and who had "no qualification to judge in the matter, having not the smallest degree of experience in building. . . ." He most certainly was referring to Elliot, who was simultaneously writing Alexander J. Davis that "the new Treasury Building had turned out to be a complete failure & is ordered to be taken down. The Architect, Mills, must go down also. He has nearly ruined the design of the Patent Office likewise."[32]

Walter indeed urged that the Treasury be removed and called for major changes in Mills's treatment of the exhibition rooms of the Patent Office. Walter questioned the thinness of the walls and their lack of horizontal bonding but reserved his chief criticism for the need to accommodate the thrust of the arches in the large exhibition spaces. For the completed room in the basement, he asked that all nine groin arches be removed and that walls be built from the center piers to each wall, that iron bars be added "at the springing line of the arches" binding the outside wall to the center pier, and that the arches then be reconstructed "upon the same plan, without danger to the edifice." He urged the same treatment for the model hall proposed directly above and the "grand exhibition room" on the upper story, predicting that the 300,000 bricks in its arches would certainly collapse if his recommendations were not heeded. Walter's approach was to convert the open exhibition areas into a series of groin-arched walled compartments open only to a center corridor rather than provide the spacious exhibition areas planned by Mills.[33]

Mills responded swiftly, setting his thirty years of experience against Walter's youthful opinion and mentioning the dozens of courthouses, customs houses, and large public buildings throughout the eastern United States whose vaults testified to his skill. Fighting theory with facts, Mills claimed not only that his walls were economically constructed but also that "walls better capable of sustaining the span of arches" involved "have never been constructed in this country," that his walls were more than sufficient to sustain the vaults, and that any further reinforcement would be wasteful of space and materials. He pointed out counterbalancing forces inherent in groin vaults and construction techniques that tended to relieve lateral pressure on the outer walls, including the use of hydraulic cement to create a taut bond through the entire vault, "relieving the lateral, and increasing the perpendicular press of the arches. . . ." Mills drew the committee's attention to the existing work, which showed no ill effects even without the aid of the full weight of the completed walls. He stood ready to strike all the supports beneath his remaining vaults, even before the walls were fully erected, to prove his faith in their strength. Mills rested his case by asserting that his techniques surpassed the textbook approach argued by Walter and "gained for the profession an important advantage, namely to economize in the construction of fire-proof structures, and remedy the evil of very thick walls in such buildings." In short, Mills had said in so many words that Walter did not know what he was talking about in regard to vaulted construction.[34]

Faced with "an unfortunate difference of opinion between Mr. Walter and Mr. Mills," the committee called on Boston architect Alexander Parris for a second opinion. Parris softened Walter's recommendations for the Patent Office, allowing the vaulting in the basement and second story to remain as constructed and adding iron tie rods to secure the second-story vaults. He went on to recommend that "all vaulting remaining to be constructed be of spheroidal form," a technique then popular in England involving a dome "hooped with iron," with "little more thrust than if it was formed of a single piece, and . . . supported at four points, like a slab of stone." Parris's approach would have eliminated Walter's compartmentalized scheme.[35]

Meanwhile, Mills made a further attempt to educate the members of the House Committee on Public Buildings. Informing them of his wish "to render the subject plain and easy to be understood," he prepared an elaborate table illustrating the difference between theory and practice in regard to the thickness of walls required to support arches of various dimensions. His figures demonstrated that his specifications for the Treasury Building and Patent Office exceeded the wall thickness theoretically required for safety and almost doubled the dimensions used in other buildings by Mills that had been standing for years.[36] It was his last word. The committee's report on March 29, 1838, recommended that the Treasury Building be torn down and its stone used to build a post office but allowed the Patent Office to stand with selected alterations proposed by the consulting architects.[37] On April 17 Levi Lincoln, speaking for both the Senate and House Committees on Public Buildings, expressed concern to the president about Mills's apparent resistance to instituting the changes at the Patent Office and cited their "*unanimous* opinion" that Mills be dismissed and a new architect named to the Patent Office work.

If Lincoln's bill to raze the Treasury Building and attempt to replace Mills on the Patent Office had been successful, Mills's professional federal career in Washington probably would have been over. After extended congressional debate and a close vote, however, work on the Treasury Building was

Opposite: Figure 4.6 Elevation and third-floor plan of the Patent Office (as built), 1840. The elevation reveals the division of spaces between offices on the eastern portion of the lower two floors and exhibition space in the remaining areas. (Machen Collection, Columbia Historical Society)

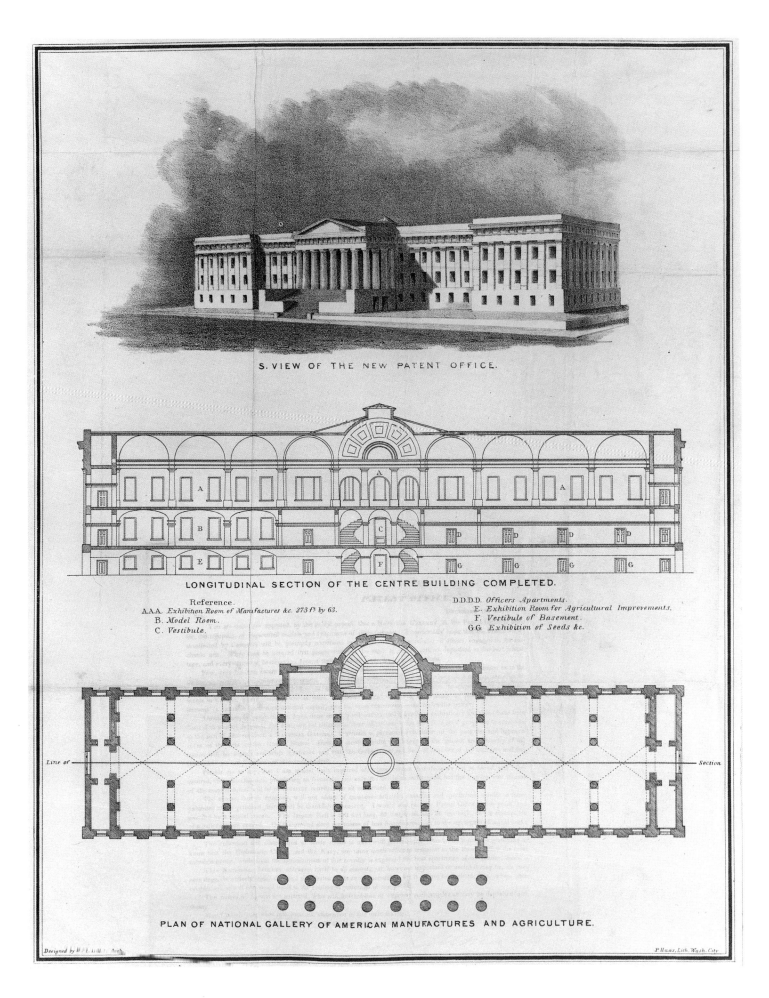

S. VIEW OF THE NEW PATENT OFFICE.

LONGITUDINAL SECTION OF THE CENTRE BUILDING COMPLETED.

Reference.
A.A.A. *Exhibition Room of Manufactures &c. 273 f.t by 63.*
B. *Model Room.*
C. *Vestibule.*

D.D.D.D. *Officers Apartments.*
E. *Exhibition Room for Agricultural Improvements.*
F. *Vestibule of Basement.*
G.G. *Exhibition of Seeds &c.*

Line of ———————————————————— Section

PLAN OF NATIONAL GALLERY OF AMERICAN MANUFACTURES AND AGRICULTURE.

allowed to proceed. In the first volume of *American Buildings and Their Architects*, William H. Pierson, Jr., extensively analyzes Mills's work on the Treasury Building and indicates that the debate eventually turned on the fact that while Congress argued, Mills continued to build and proved by removing the supports under his new vaults that his construction techniques were sound. Mills kept his position at the Patent Office, despite an effort to name Walter and Parris to the post, but was forced to institute changes to his vaulting systems, changes that altered the visual effect he had intended for the large exhibition areas and bear permanent witness to the congressional investigation.[38]

President Van Buren reacted by appointing a board of commissioners, consisting of the secretaries of state, treasury, and war, to oversee the architect and the commissioner of public buildings. The board would resolve conflicts and insulate the president from issues related to public buildings. The commissioners saw to it that most of the changes recommended by Parris were put into effect, including a suggestion for two additional rows of columns in the exhibit halls to support barrel, instead of groin, vaults (fig. 4.7; compare figs. 4.4, 4.6, 4.9). These columns in turn required two rows of supporting piers in the basement, which had already been built with groin vaults, resulting in the anomaly of piers rising to the crest of the arch yet having no function but to support the columns on the floors above (fig. 4.8). At the time Mills declared these changes superfluous and disharmonious but thought best to quiet the concern about the building's stability and to proceed as instructed.[39]

Four years later, however, Mills charged that the "unwarrantable interference of others having authority to change the plan" added $60,000 to the cost of the Patent Office and damaged the visual effect. Mills claimed that his interior would have been "much more beautiful and harmoniously light" with "lofty and airy groin vaults, springing from single columns" instead of the "dull and monotonous barrel arch . . . heavy entablature and cluster of columns." He called the space a "monument of the inroads of ignorance upon the truths of science" and deplored the lack of "architectural symmetry so apparent in the large exhibition room." In a final shot at his doubters, he reminded readers that all the formerly criticized arches in the Treasury Building and Patent Office stood firm and that he had constructed in the Patent Office an arch double the span of all the others.[40]

Despite this poignant complaint, Mills was proud of his work on the Patent Office. One senses that he

was challenged by the act of constructing it, especially the large exhibition spaces. His report on operations for 1839 is typical, with references to "the massive character of the work," the "great model room," the "immense cornice . . . grand model room arches," and the "great arch in the center." After the building opened, he described the model room in his 1841 *Guide to the National Executive Offices and the Capitol of the United States* as "the largest in the United States, taken as a whole . . . ornamented with a quadruple row of massive stone columns. . . . In the center a grand barrel arch, of forty feet span, towers above the rest. . . ." (fig. 4.9).[41] His first phase of work on the Patent Office was complete.

Mills finished all but exterior details on the Patent Office and Treasury Building by 1841 and turned his attention to completing the Post Office, which had been assigned to him in 1839. These three buildings changed the appearance of the nation's capital and set a standard for the construction of stone federal and local government offices in a monumental classical mode (see figs. 4.1, 4.2, 4.3). Commenting on Washington's public buildings in 1849, the commissioner of public buildings cited Mills's three new fireproof buildings as "the only buildings of their class having any pretensions

to architectural taste and proportion" and of the three commended the marble Post Office as "the most chaste and uniform in its construction and . . . the only one of all the public buildings of indestructible materials."[42] With completion of his work on the Post Office in 1842 and the onset of a governmentwide retrenchment, Mills's office was abolished in August 1842 and the federal construction program suspended. He turned his attention to local and privately sponsored projects, including a penitentiary (1839–41) for the District of Columbia, the building and grounds for the Smithsonian Institution (1847–55) and the Washington Monument (1845–52; completed 1879–84).

Although there was little new federal construction in Washington during the 1840s, Mills remained an active participant in planning for expanding agencies, including the Patent Office. When President Tyler established a commission to look into the "condition of the Public Buildings" in 1841, Mills presented an outline plan for the full quadrangular Patent Office and suggested that abbreviated wings—measuring 70 by 90 feet and costing $150,000—be added to complete the south facade (fig. 4.10). He wished to bring the massive portico into proportion and provide space for the newly established National Institute for the

Opposite: Figure 4.7 Altered vaulting schemes on second floor, Patent Office, with barrel arches in side bays requiring entablatures and added columns, supported by piers on the floor below. (National Portrait Gallery)

Figure 4.8 Piers added in original basement level of Patent Office rising to the apex of the vault to support additional columns above demanded by Congress in 1838. The cosmetic arches were added to the piers by the National Portrait Gallery in 1972. (Rolland G. White, National Portrait Gallery)

Promotion of Science, which aspired to become a national museum in the halls of the Patent Office. A year later he recommended this scheme to his friend Joel R. Poinsett, a founder and prime mover in the Institute,[43] enclosing a sketch made over the engraving of the building taken from his 1841 *Guide*. Significantly, it shows that Mills had originally intended to vault the exhibition rooms with two rows of supporting columns rather than the barrel vaults carried on four rows of columns, as actually constructed (fig. 4.11).

For an 1845 report on the "National Edifices at Washington," the patent commissioner called for erection of the west wing to provide room for the display of models and manufactures and possibly to "accommodate . . . professors, if appointed, under the Smithsonian fund." A year later he attached Mills's proposal for wings to his annual report.[44] Mills estimated $80,000 for the west wing, which had a cellar (because of the slope of the land), "a large room for a lecture hall" in the basement story,

a "spacious model room . . . on a level with the portico floor," and a "similar sized room above this, with a gallery running all around the whole height to the roof, which will furnish an uninterrupted surface of wall . . . for the exhibition of paintings, lighted from above." The east wing, without the cellar level, would cost $70,000. Mills stated that both wings would be entered directly from the adjacent streets at ground level or by "stairways to the upper stories, without having to use the main entrance. . . ." While none of these proposals advanced, they kept Mills associated with the building. But they provided a confusing reference point when in 1849 Congress decided to establish the Department of the Interior and appropriated $50,000 "towards the erection of the wings of the Patent Office building according to the original plan . . . to be done by contract, in the same manner as . . . the General Post Office building."[45] It was natural that Mills would be selected to supervise the work.

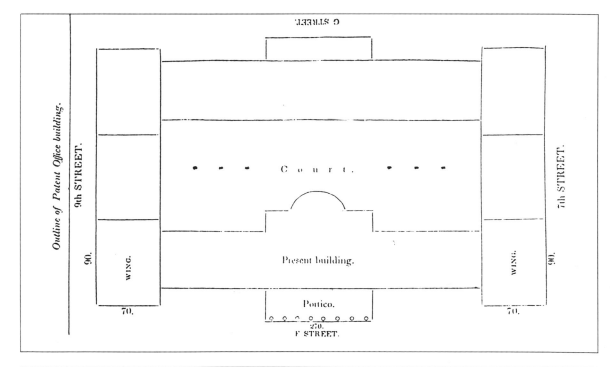

*Figure 4.10
Mills's 1841 projection of
the Patent Office wings,
showing abbreviated
versions to balance the
original wing. (Senate
Document 123, September
11, 1841)*

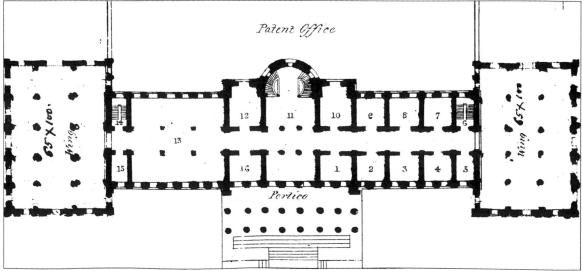

*Figure 4.11
Sketch by Robert Mills for
Joel R. Poinsett, dated
June 22, 1842, showing
how partial wings could be
added to the Patent Office
for the National Institute
and to complete the front
(south) facade. (Joel R.
Poinsett Papers, Historical
Society of Pennsylvania)*

MILLS AND THE PATENT OFFICE EXTENSIONS: 1849-51

Mills's second phase of work on the Patent Office was as stormy as the first. Questions were raised regarding the plan, funding, and Mills's management of contracts. William P. Elliot resurfaced as a critic and protector of the building for use by inventors and the Patent Office. Congress was again unclear in its intentions and funding and was drawn into extensive debate during the course of construction. Although his tenure was just over two years, Mills served under two presidents, three secretaries of the interior, and two commissioners of public buildings and faced at least two review committees. By mid-1851 Thomas U. Walter succeeded Mills at the Patent Office and edged him out for the prize of constructing the wings to the Capitol.

The Department of the Interior influenced Mills's work on the Patent Office in several ways. First, its needs for offices instead of exhibition spaces forced revisions of the internal plan. Second, Mills was an appointee of the secretary of the interior, who also supervised the commissioner of public buildings. Disputes between Mills, the commissioner, and others would be resolved within the department. Mills's position as "Superintendent of the erection of the wings of the Patent Office" lacked the stature of his earlier presidential appointment. This time there was no presidentially appointed board of commissioners to oversee the public buildings and arbitrate among opposing offices or factions. Third, the subordination of the Patent Office to the Department of the Interior and the building's use for bureaucratic offices provoked protests and grievances from inventors and constant attacks from *Scientific American* that the department was usurping the building the patentees had constructed with their own fees. Mills's dutiful service to the department's needs inevitably marked him for attack by Elliot, architect cum patent agent, who now fused personal resentment with the cause of inventors as he argued for his conception of the building.

As Mills began work in 1849, questions were raised regarding the nature of his appointment and precisely what Congress intended by the "original" plan. Mills had already issued requests for bids from contractors when Interior Department officials realized that the office of architect, abolished in 1842, had not been expressly reinstituted in the new bill. The attorney general agreed. The department ordered Mills's bid requests recalled and reissued by the commissioner of public buildings. Mills was reappointed as superintendent, although he still had considerable administrative duty in processing the bids in the ensuing months.[46]

As to the second issue, Thomas Ewing, secretary of the interior, and Mills agreed that "original" referred to the 1836 plan rather than the truncated extensions of the 1840s. Consequently, Mills's "Description and Specification" of April 20, 1849, called for two wings that would extend 270 feet, the entire length of the square. The west wing would be arranged for the Patent Office into large groin-vaulted halls, the uppermost containing a picture gallery around the room, supported on columns, for exhibiting "works of art, to be lighted from above." The east wing would be devoted entirely to offices. This arrangement conformed to the disposition of the original wing, with exhibition space at the west end and offices at the east end of the lower two floors. Mills called for white marble for the exterior facing and fireproofing throughout, reflecting federal construction standards embraced during the previous decade.[47]

The appropriation of $50,000 had been an arbitrary amount that was hardly sufficient for Mills to get started. He began foundations for both wings and exhausted the appropriation by September, before Congress returned for the winter session. Mills recommended that Ewing ask the Treasury to advance funds from the surplus of the patent fund, but Ewing would not permit him to proceed until Congress acted. Mills had to protect the structure, meet deadlines, and sustain contractors and laborers who had given favorable bids on the assumption of continuous work through the season. By the time he prepared the structure for winter, accounts were $15,000 in arrears.[48]

The following April Ewing explained his dilemma to D. S. Dickinson, chairman of the Senate Finance Committee. Ewing had decided that the public interest would be best served by laying the foundations for both wings and then concentrating on the east wing, to speed its availability for "public Archives . . . in buildings not fire-proof." Although Ewing had intended to stay within the appropriation, he claimed that "the Superintendent did not bring the work and the appropriation together so as to permit it; and I had much on my hands and could not, as the work progressed, give the accounts and the work my personal inspection." Costs to "winter it all safely, and commence the Spring Operations fairly" caused him to exceed obligations to contractors, who continued to work in the belief that the government would eventually reimburse them.[49]

A remarkable debate followed about the deficiency appropriation. Senators opposing diversion of the patent fund to serve the Interior Department argued that the mid-1840s plan for $160,000 was the "original" plan and urged that the contractor debts be paid off and the smaller building completed for the Patent Office, using the patent fund. Samuel Phelps, of Vermont, charged that the substitution of the 1836 plan was a "Yankee trick," which Mills had duped Ewing into approving. Senator James A. Pearce, a Whig from Maryland, and Henry S. Foote, a Democrat from Mississippi, took a different tack, acknowledging that "in passing this appropriation in the last session, Congress did not know what they were about . . . what the original plan was, or what . . . the wings would cost; but in all that, they did nothing more than what they have done in 100 other cases, or as often as public buildings have been erected." Pearce claimed that the 1836 plan was the original one, that the nation needed the buildings and was spending $20,000 annually to rent inferior quarters, and that the secretary had made the correct decision. Robert M. T. Hunter, of Virginia, urged that the patent fund be expended on the building to prevent it from being used to establish an agricultural bureau or otherwise interfering with the agricultural practices of his state. The debate culminated the following week when Jefferson Davis, of Mississippi, blamed Congress for its imprecision and spoke up for compensating the contractors, completing the east wing with $90,000 from the patent fund, and in due time proceeding with the west wing using general government funds. This suggestion prevailed, and work resumed on the building.[50]

What is striking in the debate is the diversity of viewpoints and the lack of partisanship. Ideological questions arose over use of the patent fund and federal interference in state and local affairs. But for the most part, the debate seemed to dwell on practical questions, without regard to party or geography. This episode provides the background against which Mills's work was performed and indicates the competing interests and lack of system still affecting decisions about federal building programs in the 1850s.

By September 1850, Mills was preparing to begin the upper level of the east wing. Zachary Taylor had died in office in July, and his successor, Millard Fillmore, appointed a new secretary of the interior, Alexander H. H. Stuart, on September 12. Greeting him as he took office was a letter from William P. Elliot, accusing Mills of "destroying the Original Plan of the building" by dividing the upper story into offices, much to Elliot's "utter astonishment" (although Mills's "Description and Specification" had clearly specified that approach). According to Elliot, this step was an affront to inventors, whose funds had paid for the construction to date and whose inventions legally deserved the space. It marred the "beauty and symetry [sic] of the Design" and damaged Elliot's "professional reputation."[51]

Elliot's reemergence as a critic of Mills's work at this time brought together the two strands of his career, that as a sometime designer-engineer and his main occupation as a patent agent. Aside from his personal association with the Patent Office, promoting the interests of inventors made good business sense for Elliot in 1850. The patent commissioner had been arguing for a decade against using the building's space for museum collections. In 1850, with 17,000 patent models overflowing the garrets and more than 1,000 more arriving annually, the Patent Office could not abide sacrificing exhibition space for bureaucrats' offices. It was time for the inventor community to take action, and Elliot and Scientific American led the way.[52]

Calling Elliot "the reputed author of the original design," Mills responded that he had never received a third-floor plan and had arranged the interior as specified by his client. He claimed to "have always regarded the Public Wants as paramount to private or professional demands; and the constant and urgent demands for office rooms . . . justified my recommendation of providing them in the East wing. . . . " While Mills believed that there was ample room for the Patent Office in the west wing, he noted that the walls and arches of the third-floor east wing were so arranged that this space could be converted into a large exhibition room, if necessary.[53]

Elliot's appeal worked. In part because of the suspension of work on the west wing, Secretary Stuart decided to accommodate the Patent Office's needs by allowing the exhibition space in the east wing. Mills was directed to take down the partitions and provide a continuous gallery on the upper floor of the building. Ironically, Elliot's intervention gave Mills the opportunity to begin to construct a large, groin-vaulted hall in the manner he had been denied in the 1838 controversy. Although completed by others, the gallery today demonstrates how Mills would have approached all the large spaces if he had had his way (fig. 4.12).[54]

CHARGES AND

INVESTIGATIONS

The controversies of 1850 continued to plague Mills in the succeeding year. In New York City Scientific American took up the cause of saving the building for inventors and promoted Elliot's views on preserving the exhibition spaces. In Washington contract alterations required by the construction delays during the deficiency bill arguments and the substitution of the exhibition space for offices in the east wing led a new team of officials to question Mills's competence, forcing him again to defend his reputation. This time he was unsuccessful and eventually saw his former critic Thomas U. Walter replace him at the Patent Office and gain the coveted job of extending the wings of the Capitol. Mills's experiences of 1851 illustrate aspects of public building practices of the day as well as his own professional behavior.

As the year began Mills had a number of projects underway in the capital. He was supervising construction of the Washington Monument, recommending the extension of the Post Office, and actively promoting his plans for enlarging the Capitol to officials ranging from President Fillmore to Jefferson Davis, chairman of the Senate committee considering the question. During the first half of the year he also made proposals for the Charleston, South Carolina, waterworks and an addition to the library at the University of Virginia, Charlottesville. But it was his work on the Patent Office that attracted controversy.

On January 31, 1851, Mills wrote to Ignatius Mudd, commissioner of public buildings, objecting to local builder William Archer's charges of Mills's "deception, impositions and frauds" at the Patent Office. Archer had accused Mills of using inferior materials, mixing sandstone and marble for an unattractive appearance, allowing inadequate construction, and overpaying contracts. Archer claimed that the full cost of the extensions would greatly exceed Congress's expectations and urged that the secretary of the interior review the "original plan" and the previous secretary's specifications for contracts and payments. He also wanted the structure examined by an experienced architect while work was stopped for the winter. Archer repeated his charges in February and March, as well as his recommendations that the Patent Office be torn down and a new building be erected on a better site with more room at less cost.[55]

Mills informed Mudd that he was "at a loss to understand the motive that had prompted this man to pursue me with his malignant and false aspersions for the last fifteen or twenty years." Pointing out that Archer had had "no visible employment" for that period, he described him as an incapable, deceitful malcontent, suggesting that his "reason has become partially dethroned." Mills informed Mudd that the "original plan" was only an outline of the foundations and that the interior arrangements had to be developed "according to the exigencies of the public service." The abbreviated plan of 1844, which Archer had suggested was the original, had been made with the needs and resources of that period in mind and with the expectation of future extensions. Mills suggested that Congress funded the extension in 1849 without an estimate of the total cost because the "public interest demanded the building at any cost." He claimed

to have reviewed the work and materials with Secretary of the Interior Ewing, who had approved the use of marble for the exterior facing and decided on the allocation of the interior space.[56]

Just as Mills's overall approach had been approved by the secretary, the contracting and payments had been administered by Commissioner Mudd. Mills reminded Mudd that all payments had been based on actual measurements made by "as honorable and upright a man as there is in this city" and approved by Mudd himself for payment. Mills viewed Archer's claim of possible overpayments of up to $70,000 as unbelievable on its face, as the work billed to date barely exceeded that amount. The terms of measurement and prices were carefully defined in all contracts, and, if anything, contractors were doing work for which they could not be paid. Mills concluded that he would no longer bear Archer's attacks or be "a patient victim of his falsehoods, when I do not doubt, for a moment, that the author of this letter is the tool of others."[57] His professional honor was at stake and he would defend it.

The next day *Scientific American* presented a "History and Description of the U.S. Patent Office Building," as designed by William P. Elliot. The article, perhaps written by Elliot, illustrated a plan purporting to be that approved in 1836, with a squared-off stair tower, and noted that the superintending architect had "injured" the design by substituting semicircular stairs, altering the vaulting systems, adding additional rows of columns, flattening the pilasters, and "changing the material so as to make the subordinate parts superior in finish to the principal."[58] This article revealed Elliot's version of the "original" plan, complete with the exhibition gallery circumventing the upper story, recently rescued by Elliot's intervention with the secretary of the interior. It also presented the patentees' resentment over the building's usurpation by the Department of the Interior. As the nation's largest patent agency, it was natural that Munn & Company would use its journal to plead the case for providing space for patent models and recognition of inventors. The Patent Office was a shrine to "American Genius"; it was featured on the magazine's masthead, and no diversion of its use would be tolerated by *Scientific American*. Arguments to save the building for inventors would add to the tensions regarding the building during the year ahead.

Mills's fortunes turned abruptly in March 1851, when Commissioner Mudd died and was replaced by William Easby. Secretary of the Interior Stuart, pressed by continuing complaints from Archer and others about Mills, asked Easby to investigate the charges. Within two weeks Easby had dismissed or threatened Mills's team of supervisors, ordered

Mills to turn over his records, and appointed an investigation committee consisting of William P. Elliot, John C. Harkness, and William W. Birth. They were to study the use of materials, measurements and basis of payments, adherence to the original plan and contracts, effects of any changes, and—reminiscent of 1838—the stability of the walls and arches. All work and practices were to be compared with Mills's "Description and Specification" of April 20, 1849.[59]

Mills learned of these actions after returning from a week on business in Virginia and fired off respectful but testy letters to Easby and Secretary Stuart. He told Stuart that he would cooperate fully with the inquiry, as he had absolutely no doubt about the integrity of the work or his staff and as all the allegations had been raised before and "declared to be unfounded by your predecessor, Mr. Ewing, a committee of the Senate . . . and . . . disregarded upon two occasions by the House." But he strenuously objected to Easby's replacement of Peter Havener, the superintendent of bricklayers and "a man of highest competence," by a stonemason

who had been one of the bidders on the work. Mills insisted on having work supervised by those fully competent in the skill itself. He questioned the propriety of handing over sensitive public papers to a committee of private citizens that he felt had not been sanctioned by law, offering instead to deliver the papers directly to Easby. Mills informed Easby that he considered Havener's replacement "entirely void" unless ordered by the secretary and that he had appealed for a ruling. Easby retorted that he would carry out his duty "without fear" and that he appreciated "this early protest for it will save much future trouble."[60]

Throughout this episode Mills presented himself as an independent appointee of the secretary of the interior with a responsibility clearly separate from that of the commissioner of public buildings. The latter was a contracting officer, disbursing agent, and maintainer of buildings and grounds. The architect, or superintendent, was the designer and supervisor of construction. Mills informed the secretary that in all his Washington career he had "never known any Commissioner of Public build-

Figure 4.12
Third-floor east wing of the Patent Office, begun by Mills in 1849, revealing vaulting schemes and effect he intended for all the large exhibition spaces in the original wing before Congress forced changes. Mills had completed a third of the vaulting shown here when he was replaced by Thomas U. Walter in July 1851. (Library, National Museum of American Art)

ings to assert that he had the power to interfere with the Superintendency of a building during its progress." The step threatened the "Concert of Action" between the two offices that Mills considered "essential to a proper execution of the public work," a cooperation that required the "most industrious efforts" to succeed.[61] Stuart was content to have Easby take his course; by the end of April Easby had dismissed Mills's superintendent of the east wing, the superintendent of laborers, and the watchman. Prophetically, the May 3, 1851, edition of *Scientific American* reported on removals in the Patent Office itself and mentioned that "Robert Mills, superintendent of buildings, is to be removed and W. P. Elliott [sic] appointed in his place."[62] Summary dismissals were the order of the day, and Mills had become a prime target.

William Easby had had long experience in local industry and politics. He had shifted his career from government service to local business at about the time Mills arrived in Washington to seek federal work. Described in his daughter's reminiscences as "an ardent Whig," he had resigned his position as master-builder at the Washington Navy Yard when Democrat Andrew Jackson became president in 1828. He then developed a shipyard and lime kilns at the juncture of the Chesapeake and Ohio Canal and Rock Creek, just below Georgetown on the Potomac. Politically, he participated in Whig inaugurals and other honorary activities over a twenty-year period and had avidly sought the commissioner of public buildings post since 1849. He had been actively involved with the local building trades and suppliers. Besides employing numerous mechanics at the shipyard, he had engaged in various engineering projects, including moving the several-ton statue of George Washington by Horatio Greenough from the Navy Yard to the Capitol in 1842. He had had a falling out with the Washington National Monument directors in 1848 when stone that he had provided was rejected as being of insufficient quality. His firm had unsuccessfully bid for foundation stone, sand, and lime contracts for the Patent Office extension. Mills and Easby could have clashed in any of these projects. According to Easby's daughter, he possessed strong mechanical aptitude, engineering skill, and "great independence of character with an indomitable will. Naturally he had enemies." Issues of temperament, politics, and personal grievance all probably contributed to his exertions to dislodge Mills from his position in the weeks ahead. As commissioner of public buildings he was perfectly placed to focus cumulative local animosities among builders, contractors, suppliers, aspiring architects, and protectors of the local status quo against federally induced changes that Mills was expected to carry out. With his stellar Whig credentials, Easby was ideally suited to engineer a transition from Mills—a traditional appointee of Democratic administrations, although studiously nonpartisan in his actions and statements—to a more politically agreeable architect for federal projects.[63]

By the end of May, Easby was able to write Secretary Stuart that he had discovered unauthorized changes by Mills in the marble and granite contracts that had more than doubled the cost of the Patent Office extensions, causing him to charge Mills with "incompetency" and "most respectfully to recommend his removal." The same day Mills accused Easby of stating "on several occasions" that Mills would be removed from office and asked that he state his reasons and authority. Easby replied that Mills was "not qualified to fill the Office with profit to the Government" and appointed a committee of architects and builders, including Thomas U. Walter, Ammi Young, and Robert Brown, to review the adequacy of the construction.[64]

The committee's line of inquiry was reminiscent of Walter's review of 1838, questioning the capacity of the third-floor walls to sustain the groin vaults Mills planned for the exhibition space. It suggested that these walls would be weakened by the relocation of chimney flues, which originally had been carried up through internal office partitions, and recommended iron tie rods to secure the arches. Easby suggested that the walls be taken down, but Mills apparently convinced Secretary Stuart of their stability and the satisfactory operation of the rerouted flues. Mills told Stuart that he had always planned to use tie rods, just as he had previously "in building the large room of equal space of Arches in the Gen'l Post Office Building." Mills's construction plans were further supported by a second examination at Stuart's request by a team of War Department engineers, whereupon Stuart rejected Easby's suggestion to remove the walls. Mills later charged that both the Elliot committee and the inquiry by architects who were his "rivals in the Plans for the Capitol" were deliberate attempts by Easby "to throw my acts under suspicion" and deny him the Capitol assignment.[65]

While neither investigating committee damaged Mills, Easby's interpretation of the written record did. Past controversies over the "original plans," suspension of work on the west wing, and the substitution of exhibition rooms for offices left a trail of changes that exposed Mills to new allegations, especially in the absence of important witnesses such as Easby's deceased predecessor I. W. Mudd. The spring of 1849, when Mills was soliciting bids, had been a chaotic period for him and then–Secretary of the Interior Thomas Ewing. The secretary had to form a new department, oversee other public building projects, and make immediate decisions regarding space and materials for the Patent Office extension. Barely eight weeks after the department's formation, bids had been submitted for construction of the two massive wings on the Patent Office. Mills found the bids "so varied and intricate" that he had to organize them into "tabular statements" for comparison and for contract awards from the commissioner of public buildings. This process included estimating "assumed quantities of . . . several kinds of work." Later changes made in response to Secretary Ewing's new needs made the written record appear as if Mills's initial estimates had been deliberately skewed. By adroitly selecting and presenting evidence from working papers, bids, contracts, change orders, and contractor complaints, Easby was able to tighten the noose rapidly on Mills, despite Mills's rebuttals. On July 29, 1851, Mills was told that Thomas U. Walter had been appointed superintendent in his place.[66]

In his appeal to Stuart the next day, Mills began a two-year effort to regain his position. He recounted the several charges and rebuttals of the previous two months, placing before Stuart the entire texts of authorizing letters and contracts, which vindicated his actions as architect, and suggesting that Easby had not passed on to Stuart much of the supporting material Mills had furnished Easby during the inquiries. When Stuart refused to reinstate Mills or allow him an official hearing, Mills appealed to President Fillmore, citing his long public service and legacy of economically executed public buildings. Mills pleaded that "it would be but justice to an old Officer to allow him to justify himself—it is due to my friends that have honored me with their confidence." Fillmore, too, declined. Now Mills was out and Walter in, with Mills viewing the outcome as the result of a concerted effort to destroy his career.[67]

Mills next turned to Congress. When the winter session began in December, he asked R.M.T. Hunter, senator from Virginia, for help, charging that Easby had come into office intending to deprive him of his post and "possessing the ear of the President he succeeded, not only to remove me from the Patent Office, but to defeat me in the charge of the Capitol extension." Mills also wrote the full Congress, asking to justify his "Public acts" in response to his removal "in consequence of the misrepresentations" presented by Easby. These appeals were part of a litany by Mills that continued through 1852, including further pleas to President Fillmore.[68]

Mills's defense was presented in the form of a "Synopsis of Charges," which included his responses to each charge. To the charge that he made changes to the building, Mills responded that all changes were sanctioned by the relevant contract or authorized by the commissioner of public buildings. Another question arose over Mills's substitutions of wall materials to meet Secretary Ewing's wish for the thinnest practical walls. Instead of using granite and marble facing over interior fill of brick and ashlar (rough, loose stone), Mills substituted thicker cuts of granite and marble facing (cubestone) and eliminated the other materials altogether. Savings in brick and ashlar contracts offset increases for cubestone. Mills claimed that these changes were made in response to the secretary's wishes, yielded additional office space, followed practices in his previous public buildings, and, most important, were allowed by the contract and authorized by the commissioner of public buildings.[69]

The third allegation was that certain contracts were not awarded to lowest bidders. The granite contract was a case in point. Between the time the bids were submitted and the contracts let, the decision had been made to face the entire courtyard with granite, instead of the foundations only. Granite purchases increased; marble purchases decreased. An erroneous bid for granite, later withdrawn and corrected, was seized by Easby as evidence that Mills had substituted high granite bids for low and defrauded the government. Mills replied that the low bid Easby mentioned was not relevant and that the tabular statements had laid out all the bids clearly for contracting by the commissioner of public buildings, a knowledgeable mechanic himself. The commissioner had reviewed all the materials with the Interior Department before executing contracts and had repeatedly reported to Congress that all contracts were made with the lowest bidders. In short, Mills asserted that by assailing him, Easby was "impugning" his predecessor, I.W. Mudd, as well as the reviewing officials in the Interior Department.[70]

None of Mills's pleas succeeded. Ironically, as Franklin Pierce succeeded Fillmore as president in 1853, Mills wrote his long-time supporter Jefferson Davis, then secretary of war, that he had informed Pierce of his interest in the positions of commissioner of public buildings or architect of the Capitol, and, if neither became vacant, he hoped to be "restored to the Professional charge of the Patent Office building, of which I was unjustly deprived by the late Administration." He ended by stating that his "pecuniary circumstances are of the most pressing need for employment," asking Davis's assistance "in procuring professional business." Mills was nearly 72, two years from death, and had dominated the practice of architecture in the nation's capital for more than twenty years.[71] But he still sought economic and professional security, much as he had two decades before—a commentary on the nature of the practice at that time and place.

MILLS'S ROLE IN DESIGNING THE PATENT OFFICE

Certain areas of Mills's work during the period of his involvement with the Patent Office deserve special focus. The first is the question of Mills's specific contributions to the design and plan of the building, in light of the controversy over the original plan. Others include various aspects of his practice, including his pay, the range of his "extracurricular" assignments, his networks for information and communication, the structure of his organization, and his role in defining standards and systems for public building projects in the nation's capital.

Two issues must be raised regarding authorship of the original design and plan. First, who designed the "Town and Elliot" plan accepted by President Jackson? Second, what changes did Mills make during construction? As to the first issue, Elliot claimed in 1842 that Town "had no hand in it," that the design was his alone, and he maintained this position throughout his life.[72] A thorough analysis by Jane B. Davies, however, has argued convincingly that Alexander J. Davis's earlier projects were the basis for the exterior characteristics, especially the strong pilasters, projecting portico, and arrangement of two stories over a raised basement (also a feature of Mills's 1834 plan). Even though Davis and Town had separated by 1836, Davis's plans were known to Elliot from the earlier competitions and may have been available in Town's office. Davis later insisted that the Patent Office was based on his designs.[73] Although Elliot had skills as a draftsman and may have been capable of furnishing an outline plan and sketch of the building, there is no evidence that he was capable of producing detailed architectural drawings. His principal career was as a patent agent and civil engineer.

Mills's own account of credits due in his 1847 *Guide to the Capitol and the National Executive Offices* and his dialogue with *Scientific American* in 1851 give insight into his specific contributions. These sources indicate that Mills was furnished the outline and exterior design in 1836 but that he had to develop all interior plans and details. Mills labeled Elliot "the mere projector of the outline of the Plan" and himself the executing architect, working without any "vertical, longitudinal, and transverse sections."[74]

In his *Guide*, Mills credited the Town and Elliot plan with the idea of the quadrangular form, based on the Louvre in Paris, and a facade using the Greek Doric order, "derived from the Parthenon . . . forming, as a whole, an imposing composition, well adapted to the objects for which it was designed." Mills added that "the beautiful engraving at the head of the Letters Patent . . . presents a perspective view of the building as completed . . ." and favorably reflected his "projection" of the building

Figure 4.13 Engraving from patent award certificate, said by Mills to reflect his own projection, c. 1846. (National Portrait Gallery)

Drawn by A.A.Von Schmidt.   Engd by W.H.Dougal

U.S. PATENT OFFICE.

(fig. 4.13). The engraving compares with a photograph of about 1846 by John Plumbe (see fig. 4.3), which also features iron railings decorated with eagles, possibly designed by Mills, and helps date the engraving.[75] Notable elements include the recessed panels below each first-floor window and boldly projecting second-floor window sills extending between the pilasters. The original basement windows were nearly square and the basement stonework was rusticated. The windows were enlarged and the stone dressed to conform to the wings in the 1850s (fig. 4.14). Mills's articulation of the window walls gave a strong horizontal effect to the building, contrasting with the vertical emphasis featured in Davis's earlier studies. The plainer treatment of the windows and more pronounced pilasters of the Davis studies seem to be reflected in a contrasting perspective view (see fig. 4.6), which may have been based on the Town and Elliot proposal circulated by the Patent Office when the building opened in 1840. An article promoting Elliot's authorship published in the February 1851 *Scientific American* criticized Mills for "the reduc-

tion of the width and depth of the pilasters," which diminished the building's "boldness and strength," and for "making the windows of the basement too prominent."[76] This reference and the visual record suggest that Mills made only slight exterior modifications to the Town and Elliot plan.

As to the interior, both Mills and Elliot agreed that Mills added the semicircular stairwell projection at the rear of the original wing (see fig. 4.5). Elliot criticized its departure from the angular Greek form, while Mills claimed it kept "the great exhibition room above . . . *unbroken* by the ascent of the stairs."[77] This approach demonstrated Mills's practicality and willingness to depart from convention and also created a striking interior effect. Additional details about the contrasting 1836 interior plans appeared in an article by Mills in the August 1851 *Scientific American*, in which he responded to criticisms in the February article that he had departed from "Elliot's" plan.

Here, for the first time, Mills outlined his recollection of the 1836 plans presented to Congress and the president. Mills stated that the only floor plans presented were of the second floor and that "nothing of the upper story arrangement was laid down." He described the "character" of the exhibition rooms in the Town and Elliot plan (see fig. 4.4) as of "long and narrow rooms each side of the passage . . . about 21 feet wide" and maintained that this scheme would have been continued above. This approach would have corresponded to the problematic initial 1836 appropriation, discussed earlier, for a brick building with wood floors. In contrast, Mills's plan showed vaulted rooms "the whole width of the building" to yield a totally fireproof structure.[78] Elliot's supporters made no rebuttal. Mills's use of vaulted masonry construction throughout was consistent with his position in the 1834 competition and his practices in his previous works. He clearly sought well-lighted, spacious exhibition areas with a minimum of walls. Elliot's plan would have had more of the character of an office building than that originally completed by Mills in 1840, with its emphasis on large, open exhibition spaces.

In summary, Mills determined the plan and detailing of the interior, separated office from exhibition spaces on the lower floors, and opened the upper level to a single gallery. He designed the gracious semicircular stairway to economize space. He introduced the groin-vault systems and would have used them throughout the exhibition rooms if Congress had not intervened. Despite claims for Elliot, there is no evidence that he deserves any credit for the interior, and, in light of Jane Davies's work, there is strong evidence that his professed responsibility for the exterior was derivative.

ASPECTS OF MILLS'S PRACTICE AND CONTRIBUTION

From the moment he arrived in Washington, Mills always depended on freelance assignments in addition to whatever steady federal position he could obtain. Initially he held federal draftsman positions, first in the General Land Office and then in the Patent Office. With these posts as a base, he took on various architectural assignments, both federal and local, from Massachusetts to South Carolina. In Washington there was a city to shape— waterworks, street paving, civic buildings, markets, landscapes, and offices—and a national capital to manifest through public buildings, monuments, and dignified spaces. Beyond Washington there was a national presence to implant and a demand for economical and tasteful buildings of all types— academic, civic, religious, and residential. And there was a nation to connect and span, by railroad

and wire. All these concerns occupied Mills during this era, and he typically balanced numerous new and continuous projects.

Compensation

When appointed architect of the Treasury Building and Patent Office by Jackson in 1836, Mills received a yearly salary of $1,800 plus $500 for drawings. The position was apparently not officially authorized by Congress until 1839, when Mills was appointed to take charge of the Post Office along with the other buildings, with a yearly salary of $2,500 and $500 for clerical work. The amounts were charged off alternately to the three buildings and the city jail, which Mills was also supervising at the time. Mills complained in 1836 that his salary was $200 less than that of his predecessors and was allowed to take on other public projects for additional pay. While serving as architect, he accepted many outside assignments, including designs for federal marine hospitals, the design and superintendence of the Alexandria Courthouse (1838–39), Alexandria, Virginia, for $300, and a library (1839–41) at the U.S. Military Academy, West Point, New York, for $50. His pay for such work was often challenged and delayed by officials unclear about the intended scope of his responsibilities. During this period, Mills's combined earnings were probably at a career peak. A decade later he received an annual federal salary of $1,600 for extending the Patent Office and $300 annually from the Washington National Monument Society for supervising that project. Even with other freelance assignments, his income then probably fell somewhat below his 1840 level. If Mills's career is a guide, architectural practice in antebellum Washington offered neither financial security nor upward mobility.[79]

Organization and Duties

When supervising construction of the Patent Office and Treasury Building in the 1830s, Mills employed a clerk, J.B. Rooker, who apparently assisted with drawing and witnessing contracts and other office assignments and was paid from both the Patent Office and Treasury construction accounts. In 1839, while working on the Post Office, Mills hired his nephew Robert M. Lusher, who had held drafting assignments in the Land Office earlier in the decade. Lusher turned over his monthly clerkship allotment to Mills, permitting Mills to be paid in effect at the rate of $3,000 per year. In addition to the clerical staff, Mills formed a supervisory team covering work on both buildings. The structure included a general superintendent, Robert Brown, who directed separate foremen at each building for stonecutters, bricklayers and stonemasons, carpenters, and laborers.[80]

The duties of chief staff members were outlined in an 1838 report by the commissioner of public buildings. Mills's responsibilities were "to make out full sets of plans and sections" and other necessary drawings and "to make estimates of all the materials . . . and to see that his plans are faithfully executed." Brown was to execute Mills's plans; specify, inspect, measure, and certify stone deliveries; see to all hauling, including "erection of all kinds of Machinery" for moving and raising stone; and "see that every man does his duty."[81] Brown also traveled to Baltimore, Philadelphia, and New York to hire masons and to Baltimore and Fredericksburg to look at stone. The foremen certified contractor deliveries of materials in their trades, kept the payroll, and kept their workers supplied with necessary materials. This structure gave Mills control but distributed authority through Brown into both projects, and it permitted resources to be shifted from one building to another.

The organization of the mid-1830s reflected a system whereby the government contracted separately for materials and labor and combined them on the job. As labor was paid by the day, Mills found it impossible to force completion within a predictable schedule and cost. Beginning with the construction of the Post Office in 1839, this system was changed to one based on fixed contracts for delivered work and materials. For the Patent Office extension in 1849, Mills issued specifications for each element of work. He indicated the dimensions, quantity, and quality required for stonework, carpentry, plastering, and other services and formed contracts for execution by the commissioner of public buildings for work and materials delivered by contractors from each trade. Payments were based on measurement of acceptable completed work.[82]

These changes influenced the organization of staff for the Patent Office extension in 1849, which consisted of Mills as superintendent, assisted by an inspector and measurer, an overseer of laborers, and a master bricklayer. The load of contracting, inspection, and payment duties created administrative burdens for Mills and the commissioner of public buildings and raised new questions about official roles. These concerns were reflected in an Interior Department report, written about 1850, which outlined the positions and responsibilities for the Patent Office and recommended an officer of the Corps of Topographical Engineers to superintend the building. It then suggested separating "links in the chain" of employees and assuring that "the person to certify amounts should not pay them." Further evidence of uncertainty concerning the appropriate structure and systems for administering the Patent Office extension was evident in Commissioner Mudd's request in 1849 to have clarified whether Mills could declare contracts and employ tradesmen on his own, especially since Mudd was to be in charge of disbursements. While Mills and Mudd seem to have had a productive relationship, Mudd's successor, as noted, dismissed Mills's assistants and challenged every aspect of Mills's authority. In this era, administrative structures and relationships could shift with the wind.[83]

Mills was extremely pressed during the summer of 1849. Aside from preparing the tabular statements of bids, he had made arrangements for city water to be brought to the work site, recommended the relocation of government greenhouses behind the building to a new location on the mall near the

Below and overleaf:
Figure 4.15
Elevation and working drawing, east wing of the Patent Office, c. 1849–50, showing Mills's enlargement of basement windows to help light offices and his adjustment of the pilaster bays to reduce the north end of the wing by three feet.
(Prints and Drawings Collection of The Octagon Museum, The American Architectural Foundation of The American Institute of Architects)

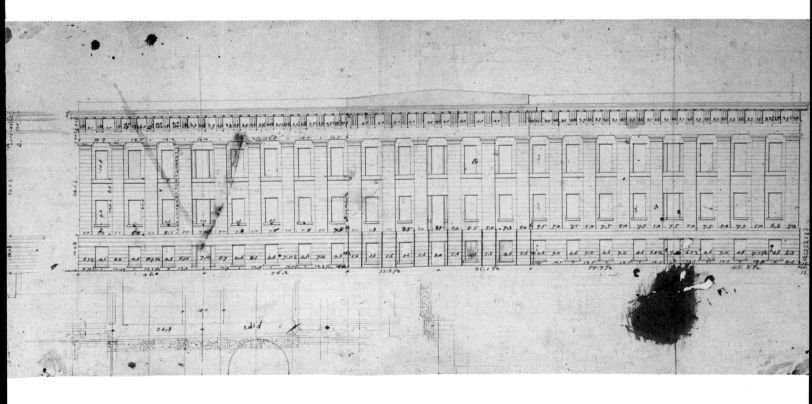

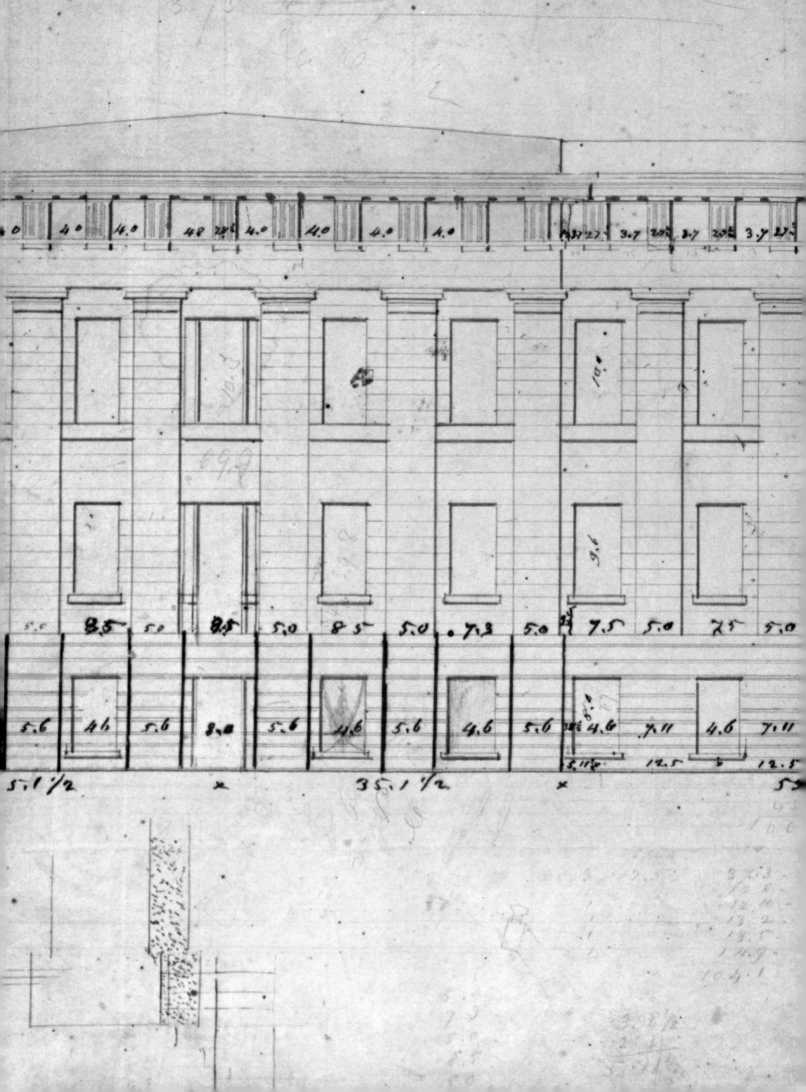

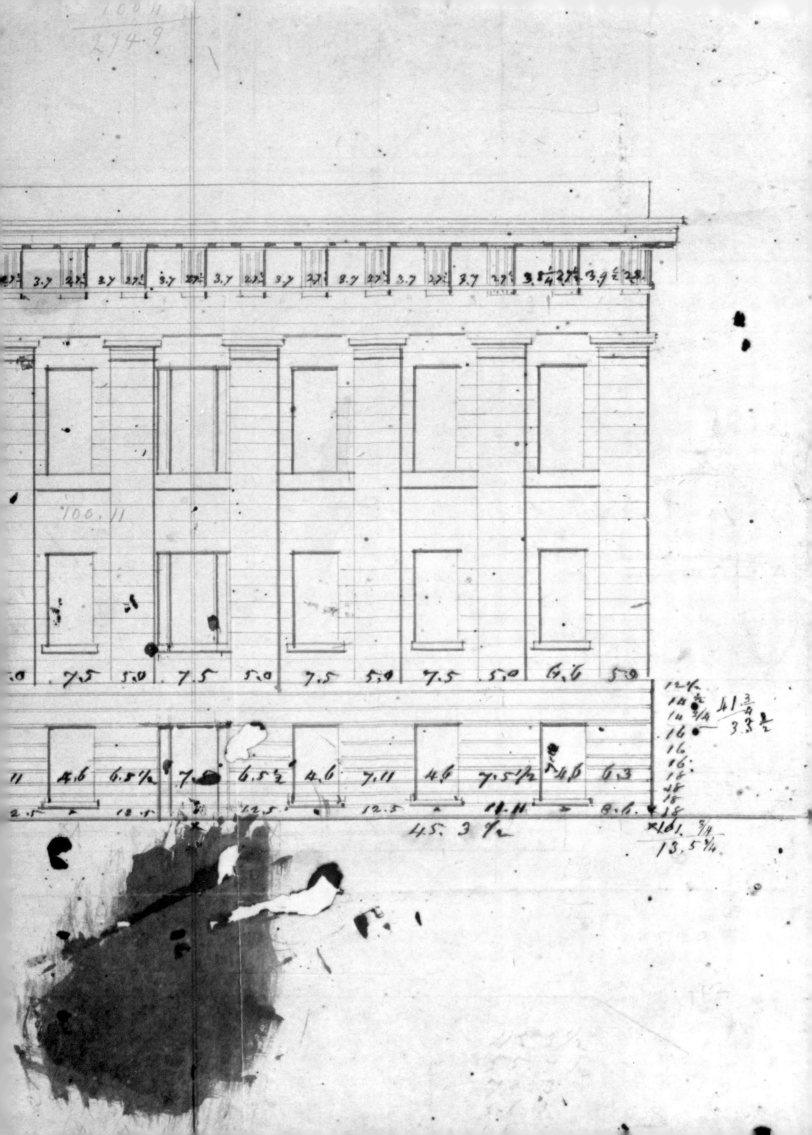

Capitol, accommodated new design needs of the secretary of the interior, and supervised foundation work, hurrying to make maximum use of the summer construction season. In late July he asked unsuccessfully for a clerk for "a brief period." He argued that he had to give time simultaneously "to outdoor operations" while the east wing "has had to be studied anew, in all its details." It required his constant effort "to put the ground plan in order, to secure correctness above," and he needed to complete all the drawings "with as little delay as possible." It seems apparent that Mills had a highly personalized operation with little supporting staff.[84]

It was probably at this time that Mills executed the only known surviving elevation of the Patent Office credited to him, a working drawing that reflects his solutions to two particular problems (fig. 4.15). First, he had to shorten the intervals between the pilasters on the north end of the wing, in order to allow steps of the north portico similar to those on the south. A letter and diagram (fig. 4.16) that Mills furnished the secretary of the interior nearly three years later showed a deficiency of three feet on the north side and gave Mills's reasons for the changes: "If this arrangement had not been made, we should have had to *abandon the Northern Portico*; the question was where the sacrifice was to be made?—I regarded the Wings as inferior, and the Main front as superior.—In *effect* the building has not suffered, by this arrangement." He gained the needed distance over the span of several bays to minimize the visual impact. The second issue was to lengthen the basement windows to provide more light for office spaces, in contrast to the squarish windows for rooms on the same level in the original wing used for storage. His approach was to drop the sills, keeping the upper line of the windows uniform with that of the original wing. The change is evident on the drawing. Mills was criticized by Elliot and *Scientific American* for the lack of correspondence between the windows, although he was responding to his client's changed requirements. Thomas U. Walter, when he replaced Mills in 1851, adjusted the basement windows on the south wing to suit.[85]

Networks and Communications

Mills actively promoted his views and positioned himself to receive timely word of new projects. From 1830 to his death in 1855, he was one of the most regular attendees of the monthly meetings of the Columbian Institute and its successor after 1840, the National Institute for the Promotion of Science. He was frequently one of only a half dozen or so present, often, surprisingly, along with William P. Elliot or William Easby, even at the time Easby was attacking him. Through this organization of local civic, media, and scientific leaders and fed-

eral officials, Mills could learn of new developments and present his ideas. Here he could offer reports on tests of building stones and the city's need for waterworks. He also published frequently —guides to federal offices in 1841, 1847–48, and 1854; regular articles in the local papers; separate publications on waterworks; a variety of memorials, or petitions, to Congress on national projects; and a steady rain of proposals and reports concerning federal and local construction needs and activities. He promoted his interests through his family and state networks, from initial associations with the Charles Nourse family to ties with South Carolinians from John C. Calhoun to Joel R. Poinsett. And he used associations from past projects to inform new work, as when he sought information on pay and materials from Philadelphia architect William Strickland and Baltimore contractor William Steuart as he began work on the Patent Office and Treasury Building in 1837.[86]

Mills relied on his allies when under duress as well as when seeking new work. During the 1838 investigation he wrote Hugh Legare, South Carolina congressman, bemoaning Legare's departure from the Committee on Public Buildings, declaring that now its members were "all strangers to me" and explaining his attempts to educate them, describing his views on retaining the Treasury Building, voicing his concern for protecting his professional standing, and expressing his hope that Legare would support him before the full House. Mills likewise solicited the aid of Jefferson Davis fifteen years later when his reputation and career were again questioned. His approach was always to state the facts of the case, provide a solution or options, and offer his professional judgment.[87]

Frequently at odds with Mills and his allies, however, were the local builders and suppliers competing, often contentiously, for public projects in which Mills participated. Congress found in 1841 that because the Treasury and the Patent Office were constructed on a "day's work" basis, costs were difficult to control and the architect, in the absence of a fixed contract, was often thrown into conflict with builders.[88] But conflicts continued, even after the fixed-contract system was introduced. It was probably inevitable that over a twenty-year period animosities would develop toward Mills and that each turnover of administration would provide new cause for appeal of old grievances. By insisting on high standards of materials, workmanship, and design and compliance to client needs, schedules, and budgets, Mills became a lightning rod, especially in the absence of supporting offices and systems. The environment included hungry contractors, economic fluctuations, congressional indecision over materials, construction methods, and funding, and a shifting array of politi-

Figure 4.16 Diagram plan of the Patent Office, 1853, indicating a deficiency of three feet for the north portico, which had to be gained by reducing the length of the east and west wings. (Records of the Department of the Interior, copies of letters sent to Commissioner of Public Buildings and Grounds, 1849–63, Record Group 48, National Archives)

cians, bureaucrats, and client requirements. Given these conditions, it is not surprising that Mills ran into controversy.

What is surprising is that Mills managed to survive as long and as productively as he did, all the while continuing to educate others by example and persuasion in the need for high professional standards and practices in public architecture. He believed that "the character of a nation is judged by the character of its public buildings." The goals of his Washington years were to use his professional talents to shape federal architecture and the "National Metropolis," as he sometimes referred to the capital city. He achieved these goals while providing stability and continuity in the development of federal projects during a period of rapid change and evolving systems of professional architectural practice.[89]

THE LEGACY OF MILLS'S YEARS IN WASHINGTON

Mills's Washington years left several legacies. Both his customs houses and marine hospitals outside the city and his federal and civic buildings in Washington set a standard in his time for fireproof masonry public architecture. His effort to design and monitor outlying federal projects from Washington anticipated the establishment in the 1850s of the office of the supervising architect of the Treasury. Mills provided models for rapidly erecting large,

durable office buildings, dealing with issues of economical arrangement of space, timely construction, light and ventilation, and coordination with suppliers, labor, and clients. His office and exhibition spaces still serve effectively. Mills argued for managing buildings by fixed contracts, paying for stone based on measurement, allowing architects "discretion . . . to select first-rate mechanics," and not requiring them to take the lowest bids at the risk of poor performance.[90] Although the controversies stand out, Mills believed in constructive relationships with contractors, labor, suppliers, and public officials. He was quick to credit them in his annual reports, and he sought fair treatment for contractors and workmen alike on many occasions when funding fluctuations or administrative caprice struck adversely. William Noland, commissioner of public buildings during the initial construction of the Patent Office and Treasury, told Congress that "there have never been public buildings of the same magnitude erected in this city with so much system and order, and with less confusion; and the superintendents . . . all declare that there has been scarcely an instance of angry strife or personal quarrel amongst them and the workman" and relatively "few complaints . . . where there were so many men employed, and of different nations."[91]

Mills's legacy reached beyond his buildings. In a highly visible and challenging role, he set an example for the professional practice of architecture in America. His contribution extended beyond his design and construction preferences to a concern for high standards of performance, quality materials, sound administrative systems, and a tasteful and economical architecture suitable to the nation. He educated a generation of politicians, administrators, and other clients in the qualities required for dignified and lasting federal architecture and demonstrated these qualities from New England to New Orleans. His involvement with the Patent Office shows the challenges of directing federal building projects in antebellum Washington. Given those challenges, Mills provided a model of professional conduct and accomplishment for his age and ours.

1. Robert Mills to John C. Calhoun, c. October 1826, in *Some Letters of Robert Mills* (Columbia, South Carolina: The Historical Commission of South Carolina, 1938), 6.

2. Mills to Charles Nourse, March 31, 1827, in *Some Letters*, 9. Congress's slow response to President Adams's request for increased public works projects is detailed in George Dangerfield's *The Awakening of American Nationalism, 1815–1828* (New York: Harper and Row, 1965), 238. Charles Nourse was Mrs. Mills's cousin; his father was register of the Treasury Department.

3. For Mills's appointment in 1814 and longstanding relationship with Baltimore's Washington Monument, see H.M. Pierce Gallagher, *Robert Mills, Architect of the Washington Monument, 1781–1855* (New York: Columbia University Press, 1935), 107-10. Mills to John C. Calhoun, May 5, 1827; Mills to General Macomb, November 8, 1827; Mills to Andrew Jackson, August 15, 1829; in *Some Letters*, 10, 11, 14, respectively.

4. For Eliza's preparations, see Eliza Mills to Robert Mills, February 6 and 13 and May 10, 1830, *Papers of Robert Mills*, South Carolina Historical Society. For prospects in Baltimore and Washington, see Robert Mills to Robert Gilmor, January 4, 1830, Washington Monument Papers, Maryland Historical Society; Robert Mills to Eliza Mills, January 17, 1830, *Papers of Robert Mills*, South Carolina Historical Society; Robert Mills to Eliza Mills, February 19–21, 1830, Robert Mills Family Papers, Archives of American Art, Smithsonian Institution.

5. Glenn Brown, *History of the United States Capitol* (Washington, D.C.: Government Printing Office, 1900), 61. Mills to the Committee on Public Buildings, February 4, 1832, in George C. Hazelton, Jr., *The National Capitol: Its Architecture and History* (New York: J.F. Taylor and Company, 1897), 282-83. Mills's letter indicates he had offered advice on the Capitol's acoustics in 1821 and 1827 but that Bulfinch had opposed his ideas.

6. Mills to Gulian C. Verplanck, March 15, 1830, Verplanck Papers, Box 10, no. 81, New York Historical Society.

7. Committee on the Public Buildings, *A Bill Making Appropriations for the Public Buildings, etc.*, H.Rept. 407, April 5,1830, File no. 11–517–217, *Papers of Robert Mills*, South Carolina Historical Society.

8. Mills to Robert Gilmor, June 3, 1830, Washington Monument Papers, Maryland Historical Society.

9. Allen C. Clark, "The Trollopes," *Records of the Columbia Historical Society*, 37–38 (1937): 85. For Baltimore's early development see George W. Howard, *The Monumental City* (Baltimore: J. D. Ehlers and Company, 1873), 22–23. For the early development of Washington see Frederick Gutheim, *Worthy of the Nation: The History of Planning for the Nation's Capitol* (Washington, D.C.: Smithsonian Institution Press, 1978), 11–59.

10. Mills, "Statement," October 11, 1830, Papers of Robert Mills, Manuscript Division, Library of Congress. Mills, October 9, 1830 (draft), *Papers of Robert Mills*, South Carolina Historical Society. Mills to Walter Lowrie, December 10, 1830, Office of the First Auditor, Misc. Treasury Accounts, no. 60316, Record Group 217, National Archives. Mills, September 9, 1830, ibid., no. 58158. Mills to Robert Gilmor, November 25, 1830, Washington Monument Papers, Maryland Historical Society. Asbury Dickins to Mills, November 1, 1830, *Papers of Robert Mills*, South Carolina Historical Society.

11. Select Committee on the Patent Office, Congressional Document, March 1, 1827, in House Committee Records, Select Committee on the Patent Office, HR19A, D23.13, Record Group 233, National Archives.

12. Andrew Jackson, *Presidential message . . . for the accommodation of the Patent Office*, April 4, 1832, H.Doc. 195. Leonard Jarvis, draft report, House Committee Records, Committee on Public Buildings and Grounds, 22nd Cong., 1st sess., 1832, Record Group 233, National Archives.

13. Jane B. Davies, "A. J. Davis' Projects for a Patent Office Building, 1832–1834," *Journal of the Society of Architectural Historians* 24 (October 1965): 231, 237, 234. Mills to Gulian C. Verplanck, March 27, 1832, Verplanck Papers, Box 10, no. 74, New York Historical Society.

14. Elliot's career and papers available to family friend Robert W. Fenwick are presented in Fenwick's "Old and New Patent Office" in *Patent Centennial Celebration, Washington, D.C. 1891, Proceedings and Addresses* (Washington, 1892), 453–71. For study with Hadfield see *Daily National Intelligencer*, February 20, 1835; Hadfield's friendship with William Elliot is mentioned in John Walker, "The High Art of George Hadfield," *American Heritage* 37 (August-September 1986): 81. For other sources on the Elliots and an account of Mills's competition with Town and Elliot for the Patent Office see Louise Hall, "The Design of the Old Patent Office," *Journal of the Society of Architectural Historians* 15 (March 1956): 27–30. The William Thornton Papers project has also prepared biographical materials on the Elliots. Elliot's obituary was published in the *Daily National Intelligencer* on November 6, 1854. Although Elliot advertised architectural services, there is little evidence of any appreciable architectural practice. No drawings signed by Elliot have been found, although he was paid $300 for the Patent Office design. The Navy paid him $20 for a plan for barracks in October 1836, and he appears to have redecorated a theater that he offered for lease in November 1836 (H.Doc. 458, June 1838). He was paid $5.00 for "making elevation to President's Stable" in 1834 (No. 66377, Record Group 217, National Archives). These were random assignments. His principal occupation was as deputy city surveyor from 1834 to 1838 and surveyor from 1838 to 1845, succeeding his father, with increased activity as a patent agent beginning in the mid-1830s; see note 52.

15. Additional materials concerning the Elliots and the Patent Office in their period are held in the Federico Patent Office Papers, Archives Center, National Museum of American History, Smithsonian Institution. The vocal opposition of various Elliots to Jackson's election probably doomed William's chances of survival at the Patent Office. See excerpts from *U.S. Telegraph*, April 9 and 11, 1829, and *National Journal*, April 11, 1829, in the "William and William Parker Elliot Notebook," Federico Papers. For William Elliot's departure see William Elliot to Martin Van Buren, March 30 and May 11, 1829, "Thomas P. Jones Notebook," ibid. For William Parker Elliot's tenure see William P. Elliot to Louis McLane, June 26 and December 11, 1833, Patent Office Letterbook, Letters Received, Federico Papers; William P. Elliot to Louis McLane, December 16, 1833, "Conduct Notebook," ibid.; William P. Elliot, advertisement as patent agent, *Daily National Intelligencer*, January 22, 1834.

16. Mills mentions training northern mechanics in *New Treasury and Post Office Buildings*, March 29, 1838, H.Rept. 737, 23.

17. Davies, "A. J. Davis' Projects," 243. John Craig to William Noland, April 5, 1834, Letters Sent, Record Group 42, National Archives.

18. Mills to William Noland, April 9, 1834, House Committee Papers, Select Committee on Patents and Patent Law, HR 23A-D23.1, Record Group 233, National Archives.

19. Mills to William Noland, April 15, 1834, ibid. Mills to William Noland, April 15, 1834, Letters Received, no. 2825, Commissioner of Public Buildings, Office of Public Buildings and Grounds, Record Group 42, National Archives. Mills's preference for solid masonry rather than iron construction for fireproof buildings is detailed in Louise Hall's "Mills, Strickland, and Walter: Their Adventures in a World of Science," *Magazine of Art* 40 (November 1947): 266–71.

20. Mills to William Noland, April 9, 1834, op. cit.

21. Jane B. Davies, "Six Letters by William P. Elliot to Alexander J. Davis, 1834–1838," *Journal of the Society of Architectural Historians* 26 (March 1967): 71, 72.

22. Henry Ellsworth to John Forsyth, September 29, 1835, Patent Office Letterbook, 236, Federico Papers, op. cit. Robert E. Riegel, *Young America 1830–1840* (Norman: University of Oklahoma Press, 1949), 49.

23. Select Committee on the Patent Office, S.Rept. 338, April 28, 1836, 7, 8.

24. Ibid.

25. Mills to Andrew Jackson, July 4, 1836, Notable Employees of the Treasury Department, File no. 1809, Record Group 56, National Archives.

26. Leonard Jarvis to Andrew Jackson, July 4, 1836, ibid. Andrew Jackson's Appointment Statement, July 4, 1836, *Patent*

Centennial Celebration, 461.

27. Jackson's Appointment Statement, ibid.

28. Mills to Martin Van Buren, March 27, 1837, Martin Van Buren Papers, Library of Congress. Mills to Andrew Jackson, August 3, 1836, Andrew Jackson Papers, Library of Congress. Commissioner of Public Buildings, *Annual Report*, December 7, 1836, S.Doc. 10. Mills to Van Buren, March 27, 1837.

29. Davies, "Six Letters," 73. *Daily National Intelligencer*, December 13, 1836.

30. J. N. L. Durand's *Precis des Lecons d'Architecture* (Paris, 1802–9) provided numerous designs for modularly constructed vaulted public building types, including halls, galleries, and museums.

31. Commissioner of Public Buildings, *Annual Report*, December 15, 1837, H.Doc. 28. Louise Hall describes Mills's construction techniques in "Mills, Strickland . . ." (n. 19) and points out that Mills's masonry vaults in the Patent Office survived a fire in 1877 that destroyed later iron and brick ceilings.

32. Mills to Levi Lincoln, January 4, 1838, House of Representatives, Committee Papers, Committee on Public Buildings and Grounds, HR 25A-D20.1, Record Group 233, National Archives. Davies, "Six Letters," 73.

33. Committee on Public Buildings and Grounds, *New Treasury and Post Office Buildings*, March 29, 1838, H.Rept. 737, 16–17.

34. Ibid., 19–27.

35. Ibid., 33.

36. Ibid., 27–28.

37. Ibid., 10.

38. Levi Lincoln to the President of the United States, April 17, 1838, Records of the Office of Public Buildings and Grounds, Commissioner of Public Buildings and Grounds, General Correspondence, Letters Received, Record Group 42, National Archives. Commissioner of Public Buildings and Grounds, April 17, 1838, Letters Sent 8, 151, Record Group 42, National Archives. William H. Pierson, Jr., in *American Buildings and Their Architects*, 1 (New York: Anchor Books, Doubleday, 1976), 404–17, discusses at length Mills's work on the Treasury Building and the investigation of that building.

39. Martin Van Buren to Levi Woodbury, John Forsyth, and Joel R. Poinsett, April 23, 1838, Records of the Office of Public Buildings and Grounds, Board of Commissioners of Public Buildings and Grounds Proceedings, Record Group 42, National Archives. Mills to William Noland, April 28, 1838, Records of the Office of Public Buildings and Grounds, Commissioner of Public Buildings and Grounds, Letters Received, no. 2924, Record Group 42, National Archives.

40. Mills, *Memorial*, May 10, 1842, H.Rept. 460, 4–5. Robert Dale Owen, one of the period's foremost architectural critics and a Mills ally, blamed interfering "Building Committees" for the introduction of a nonfunctioning column screen that distorted the grand central court of the upper floor, urging them either to learn architecture or "have discretion enough to leave its details to those who have studied them" (*Hints on Public Architecture* [New York: G. P. Putnam, 1849], 14).

41. Commissioner of the Public Buildings, *Annual Report*, December 30, 1839, H.Doc. 32, 6–7. Mills, *Guide to the National Executive Offices and the Capitol of the United States* (Washington, D.C., 1841), 30–32.

42. Committee on Public Buildings and Grounds, *Annual Report for 1849*, January 21, 1850, H.Rept. 30, 12. Mills's work on the Post Office is detailed by Denys Peter Myers in "Historic Report of the General Post Office Building," prepared in 1980 for the General Services Administration, Washington, D.C. Copies are available at the Robert Mills Papers and the Office of Architectural History and Historic Preservation at the Smithsonian Institution. A forthcoming article by Pamela Scott, based on her lecture "Robert Mills's Washington," delivered at the Annual Meeting of the Society of Architectural Historians (Washington, D.C., 1987), discusses Mills's iconographic intentions in his Washington buildings, including the Patent Office, Post Office, Treasury Building, and Washington Monument.

43. President of the United States, *Message . . . into the condition of the Public Buildings . . .* , September 11, 1841, S.Doc. 123, 22–23. The National Institute wished to gain the half-million dollar bequest to found the Smithsonian Institution, then being debated by Congress, for use as a national museum. Led by Joel R. Poinsett, secretary of war, the members had several shiploads of collections from the United States Exploring Expedition to the Pacific placed in the Patent Commissioner's "National Gallery" to demonstrate their cause, creating pressures by 1842 to extend the building. Mills to Joel R. Poinsett, June 22, 1842, Poinsett Papers, vol. 16, folder 13, Historical Society of Pennsylvania. Mills had frequent contact with fellow South Carolinian Poinsett in relation to War Department projects and interests of the National Institute. When the Whigs succeeded the Democrats and Poinsett left Washington in 1841, both the Institute and Mills lost an effective ally.

44. Committee of Public Buildings and Grounds, *National Edifices at Washington*, February 25, 1845, H.Rept. 185, 8.

45. Commissioner of Patents, *Annual Report*, February 24, 1846, H.Doc. 140, 24.

46. Reverdy Johnson to D. G. Goddard, April 19, 1849, Opinions of Attorney General Concerning Public Buildings in the District of Columbia, 1849, Record Group 48, National Archives.

47. Mills, "Description and Specification," April 20, 1849, Construction of the Patent Office Building, 1849–75, Record Group 48, National Archives.

48. Mills to Thomas Ewing, September 22, 1849, ibid.

49. Thomas Ewing to D. S. Dickinson, April 2, 1850, Letters Sent, Patents, vol. 1, 1850, Record Group 48, National Archives.

50. *Congressional Globe*, April 12, 1850, 725–30.

51. William P. Elliot to A. H. H. Stuart, September 11, 1850, Letters Sent to Committee on Public Buildings and Grounds, 1849–63, Record Group 48, National Archives.

52. Elliot advertised in the 1850 *Washington City Directory* (p. 197) that his patent agency opposite the Patent Office could secure United States and foreign patents and have "models, drawings, specifications, &c. prepared from sketches and descriptions" sent to Elliot. He cited "more than twenty years" experience "in and out of the Patent Office." Patent statistics are from Commissioner of Patents, *Annual Report*, January 1, 1851, Ex.Doc. 32, 353.

53. Mills to D. G. Goddard, September 11, 1850, Letters Sent, Committee on Public Buildings and Grounds, 1849–63, no. 262, Box 2, Record Group 48, National Archives.

54. Thomas U. Walter reported that when he took over from Mills on July 29, 1851, the exterior walls had been erected to the cornice line and "about one third of the arching in the upper story was completed. . . ." By December 1851 Walter had completed the exterior walls, set "the double piers for supporting the remaining arches of the upper story," and finished the arching. See Millard Fillmore, *Report of the Architect for the Extension of the Capitol . . .* , February 11, 1852, S.Doc. 33, 9.

55. William Archer to A. H. H. Stuart, January 14, 1851, Commissioner of Public Buildings and Grounds, Letters Received, no. 3152, Record Group 42, National Archives. William Archer to A. H. H. Stuart, February 21, 1851, Secretary of Interior, Misc. Div., Patent Office Building, Robert Mills Architect, File 84, Record Group 48, National Archives. William Archer to William Easby, March 26, 1851, Office of Public Buildings and Grounds, Commissioner of Public Buildings and Grounds, Letters Received, no. 3170, Record Group 42, National Archives.

56. Mills to I. W. Mudd, January 31, 1851, Office of Public Buildings and Grounds, Commissioner of Public Buildings and Grounds, Letters Received, no. 3154, Record Group 42, National Archives.

57. Ibid.

58. *Scientific American* 6 (February 1, 1851): 156.

59. William Easby to William P. Elliot, John C. Harkness, and William W. Birth, April 1, 1851, Commissioner of Public Buildings and Grounds, 1849–63, Letters Received, Record Group 48, National Archives.

60. Mills to A. H. H. Stuart, April 7, 1851; Mills to William Easby, April 7, 1851; William Easby to Mills, April 7, 1851; all in Construction of the Patent Office Building, 1849–75, Record Group 48, National Archives.

61. Mills to A. H. H. Stuart, April 7, 1851, Construction of the Patent Office Building, 1849–75, Record Group 48, National

Archives.

62. *Scientific American* 6 (May 3, 1851): 261.

63. Wilhelmine M. Easby, "Personal Recollections of Early Washington and a Sketch of the Life of Captain William Easby," June 4, 1913, Columbia Historical Society. Thomas Carbery to P. R. Fendall, Peter Force, Walter Lenox, etc., August 10, 1848, Washington National Monument Papers, William R. Perkins Library, Duke University. William Easby to Millard Fillmore, December 3, 1849, Millard Fillmore Papers, Library of Congress.

64. William Easby to A. H. H. Stuart, May 24, 1851, Construction of the Patent Office Building, 1849–75, Record Group 48, National Archives. Mills to William Easby, May 24, 1851, Office of Public Buildings and Grounds, Commissioner of Public Buildings and Grounds, Letters Received, no. 3189, Record Group 42, National Archives. William Easby to Mills, May 26 and June 5, 1851, Construction of the Patent Office Building, 1849–75, Record Group 48, National Archives.

65. Mills to A. H. H. Stuart, "Report on CPB Recommendation to Take Down the Walls of the East Wing of the Patent Office, etc.," late 1851, Miscellaneous Division, Patent Office Building, Robert Mills, Architect, 1849–53, file no. 84, Record Group 48, National Archives. Mills to R. M. T. Hunter, December 12, 1851, accession no. 25064, Virginia State Library.

66. A. H. H. Stuart to Mills, July 29, 1851, Office of Public Buildings and Grounds, Commissioner of Public Buildings and Grounds, Letters Received, no. 3207, Record Group 42, National Archives. Mills to A. H. H. Stuart, July 30, 1851, Letters Sent to Committee on Public Buildings and Grounds, 1849–63, Record Group 48, National Archives.

67. Ibid. Mills to Millard Fillmore, August 4, 1851, Letters Sent to Commissioner of Public Buildings and Grounds, 1849–63, Record Group 48, National Archives.

68. Mills to R. M. T. Hunter, December 12, 1851, and Mills to the Senate and the House of Representatives, December 16, 1851, House Committee Papers, Committee on Public Buildings and Grounds, Various Subjects, HR32A-G18.3, Record Group 233, National Archives.

69. Mills, "Synopsis of Charges . . . ," September 10, 1852, Letters Sent to Commissioner of Public Buildings and Grounds, 1849–63. Mills to A. H. H. Stuart, July 20, 1851, Construction of the Patent Office Building, 1849–75, Record Group 48, National Archives.

70. Ibid. Mills to Millard Fillmore, October 15, 1852, Letters Sent to Commissioner of Public Buildings and Grounds, 1849–63, Record Group 48, National Archives.

71. Mills to Jefferson Davis, May 21, 1853, Jefferson Davis Papers, Transylvania University.

72. *Daily National Intelligencer*, May 9, 1842; Elliot's position was sustained by family friends after his death (see note 15).

73. Davies, "A. J. Davis' Projects," 247.

74. Mills, *Scientific American* 7 (October 18, 1851): 38.

75. Mills, *Guide to the Capitol and the National Executive Offices of the United States* (Washington, D.C.: Wm. Greer, Printer, 1847–48), 68. The use of twenty-nine stars probably reflects the entry of Iowa into the Union as the twenty-ninth state in 1846.

76. *Scientific American* 6 (February 1, 1851): 156.

77. Mills, *Guide*, 68.

78. Mills, *Scientific American* 7 (August 23, 1851): 387.

79. John Tyler, *Reports of Commissioners appointed to inquire into the condition of the Public Buildings . . .* , September 11, 1841, S.Doc. 123, 5, 38. Mills to Committee on Public Buildings, March 6, 1838, House Committee Papers, Committee on Public Buildings and Grounds, Various Subjects, HR 25-D20.4, Record Group 233, National Archives. Mills to Andrew Jackson, August 8, 1836, Andrew Jackson Papers, Library of Congress. House of Representatives, *Architectural Plans and Drawings Since 1836*, July 7, 1838, H.Doc. 458.

80. Board of Commissioners of Public Buildings, May 15, 1839, Office of Public Buildings and Grounds, Board of Commissioners of Public Buildings Proceedings, Record Group 42, National Archives. William Noland, January 1, 1837, Abstracts of Expenditures for Patent Office, Treasury, General Accounting Office, First Auditor, Miscellaneous Treasury Accounts, nos. 71532, 71531, Record Group 217, National Archives. Mills,

June 1, 1839, Invoice and Receipt, no. 77474, ibid.

81. William Noland to John Forsyth, Levi Woodbury, and Joel R. Poinsett, May 1, 1838, Office of Public Buildings and Grounds, Commissioner of Public Buildings and Grounds, Letters Sent, Record Group 42, National Archives. Brown to William Noland, April 27, 1838, Letters Received, no. 2925, ibid.

82. William Noland, October 18 and December 1, 1836, General Accounting Office, First Auditor, Miscellaneous Treasury Accounts, nos. 70925, 71275, Record Group 217, National Archives. Mills, *Memorial*, May 10, 1842, H.Rept. 460, 2. Mills to A. H. H. Stuart, September 3, 1851, Construction of Patent Office Building, 1849–75, Record Group 48, National Archives.

83. Department of Interior, "Officers, Contractors &c. Employed on Patent Office Building," c. 1850, Letters Sent to Commissioner of Public Buildings and Grounds, 1849–63, Record Group 48, National Archives. Ignatius Mudd to Thomas Ewing, May 28, 1849, Office of Public Buildings and Grounds, Letters Received, no. 3109, Record Group 42, National Archives.

84. Mills to Thomas Ewing, July 25, 1849, Construction of Patent Office Building, 1849–75, Record Group 48, National Archives.

85. Mills to A. H. H. Stuart, February 18, 1853, Miscellaneous Division, Patent Office Building, Robert Mills, Architect, 1849–53, File 84, Record Group 48, National Archives. Millard Fillmore, *Report of Architect for the Extension of the Capitol . . .* , February 11, 1852, S.Doc. 33, 9.

86. Columbian Institute members in the 1830s included William Seaton and Joseph Gales, publishers of the *Daily National Intelligencer*; Asbury Dickins, secretary of the Senate; District Judge William Cranch; M. H. C. Clarke, clerk of the House; John Calhoun; William Noland; and William Elliot. Participants in the National Institute in the 1840s included Poinsett, Smithsonian Secretary Joseph Henry, Peter Force, and key local officials. Many of the same officials (for example, Gales, Force, and Cranch) were active after 1833 in the Washington National Monument Society, which also employed Mills. "Minutes," Columbian Institute, February 4, 1833, Peter Force Papers, Series D, Item 24, Library of Congress. "Minutes," National Institute, June 3, 1850, Record Unit 7058, Box 11, Journals of Proceedings of Meetings, 3, Smithsonian Institution Archives. William Steuart to Mills, April 6, 1837, and William Strickland to Mills, same date, Martin Van Buren Papers, 286, Library of Congress.

87. Mills to Hugh S. Legare, March 27, 1838, South Carolina Library, University of South Carolina.

88. John Tyler, S.Doc. 123, 9.

89. Secretaries of War and Navy, *Additional Buildings for War and Navy Departments*, January 25, 1843, H.Doc. 85, 16.

90. Mills, *Memorial*, 7–9.

91. William Noland, "Letter in relation to the report of the Commissioner," April 20, 1842, 3.

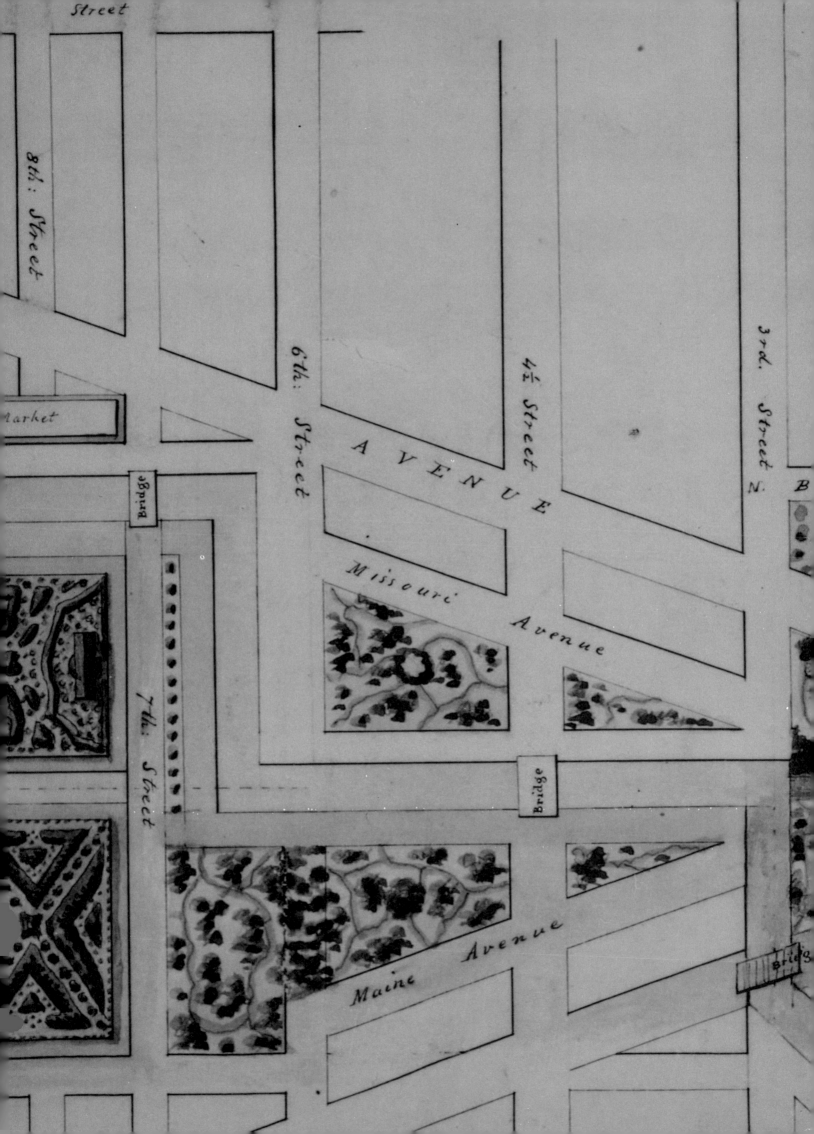

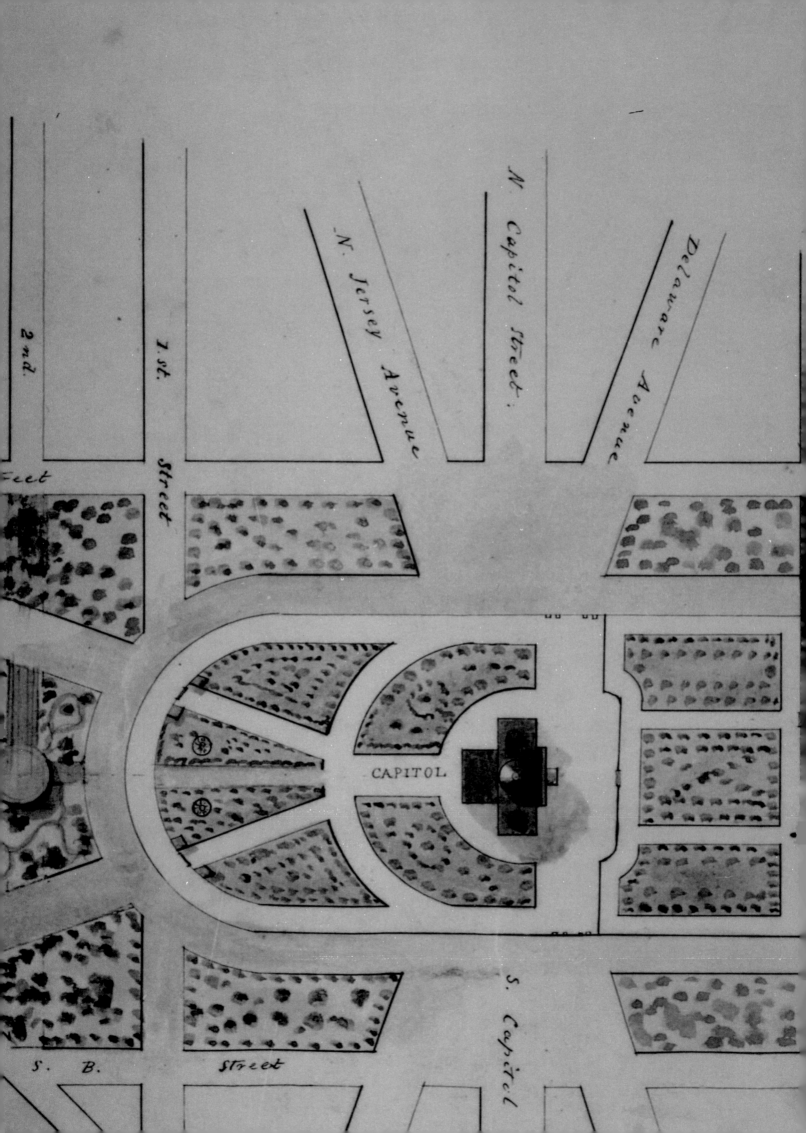

2nd.

1st. Street

N. Jersey Avenue

N. Capitol Street;

Delaware Avenue

Feet

CAPITOL

S. Capitol

S. B. Street

CHAPTER 5

ROBERT MILLS

AND AMERICAN MONUMENTS

Pamela Scott

ive days after the signing of the Declaration of Independence, on July 9, 1776, Joseph Wilton's lead statue of King George III, erected on Bowling Green in New York City only six years earlier, was toppled by an angry mob. The pedestal, however, was left standing, and in 1792 William Sullivan's wood statue of George Washington was raised on it. The Continental Congress (1774–89), recognizing the symbolic importance of monuments to promote national feeling, proposed numerous monuments to individual fallen heroes and battles. Benson Lossing, in his *Pictorial Field-Book of the Revolution* (1852), noted nineteen monuments actually built commemorating the Revolution, most of which were erected in the 1820s. Many were small and are little known today, but some were prominent, such as the Bunker Hill Monument (1825–43), in Charlestown, Massachusetts, the Baltimore Washington Monument (1813–42), and the Greene and Pulaski Monument (1829) in Savannah.[1]

The most important monument voted by the Continental Congress was an equestrian statue of George Washington proposed for the yet-to-be selected national capital. A resolution dated August 7, 1783, decreed that Washington be depicted in Roman dress with a laurel wreath on his head and a truncheon in his raised right hand. The bronze statue was to stand on a marble pedestal decorated with relief-sculpted tablets depicting four major events that Washington directed: the evacuation of Boston, the battles at Trenton and Princeton, and the surrender of Cornwallis at Yorktown. The use of

Roman dress, rather than Washington's uniform, was selected to convey timelessness, a metaphor to demonstrate that the "sitter's fame is beyond all strictures of time and circumstance, that it belongs to all ages and all countries." However, Washington was depicted wearing his uniform in all three statues commissioned of major European sculptors by state legislatures.[2]

The deification of Washington begun during the Revolution was intensified by his death on December 14, 1799, and was expressed by a proliferation of character sketches, engraved portraits, memorial objects, eulogies, and good intentions to erect monuments to his memory.[3] Congress immediately proposed to build a mausoleum to house his remains in the city of Washington, and both the English architect George Dance and Benjamin Henry Latrobe submitted pyramidal designs on a grand scale. The symbolism that Latrobe suggested was largely inherent in the form ("as durable as the Nation that erected it") and in the thirteen steps of its base.[4]

The first monument both proposed and carried out to commemorate the Revolution rather than its heroes was the Beacon Hill Memorial Column, suggested by its architect, Charles Bulfinch, in 1789. Built from 1790 to 1791, the 60-foot-tall brick and stone column stood on a rectangular base with inset, inscribed panels and was surmounted by an eagle atop a globe that served as a weather vane. Nearly contemporaneously the Italian sculptor Giuseppi Ceracchi sent to Congress drawings and a description of a monument to American liberty. An equestrian statue of Washington in antique armor standing on a rock 300 feet in circumference and 100 feet high was to be surrounded by four allegorical groups drawn from the Olympian pantheon. Mars represented republican government, Apollo the history of the states, and Minerva the arts and sciences, while the Triumph of America oversaw the arts, agriculture, and commerce. On his second trip to America in 1794, Ceracchi exhibited in Philadelphia a revised design in which the equestrian of Washington was replaced by a statue of liberty with nature, revolution, legislation, and the sciences and arts represented by allegorical figures. Both of these series of sculptural groups, emblematic more of the Revolution's values than of its events, employed an iconographical complexity that would have been incomprehensible to many Americans but also called for a broader conception of how to honor the American struggle for independence.[5] Unfortunately no image of either monument survives.

Famous victories were deemed as worthy of American monuments as the heroes who won them. On October 29, 1781, the Continental Congress voted for "a marble Column, adorned with emblems of the alliance" between the United States and France and "inscribed with a succinct narrative of the surrender of Earl Cornwallis," to be erected at the site of the victory in Yorktown, Virginia. In 1794 a columnar monument to Major General Joseph Warren and his compatriots who died defending Bunker Hill was erected on Breed's Hill in Charlestown, Massachusetts. The Lexington Monument, erected in 1799 on the site of the first battle of the Revolution, was a truncated granite obelisk raised on a high base, a type commonly used for both sepulchral and commemorative monuments in eighteenth-century Europe.[6] This nucleus of American monuments, both realized and promised, provided a foundation upon which later designers could legitimately draw. The struggle to create "American" monuments was a struggle to reconcile or adapt the architectural and symbolic vocabularies of European traditions to American circumstances and history.

Robert Mills was the designer of two of the monuments cited by Lossing—the Baltimore Washington Monument (1813–42) and the DeKalb Monument (1824–27) in Camden, South Carolina—and entered the competition for a third, the Bunker Hill Monument. In his lifetime Mills was probably the preeminent architect of monuments in America; six were built following his designs and he provided plans for at least a dozen more, including a national cemetery and a national mausoleum. Mills's earliest known monument was incorporated in his 1812 design for the Monumental Church in Richmond; his latest were unrealized designs for monuments to Thomas Jefferson in Charlottesville, Andrew Jackson in Washington, D.C., and George Washington in Charleston, done during the last three years of his life. Six of Mills's monuments were sepulchral in nature, the rest commemorative. Twelve were prompted by the revolutionary era, and five were monuments to George Washington.[7]

Monuments were for Mills a major form of both architectural and personal expression. He was born during the Revolution, and his avowed patriotism, like his religious fervor, although not uncommon among his contemporaries, provides a salient clue to his intense interest in public architecture. His oft-repeated, proud boast that he was America's first native-born architect and his interest in and knowledge of the history of the revolutionary era went hand in hand. When the "Essay on Architectural Monuments" was published in the April 1820 *Analectic Magazine*, Mills was justly famous as the architect of the Baltimore Washington Monument, planned to be the tallest memorial column in the world. Both his chief biographer, H. M. Pierce Gallagher, and Talbot F. Hamlin attributed the essay to Mills, partly because of Mills's preeminence as an American designer of monuments, partly because it is signed *M*, and partly because they saw in it knowledge and sentiments that they felt Mills possessed.[8] Mills's published works, both his books and short essays, belie these assumptions, as does his general correspondence, journals, and unpublished works. He may have had the scholarly knowledge of the history of ancient and modern monuments displayed in the essay, yet no literary remains of that knowledge have survived, and Mills's own designs indicate the repetition of set themes. The use of language in the essay is in no way similar to Mills's turns of phrase in any of his writings, which were pragmatic, often revealing a scientific bent of mind. His historical interest—amply seen, for instance, in his *Statistics of South Carolina*—was American history. Nowhere in the essay is America mentioned.

To attribute this essay to Mills is tempting because he brought such wide-ranging knowledge of historical monuments to his own work. Obelisks, columns, and sarcophagi were his favored formal prototypes. Although variations on these three typologies were common among other designers of monuments at the time, Mills's monuments were distinctly his own, marked by large (often huge) scale, eclecticism of architectural form and detail, and overt symbolic content. Early Mills scholars characterized his works as exemplifying the simplicity and purity of geometric form that they associated with the Greek Revival style in America. In actuality, Mills's designs for monuments were extremely elaborate, richly ornamented with emblematic and narrative sculpture. The severe geometric forms much admired in the twentieth century reflect modifications forced by the building process and economic realities.

THE MONUMENTAL CHURCH

A commemorative and sepulchral monument to the more than seventy victims of the Richmond Theatre fire of December 26, 1811, brought Mills into direct competition with his teacher and mentor Latrobe and caused their eventual estrangement. Both architects had offered designs to prominent Richmond citizens, as no formal competition was held. Latrobe's design was for a pyramid, and, as the victims were to be interred at the site of the conflagration, reviving his Washington mausoleum design was entirely appropriate. He felt that permanence was the most desirable attribute and that "plainness instead of sculpture and allegory" would best achieve this. Mills's suggestion that the monument take the form of a church was accepted by May 20, 1812.[9]

Six Doric columns adapted from the Temple of Apollo at Delos were set in antis on three sides of the porch, providing an unusually open setting for a tomb in the center (fig. 5.1). Mills replaced the triglyphs (rather than the metopes) of the frieze with lachrymatories. The entire form of the porch from its shallow pediment and acroteria and its low vaulted ceiling, similar to those in tomb chambers, took on the character of a Roman tomb. For the tomb Mills combined a Roman-inspired urn with a sarcophagic base that was a melding of Roman and Egyptian forms and decoration. The marble urn, decorated with wreaths, stars, ribbons, and a flame,

was sculpted by Antonio Capellano. The exaggeratedly battered walls of the sarcophagus curved into a cavetto cornice with winged orbs giving the whole a predominantly Egyptian character. The shallow pediments terminating the sarcophagus and the urn add some classical flavor.[10]

The Monumental Church is the earliest of Mills's major works to survive, and the building reflects a conscious reordering of the syntax of the historical language of architecture to create something new. Mills repeatedly asserted that his architectural designs were not imitative but innovative, and his thinking and designs can best be understood in the context of eclecticism, one strain of advanced neo-classicism that emerged as a strong current of thought in the mid-eighteenth century.

Although present as early as 1721 with the publication of Fischer von Erlach's *Entwurf einer historischen Architektur*, combinations of generalized characteristics of ancient forms having associated meaning became by mid-century a basis for renewing antiquity for modern usage. In 1753 the Comte de Caylus (1692–1765), in publishing a reconstruction of the Mausoleum of Halicarnassus, combined Greek and Egyptian features. He maintained that such historical eclecticism was appropriate for the cultural diversity existing in the time and place in which the mausoleum was built. Giovanni Battista Piranesi (1720–78) popularized eclectic mixtures of disparate forms in his numerous publications beginning with *Diverse Manière d'adornare i cammini* (1769). His etchings influenced the less doctrinaire among archaeologically

Figure 5.1
Sarcophagus tomb
on the porch of the
Monumental Church
(1812–17),
Richmond, Virginia.
(Pamela Scott)

inspired neoclassicists, who recognized the creative possibilities of the imaginative reconstruction of antiquity. Quatremère de Quincy (1755–1848), whose writings codified the theoretical basis for nineteenth-century eclecticism, defined invention as "finding new combinations of pre-existing elements."[11] Eclecticism was the leitmotif of Mills's monument designs, and he intended that their historically derived elements convey symbolic meaning appropriate for America.

THE BALTIMORE WASHINGTON MONUMENT

Of Mills's entire architectural output the best documented in terms of the evolution of his ideas and the strictures of reality is the Baltimore Washington Monument.[12] On January 6, 1810, the Maryland legislature authorized a lottery to raise funds for the monument in response to a citizen's petition circulated in December 1809.[13] After accumulating funds for three years, the board of managers of the Baltimore Washington Monument voted on February 15, 1813, to offer a premium of $500 for a design costing not more than $100,000 to construct. Two experienced, European-trained architects practicing in America, Maximilian Godefroy and Joseph Ramée, both entered designs for triumphal arches sheltering statues of Washington. Only three other entries survive, the winning design by Robert Mills and two by unknown architects.[14]

Mills's design for the monument went through four distinct phases, a process by which a very complex design and an equally complex iconographical program were gradually simplified. The first phase was marked by preliminary plans dating from November 1813; the second, by Mills's successful entry in the competition submitted on January 12, 1814, and selected on May 2; the third, by the design for which the cornerstone was laid on July 4, 1815; and the fourth, the period of construction lasting until 1842 when the cast-iron fence enclosing the base was completed. The major construction was completed by 1825, when the monument reached 165 feet 4 inches. In 1829 Mills superintended the raising of Enrico Causici's standing figure of Washington to the summit.

This evolutionary process resulted in a column closely resembling the Vendôme Column (1806–10) in Paris, designed by Denon, Gondouin, and Lepère, but which was ultimately derived from Trajan's Column in Rome. From initial design to final reality Mills's monument was columnar in nature, with a base and a statue of Washington, but the conventional, acceptable, and very beautiful monument that was built was more distinctly "European" than his earlier eclectic designs, which Mills perceived of as "American" (fig. 5.2).

Apparently Mills's drawings for six alternative preliminary designs done in 1813 have been lost, but a short essay by Mills described an octagonal column divided into four levels.[15] A brass equestrian statue of Washington dressed in his uniform and riding a horse "of a color and form that will represent his old charger," stood on top of the column. The base was substantial. The shaft was buttressed by half-columns 8 feet high and surrounded by a series of "white marble posts" 6 feet in height and "of diagonal form." Eight of these posts, placed at the angles produced by the octagonal shaft, were surmounted by partial caryatid figures "expressive of modesty & innocence"; Mills designated them "virgin posts." Entry to the monument's inner precinct was from all four cardinal directions through arched gateways, each bearing the arms of the United States. An outer precinct, a gravel walk 11 feet wide, was enclosed by a wood fence following the octagonal lines established by the base and monument. Each angle was marked by an ornamental shade tree.

For the column shaft Mills planned a series of thirty-two relief panels depicting "an emblematical history of Washington's public life." In addition to conceiving of the entire program, Mills also imagined designs for several panels, for he occasionally described the demeanor of participants or the composition of scenes. The first course consisted of eight panels narrating the history of the Revolution, beginning with Benjamin Franklin's petition to the British Parliament and ending with Washington's farewell to his officers in 1784. Only three of the panels were associated with revolutionary war battles; at two of these battles—those at Princeton and Yorktown—Washington commanded the American troops.

Washington's presidency provided the schema of the second tier. Principal events, such as the meeting of the First Federal Congress, as well as various social and political conditions of the period, such as the "arts of civilized life imparted to the savages," were represented. Washington in the role of Cincinnatus, privately practicing civic virtues after his retirement to Mount Vernon, was recorded in the third band of sculpture.[16] Panels portraying Washington freeing a slave, voting, serving on a jury, and inspecting a school were among those included. The top range of relief panels was the most abstract, representing freedom and independence, which Washington had secured for America. These beneficences were expressed by emblems of various trades and professions, including agriculture, fishing, mechanical arts, manufactures, the sciences, commerce and navigation, and "na-

Figure 5.2
Washington Monument
(1813–38), Baltimore,
Maryland. (Pamela Scott)

tional bravery & nautical skill." For the last two, traditional mythological figures—Neptune and Mars—were used to represent the ocean and war. Otherwise, tools of the trades as well as individual Americans—Benjamin Franklin and the scientist David Rittenhouse—were used to convey the meaning of individual panels.

Mills offered two simpler iconographic programs should the "emblematical history" of Washington be deemed "too numerous, complex, expressive, unappropriate, or inexpedient." In both cases he suggested more abstract themes, such as "a state of peace the best policy of the nation," rather than a sculpted cycle of American history. The first set of these themes was expressed through generalized imagery, somewhat biblical in inspiration, such as peace represented by animals living in harmony. Mills's second set of alternative themes was drawn primarily from easily recognizable classical allusions, such as Mars, Minerva, and Ceres. The goddess of liberty was also included.

Mills concluded his description of the 1813 design by reflecting on the nature of commemorative monuments. He believed that his design conformed to established criteria for a Winkelmanian definition of classical beauty—"comparatively small, smooth, [and] variety in the direction of the parts." Washington's virtues and public character were expressed by devices and inscriptions that he contended were "simple, expressive and significant." The purpose of monuments was to inspire love of liberty and political independence among Americans.

What Mills's first design would have actually looked like is difficult to imagine, since octagonal columns were not part of the classical tradition. The relationship of narrative sculpture to architectural form that Mills described was more reminiscent of Lorenzo Ghiberti's bronze doors for the Baptistry (1401–24) at Florence than the helical sculptural program of Trajan's or Hadrian's columns. Rough sketches for an octagonal column constructed of wood are bound together with Mills's 1813 description but the structure depicted does not seem to correspond to the formal or iconographic complexity that Mills described.

Mills's formal submission of his entry on January 12, 1814 (he had been granted an extension of time), consisted of seven watercolor drawings, a descriptive essay, and a cover letter citing his qualifications. Two elevations (figs. 1.8, page 12; 5.3) depicted the column in a quasi-formal landscape setting, since the program had alerted competitors that the monument would stand in a square 140 by 300 feet, with its major axis traversed by a principal street. Mills emphasized this longitudinal axis by lining the street, running north and south, with willow and cypress trees and by piercing the base with a barrel vault so that the street passed under the column. The east and west facades of the base were approached by staircases leading to a sunken arched doorway composed in a markedly Ledocian manner; on all four facades the arched openings were flanked by double Greek Doric columns.[17] Latrobe's influence, particularly in the use of the archaic Doric order, is evident. The 65-by-50-foot base provided the buttressing necessary for raising the column above an arched opening as well as access to the column's staircase. Mills noted in his essay accompanying the drawings that a monument encircled by a city should be towering, "otherwise its *popular* intention is frustrated."[18] The monument's intended height (140 feet) and its extensive base determined the scale of Mount Vernon Square, where it is located.

Mills characterized the column shaft itself as Greek Doric, although it was unfluted. Presumably the broad splay of the echinus and its placement directly on the stylobate of the base were the elements that in Mills's eyes distinguished it from Roman columns, although memorial columns were more traditionally Roman.[19] Mills's column shaft was divided into seven levels by balconies set at decreasing intervals toward the top, presumably for perspective control. Detailing of these balconies was derived not from the classical language, as was the rest of the monument, but from the medieval architectural vocabulary, as the balustrades were composed of a frieze of quatrefoils rather than Renaissance balusters. With the exception of the lowest level, the shaft was decorated with inscriptions and minor emblematic sculpture. Visitors could ascend staircases within the double wall and exit onto the six balconies to read these historical inscriptions and view the city.

The iconography of this second design was formulated around Washington as a military hero. The major sculptural program consisted of a quadriga, or triumphal car, driven by George Washington guided by Liberty on top of the column, a band of relief sculpture around the column's base, and four large groups of trophies of victory marking each corner of the monument's base. The progress of the Revolution could be followed, starting at the top with 1776 and descending year by year to 1781 at the base of the column. The names of heroes and battles were inscribed on the six top levels; a relief sculpture of Lord Cornwallis's surrender at Yorktown encircled the column base, beginning 20 feet above ground level. Mills suggested that Washington's resignation of his commission at Annapolis would provide another appropriate subject for a relief sculpture, since he wished to emphasize the participation of Maryland in revolutionary era events and to laud the patriotism of its citizens in raising the monument. Only a few elements from

his November 1813 design were repeated. The voussoirs in the archways represented the states, and the arms of the United States were sculpted on the keystones.

Mills suggested alternative metaphorical symbolism if the four trophies of victory on each corner of the base were not acceptable. Statues of distinguished generals might be placed there or allegorical representations of the "Unity of the people, the

ELEVATION
OF THE PRINCIPAL FRONTS.

gratitude of Maryland, [or] the Genius of America." The quadriga, or "Chariot of Victory," was to be cast in brass, as was the platform on which it stood; the column's double walls had a hollow center to allow for an open view up to the quadriga.[20] The shaft and base were to be of white marble quarried near Baltimore. Minor emblematic sculpture included wreaths, inverted torches, and stars, all of which Mills identified as "sarcophagic emblems" associated with fame and immortality.

allied ancient traditions, may be due to Mills's naiveté or to a conscious decision to carry further his "invention" of an American architectural vocabulary begun at the Monumental Church.

Mills's design was not received favorably. Maximilian Godefroy denigrated Mills's monument as the pagoda of "Bob the Small," reacting against the six balustraded balconies. Mills may well have had pagodas in mind when adding this feature to his monument. The Nanking pagoda, set in a monu-

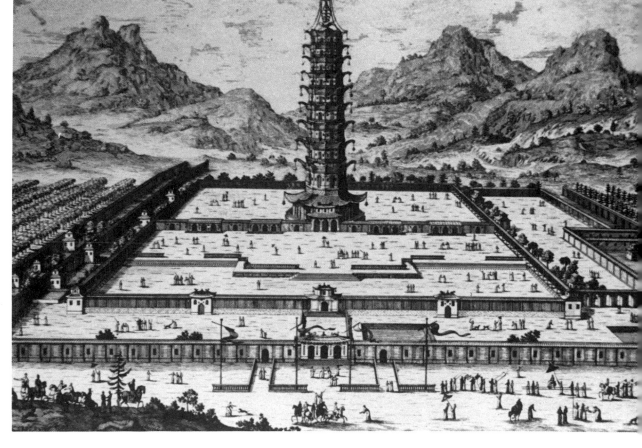

In the remarks accompanying his design, Mills noted that monuments should be characterized by solidity and simplicity of form but also "cheerfulness" so as not to evoke "gloom or disgust," qualities that he apparently associated with the "frivolity of Heathen superstition, as the gloom of Egyptian darkness." This attitude may account for the introduction of medieval—that is, Christian—details into a design derived from classical prototypes. Certainly Mills had some specific architectural or symbolic intention in mind, for his careful planning of the design and the iconographic program indicates that all aspects of his design were purposeful.

The inclusion of Greek, Roman, and medieval elements suggests not only a temporal span but also a geographic range. Mills may have believed that he was expressing the diversity of American society by such eclecticism.[21] This daring departure from European eclecticism, which at this time was confined to altering or combining elements from the closely

mental urban setting similar to and as grand as that provided for Trajan's Column, was published in Fischer von Erlach's *Entwurf*, the first European work in which world architecture was seen on a par with the classical tradition (fig. 5.4).[22] Sir William Chambers's pagoda at Kew Gardens was published in his *Plans, Elevations, Sections and Perspective Views of the Gardens and Buildings at Kew in Surrey* (1763), thus reinforcing the form as acceptable within a universe of architectural prototypes.

In 1851 Rembrandt Peale recalled that Mills's design had been ridiculed by Philadelphia artists, presumably when Mills exhibited four drawings at the fourth annual exhibition of the Columbian Society of Artists in May 1814. Latrobe's response to the design was unfavorable. He complained in a letter to Godefroy that "Mills is a copyist, and is fit for nothing else. His Christian monument is an imitation of a design proposed for Lord Nelson. It is anything but a fit mausoleum for Washington."[23] In

1809 Latrobe had invented two American orders of architecture for the U.S. Capitol, one based on corn and the other on the cotton flower. In these designs, as well as his classically derived orders used at the Capitol, Latrobe practiced what might be called a form of eclecticism common to the design process of all architects of all times by combining and integrating elements from earlier prototypes. In his Washington Monument design Mills probably considered that he was putting into practice basic tenets that he had learned under Latrobe's tutelage. By January 12, 1818, when construction demanded that a decision be made on the balconies, Mills expressed concern in a letter to Robert Gilmor, president of the monument's board of managers, that the novelty of this feature of the design might be criticized.

At the cornerstone ceremony on July 4, 1815, Rembrandt Peale displayed a portrait of Washington, and Henry Warren, a local theatrical scene painter, exhibited a painting of what the proposed monument would look like. Warren's painting has been lost, but an engraving of it, published by John Horace Platt in *An Authentic Account of the Proceedings on the Fourth of July, 1815*, shows a standing figure of Washington atop a Doric column; the whole was raised on a compact rectilinear base, the vaulted archway of the winning design having disappeared (fig. 5.5). Four low-arched entrances, with keystones apparently decorated with the insignia of the states, were approached by substantial

staircases. Monumental sculptural groups of trophies placed on the corners of the base were carried over from the winning design, but decoration of the column's shaft was reduced to only three bands of bronze ornaments. Two widely spaced bands of wreaths divided the column into thirds, while a frieze of thirteen shields and spears above a ring of stars decorated the base. Mills's introduction of wreaths into his vocabulary of appropriate symbolic ornament was a significant one. In antiquity, wreaths of laurel or oak were symbols of fame, and Mills used them alone, hung with swords, or as a frame for important elements in most of his subsequent monument designs.

A major change in the monument was the substitution of a standing figure for the quadriga, since Washington was to be depicted resigning his commission at Annapolis. On May 16, 1816, Mills sent the building committee two sheets of drawings indicating several possible ways to vary the decorations (fig. 5.6). Mills suggested that letters be addressed to the governors of the original states requesting that each state legislature contribute to the cost of the bronze or brass shields, which would have the state seals embossed on them. He offered designs for three alternative sculptural groups to crown the summit of the column—a standing figure, an equestrian statue, or a quadriga. He also suggested figural sculpture to replace the trophies of victory—statues of presidents, cabinet officers, or generals. The symbolism was constant—emblems to express Washington's military and civic achievements—but the means of conveying it varied. The trophies of victory, equestrian statue, and quadriga were symbolic of Washington's military career, while the standing figure depicted him returning to private life. Two years later, on April 7, 1818, Mills again wrote Robert Gilmor concerning the decorations. The series of thirteen shields representing the states were still to ornament the base of the column, but for each corner of the base Mills now planned four Roman eagles "passing thro' wreathes, & connected together by a feston'd garland or draparey."[24]

Construction of the monument was rapid during the first five years. By the end of 1819 the column was 137 feet 4 inches high; by the end of 1820 it was completed at 140 feet 4 inches. By 1825 the abacus, cornice, parapet, and pedestal for the statue were complete. The total height—165 feet 4 inches—made it the tallest column in the world. The shaft, as completed, was entirely without ornament, and the base carried the simplest of inscriptions in bronze letters, the design and content of which Mills provided.[25] On September 30, 1826, his advertisement for designs of a colossal statue of Washington and for bronze decorations, principally tripods to mark the four corners of the base,

Figure 5.5
Frontispiece from John Horace Platt, **An Authentic Account of the Proceedings on the Fourth of July, 1815,** *1815.*

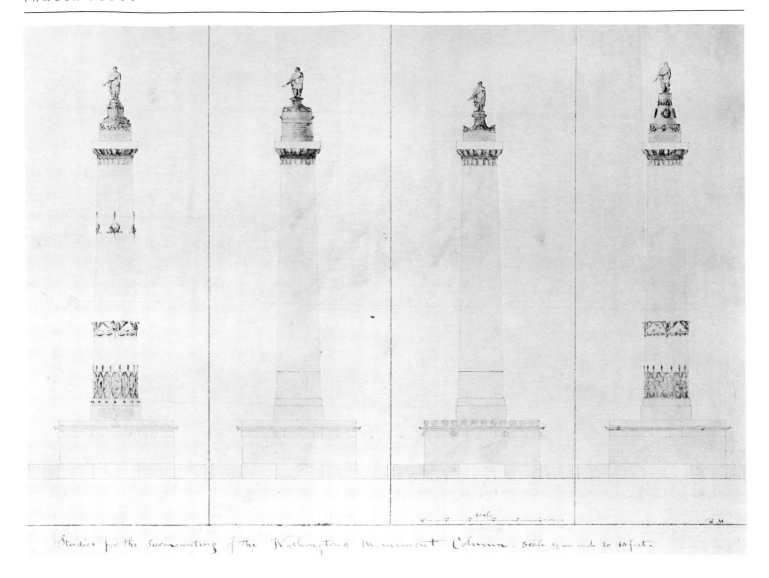

Studies for the surmounting of the Washington Monument Column. scale ½ in. inch to 10 feet.

Above and overleaf:
Figure 5.6
Studies for the Baltimore
Washington Monument,
c. 1815–20. (Maryland
Historical Society)

appeared in *Niles Weekly Register*. Mills continued to work intermittently on details of the monument throughout the 1820s and 1830s, although he was forced to leave Baltimore in 1820 in order to find work.

In 1829, with the aid of his friend James D. Woodside, Mills undertook to raise Enrico Causici's 14-foot marble statue of Washington to the summit.[26] The final block of the four-part statue was put in place on November 25, 1829, during a grand ceremony. Mills's basic columnar form survived, as did the statue of Washington, which alluded to Maryland's participation in revolutionary era events, but the emblematic sculpture to which he had given so much thought was not yet part of the monument.

Mills's final major contributions to the monument's design were the cast-iron fence and the tripods that replaced the earlier trophies and figural sculpture. The fence is perhaps the finest extant American cast-iron fence of the period (fig. 5.7).[27] Mills transferred to it his efforts to ornament the monument and imbue it with appropriate symbolic meaning, and, like the column itself, it went through numerous permutations. Mills began studies for the fence in 1830, but a contract was not

made with the Savage Manufacturing Company until June 26, 1836. The four gates initially were to be decorated with the arms of Maryland; the posts, cannon modeled on those used in the Revolution, were to function as lamps; and the railing was to be composed of a series of anthemion set within circles. By 1837 Mills had redesigned the gates to incorporate stars, changed the stanchions from up-ended cannon to fascial columns surmounted by eagles, and designed a railing of simple spears. In a final change he used for the posts a fascial column with ax head that he found in Michel-François Dandré-Bardon's *Costume des anciens peuples* (1772), which he consulted at the Library of Congress.[28]

The change from trophies, figural sculpture, and eagles to tripods was undoubtedly due to financial considerations, since the monument's board of managers was dependent for funding on the Maryland legislature during that time. Tripods, which then became a part of Mills's vocabulary, had various meanings in antiquity. A huge tripod at Delphi commemorated the Greek victory over the Persians in 479 B.C.. They were also given as prizes in choragic contests, and monuments were built to display them, the most famous of which was the

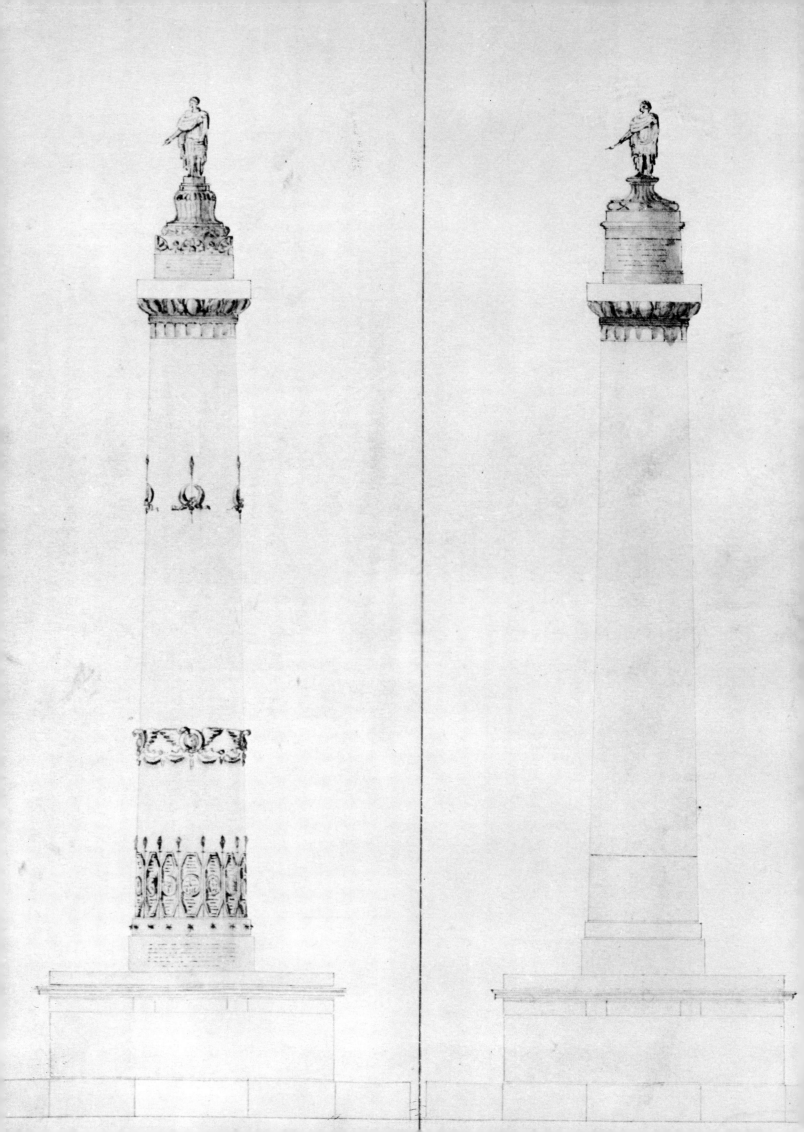

Choragic Monument to Lysicrates in Athens (334 B.C.), known in Mills's day as the Lantern of Demosthenes. Thus tripods had the desirable feature of combining both military and civic associations, and Mills incorporated them in some form in all of his contemporaneous and subsequent monument designs.

DESIGN FOR THE BUNKER HILL MONUMENT

On March 20, 1825, Mills sent to the building committee of the Bunker Hill Monument two alternative designs, an obelisk and a column. In his accompanying description Mills promoted the obelisk design on the grounds that the Baltimore Washington Monument had already provided the country with a monumental column. Equating size with the greatness of the American people, Mills's obelisk rose 220 feet in height. The steps approaching it formed a stepped pyramid for its pedestal. A quarter century later Mills suggested a stepped pyramid base for the 600-foot obelisk of his Washington National Monument if his complete design were not to be built. He apparently felt that American obelisks (and columns) needed to be combined with another architectural form to be valid and also, because of their great height, required the visual support of a base.[29]

The Bunker Hill Monument shaft was intersected by three iron balconies supported by "winged globes." The balustrade itself probably was composed of some additional Egyptian motif, for Mills stated in 1832 that "the outline of the gallery showed the monumental character used by the Egyptians." Thirteen shields, representing the original states and decorated with their state seals, surrounded the base of the obelisk, while eleven tablets surrounding a star represented the subsequent states constituting the union. Above this was a second frieze of spears and wreaths. Additional wreaths hung with spears decorated each face of the obelisk on the three remaining levels. The wreaths encircling the letter W—to commemorate Joseph Warren, the hero of Bunker Hill—also served as window frames. Inscriptions near the base of the obelisk were to be in a different language on each face—Latin, Greek, English, and French. These inscriptions honored Warren and his compatriots as well as the French contribution to the Revolution. Mills specifically mentioned the Marquis de Lafayette, who was making a triumphal tour of America in 1825. On the summit of the Bunker Hill obelisk was to be a tripod fed with gas so that the monument could also serve as a lighthouse. Most of these elements had appeared in one or more of Mills's Baltimore Washington Monument designs.

Solomon Willard's plain, 225-foot obelisk was built beginning in 1825, but seven years later Mills claimed credit as the author of the monument, asserting that the building committee had erred in omitting his ornamentation.[30] In the original description accompanying his drawings in 1825, Mills had given a short disquisition on the history of

Figure 5.7
Fence (1838) for the
Baltimore Washington
Monument.
(Pamela Scott)

obelisks. His interests were the scale and the abstract possibilities inherent in the form: "The *obelisk* form is peculiarly adapted to commemorate *great transactions* from its lofty character, great strength, and furnishing a fine surface for inscriptions." Mills derived his information from Book 1, "De Origine et Erectione Obeliscorum" of Athanasius Kircher's *Obeliscus Pamphilius* (1650), which illustrated obelisks with square, often multilevel bases, with their surfaces embossed with hieroglyphics and, occasionally, having shallow pyramidiums.[31]

SMALLER MILLS

MONUMENTS

Mills's Washington Monument was the most prominent among numerous nineteenth-century monuments that gave to Baltimore the title "Monumental City." Most of these monuments commemorated heroic actions of Baltimoreans during the War of 1812, including the Aquilla Randall, or North Point, Monument, designed by Jacob Small, Jr. (1772–1851), and raised by Randall's compatriots of the First Mechanical Volunteers to commemorate his death. An undated drawing by Mills for the Aquilla Randall Monument (fig. 5.8) of an obelisk-on-base type depicts a base organized horizontally with sculptural and inscriptive panels inset within a wide, flat frame.[32] The plain, hard-edged quality of the frame contrasting with the sculpted surfaces of the panels became an identifying characteristic of Mills's smaller monument designs. Mills drastically reduced the pyramidium of the obelisk to act as a pedestal for a tripod cradling a globe. Proportionally the footed tripod was the same height as the base, and all of its surfaces were articulated by light relief sculpture. The scale of the tripod suggests that Mills may have intended that the globe serve some purpose (such as a beacon) in addition to acting as a symbol of immortality, but as no written description by him survives, his intention is uncertain. Bronze wreaths hung with swords, arrows, stars, and the inscription "North Point, 1814" decorated each face of the obelisk. The whole was enclosed by a cast-iron fence, the stanchions of which were upended cannon.

Neither drawings nor a description by Mills for his monument to the revolutionary war general Baron Johann DeKalb (1721–80), erected in Camden, South Carolina, on the grounds of his Bethesda Presbyterian Church, have survived (see fig. 1.9, page 13). Although the monument marked DeKalb's grave, its isolation and large scale (it is 15 feet in height) imbued it with more of a commemorative character than a sepulchral one. Inscriptions on the base written by revolutionary war historian David Ramsey recount DeKalb's role in the Revolution and note that the citizens of Camden raised the monument in his memory.[33]

The DeKalb Monument, a truncated marble obelisk set on a base derived from a Roman sarcophagus, was based on the same topos as the Lexington Monument. The whole is raised on a wide, double-tiered platform that has an iron fence with an anthemion motif around its perimeter. A single star near the apex of the obelisk and a wreath encircling the inscription "To Baron DeKalb" near its base were the only emblematic devices. Although obelisks or sarcophagi alone were often found in cemeteries or used as commemorative monuments in this country, Mills may have believed that their combination produced a type of monument peculiarly appropriate for military heroes. A monument combining the two forms had been used to mark Maréchal Lefebvre's grave at Père Lachaise cemetery in Paris. Illustrated in Marchant de Beaumont's *Vues pittoresques* (1821) and located next to the grave of the Maréchal Masséna, the ensemble was entitled "The Heroes' Last Rendez-Vous."[34]

Mills's contemporaneous Maxcy Monument (1824–27), located on the grounds of the South Carolina College in Columbia, was to honor the first president of the college, Jonathan Maxcy (1768–1820) (see fig. 3.18, page 100).[35] Although composed of the same two ancient architectural prototypes as the DeKalb Monument, the Maxcy Monument was a fusion of obelisk and sarcophagus rather than a composition of both forms, similar to Mills's 1812 sarcophagus for the Monumental Church. The sarcophagus was subsumed into the

Figure 5.8
Design for the Aquilla Randall Monument, Baltimore, Maryland, c. 1814. (Peale Museum)

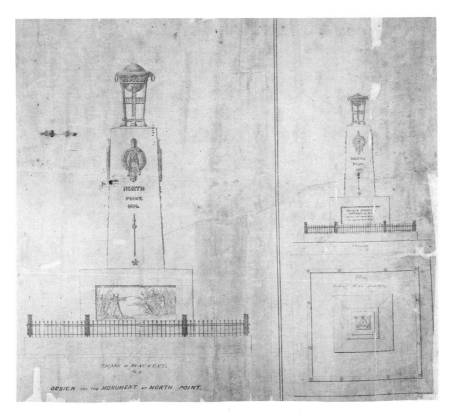

obelisk by merging the angles of the two forms yet retaining the essential character of each. The shaft of the obelisk was divided into thirds by a cavetto cornice (ornamented with winged orbs) and a heavy belt course decorated by alternating stars and the letter *M*. A tripod cradling a globe, another symbol of immortality in Mills's vocabulary, surmounted the obelisk. The insignia of the college's Clariosophic Society, which raised the Maxcy Monument, was sculpted on each face of the obelisk below the cornice. The obelisk itself was white marble, and small marble panels were recessed in the substantial gray granite base.

As constructed, Mills's South Carolina monuments, because of the inclusion of his sculpted emblematic symbols, probably represent Mills's intentions more fully than his better known commissions and proposed designs. The DeKalb and Maxcy monuments were large in scale in relation to their sites and shared a typology that particularly lent itself to Mills's eclectic transformations. The creative melding of forms that Mills employed for the Maxcy Monument was carried further in his Charles Bennett Monument (1841), erected on the grounds of Christ Church in Alexandria, Virginia (fig. 5.9).[36] Austere in its purity of form, the obelisk-

Figure 5.9
Charles Bennett
Monument (1841),
Alexandria, Virginia.
(Pamela Scott)

cum-sarcophagus was broken once by a pedimented cavetto cornice, recalling Mills's sarcophagus for the Monumental Church twenty-seven years earlier.

Mills designed two other monuments during his South Carolina years about which very little is known. In a letter to Robert Gilmor dated March 1, 1826, Mills mentioned his design for a Kosciuszko monument, but no drawings or description is known to have survived. Mills probably entered a design in the competition held by West Point cadets resulting in the erection of John H. B. Latrobe's monument in 1828. A second monument was to commemorate the Battle of Eutaw Springs, which took place on September 8, 1781. A copy of an address purporting to have been given by Mills in 1826 "before the citizens of South Carolina on the erection of a mon't to the Soldiers of the Revolution" may be for the Eutaw monument. The American troops, led by Nathaniel Greene, had suffered heavy losses, and Mills exhorted his audience in 1826 to remember the heroes of the Revolution by inscribing "their deeds upon the tablets of fame," as apparently all South Carolina heroes and statesmen of the Revolution were to be remembered by name on "the Monumental cenotaph."[37]

WASHINGTON

NATIONAL

MONUMENT

Mills's move to Washington in 1829 marked the beginning of his mature style, and the culmination of his ideas about monuments was realized in the Washington National Monument. The process of erecting a national monument was a protracted one, and Mills was involved in it from the beginning. The centennial of Washington's birth in 1832 prompted Congress to fulfill its 1783 pledge to erect a monument to his memory in the national capital and was accompanied by renewed efforts to have Washington reinterred in the Capitol crypt. The need for a Washington monument associated with his tomb was real, for the crowds visiting Mount Vernon necessitated a building to protect his burial place. On March 17, 1830, Mills wrote Maryland Congressman George E. Mitchell, suggesting that a white marble tomb in the crypt of the Capitol be surmounted by a tripod, symbolizing immortality and perhaps serving as a perpetual lamp. He also proposed a colossal figure of Washington (8 to 9 feet in height) in modern dress as part of the monument. An undated Mills sketch relates to this proposal for a "Cenotaphic Monument to Washington" that he proposed to Leonard Jarvis, chairman of the House Committee on Public Buildings. A "colossean" statue of Washington in modern dress depicted resigning his commission (similar to Causici's statue atop the Baltimore monument) was raised on a pedestal above the floor of the Capitol rotunda. Four staircases descended to the crypt below for viewing Washington's tomb. Mills's suggestion may have contributed to Congress's commissioning in 1832 the American sculptor Horatio Greenough to execute a figural sculpture. His controversial seated Washington in a Roman toga was installed in the Capitol rotunda in 1842 under Mills's supervision.[38]

The Washington National Monument Society was founded on September 26, 1833, by a group of Washingtonians who were dismayed that the Greenough statue was not on a scale suitable to vie with the Baltimore Washington Monument or those proposed for New York and Philadelphia.[39] Former Librarian of Congress George Watterston wrote the society's constitution, adopted at the second meeting on October 31, and delivered an address in which he explicated the society's sole purpose: to erect "a monument [to Washington] whose dimensions and magnificence shall be commensurate with the greatness and gratitude of the nation which gave him birth [and] whose splendor will be without parallel in the world."[40]

To realize a monument of such grandeur the society planned to raise a million dollars. Since the society intended that the monument be erected by the American people as a whole, not more than one dollar was to be accepted from any individual. In 1838, after five years of collecting funds, a sum total of only $30,779.84 was on hand, and skepticism about the eventual completion of the monument was widespread, especially since no design had been announced.[41] The second problem facing the society was a suitable site. As it was a private organization, congressional authorization was necessary for use of public grounds. After consideration of privately donated sites and protracted negotiations, Congress authorized on January 31, 1848, the public reservation originally designated by Pierre Charles L'Enfant as the monument grounds.

The first mention of a design for the monument was on September 23, 1835, at a meeting of the society's board of managers:

It is proposed that the contemplated monument shall be like him in whose honor it is to be constructed, unparalled in the world, and commensurate with the gratitude, liberality, and patriotism of the people by whom it is to be erected. A premium will be offered by the Society, for the best design by an American architect, and therefore no definite idea can as yet be given of the plan which may be adopted, but it is the wish of the Society, that it should blend stupendousness with elegance, and be of such magnitude and beauty as to be an object of pride to the American people, and of admiration to all who see it. Its material is intended to be wholly American, and to be of marble and granite brought from each State, that each State may participate in the glory of contributing in material as well as in funds to its construction.[42]

Ten months later a notice calling for designs predicated on not less than a million dollars was prepared for insertion in newspapers. None of the designs submitted was found to be "coextensive with the Nation" and so did not meet with approval of the board of managers.[43]

In November 1844 a committee of the society consisting of Watterston, Peter Force, and William Seaton was appointed "to procure a suitable design" for the monument. On April 26, 1845, this committee offered the resolution that "the plan furnished by Mr. Mills & estimated by him to cost, when completed $200,000; with a shaft to cost $50,000 be adopted as the plan of the projected monument." Samuel Smith, treasurer of the society since its founding, offered a substitute resolution calling for another public competition and limiting the total expenditure to $50,000. On November 18, 1845, Mills's design was adopted, and on December 13 he was paid $100.[44]

Mills's accepted design for an obelisk 600 feet tall rising from the center of a circular pantheon base 250 feet in diameter (fig. 5.10) was probably not the same design that he submitted to the 1836 competition. Three designs identified as Washington monuments are among the many sketches for monuments in Mills's journal of 1836–40. One, apparently housing a statue of Washington, was medieval revival in style, a definite departure from Mills's usual thinking about monuments. It may have been prompted by the very serious consideration the society gave to a Gothic Revival design by John McClelland. Mills had designed a medieval building in 1841 for the Smithsonian (or the National Institution, whichever should be built first), in which he combined features from "the ancient English Saxon and Norman" styles of architecture, typically combining features of two allied traditions.[45]

The second Washington monument design illustrated in Mills's journal was for a 110-foot-tall robed figure of Washington astride a 100-foot cubical base with a great catacombed interior. The exterior of the base was decorated with panels of unidentified relief sculpture. A third candidate from the journal was a triple-tiered monument beginning with a triumphal arched base supporting a Greek Doric temple that sheltered a standing figure, the whole surmounted by a variation of the Choragic Monument to Lysicrates.

Another indication that Mills was considering several alternative ideas between the time of the original competition and the final selection of his design nine years later is found on his 1841 drawing for the mall that accompanied his Smithsonian design (fig. 5.11). On the site originally selected by L'Enfant for the equestrian statue of Washington, Mills placed a colossal double rotunda. Wider than the Capitol, it was a gigantic folly amidst the varied landscape and plantings of a picturesque garden, the first large-scale public picturesque park proposed for America. Neighboring smaller monuments, or perhaps pavilions, were within the monument grounds, while the adjoining Smithsonian grounds were appropriately modeled on medieval medicinal gardens.

Enormity of scale was a consistent theme in all of Mills's monument designs, but nowhere was it expressed so extravagantly as in an undated description in Mills's hand entitled "National Monument to Washington." He envisaged a stepped pyramid 680 feet high surmounted by a 100-foot-high statue of Washington. The entire surface of the pyramid was rusticated, and colossal buttresses at each corner supported 350-foot obelisks. The body of the structure was pierced throughout by vaulted galleries on seven levels of decreasing height. The first stage had thirteen arched doorways on each face, representing the original union of states, with the names of each state in bronze letters on the voussoirs. The second stage had nine arched openings, each of which was to contain a 33-foot statue of a hero or statesman of the Revolution. This second level opened onto a 150-foot-wide balcony, or "terrace walk." The third level had seven arched entries and 60-foot-wide balconies; the fourth, five openings and 50-foot terraces; and the fifth, three arches. Statues of additional unspecified "worthies of the Revolution" would be contained on the third level, but Mills did not specify any sculpture for the next two stages. The sixth level consisted of a 40-foot-high pedestal for the statue of Washington, which was on the seventh level. The lower part of the pedestal was enriched with inscriptive panels recounting events in Washington's life, while each face of the upper part was decorated with a wreath encircling Washington's name. Visitors would walk or drive carriages up "inclined planes" on all four 1,000-foot sides to reach the summit.[46]

Mills's accepted design for the Washington National Monument exhibited nearly the same grandiosity as his pyramid scheme; perhaps the pyramid design had been proposed to the Washington National Monument Society but had been rejected. The accepted design was composed of two parts, a 600-foot-tall obelisk surrounded by a colonnaded pantheon base 250 feet in diameter and 100 feet high. Mills's detailed description of

Figure 5.10
Sketch for a Washington
National Monument,
1845. (National Archives)

SKETCH OF

WASHINGTON

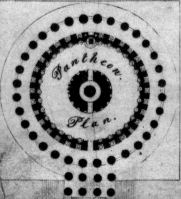

Pantheon Plan.

NATL: MONUMT:

BY

ROBT: MILLS,

ARCT.

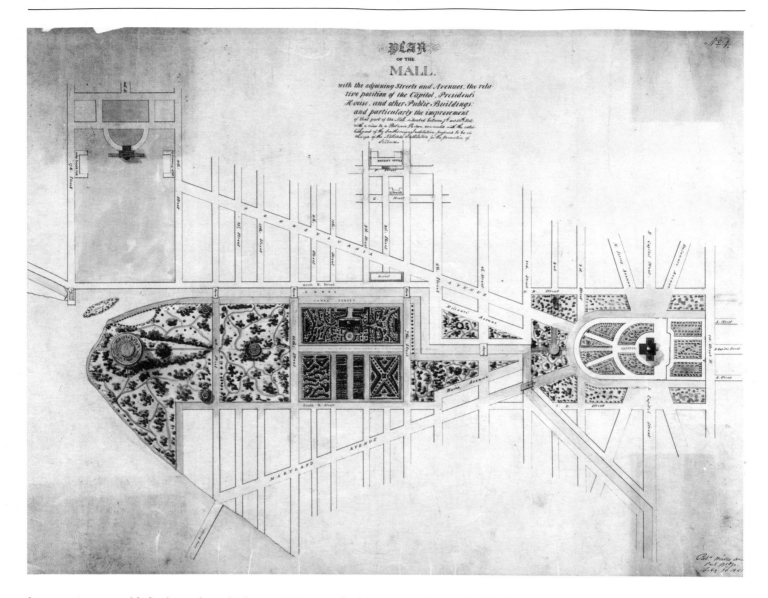

Figure 5.11
Design for the Mall,
Washington, D.C., 1841.
(National Archives)

the monument, published in a broadside in 1848, indicated that its scale was matched by a complex iconographical program. The pantheon base consisted of thirty Doric columns, 45 feet high and 12 feet in diameter, encircling a rotunda. The antae set behind the columns on the exterior wall of the cella projected 7½ feet and were 10 feet wide. Statues of the signers of the Declaration of Independence were in niches cut in the rotunda wall. The thirty columns represented the number of states in 1845, and bronze civic wreaths enclosing each of the state seals were placed above each column in the entablature.[47] A tetrastyle portico, the entablature of which contained sculpture symbolic of the United States, projected to the west.

The cella of the pantheon continued the lavish use of allegorical and portrait sculpture begun on the exterior and introduced a cycle of historical paintings. The internal gallery encircling the obelisk base contained niches for statues of the fathers of the Revolution; paintings on the walls above them depicted scenes of the founding of the Republic. Initially, Mills planned to place a colossal statue of Washington within this rotunda. In the basement were catacombs for the tombs of distinguished Americans, including Washington.

The roof of the pantheon formed a balustraded terrace 700 feet in circumference, with four cupolas to provide light and a view of the statues in the gallery below. The projection of the terrace over the portico served as a pedestal for a quadriga. On the perimeter of the terrace, staircases descended to an intermediate gallery containing rooms for an art museum and the monument's archives.

The obelisk rose 500 feet above the terrace level, which was 600 feet from the ground, and relief sculpture of Roman imperial symbols, "tripods of victory and fascial columns with their symbols of authority," would be sculpted on each face. Above these ancient civic symbols further bas reliefs of four leading events in Washington's military career were to be sculpted. A single star, "emblematic of the glory which the name of WASHINGTON has attained," was at the summit of the obelisk. Charles Fenderich's lithograph (1846), commissioned by the society, depicted the monument from the west, showing the entrance portico (fig. 5.12). The cheek blocks of the staircase supported sculpted figures that appear to be river gods. Mills probably knew the anonymous *Essai sur la ville de Washington*

*Above: Figure 5.12
Charles Fenderich, detail
of Mills's design for the
Washington National
Monument, 1846.
(Library of Congress)*

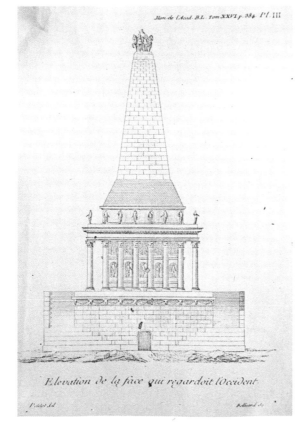

*Figure 5.13
Comte de Caylus,
Reconstruction of the
Mausoleum of
Halicarnassus, 1759.
(Memoires de litterature,
tirés des régistres de
Académie Royale des
Inscriptions et Belles-
Lettres)*

(1795), which described sculptural groups of river gods representing great American rivers, such as the Potomac and Hudson, to be placed on the west terrace of the Capitol.[48] Mills may have been reviving this idea, or he may have wanted to further enrich his monument with another venerable element of the European urban tradition.

Mills's possible sources for his obelisk and pantheon design indicate how knowledgeable he was concerning both the architecture of his own time and historical examples. Reconstructions of two great tombs of antiquity, the Mausoleum of Halicarnassus and Hadrian's Tomb, in conjunction with modern variations on their forms provided Mills with his basic prototype. The Comte de Caylus's 1759 reconstruction of the Mausoleum of Halicarnassus, in which he combined Egyptian and Greek features—an obelisk with a colonnaded base—initiated a modern series of monument designs that were particularly associated with revolutionary heroes (fig. 5.13). A monument from this series, one commemorating the role of the poet Mirabeau in the French Revolution by the architects Jean Molinos and Jacques LeGrand, may well have been known to Mills (fig. 5.14). Published in 1792 by

Armand Guy Kersaint in his *Discours sur les monumens publics*, the Mirabeau monument was to be raised on the site and make use of the ruins of the Bastille.[49] Mills may also have derived elements for his rotunda from a seventeenth-century reconstruction of Hadrian's Tomb (now Castel Sant' Angelo), which depicted its colonnaded rotunda with niches cut into the wall and extensive use of exterior sculpture, including a quadriga (fig. 5.15).[50] Mills would have composed his Washington National Monument design from these sources because of their historical importance, immense scale, and sepulchral associations.

Additional sources offering appropriate associations include designs by A. T. Brongniart dating from about 1812 to 1815 for mausolea and a monument to a "grand personnage" for Père Lachaise Cemetery in Paris.[51] In 1829 Mills had submitted to Congress a design for a national cemetery (fig. 5.16) in Washington located in a picturesquely landscaped square originally designated on L'Enfant's plan of the city as the site of the national pantheon. Mills combined catacomb with monument, placing statues of heroes in niches alternating with Egyptoid pilasters on the exterior wall of a rotunda 100 feet in diameter.[52] Rising 76 feet from the center of the mausoleum was a column, also with Egyptian overtones but ornamented with wreaths hung with swords, the whole surmounted by an unidentified seated figure, probably Washington. In both form and function Mills's national cemetery design was closely related to Brongniart's mausolea designs.

The basic parti of a colonnaded base encircling a

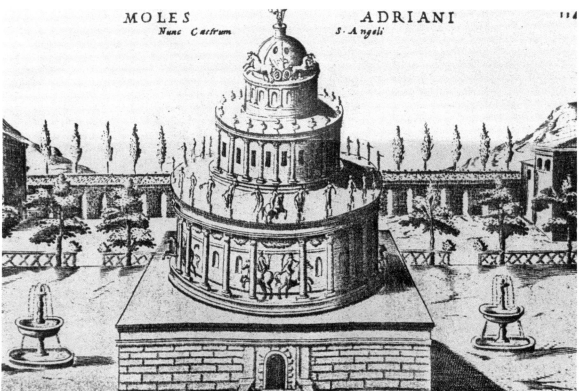

Above: Figure 5.14 Jean Molinos and Jacques Le Grand, Monument to be Raised on the Ruins of the Bastille. (Armand Guy Kersaint, Discours sur les monumens publics, 1792).

Left: Figure 5.15 Reconstruction of Hadrian's Tomb, 17th century. (E.P. Rodocanachi, Le Château Sant-Ange, 1909).

Opposite: Figure 5.16 Design for a national cemetery, Washington, D.C., 1829. (National Archives)

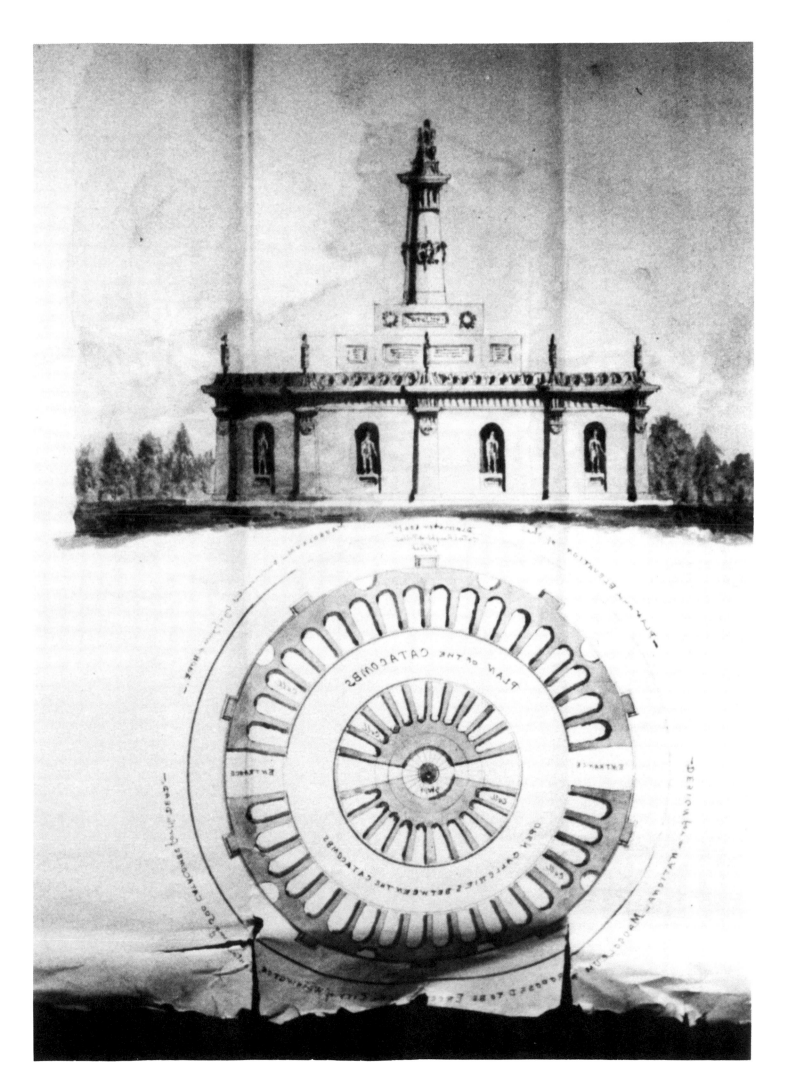

vertical shaft was not confined to monuments. While he was a student in Latrobe's office, Mills had first-hand exposure to Latrobe's use of the type for his lighthouse (1805–19) at Frank's Island, Louisiana, at the mouth of the Mississippi (fig. 5.17). Latrobe used a colonnaded rotunda to buttress the weight of a stone column built on swampy land, replacing the usual New Orleans system of floating wood piles. Iconographically Latrobe was building, at the behest of President Jefferson, a beacon to signify the entry into the interior of America, an area that Jefferson believed of paramount importance to the country.[53]

The change from a monument to honor Washington alone to a pantheon of American revolutionary heroes is a significant one, reflecting the changing perception of the role of great men in history. Although the theme can be traced to Plutarch's *Lives,* it gained new currency in the nineteenth century. G. W. F. Hegel's *Die Philosophie der Geschichte* (1837), Thomas Carlyle's *On Heroes, Hero Worship and the Heroic in History* (1840), Friedrich von Schlegel's *The Philosophy of History* (English translation, 1846), and Ralph Waldo Emerson's *Representative Men* (1849) codified ideas expressed as early as 1804 by Joseph Marie de Gerando in *Histoire comparée des systèmes de philosophie,* by Ralph Cudworth in *The True Intellectual System of the Universe* (1820), and by Victor Cousin

in *Introduction to the History of Philosophy* (English translation, 1832).[54] Great men as exemplars capable of motivating their own and future generations was at the core of this theory of history, yet the leader or man of action was seen as having a symbiotic relationship with his compatriots.

National monuments, as the embodiment of the moral and civic paradigm of the great man, inspired patriotism and contributed to the formation of the country's character and ideals. The extension of the original program of the Washington National Monument, initially honoring Washington alone, into a complex iconography of the American Revolution, reflected this evolving view of an interdependent relationship among men engaged in a great enterprise. In Mills's accepted monument design, Washington was at the center of the monument, both figuratively and symbolically, but he was joined by the signers of the Declaration of Independence and revolutionary war heroes. The result was a kind of secular Parnassus or Walhalla.[55]

On January 25, 1843, Henry Wheaton, the American minister to Prussia, sent to the National Institute for the Promotion of Science in Washington a thirty-nine page letter describing works of art in the Bavarian capital, including a detailed account of the opening ceremonies of the Walhalla (1832–42) near Regensburg, designed by Leo von Klenze (1784–1864). The letter was read at the institute's

Figure 5.17
Lighthouse (1805–19,
Benjamin Henry Latrobe),
Frank's Island, Mississippi.
(National Archives)

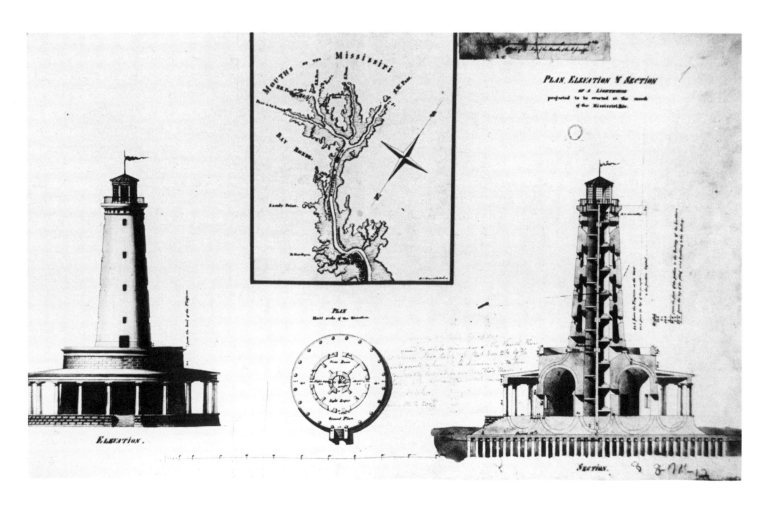

May 8 meeting, attended by Mills, one of the founding members.[56] Wheaton outlined the history of the Walhalla, describing in detail its iconographical program, in which Norse mythology was used as a metaphor for Prussian greatness. His critical discussion of the architecture and sculpture of the Prussian temple of fame included identification of each of the artists involved and a discourse on the tenets and principles of contemporaneous German neoclassical architecture. Wheaton's description, in conjunction with the plans of the Walhalla that he sent, provided a more in-depth knowledge of this significant building than coverage in journals or even in von Klenze's own illustrated *Die Walhalla in artistischer und technischer Beziehung* (1843). Mills and the other institute members who were on the board of managers of the monument society were thus exposed to a major national monument hailed as a modern masterpiece shortly after its completion, and it surely influenced their thinking about the nature of the Washington National Monument.

Unfortunately very little is known about Mills's private library, and the contents of Latrobe's library are still known only to specialized scholars. Resources available to Mills, such as Henry Wheaton's contributions to the National Institute, may have been more various (and much more current) than previously believed. Education through public lectures had been one of the most prominent features of Mills's 1841 Smithsonian Institution design.

The scale on which Mills conceived of the Washington National Monument was in keeping with the tradition of national monuments, which equated the worth of great men with monumentality. Colossal size was the identifying characteristic of the eighteenth-century aesthetic category of the sublime, capable of stimulating wonder, awe, admiration, reverence, and astonishment. Jacques-François Blondel, in his *Cours d'architecture* (1771), included monuments to heroes as an appropriate category for sublime architectural effects.[57] In addition to the Walhalla, another national monument of great size was Jean-François Chalgrin's Arc de Triomphe (1806–36), built to exemplify how Napoleon intended to "rendre sensible la grandeur de l'Empire."[58]

The only monument mentioned in the papers of the Washington National Monument Society as a possible prototype was that raised to Thaddeus Kosciuszko near Cracow, Poland, in the 1820s.[59] An enormous conical Boulléesque mound of earth transversed by a diagonal pathway to the summit, the Kosciuszko Monument was appropriate as a model for the American people, both because of his involvement in the American Revolution and because it was built by thousands of Poles, including nobility, who made pilgrimages to deposit handfuls

of dirt on the mound. The monument society, by initially limiting contributions to one dollar per American, wished symbolically to replicate this Polish act of patriotism.

The society may have been responding to sentiments expressed by the most important surviving link to Washington. In an address on January 11, 1836, George Washington Parke Custis commented on an appropriate Washington monument:

> Tell me not of models to be derived from the antique— the tomb of Hadrian, or the columns of Trajan or Antoninus; the Yankees will have their monument after their own fashion, sui generis, and this let it be. To rear a mound two hundred feet square, by one hundred feet high, that the base may be earth-fast, and upon the apex of this mountain, this time-defying pedestal, place the colossal statue of the Pater Patriae.[60]

Rival attempts to raise monuments to Washington were an immediate stimulus to transform the Washington National Monument into a monument to the revolutionary era. The best known was Calvin Pollard's proposed design for New York in 1843, billed as "one of the most splendid Monumental Edifices ever reared in the world."[61] Gothic Revival in style, pentagonal in form, and containing libraries and art galleries, it combined monument with museum and embraced a rich iconographical program in which the history of the country's founding was recounted. In addition to portrait and emblematic sculpture, a cycle of historical paintings illustrating the events of the Revolution was to be included.

On April 12, 1844, Congressman Zadock Pratt, chairman of the House Committee on Public Buildings and Grounds, proposed to Congress a design by the Philadelphia architect William Strickland for the national monument, since the society had not been successful in obtaining either a design or a monument site.[62] A neoclassical rotunda based on Robert Adam's mausoleum at Bowood (1761–64), the program of the Strickland-Pratt design reflected the rising interest in establishing an American pantheon, and this, in turn, was reflected in Mills's design:

> The committee have given their best consideration to the most useful kind of monumental architecture, and have come to the conclusion that the *temple form* is the best; and to be built upon such a scale as to be capable of containing the busts and statues of the Presidents of the United States, and other illustrious men of our country, as well as paintings of all the historical subjects which have or may be designed by our artists through ages yet to come.[63]

On July 31, 1850, when the future of the pantheon base of the Washington National Monument was uncertain, Mills revived his 1829 scheme for a national cemetery, submitting to Congress a pro-posal for a national mausoleum, the drawings for which have unfortunately been lost.[64] In this scheme Mills planned two rotundas, probably simi-lar to the national cemetery design, connected by a 200-foot terrace. Each rotunda was 30 feet high with niches for tombs of the illustrious dead. Rising above one would be a 60-foot tripod and above the other a fascial column of equal height. One rotunda would be the burial place of presidents and the other of congressmen. The national mausoleum could also shelter the statues of Washington and Jefferson, which were exposed on the Capitol and White House grounds.

The scale of Mills's Washington National Monu-ment, particularly the height of the obelisk, was questioned while the society was still deliberating on the design. On June 14, 1845, Mills wrote Judge William Cranch, a member of the society, that the reason he could estimate his proposed design any-where from $100,000 to one million dollars "with-out any change in architectural character" was the "ratio of the Magnitude of the work."[65] In other words, the same design might come in small, me-dium, large, or gigantic. In March 1848 George Watterston chaired a committee of the society's board of managers to consider whether the height of the monument ought to be limited to 300 feet. The difficulties already encountered in raising funds led Watterston's committee to conclude that since no monument in the world exceeded 300 feet, the society would be acting both prudently and in concert with their original intentions to limit the height. Watterston quoted Mills:

The imposing character of a Column raised to the height of 300 feet would fill the mind with admiration, espe-cially when it is united to the thought that this lofty pillar is dedicated to the Father of his country. [In this design] will be found originality, magnitude and utility, which last rarely enters into Monuments of this description, every venerated name of the Revolution may be represented and recorded, and the foul stain of ingratitude be forever blotted out, and succeeding Generations shall call the founders of this glorious work Blessed.[66]

The board referred the question to Mills and the young architect James Renwick (1819–95), who were to consider cost and possible modifications to the design at heights between 300 and 500 feet. Their report, dated March 28, 1848, suggested that a pyramidal termination to the obelisk (lacking in the original plan) would increase the apparent height of the monument. They also felt that using Egyptian-inspired shafts for the columns of the pantheon with "details derived from production purely American" would give the monument a na-tional character, which they defined as deriving from its "differing in detail from all previous monu-

ments."[67] The results of both these decisions are seen in an 1852 lithograph of the monument by Benjamin Franklin Smith, Jr. (fig. 5.18).[68]

The Doric columns originally planned for the colonnade were changed to "the American order," presumably the corn capitals invented by Latrobe in 1809 for the vestibule of the Supreme Court of the U.S. Capitol. Mills apparently stimulated a re-surgence of interest in reviving the American orders at mid-century. Robert Dale Owen illustrated La-trobe's corn order in his Hints on Public Architec-ture (1849) and promoted the development of an American vocabulary of architectural detailing, as did Andrew Jackson Downing in The Architecture of Country Houses (1850). Downing illustrated his own design for the corn order and suggested to-bacco, cotton, and magnolia flower capitals to give "national character" to American domestic ar-chitecture. Alexander J. Davis used the corn order on the portico of Smith Hall (1850–52) at the Uni-versity of North Carolina, in Chapel Hill, and for Grace Hill (1854–57), the Litchfield villa, in Brook-lyn, New York. In 1859 James Renwick used a corn capital variant of the Corinthean order on the Cor-coran Museum of Art (now the Renwick Gallery) in Washington.[69]

Another major change suggested by Mills and Renwick was to offer an intermediate design in case the pantheon was too costly for immediate erec-tion. Depicted on certificates issued after 1848 by the monument society for contributions of $5 or more (fig. 5.19), this design substituted massive steps—25 to 50 feet in height, depending on the obelisk's height—for the pantheon and preserved the national character of the monument by cutting the "names of the Statesmen and Heroes of the Revolution" into the steps. The stepped pyramid substructure was 76 feet square, while the base of the obelisk was 55 feet square with walls 15 feet thick, making the interior core 25 feet square at the base.

Although Mills was not hired in any professional capacity when his design for the monument was initially accepted, he undertook various miscella-neous duties. On February 22, 1848, he presented to the society a report entitled "Plan of Operations proposed connected with the ceremonies of the fourth of July, 1848, in laying the cornerstone of the National Washington Monument."[70] On May 1, 1848, the board of managers voted him an addi-tional compensation of $100 for his services to that date and retained him as "architect and engineer" of the monument for $500 per annum.

The site favored by the monument society, on the mall next to the canal between Seventh and Ninth streets, is depicted in Charles Fenderich's 1846 lithograph. It would have been on axis with the Patent Office, which occupied the site that

Figure 5.18
Benjamin Franklin
Smith, Jr., detail of
"A View of the Mall,"
Washington, D.C., 1852.
(Library of Congress)

THE MONT COMPLETE
WITH THE PANTHEON

WASHINGTON
NATIONAL MONUMENT

HEIGHT of OBELISK 500 feet DIAMETER of the PANTHEON 250 feet Height 100 feet

DIMENSIONS of the OBELISK 55 FEET SQUARE AT THE BASE 35 feet at Top with an opening for the IRON STAIR CASE of 25 feet to Top!

THE OBELISK OF THE

WASHINGTON
NATIONAL MONUMENT

contributed ___ ha___ Dollar

in aid of the erection of the

WASHINGTON NATIONAL MONUMENT

which entitles ___ to all the

privileges of Membership in the

Washington National Monument Society.

Z. Taylor. President.

Geo. Watterston Secretary

Elisha Whittlesey. Genl. Agent.

Agent

Lith. by E. Weber A. C. Baltimore

L'Enfant had designated for the national pantheon. The monument's actual site has perplexed historians who have repeatedly stated that it was not in axial alignment with either the White House or the Capitol because of the difficulty of locating secure foundations in the center of the mall, although there is no evidence in the society's records to support this assertion.[71] It is probable that the monument's placement to the south and east of the crossing of the city's two major axes was due to both historical and aesthetic reasons rather than a pragmatic one. A venerable object, the Meridian Stone, already occupied the center of the mall because of its function. It had been erected in 1804 by President Jefferson and was more prominent in 1848 than it is today, measuring 13 feet 1⅝ inches. In addition, the mall's "visible" center in 1848 did not coincide with its actual center because acreage on its north side had been incorporated in the canal designed by Latrobe in 1804.[72] When the canal was widened in 1832, from 80 to 150 feet, the imbalance was increased.

Although Mills showed a Washington monument on axis with the center of the Capitol on his 1841 plan of the mall, the monument was built in the center of the garden proper (discounting the canal). It is likely that since the monument was to be one of two great objects on the mall—the other being the Smithsonian Institution—it was planned so that each could be seen in its entirety and in a balanced

relationship to each other from the Capitol terrace, the principal belvedere in the city. E. Weber's "View of Washington City" (fig. 5.20) of about 1848 demonstrates how the placement of the monument to the north and west of the already extant Smithsonian gave each building a separate but equal visual field when viewing the panorama of the city. Mills described such a panorama in the 1848 and 1854 editions of his *Guide to the Capitol.*[73]

The cornerstone was laid on July 4, 1848, before "masses such as never before were seen within the shadows of the Capitol." The Baltimore and Susquehanna Railroad and the Steam Navigation Company of New York offered half-price fares for those attending from Baltimore, New York, and Boston. A grand parade included dignitaries from America and abroad and numerous organizations, from the Order of Red Men to fire companies. All the former first ladies attended, led by Dolley Madison, age 82. The "carriage containing the architect of the Monument, having in charge the books and other articles to be deposited in the cornerstone" was last in the procession. Robert C. Winthrop, speaker of the House, gave the oration. He extolled the virtues of the first president and commented on all of the statues of Washington that had been erected in the state capitols but did not mention the Baltimore Washington Monument. He alluded to the Washington National Monument design in his concluding remarks:

*Figure 5.19
Certificate of the
Washington National
Monument Society,
c. 1848. (Library of
Congress)*

*Opposite: Figure 5.20
E. Weber, detail of "A
View of Washington City,"
c. 1848. (Columbia
Historical Society,
Washington, D.C.)*

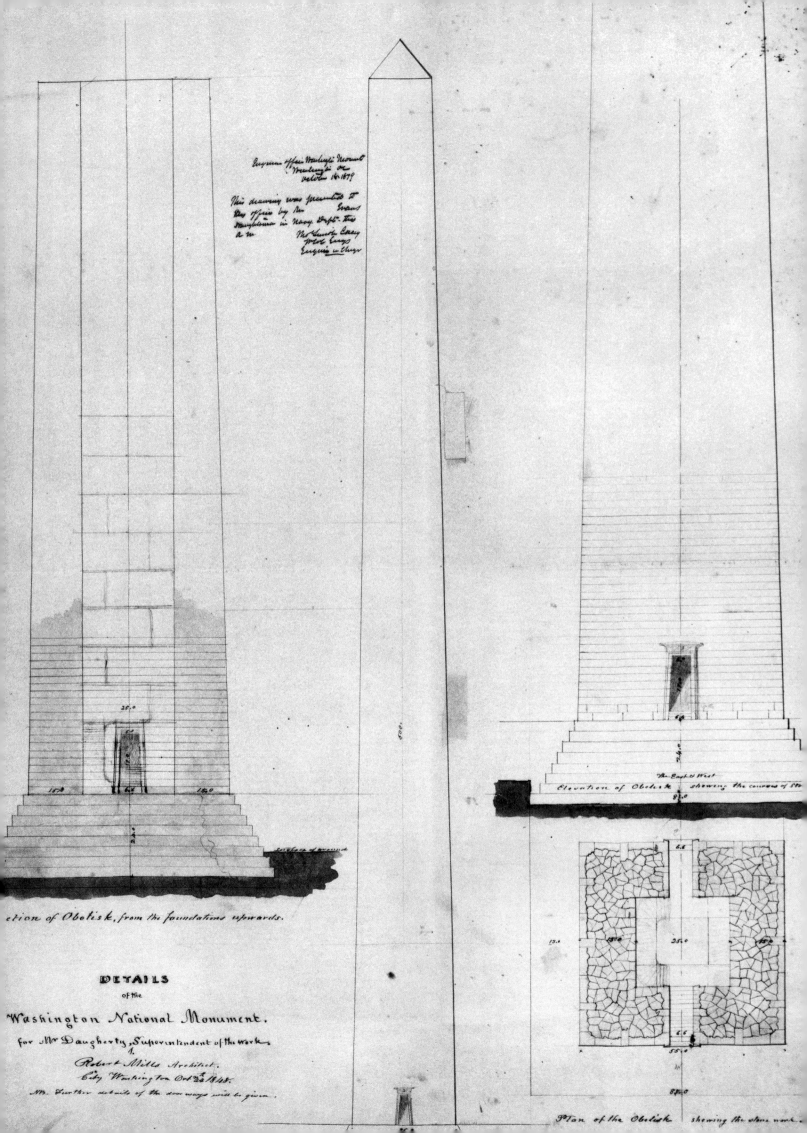

Engineer office Washington Monument
Washington DC
October 14 1879

This drawing was presented to
this office by Mr _____ Evans
draughtsman in Navy Dept. this
a.m.   Thos Lincoln Casey
              Lt Col Engrs
              Engineer in Chief

Section of Obelisk, from the foundations upwards.

25.0

15.0   25.0   15.0

Section of Obelisk, from the foundations upwards.

DETAILS
of the
Washington National Monument.
for Mr. Daugherty, Superintendent of the work.
1.
Robert Mills Architect.
City Washington Oct 2d 1848.
NB. Further details of the door ways will be given.

Elevation of Obelisk showing the courses of stone

The East & West

24.0

81.0

Plan of the Obelisk showing the stone work

6.5

13.0   15.0   25.0   15.0

6.6

55.0

87.0

600.

Build it to the skies; you can not outreach the loftiness of his principles! Found it upon the massive and eternal rock; you can not make it more enduring than his fame! Construct it of the peerless Parian marble; you can not make it purer than his life! Exhaust upon it the rules and principles of ancient and of modern art; you can not make it more proportionate than his character![74]

On October 24 Mills's working drawings with "verbal explanations" were submitted to the board members, and thereafter any changes required their approval (fig.5.21).[75] The marble used, Symington's crystal marble from quarries near Baltimore, was severely criticized, and Mills replied by citing tests carried out by order of the secretary of the interior that this marble was equal in strength to granite. Mills and Renwick in their report suggested white marble not only for its durability and beauty but for "the purity of its colour, as better fitted to express the object of the structure than any other material." Mills changed the height of the monument's entrance, lowering it by three feet after calculating the relative heights of the other public buildings and spaces in the city. The roof of the pantheon had always been intended as a platform for viewing the city, as was the summit of the obelisk.[76] With the resumption of the building season in the spring of 1849, the question of ascending the monument arose. In his description, published as a broadside, Mills proposed "to ascend to the summit of the column, the same facilities as below are provided within the shaft, by an easy graded gallery, which may be traversed by a railway." Mills may have been trying to work out the mechanics of an elemental elevator or to adapt the principle of a cog railway to a very limited circumference.[77]

The redemption of a pledge made in 1835 to utilize materials from all over America led to the events halting construction of the monument in 1854. In the early summer of 1849 the society invited every state to send native stones to be placed on the interior walls, with Mills supplying designs for the coats of arms of the states and various societies as well as suitable inscriptions. The popularity of the state stones led quickly to the acceptance of stones from other nations. News of a gift by the Vatican was reported in the *National Intelligencer* on February 2, 1852, and aroused a violent reaction from the Know-Nothing Party, whose platform was anti-Catholicism.[78] On October 18, 1853, a stone sent by the Vatican from the Temple of Concordia arrived in Washington. Six months later it was stolen by sixteen members of the Know-Nothing Party and apparently sunk in the Potomac River. At an illegal election held at the annual meeting of the monument society on February 22, 1855, the Know-Nothings gained control and were not ousted for three years. A depleted treasury, the death of many of the original mem-

bers, and public weariness with the entire project contributed to suspension of work until the centennial. On March 1, 1855, the new board of managers voted to apply to Congress for a charter in hopes of gaining government support. Mills may not have been cognizant of this development as he died two days later.

FINAL MONUMENT DESIGNS

On August 13, 1850, Mills received a letter from Dr. Smith Fuller commenting on his drawing and suggestions for a proposed monument to George Washington in western Pennsylvania. The Fort Necessity Washington Monument Association had been incorporated on April 6, 1850, to erect a monument on the site of Washington's first battle, a skirmish during the French and Indian Wars in 1754. Particulars of Mills's design known from Fuller's letter are confirmed by the printed public appeal for funds.[79] The monument was to be 50 feet in height. Mills suggested a pedestal composed of stones contributed by each of the states, but Fuller rejected this proposal as being too costly. Mills designed "emblematic guns" for the pedestal, as well as some other form of ornament, the description of which has been obliterated in Fuller's letter. An unusual feature of the design was that the 50-foot shaft was to be of iron, perhaps to promote use of the region's major industrial product. Its form—obelisk or column—is not certain. Since its base was to measure 5 feet square, an obelisk is suggested, although Fuller referred to it as a column. The hollow structure was "composed of plates with suitable devices and inscriptions." This may have been the first substantial metal architectural work proposed in America.[80] The cornerstone of the Fort Necessity Monument was laid on July 4, 1854, but it was never completed.

Sometime between 1848 and 1851 Mills was consulted by Congressman Charles S. Morehead about the "plan, cost &c" of the Kentucky War Monument. Although the extent of Mills's involvement with the monument, executed by Robert Launitz in 1850–51, is not known, it is probable that the monument's height (62 feet) was his suggestion.[81]

Additional monuments for which Mills provided designs during the 1850s included the Richmond Washington Monument, a Thomas Jefferson monument for Charlottesville, Virginia, and a Washington monument for his native city, Charleston, South Carolina. Mills's surviving description and drawings for the Richmond Washington Monument indicate that he again proposed an ornamented column rising from a base decorated with

Figure 5.21
Drawing of the
Washington National
Monument, 1848. (Society
for the Preservation of
New England Antiquities)

both figural and emblematic sculpture. In a letter to Gov. John B. Floyd dated January 4, 1850, Mills stated that his design was "original and peculiarly American in its composition, its decorations being formed of the '*Star-Spangled banner*,'" which he placed under the abacus of the capital and supported by four American eagles with wings spread.[82] Bronze shields and spears, familiar from the Baltimore Washington Monument and the Bunker Hill column design, ornamented the base of the column. The monument's base was composed of bas reliefs of Washington's major military victories flanked by pedestals embossed with bronze fasces-with-ax head columns. Seated figures in Roman dress reminiscent of Greenough's statue of Washington in the Capitol were placed on all four corners of the upper base. Bronze sculptures of tripods holding fasces with ax heads ornamented a lower base.

Thomas Crawford's equestrian statue of Washington, including a complex base composed of statues of Virginia heroes of the Revolution, was selected for the Richmond monument, with Mills named as the superintending architect.[83] During early stages of construction, while Crawford was in Rome working on his figural sculpture, Mills began to implement changes to bring the base more in conformity with his own design. Crawford's acerbic response in a letter to Mills dated September 15, 1851, indicated that what might have been considered appropriate as a monument to the Revolution in 1814 was not universally acceptable thirty-five years later: "You propose to place the main feature of my design (I allude to the Grand pedestal and the Equestrian Group) upon the ground, and offer to me as a substitute, the most hackney'd of all architectural forms, a kind of bastard Column that you would dignify if possible by the sounding appellation of 'the Column of the Revolution.'"[84]

Little is known of Mills's last monument designs. On July 19, 1852, the renderer Emil Friedrich billed Mills for drawings of both the Jefferson monument and an Andrew Jackson monument, but no images of either survive.[85] In 1851–52, while employed at the University of Virginia making an addition to the rotunda, he designed a monument to Jefferson based on the Lantern of Demosthenes (the Choragic Monument of Lysicrates). In a letter to Mills dated March 3, 1826, Jefferson noted that he himself had once suggested that a monument to Washington be based on this ancient form. In his contemporaneous national mausoleum design Mills also suggested that the segment devoted to Jefferson be based on this prototype.

About 1854 Mills designed an equestrian monument to Washington for Charleston, South Carolina. Washington was in Roman military dress holding a scroll inscribed with his farewell address.

The three-part pedestal (terrace and fountain at base, 8-foot-square plinth, and 22-foot circular top) was embellished with elements common to Mills's vocabulary—figures denoting fidelity, stars, and shields representing the states. Inscriptions recounted the most important acts of Washington's life, and through these "the outline of the American Revolution will also be recorded."[86]

MILLS'S MONUMENTAL LEGACY

Does the consistency of form and emblem found in Mills's monuments indicate a poverty of architectural thought or an unswerving dedication to an ideal? In his January 12, 1814, description of the Baltimore Washington Monument, Mills referred to his design as "a *Triumphal* monument having much to record of *historical* fact." Nearly four decades later he called the Richmond Washington Monument "the Column of the Revolution." The Washington National Monument was the ultimate celebration of the deeds and heroes of the Revolution. Mills identified directly with this era. As a young man he saw Washington in the newly founded capital; he was nurtured by Jefferson and corresponded with him until just a few months before his death; he was present when the Marquis de Lafayette laid the cornerstone for his own De-Kalb Monument. Both the richness of his sculptural programs and the scale of his monuments—two of their most salient features—were integral to the purpose of commemorating the Revolution and its heroes.

Mills himself stated that the size of his monuments was commensurate with the greatness of the enterprise they recorded. His repeated use of the same symbolic emblems must be seen as an attempt to establish an iconography for America, since he always related these symbols to specific virtues or attributes of heroes, to some historic event, or to the original thirteen states. He viewed his eclectic combinations of ancient architectural forms as an American innovation in architecture. Mills's numerous efforts throughout his career to erect a monument to the Revolution was an effort to embody the history of America's founding in a uniquely American architectural form. The traditional view of Mills as a Greek Revival architect with a penchant for the purity of classical forms is challenged by a careful analysis of his monument designs. His vision was an intensely romantic one in which he fused the classical, the sublime, and the picturesque into what he considered to be the essence of the American experience.

1. Arthur S. Marks, "Statue of King George III in New York and the Iconology of Regicide," *American Art Journal* 13 (1981): 61–82; Margaret Brown Klapthor and Howard Alexander Morrison, *George Washington, A Figure Upon the Stage* (Washington, 1982), 18–21; and I. N. Phelps Stokes, *The Iconography of Manhattan Island*, 5 (New York, 1925), 992. Lossing noted numerous other monuments either proposed but never built or erected over the graves of heroes who survived the Revolution and were later honored by their communities. Apparently the first attempt to mark a revolutionary-era event was a proposed obelisk to be erected under the Liberty Tree on Boston Common commemorating the repeal of the Stamp Act (1766). Clarence S. Brigham, "Paul Revere's Engravings," *American Antiquarian Society* (1954), plate 6. Pre- and post-revolutionary era commemorative celebrations, orations, pamphlets, and proposed monuments are discussed in Albert Matthews, "Centennial Celebrations," *Transactions of the Colonial Society of Massachusetts* (1926), 26: 402–26.

2. Quoted in Frederick L. Harvey, *History of the Washington National Monument and Washington National Monument Society*, 57th Cong., 2d sess., 1902–3, S. Doc. 224, 14–15. Pierre Charles L'Enfant placed this equestrian Washington monument at the crossing of the two major axes of the White House and the Capitol in his 1791–92 plan for the national capital. H. W. Janson, "Observations on Nudity in Neoclassical Art," *16 Studies* (New York, 1973), 191. The state statues were by Jean-Antoine Houdon for Virginia in 1785, Antonio Canova for North Carolina in 1816, and Sir Francis Chantry for Massachusetts in 1826.

3. The literature is extensive. For portraits and memorial objects see *George Washington, An American Icon* (Washington, D.C., 1890); William S. Baker, *The Engraved Portraits of Washington* (Philadelphia, 1880); Betty Strauss, "The Memorial Iconography of George Washington" (Master's thesis, University of Delaware, 1966); and Mark Thistlethwaite, "The Image of George Washington" (Ph.D. diss., University of Pennsylvania, 1977). For eulogies see Margaret Bingham Stillwell, *Washington Eulogies, A Checklist of Eulogies and Funeral Orations on the Death of George Washington, December 1799–February 1800* (New York, 1916). For reminiscences, character studies, biographical sketches, and full-scale biographies, see William S. Baker, *Character Portraits of Washington as Delineated by Historians, Orators and Divines* (Philadelphia, 1887), and *Bibliotheca Washingtoniana* (Philadelphia, 1889); William Alfred Bryan, *George Washington in American Literature, 1775–1865* (New York, 1852); and Franklin B. Hough, *Bibliographical List of Books and Pamphlets Containing Eulogies, Orations, Poems, or Other Papers, Relating to the Death of General Washington, or to the Honors Paid to His Memory* (Albany, New York, 1865).

4. John Trumbull's description of the Dance design is contained in a letter from him to Christopher Gore, February 28, 1800, Thomas Sedgwick Papers, Massachusetts Historical Society. The Dance design is discussed by Damie Stillman, "Death Defied and Honor Upheld: The Mausoleum in Neo-classical England," *The Art Quarterly* 1 (1978): 175–213. In 1819 Trumbull himself designed a statue of Washington; see Charles R. King, ed., *The Life and Correspondence of Rufus King* (New York, 1900), 6: 220–21. Latrobe's description and correspondence concerning his design are included in John C. Van Horne and Lee W. Formwalt, eds., *The Correspondence and Miscellaneous Papers of Benjamin Henry Latrobe* (New Haven, 1984), 1: 160–67.

5. The Beacon Hill Memorial Column was demolished in 1811. Its history is recounted in Harold Kirker, *The Architecture of Charles Bulfinch* (Cambridge, 1969), 33–36. Ceracchi's description date, October 31, 1791, is in the Papers of George Washington, Manuscript Division, Library of Congress. A broadside dated February 14, 1794, and signed by Washington promoting the monument (then called the Monument to the American Revolution), is in the Horatio Gates Papers, New York Historical Society. For this aspect of Ceracchi's American career, see Wayne Craven, *Sculpture in America* (New York, 1959), 53–54; Ulysses Desportes, "Giuseppe Ceracchi in America and His Busts of George Washington," *Art Quarterly* 26 (1963): 140–79; and Gérard Hubert, *Les Sculpteurs italiens en france sous*

la Révolution, l'Empire et la Restauration, 1790–1839 (Paris, 1964), 25–28.

6. The Yorktown monument was noted in Journals of the Continental Congress, 1774–1789 (Washington, 1908), 20: 1081. The second Bunker Hill Monument was begun in 1825, but a model of the original column was incorporated into the base of the new obelisk. The fundamental history of the Bunker Hill Monument is still William W. Wheildon, Memoir of Solomon Willard, Architect and Superintendent of the Bunker Hill Monument (Boston, 1865). The history of the Lexington monument is recounted in Charles Hudson, History of the Town of Lexington (Boston, 1868), 215–17, and Caleb Snow, History of Boston, 2d ed. (Boston, 1828), 302–3.

7. Two grave markers probably designed by Mills were for family members. The Davison Monument (1816), Winchester, Virginia, a beveled obelisk on a rectangular base, was for Eliza Smith Mills's uncle. A small marble obelisk on a base marks the grave of Mills's son, John Smith Mills, who died on July 12, 1822, in Columbia, South Carolina.

8. H. M. Pierce Gallagher, Robert Mills, Architect of the Washington Monument, 1781–1855 (New York, 1935), 98. Gallagher and Hamlin also attribute to Mills the design for a proposed monument to Capt. Charles Ross, illustrated in the same issue of the Analectic Magazine. The rectangular stone monument raised on a stepped plinth was surmounted by a bronze helmet resting on crossed swords. The face of the monument was decorated with a sculpted wreath enclosing the date of Ross's death flanked by two amphora. The whole was enclosed by a fence. Hamlin saw this design as resembling in "many details" Mills's DeKalb Monument. This author does not accept an attribution to Mills for the Ross Monument, as the form was not derived from any ancient sepulchral type.

9. An excellent history and interpretation of the project is Margaret Pearson Mickler, "The Monumental Church" (Master's thesis, University of Virginia, 1980). Latrobe wrote John Wickham on January 21, 1812, concerning his design, cited in Mickler, p. 14. Mills probably suggested that the monument be combined with a church because of his success as a designer of churches. Robert L. Alexander's unpublished "A Year in the Life of Robert Mills," a detailed study of Mills's 1816 Journal, gives a useful chronology for the Monumental Church. Construction was completed on the church before the porch was begun.

10. Mickler notes that Sir John Soane used a similar ceiling at his house at Lincoln's Inn Fields in the room where his collection of sarcophagi was displayed ("The Monumental Church," 31). Mills's drawing for the urn is on the cover of his 1816 Journal preserved in the Manuscript Division, Library of Congress. Baughman and Hore, stonemasons from Baltimore, were the carvers. Capellano's bill for "cornices" for the monument is dated August 11, 1817; he was one of the numerous Italian sculptors who came to work on the U.S. Capitol. See Clarence Cook, Art and Artists of Our Time (New York, 1888), 3: 231–33; Glenn Brown, History of the United States Capitol (Washington, 1900–1903), 1:75; T. Frary, "The Sculpted Panels of Old St. Paul's Church, Baltimore," Maryland Historical Magazine 34 (1939): 64–66.

11. Comte de Caylus, "Dissertation sur le Tombeau de Mausole," Memoires de litterature, tirés des régistres de Académie Royale des Inscriptions et Belles-Lettres (1759), 26:321–34. Piranesi proposed in the Diverse manière the inventive combination of "the Grecian, the Tuscan, and the Egyptian together." John Harris, "LeGeay, Piranesi and International Neo-classicism in Rome 1740–1750," in Donald Fraser, Howard Hibbard, and Milton J. Lewine, eds., Essays in the History of Architecture Presented to Rudolf Wittkower (London, 1867), 189–96. Antoine Chrysosthôme Quatremère de Quincy, Dictionnaire Historique d'Architecture (Paris, 1832), quoted in Quatremère de Quincy, De L'Imitation (Paris, 1980), 55. He published the same thought much earlier in his entry for "invention" in the Encyclopédie méthodique (Paris, 1788), 1: 461–65.

12. The Papers Relating to the Washington Monument are in the Maryland Historical Society, MS 876. All references to documents relating to the monument, unless otherwise stated, are to these papers. The genesis and building of the monument have been studied in detail by J. Jefferson Miller II, "Baltimore's

Washington Monument" (Master's thesis, University of Delaware, 1962), and "The Designs for the Washington Monument in Baltimore," Journal of the Society of Architectural Historians 23 (1964): 19–28. The most important member of the board of managers was Robert Gilmor, Jr., with whom Mills consulted about the details of the monument for a quarter century. Other key members were the members of the building committee: Gilmor, James A. Buchanan, William H. Winder, Isaac McKim, Eli Simkins, Fielding Lucas, Jr., and David Winchester.

13. The tenth anniversary of Washington's death and the desire to protect property values in the area of the originally proposed site on the courthouse square have both been suggested as motivations for erecting the monument. William D. Hoyt, Jr., "Robert Mills and the Washington Monument," Maryland Historical Magazine 34 (1939): 144–60, suggested the anniversary of Washington's death; many key early documents, including Mills's descriptions, are reproduced by Hoyt. Miller suggests that more pragmatic factors should be considered. Lotteries and public subscriptions were more common than monies from public treasuries to raise monuments during the early nineteenth century.

14. The managers had initially discussed contacting Antonio Canova about a design, but the notice inserted in Maryland newspapers in March 1813 suggested a desire on the board's part to award the prize to an American. For Godefroy's design and his involvement dating from before the competition in 1811, see Robert L. Alexander, "The Public Memorial and Godefroy's Battle Monument," Journal of the Society of Architectural Historians 17 (1958): 19–24, and The Architecture of Maximilian Godefroy (Baltimore, 1974), 71–75. Latrobe wrote Godefroy that he would not enter the competition because he did not wish to compete with him. Robert Gilmor, however, believed that a pyramid design was Latrobe's work (Miller, "Baltimore's," 23–27). Rembrandt Peale in his "Reminiscences," The Crayon 3 (1856): 5–6, said drawings were displayed by numerous entrants.

15. The text of the essay is given in full in Hoyt, "Robert Mills," 145–52. Bound into the small volume containing the manuscript are four small drawings, which are probably not those that Mills referred to as accompanying his description.

16. The theme of Washington as Cincinnatus during this period is discussed by Garry Wills, Cincinnatus, George Washington and the Enlightenment (New York, 1984).

17. The influence of Claude Nicholas Ledoux on American architecture has been studied by Rich Bornemann, "Some Ledoux-Inspired Buildings in America," Journal of the Society of Architectural Historians 13 (1954): 15–17.

18. Negotiations to change the site from the courthouse square began in August 1914 before that site was selected for Godefroy's Battle Monument. Howard's Park, a 200-foot-square site 100 feet above sea level on the north edge of Baltimore, was donated for the monument by John Eager Howard in 1815. Although selected to be on axis with Charles Street, it was not until 1817 that Howard petitioned the city to extend and grade the street up to the monument. In 1831 Howard's descendants donated additional land on all four sides of the square, providing a cruciform park framing the completed monument. Mills landscaped this cruciform park, two arms of which were on a steep incline toward the city on the south and west.

19. The column as built was derived directly from that of the Temple of Apollo at Delos (426 B.C.), with the top and the bottom of the shaft fluted. Mills used this order repeatedly throughout his career.

20. This type of construction—with the hollow core open at the top and bottom—was carried out at the Bunker Hill Monument, presumably for ventilation. Lack of provision for light in the Baltimore Washington Monument was noted by the Scottish traveler John M. Duncan in his Travels Through Part of the United States and Canada in 1816 and 1819 (Glasgow, 1823), 223.

21. I have suggested elsewhere that Mills's eclectic approach in his public architecture for Washington was motivated by this same intention (Scott, "Robert Mills' Washington," lecture delivered at the annual meeting of the Society of Architectural Historians, Washington, April 1986).

22. Godefroy's comment is quoted in Alexander, Godefroy,

72. The *Entwurf* was in Latrobe's library and was known to Mills in the mid-1830s, when he referred to details of the Temple of Diana at Ephesus originating with it.

23. Jeffrey A. Cohen has explored the possible monuments to Nelson that Latrobe might have been referring to (Van Horne, *Correspondence* [New Haven, 1988], 3: 581–82).

24. These letters are in the Richard X. Evans Collection, Special Collections Division, Georgetown University Library. The undated drawings are at the Maryland Historical Society, which has several miscellaneous drawings relating to the monument. Mills saw the equestrian in the "character of an apotheosis, a winged horse in the act of taking flight."

25. Trajan's Column, in Rome, is 140 feet tall. Mills preferred inscriptions in four languages (Greek, Latin, English, and French), for he felt the meaning would be distorted by changes in English over time (Mills to Gilmor, August 22, 1826). As the sculptural program was increasingly simplified, so was the content of the inscriptions. Initially they were a paean to Washington's virtues and achievements; as completed they were a simple record of the major dates and events of his career.

26. Mills's contract with Causici was made on January 22, 1828, and the statue was completed by September 3, 1829. Other sculptors who submitted models were Antonio Capellano and Nicholas Gevelot. All three foreign-born and -trained sculptors had worked on the U.S. Capitol. Mills had subcontracted with Enrico Causici to raise the statue. He paid Woodside, a captain in the Navy, $200 plus expenses to hoist the four blocks.

27. Some of Mills's designs in iron are discussed by Robert L. Alexander, "Neoclassical Wrought Iron in Baltimore," *Winterthur Portfolio* 18 (1983): 147–86.

28. Mills had used the anthemion motif in 1827 for the fence around the DeKalb Monument and used it for the Patent Office fence in 1840. Both are nearly the same design used by Charles Bulfinch at the U.S. Capitol (about 1826) and William Strickland for the fence at the Second Bank of the United States (1818–24), Philadelphia. The present paving at the Baltimore Washington Monument (red, white, and blue) is not original and probably dates from the centennial for 1876. The original flagging was silver gray and was contracted for on August 26, 1837, from William Steuart of Baltimore. On May 20, 1837, Mills wrote Gilmor that Ferdinand Pettrich, the German sculptor with whom Mills was working in Washington, had designed the eagles. Six months later Pettrich and Mills consulted Audubon's *Ornithology* seeking a true likeness of the American eagle, possibly for colossal eagles to mark the corners of the base. About 1840 Mills used eagle finials on the cast-iron fence at the Patent Office. As early as November 21, 1831, Mills had included in his estimate for the Baltimore monument $10,500 for bronze shields and four bronze eagles. For Pettrich, see R. L. Stehle, "Ferdinand Pettrich in America," *Pennsylvania History* 33 (1966): 389–411. Dandré-Bardon is cited in Alexander, "Neo-classical," 181; the design is in volume 1, part 2, plate 60. Mills's fence for the Post Office in Washington, D.C., was composed of fascial column posts.

29. Mills's drawings for the obelisk cannot be presently located by the Bunker Hill Monument Association, the repository of all the records. According to the published history of the Bunker Hill Monument, Mills sent a second, larger drawing of the obelisk, apparently lost at the time (see Whieldon, *Memoir*). Mills's alternative columnar design is in the association's museum in Charlestown, Massachusetts. Mills's statement equating the size of the monument with America is, "The genius of our people and government, in all their national works, embraces *greatness* of outline."

30. Whieldon, *Memoir*, 87–89. Mills's letter of July 1, 1832, was addressed to Richard Wallach but came to Willard's attention.

31. Mills cited just "Kerker" as his authority. Kircher's numerous publications illustrated many marvels of the world, including those drawn from his travels in China. He wrote a second book on obelisks, *Obelisci aegyptiaci* (Rome, 1666).

32. [Wilbur H. Hunter], *In Commemoration of the "Star Spangled Banner" Sesquicentennial 1814–1864* (Baltimore, 1964), discusses and illustrates seven of these monuments. Small's monument was of the same type as Mills's project but undeco-

rated except for the inscriptive panels on all four sides of the base. Small was a Baltimore builder and architect, the father of the architect William Small (1798–1832) (undated newspaper clipping in the Scrapbook of Nicholas Rogers, Ms. 1494, Maryland Historical Society). I wish to thank Robert L. Alexander for this citation. Mills's drawing is in the Peale Museum in Baltimore.

33. Mills claimed authorship in his unpublished *Autobiography*, and a broadside published by the Kershaw Masonic Lodge on December 27, 1827, cited Mills as the architect. In his March 20, 1825, letter to the building committee of the Bunker Hill Monument Association, Mills stated that he had been present when the Marquis de Lafayette laid the cornerstone of the DeKalb Monument only eleven days earlier, on March 9. DeKalb was reinterred in front of the church when the monument was erected. The Continental Congress had resolved on October 14, 1780, to erect a monument to DeKalb at Annapolis; although it did not specify what form the monument should take, it did have prepared a lengthy inscription heralding DeKalb's bravery. See *Journals of the Continental Congress, 1774–1789*, 18, 923. A DeKalb statue was erected in Annapolis in 1886.

34. The plate from François-Marie Marchant de Beaumont, *Vues pittoresques, historiques et morales du Cimetière de P. La Chaise*, is illustrated in Richard A. Etlin, *The Architecture of Death* (Cambridge, Massachusetts, 1984), plate 258.

35. Documents recounting the history of the Maxcy monument are cited in John M. Bryan, *An Architectural History of the South Carolina College, 1801–1855* (Columbia, South Carolina, 1983), 63–71. William Brown was the stone carver; Mills obtained the metal tripod from an unidentified source.

36. The city of Alexandria commissioned the monument from Mills on February 21, 1841, to commemorate Bennett's financial and civic contributions to the city. See Penny Morrill, *Who Built Alexandria?* (Alexandria, Virginia, 1979), 23–24.

37. Mills claimed a design for the Eutaw Monument in a letter dated 1829. The address (not in Mills's hand) is in the Richard X. Evans Collection, Special Collections Division, Georgetown University Library. A search of Charleston newspapers about the time of the anniversary of the battle did not turn up any mention of the Eutaw monument.

38. Mills to Mitchell, Maryland Historical Society, MS 1948; Mills to Jarvis, Record Group 200, National Archives. [Charles Warren], "How Politics Intruded into the Washington Centenary of 1832," *Proceedings of the Massachusetts Historical Society* (1932) 65: 37–62; Wayne Craven, "Horatio Greenough's Statue of Washington and Phidias' Olympian Zeus," *Art Quarterly* 26 (1963): 429–40; and Natalia Wright, "Horatio Greenough's Memorial to Congress Praying the Removal of his Statue of Washington from the Capitol," *Art Quarterly* 20 (1957): 400–406.

39. Dorothy C. Barck, "Proposed Memorials to Washington in New York City," *The New York Historical Society Quarterly Bulletin* 15 (1931): 79–90, and Ellis P. Oberholtzer, *Philadelphia: A History of the City and its People, A Record of 225 Years* (Philadelphia, 1912). The materials presented here were drawn from the author's "Robert Mills's Washington National Monument" (Master's thesis, University of Delaware, 1985).

40. An abridged version of Watterston's address was prepared for publication in newspapers on February 22, 1835. Annual meetings of the society were held on Washington's birthday, and the cornerstone ceremony was originally planned to take place on February 22, 1848. The fundamental history of the monument is Harvey, *History*, with the concentration of discussion on the society and the political history of the monument rather than on its design. The society's voluminous records are in the Papers of the Washington National Monument Society, Office of Public Buildings and Grounds, Record Group 42, National Archives. All references, unless other noted, are to this collection of papers. For Watterston see William Matheson, "George Watterston, Advocate of the National Library," *Librarians of Congress* (Washington, 1977), 57–75. At the October 31 meeting former Chief Justice John Marshall was elected president; Judge William Cranch, first vice president; Mayor of Washington John P. Van Ness, second vice president; and the

journalist Samuel H. Smith, treasurer. The board of managers consisted of Gen. Thomas S. Jesup, Col. George Bomford, Col. James Kearney, Roger C. Weightman, Col. Nathan Towson, William Brent, Peter Force, Col. Archibald Henderson, Thomas Carbery, Thomas Monroe, Matthew St. Clair Clarke, William A. Bradley, and John McClelland.

41. An elaborate system in which bonded collectors for every county was established. Initially collectors retained 10 percent, then 15 percent, and eventually 20 percent of the proceeds from their work. As limiting contributions to one dollar proved too idealistic, the society did away with this provision. The person responsible for the society's eventual financial success was former Congressman Elisha Whittlesey, who was named general agent in charge of fund raising on June 1, 1847. Competition for public support came from contemporaneous proposed Washington monuments in both New York and Philadelphia.

42. Board of Managers Record Book, 1833–49.

43. Ibid., August 10, 1836, and February 1, 1837. No premium for the architect was offered, the honor of being selected being ample reward. Drawings were to be done on paper 16 by 22 inches so that all could be bound together for the society's archives. On June 7, 1837, the society's thanks were voted to the original competitors: John McClelland of Baltimore, S. M. Stone and Benne and Platte of New Haven, E. Barame of Baltimore, William P. Elliot of Washington (for his teacher, George Hadfield, who had died in 1826), and Robert Mills. On September 18, 1835, Gideon Shryock wrote from Louisville asking for more information, but no known design by him survives. Other competitors are discussed by Robert Belmont Freeman, Jr., "Design Proposals for the Washington National Monument," *Records of the Columbia Historical Society* (1973–74), 151–86, and Bates Lowry, ed., *The Architecture of Washington, D.C.* (1976), 2: chapter 5.

44. Board of Managers Record Book, 1833–49. The decision to accept Mills's design took place shortly after Smith's death. The implication in the society's records is that Smith was unhappy about circumventing the democratic process by "selecting" Mills's design and its projected cost.

45. Mills's letter to Joel R. Poinsett dated February 16, 1841, and the accompanying designs are in Record Group 77, Cons. 90–2, National Archives. This letter is discussed by Terese O'Malley, "The Smithsonian Castle and Its Mall," *Design Action* 2 (1983), 6, and Pamela Scott, "Design for the Mall, Washington, D.C.," in James O'Gorman, Jeffrey A. Cohen, George E. Thomas, G. Holmes Perkins, eds., *Drawing Towards Building* (Philadelphia, 1986), 87–88.

46. This document is in the Maryland Historical Society, VF-Mills. Although it is unlikely that Mills would have ever known of it, a model for a similar scheme for a British National Monument proposed in 1815 by Matthew Cotes and Philip Wyatt was exhibited to the public at the Duke of York's house on Pall Mall. This stepped pyramid was 360 feet tall with twenty-two levels decorated with sculpture. For an illustration and discussion see John Martin Robinson, *The Wyatts, An Architectural Dynasty* (Oxford, 1979), 179–81.

47. The ancient prototype for wreaths in a frieze was the Choragic Monument of Lysicrates. Mills included them in most of his monument designs subsequent to his 1815 Baltimore Washington Monument scheme. In the 1820s they became an important element in American architectural decoration. Charles Bulfinch used them in the frieze of the rotunda of the U.S. Capitol, in about 1825, and John Haviland used them on the exterior frieze of his Walnut Street Theatre in Philadelphia in 1828. It is likely that Henry Bacon was cognizant of Mills's use of the columns with wreath frieze to represent the states, as he used the same scheme on the Lincoln Memorial (1916–22).

48. Citoyen des Etats Unis, *Essai sur la ville de Washington* (New York, 1795), 3–4.

49. This book would have been available to Mills in 1845 in Washington, D.C., as it was sold to the Library of Congress in 1815 by Thomas Jefferson. William B. O'Neal, *Jefferson's Fine Arts Library* (Charlottesville, 1976), 165–66. The topos actually began with Fischer von Erlach's reconstruction of the Mausoleum of Halicarnassus, published in his *Entwurf*, 25. A colon-

naded, stepped pyramid (c. 1789) by either Louis-Jean Desprez or P.-A. Paris is illustrated by Nils Wollin, *Desprez en Suède* (Stockholm, 1919). Several examples proposed during the French Revolution are illustrated by Jean Humbert, "Les Obelisques de Paris projets et réalisations," *La Revue de l'Art* 23 (1974): 9–29.

50. The author of this reconstruction is unknown. It was published by Mariano Borgatti, *Castel Sant'Angelo in Roma* (Rome, 1890), fig. 26, and Emmanuele Pierre Rodocanachi, *Le Château Sant Ange* (Paris, 1909), 4. It probably derives from Etienne Du Perac's reconstruction done for his map, *Roma antica nei suoi monumenti* (1574).

51. Brongniart's projects are discussed and illustrated in Richard A. Etlin, *The Architecture of Death* (Cambridge, Massachusetts, 1984), 310–28.

52. Mills's design and accompanying description are in "Records of the House of Representatives," Record Group 233, National Archives. Other examples of Mills's invented orders are discussed by Robert L. Alexander, "The Special Orders of Robert Mills," in *The Documented Image, Visions in Art History*, G. P. Weisberg and L. S. Dixon, eds. (Syracuse, New York, 1987), 243–56, and in Michler, "Monumental," passim.

53. The watercolor by Latrobe's son, John H. Boneval Latrobe, dated November 7, 1816, is in "Records of the Lighthouse Board," Record Group 26, National Archives. Michael Fazio, "Benjamin Henry Latrobe's Lighthouse for the Mouth of the Mississippi River" (Paper delivered at the annual meeting of the Society of Architectural Historians, Phoenix, April 1983).

54. See Robert Stover, "Great Man Theory of History," in *The Encyclopedia of Philosophy* (New York, 1972), 3: 379–82; Paul F. Bloomhardt, "The Great Man in History," *Ohio State Archaeological and Historical Quarterly* 50 (1941): 233–47; and Benjamin H. Lehman, *Carlyle's Theory of the Hero: Its Sources, Development, History and Influence on Carlyle's Work; A Study of a Nineteenth Century Idea* (New York, 1966).

55. Studies of national monuments include Georg Germann, "The German National Monument," *Gothic Revival in Europe and Britain: Sources, Influences and Ideas* (Cambridge, Massachusetts, 1972), 81–97; Nikolaus Pevsner, "National Monuments and Monuments to Genius," *A History of Building Types* (Princeton, 1976), 11–26; and James Stevens Curl, in "Some Grander Buildings to Celebrate Individuals and National Events," *A Celebration of Death* (London, 1980), 338–56. Early nineteenth-century monuments built to commemorate a collective action of a group of heroes include Jean-Francois Chalgrin's Arc de Triomphe de l'Etoile (1806–36), Paris; Leo von Klenze's Walhalla (1832–42), built near Regensburg for Ludwig I of Bavaria; and Charles Cockerell and William Playfair's partially completed Scottish National Monument (1824–29), Edinburgh.

56. Between 1841 and 1844 Wheaton regularly sent to the National Institute numerous journals, maps, prints, and descriptions of places and events relating to the arts, culture, and sciences in modern Germany. Mills regularly attended these meetings as he had those of its predecessor organization, the Columbian Institute. See National Institute Records, 1839–63, RU 7058, Smithsonian Institution Archives.

57. "Sublime architecture is also appropriate for cathedrals and public buildings, tombs of great men, and generally for all monuments raised to commemorate great deeds and important events, to honor princes, heroes, and great leaders" (Blondel, *Cours*, 1: 380; translation by author).

58. Louis Hautecoeur, *Histoire de l'architecture classique en France* (Paris, 1953), 5: 148. Hautecoeur quotes Napoleon's architect Pierre Fontaine as saying, "The Emperor did not look for beauty except in large objects; he did not realize that one could be separate from the other" (translation by author).

59. An engraving of the Kosciuszko Monument was published as the frontispiece of Karl Falkenstein's biography, *Thaddeus Kosciuszko, nach seinen offentlichen und hauslicken Leben* (Leipzig, 1834). Watterston, in a broadside of about 1845 addressed "To the People," referred to the Kosciuszko Monument as a reproach to the American people who "manifest less patriotism and veneration for her great and glorious Son than Poland has shown to her illustrious Chief."

60. Custis's address was reproduced in full in the *Washington*

National Intelligencer, January 13, 1836, 2. He went on to imagine the day when the cornerstone of the Washington monument would be laid. Americans "from all parts of the Republic" would lift spades of earth to add to the pile.

61. Pollard's description of the monument accompanied an illustration of it on the front page of the *New York Daily Tribune*, August 17, 1843.

62. *National Monument*, 28th Cong., 1st sess, April 12, 1984, H. Doc. 434. Pratt was chairman of the House Committee that was to decide whether to grant the Washington National Monument Society a site for their monument on public grounds. As early as 1813 Strickland had proposed a Washington Monument in Philadelphia, and he designed a second one in response to Lafayette's visit to the city in July 1825. "Strickland had designed a work copied after 'the famous Choragic Monument of Thrassylus at Athens.' It was to be 120 feet in height, and would cost probably $67,000 of which only $11,000 were in hand. It was several years before the cornerstone was set in place (Washington's Birthday, 1833)" (Oberholtzer, *Philadelphia*, 140–41). Further discussion of Washington Monument projects for Philadelphia are discussed by Jeffrey Cohen in O'Gorman et al., *Drawing*, 65–68.

63. *National Monument*. The site suggested by Pratt for this rotunda was north of the Capitol. Six weeks later, on May 25, 1844, Pratt amended the site to that favored by the society, on the mall between Seventh and Twelfth streets, N.W.

64. No drawings survive, but two copies of his lengthy description do. One is in Record Group 233, "Records of the House of Representatives," HR 31A-D17.1, National Archives, and the other is in the Papers of Robert Mills, Library of Congress. Mills resubmitted the scheme to Congress in 1852.

65. Mills's letter to Cranch is in the Richard X. Evans Collection, Special Collections Division, Georgetown University Archives.

66. Records of the Washington National Monument Society, Board of Managers Record Book, 1833–49, March 21, 1848, Record Group 42, National Archives.

67. This report is in the Thomas Lincoln Casey Papers, Society for the Preservation of New England Antiquities. I wish to thank Earl Shuttlesworth for bringing it to my attention. At this time Mills was acting as the assistant architect in charge of constructing Renwick's design for the Smithsonian Institution. Renwick's entry for the Richmond Washington Monument also had an invented order based on a fascial column.

68. Correspondence between Smith and Mills in the Papers of Robert Mills, Manuscript Division, Library of Congress, indicates that Mills provided drawings and probably detailed descriptions of all of his buildings that appear in Smith's view. In April 1852 Smith complained that the "sketch was not defined enough." Another lithograph of the monument of about 1850 by Currier and Ives also shows the "American order"; a copy is at the Columbia Historical Society.

69. John V. Alcott, "Scholarly Books and Frolicsome Blades: A. J. Davis Designs a Library-Ballrooom," *Journal of the Society of Architectural Historians* 33 (1974): 145–54. Charles E. Brownell, "In the American Style of Italian: The E. C. Litchfield Villa" (Master's thesis, University of Delaware, 1970). Jay Cantor, "The Public Architecture of James Renwick, Jr." (Master's thesis, University of Delaware, 1967), 126.

70. On February 29 Whittlesey "presented to the Board a copy of a Latin inscription for the Monument given to him by Robert Mills architect from the original in his possession written by Professor Henry of Columbia College South Carolina."

71. Nowhere in the society's early records is there any indication that locating the monument was a problem. Apparently the myth dates from an 1874 report of the Army Corps of Engineers stating that the current foundations were insufficient to bear the weight of the 600-foot obelisk. The major authority, Harvey, *History*, without citing any specific records, stated that the misalignment was due to foundation problems.

72. Cornelius W. Heine, "The Washington City Canal," *Records of the Columbia Historical Society* (1956), 53–54: 1–27.

73. The monument in the foreground of the Weber view is the Tripoli, or Naval, Monument, executed in Italy and erected in the Washington Navy Yard under Latrobe's direction in

1808. Mills supervised its removal to the west terrace of the Capitol in 1831, designing its cubic base with square fascial piers at the corners. In 1860 it was moved to the grounds of the Naval Academy in Annapolis. For its history see C. Q. Wright, in "The Tripoli Monument," *U.S. Naval Institute Proceedings* (1922), 1931–41.

74. Recalling Thomas Jefferson's remarks on the difficulty of America's achieving its own culture and society while linked to Europe, Winthrop concluded that the "great moral of the events of the day" was the "*influence of the New World upon the Old.*" He was alluding to contemporaneous European revolutions.

75. They did decide to place Washington's sarcophagus (if his remains were ever obtained) "on the floor above the foundation of the Obelisk." Mills's working drawing is in the Thomas Lincoln Casey Papers, Society for the Preservation of New England Antiquities. It shows the Egyptian doorway with the winged orb that was built in the late 1840s but is no longer extant.

76. Potomac gneiss was used for both the foundations and the interior. On October 22, 1848, Mills recommended that the height of the foundation above the ground surface be adjusted from 20 to 17 feet (Records of the Society). See John Zukowsky, "Monumental American Obelisks: Centennial Vistas," *Art Bulletin* 58 (1976): 574–81, for a discussion of monuments as belvederes.

77. In a printed statement dated October 20, 1849, Whittlesey stated that the monument "will be ascended by stairs in the inside, and by machinery," without defining the machinery. Elisha Otis's elevator was first introduced in a bedstead factory in New York in 1852.

78. Harvey, *History*, and later writers have always maintained that the Pope's Stone, as it was dubbed, was the sole cause of halting the work. Examination of the society's records, however, reveals that the dozens of stonemasons, bricklayers, and laborers employed on the monument were predominantly Irish, suggesting that anti-Irish sentiment may have been an underlying cause.

79. The badly damaged letter, illegible in many parts, is among the Papers of Robert Mills, South Carolina Historical Society. Dr. Smith Fuller served on various committees of the Fort Necessity Washington Monument Association. I wish to thank William O. Fink and Steven Strach of the National Park Service for bringing to my attention *Fort Necessity and Historic Shrines of the Redstone Country* (Uniontown, Pennsylvania, 1932), 42–48.

80. Diana S. Waite, *Architectural Elements* (New York, 1972), 5, notes that Hinkle, Guild and Company, of Cincinnati had been fabricating iron building elements as early as 1845.

81. The Kentucky War Monument was Launitz's most monumental work. See Robert Eberhard Launitz, *Collection of Monuments and Head-Stones* (Boston, 1866). For Mills's involvement see Charles Morehead to Millard Fillmore, June 23, 1851, Record Group 48, Appointments Division, National Archives.

82. Mills's drawings are at the Virginia Historical Society; his correspondence with Gov. John Floyd about the monument is in the Capitol Square files, Washington Monument, Virginia State Library. During the same period (March 4, 1851), Mills submitted to the Virginia Senate a design for a building to house Houdon's "Washington."

83. Thomas B. Brumbaugh, "The Genesis of Crawford's Washington," *The Virginia Magazine of History and Biography* 66 (1958): 448–53. "The Evolution of Crawford's 'Washington'," *The Virginia Magazine of History and Biography* 70 (1962): 3–29.

84. Quoted in a letter from Crawford to Conway Robinson dated August 12, 1852 (Virginia Historical Society, MS, IR 5685 b 374). On October 31, 1852, Mills's services as superintending architect of the monument were terminated.

85. Friedrich's bill is in the Papers of Robert Mills, Manuscript Division, Library of Congress.

86. Mills's undated draft describing the monument is in the Papers of Robert Mills, Manuscript Division, Library of Congress.

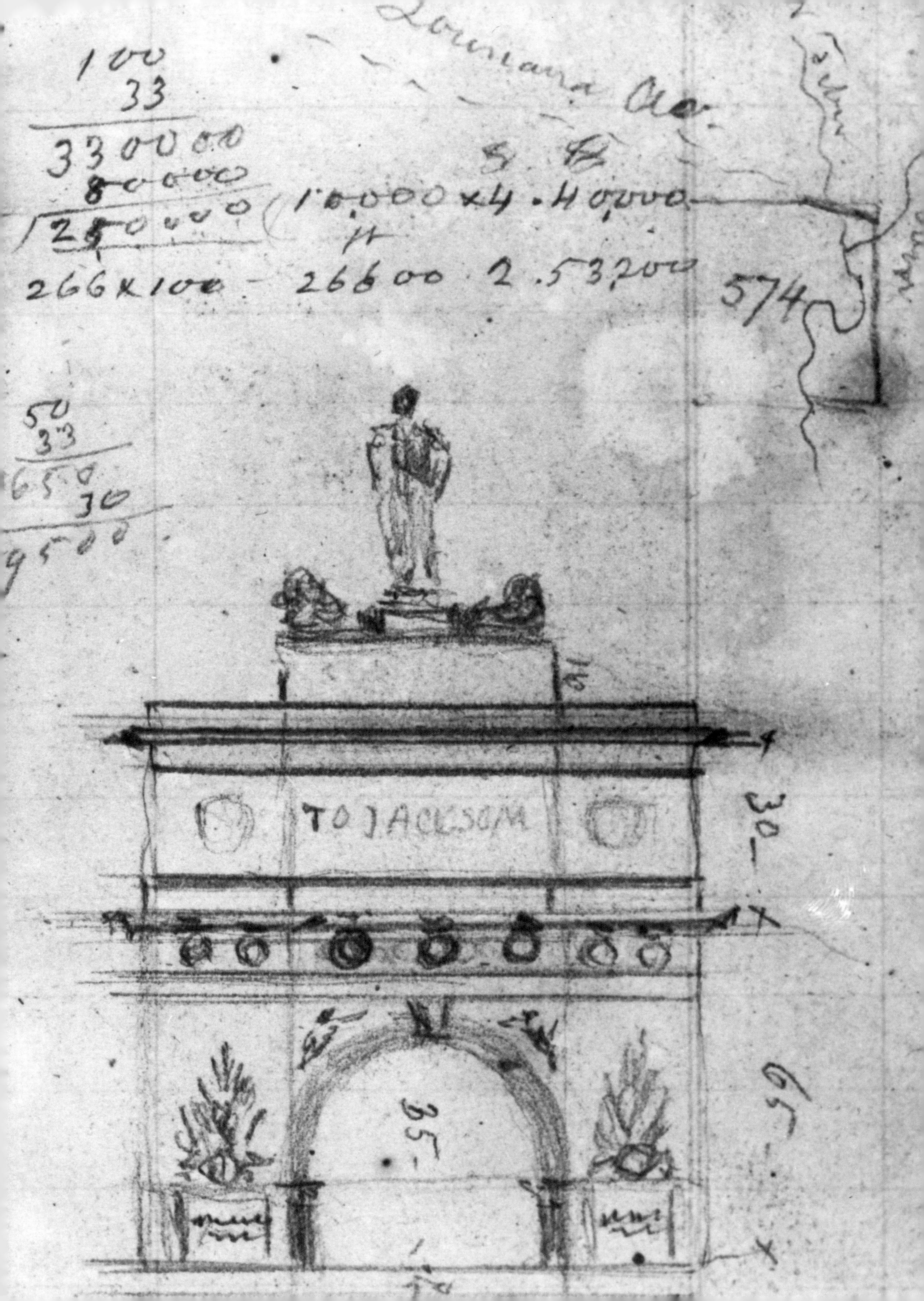

Louisiana Av.

100
33
_____
33000 0
8000 0
_____
250000 (10.000 x 4 . 40,000
                    4
266 x 100 = 266 00 2.53,200   574

50
33
_____
6550
  30
_____
9500

S. E.

TO JACKSON

30-

35-

65

R O B E R T   M I L L S :

A   L I S T   O F   W O R K S,

P R O J E C T S,   A N D

W R I T I N G S

This list is preliminary and will require modification when the Papers of Robert Mills, to be published by Scholarly Resources, are fully available. Each entry is made on the basis of documentation or attribution by one or more of the editors of the Papers. For additional letters and estimates published as a part of congressional reports, see the Papers of Robert Mills.

Opposite:
Sketch of a monument to
Andrew Jackson, c. 1838.
(Papers of Robert Mills,
Library of Congress)

	Works	Projects	Writings
1 8 0 2		South Carolina College, Columbia, S.C.	
1 8 0 3		John's Island Church, John's Island, S.C., c. 1803	
1 8 0 4	Circular Congregational Church, Charleston, S.C., 1804–6	St. Michael's Church (alteration), Charleston, S.C.	
1 8 0 6	South Carolina Penitentiary, 1806–8		
1 8 0 7	First Presbyterian Church, Augusta, Ga., 1807–12		
1 8 0 8	Burlington County Jail, Mount Holly, N.J., 1808–10	Reaping machine	
1 8 0 9	Franklin Row, Philadelphia, Pa., 1809–10 State House (Independence Hall) Wings, 1809–14, Philadelphia, Pa.	Pennsylvania Academy of Fine Arts (addition), 1809–10	
1 8 1 0	Gideon Fairman House, Philadelphia, Pa. Richard H. Willcocks House, Philadelphia, Pa. Benjamin Chew House, Philadelphia, Pa., 1810–12	Isaac Harvey Office Building, High Street, Philadelphia, Pa. State Capitol, Harrisburg, Pa.	
1 8 1 1	Sansom Street Baptist Church, Philadelphia, Pa., 1811–12		

	Works	Projects	Writings
1 8 1 2	First Unitarian (Octagon) Church, Philadelphia, Pa., 1812–13 Eighth Street Houses, Philadelphia, Pa., 1812–14 Monumental (Episcopal) Church, Richmond, Va., 1812–17		
1 8 1 3	Upper Ferry Bridge (Lancaster-Schuylkill Bridge) Cladding and Toll Houses, Philadelphia, Pa., 1813–14 Washington Monument, Baltimore, Md., 1813–42		
1 8 1 4	Cunningham-Archer House, Richmond, Va., 1814–15 Washington Hall, Philadelphia, Pa., 1814–16		
1 8 1 5	John Ambler House (renovation), Richmond, Va., 1815 Howard's Neck (Cunningham House), Goochland County, Va., c. 1815 Hanover House, Richmond, Va., 1815–17 Carter Page House, Richmond, Va., 1815–16	Merchants' Exchange, Baltimore, Md., 1815–16	"The Art of Painting," *National Intelligencer,* Washington, D.C., April 1, 1815, 3–4.
1 8 1 6	James Buchanan House (addition), Baltimore, Md. Davison Monument, Winchester, Va. Patapsco Factory Furnace, Baltimore, Md. Winchester Monument, Baltimore, Md. Brander House, Richmond, Va., 1816–17 Joseph Marx House, Richmond, Va., 1816–17 Aquilla Randall Monument (North Point Monument), Baltimore, Md., c. 1816–17 First Baptist Church, Baltimore, Md., 1816–18 Belvidere Street (extension), Baltimore, Md., 1816–19	Canal at the "Rockets," the falls of the James River, Richmond, Va. Courthouse, Richmond, Va., 1814–16	
1 8 1 7	John Brockenbrough House, Richmond, Va., 1817–18 Hampton-Preston House (First Ainsley Hall House), Columbia, S.C., 1817–18 St. John's Episcopal Church, Baltimore, Md., 1817–18 Richard Potts House, Frederick, Md., 1817–19 Waterloo Row, Baltimore, Md., 1817–19	Henry Didier ("Dedian") House, Baltimore, Md. Powder magazine, Baltimore, Md. Improvement of Jones Falls, Baltimore, Md. Library, Baltimore, Md. Branch Bank of U.S., Baltimore, Md.	"Report on the Survey of Jones Falls," *Baltimore American,* October 3, 1817.

	Works	Projects	Writings
1 8 1 8	Courtland Street Row, Baltimore, Md., 1818–19 Belvidere Bridge, Jones Falls, Baltimore, Md., 1818–20 First Baptist Church, Charleston, S.C., 1818–22	House of Industry, Baltimore, Md. Bank of U.S., Philadelphia, Pa.	
1 8 1 9	Robert Oliver House, Baltimore, Md., 1819–20 Calhoun-Buchanan Vault, Baltimore, Md., c. 1819 James Sloan House (addition), Baltimore, Md., c. 1819		
1 8 2 0	John Hoffman House, Baltimore, Md., 1820–22	Susquehanna to Potomac Canal, Md. and Va. City Hall, Washington, D.C.	*A Treatise on Inland Navigation, Accompanied by a Map.* Baltimore: F. Lucas, 1820. (103 pp.)
1 8 2 1	Colleton County Courthouse (redesign), Walterborough, S.C., 1821–22 Colleton County Jail, Walterborough, S.C., 1821–22 Fairfield County Courthouse, Winnsborough, S.C., 1821–22 Lancaster County Jail, Lancaster, S.C., 1821–22 Bethesda Presbyterian Church, Camden, S.C., 1821–23 Columbia Canal, Columbia, S.C., c. 1821–23 Newberry County Courthouse, Newberry, S.C., 1821–24 Greenville County Courthouse, Greenville, S.C., 1821–24 York County Courthouse, York, S.C., 1821–24 Williamsburg County Courthouse, Kingstree, S.C., 1821–25	Survey, Savannah–Broad River Canal, Beaufort County, S.C. Columbia to Charleston Canal Charleston to Ohio River Canal System	*Inland Navigation. A Plan for a Great Canal Between Charleston and Columbia and for Connecting Our Waters with Those of the Western Country.* Columbia: Telescope Press, 1821. (93 pp.)
1 8 2 2	Spartanburg County Jail, Spartanburg, S.C., 1822–23 Union County Jail, Union, S.C., 1822–23 Charleston County Jail (addition), Charleston, S.C., 1822–24 Georgetown County Courthouse, Georgetown, S.C. 1822–24 Marlborough County Courthouse, Bennettsville, S.C., 1822–24 Marlborough County Jail, Bennettsville, S.C., 1822–24 Williamsburg County Jail, Kingstree, S.C., 1822–24 County Records Office (Fireproof Building), Charleston, S.C., 1822–27 Powder Magazine Complex, Charleston, S.C., 1822–27 South Carolina Asylum, Columbia, S.C., 1822–28		*Internal Improvements of South Carolina, Particularly Adapted to the Low Country.* Columbia: State Gazette Office, 1822. (28 pp.)

	Works	Projects	Writings
1 8 2 3	Horry County Jail, Conway, S.C., 1823–24 Ainsley Hall House, Columbia, S.C., 1823–25 Marion County Courthouse, Marion, S.C., 1823–25 Horry County Courthouse, Conway, S.C., 1823–25 Marion County Jail, Marion, S.C., 1823–25 Union County Courthouse, Union, S.C., 1823–25	Charleston Harbor Improvements, 1823–24 State Capitol, Columbia, S.C., c. 1823	
1 8 2 4	DeBruhl-Marshall House, Columbia, S.C., c. 1824 St. Peter's Church, Columbia, S.C. DeKalb Monument, Camden, S.C., 1824–27 Maxcy Monument, Columbia, S.C., 1824–27 Darlington County Courthouse, Darlington, S.C., 1824–26		"Rotary Steam Engine" (unpublished manuscript)
1 8 2 5	Edgefield County Jail, Edgefield, S.C., 1825–26 Chesterfield County Courthouse, Chesterfield, S.C., 1825–27 Kershaw County Courthouse, Camden, S.C., 1825–30	Charleston Water Company Bunker Hill Monument, Charlestown, Mass.	*Atlas of the State of South Carolina.* Baltimore: F. Lucas, 1825. (28 plates)
1 8 2 6	Newberry Jail, Newberry, S.C., 1826–27 Orangeburg County Courthouse, Orangeburg, S.C., 1826–28 Orangeburg County Jail, Orangeburg, S.C., 1826–28	Elevated railroad, Washington, D.C., to New Orleans	*Statistics of South Carolina.* Charleston: Hurlbut and Lloyd, 1826. (829 pp.)
1 8 2 7	Anderson County Courthouse, Anderson, S.C., 1827–29	Model railroad, Baltimore, Md., c. 1827	"Manual on railroads" (unpublished manuscript) "Abstract of a Plan of a Rail-Road," *Baltimore Gazette and Daily Advertiser*, vol. 68, no. 10323, July 7, 1827. "The Maxcy Monument," *Columbia Telescope, South-Carolina State Journal* 13, no. 56 (December 28, 1827).
1 8 2 8	Methodist Parsonage, Abbeville, S.C., c. 1828 Abbeville County Courthouse, Abbeville, S.C., 1828–30	South Carolina railroad estimates South Carolina monument to revolutionary worthies, c. 1828	
1 8 2 9	Greenville County Jail, Greenville, S.C., 1829–30		
1 8 3 0	U.S. Senate (renovation), Washington, D.C. Customs House, Mobile, Ala., 1830–35		Memorial concerning improving the acoustics in the House of Representatives, H. Rept. 83, 21st Cong., 1st sess., 1829–30. (5 pp.) *(continued)*

	Works	Projects	Writings
			Water for the Capitol, H. Rept. 344, 21st Cong., 1st sess., 1830. (4 pp.)
1 8 3 1	Tripoli Naval Monument (relocation), Washington, D.C. Marine Hospital, Charleston, S.C., 1831–33 Washington Canal, Washington, D.C.	Naval depot, Annapolis, Md. Prison, Washington, D.C. [?] National clock tower, Washington, D.C. 1831–c. 1839	
1 8 3 2	Executive Offices and White House (water systems), Washington, D.C. House of Representatives (alterations), Washington, D.C. Aqueduct Bridge, Alexandria Canal, Alexandria, Va., 1832–43	Richard Dorsey House, iron railing, Baltimore, Md. Improvements, Pennsylvania Ave., Washington, D.C., 1832–40	*The American Pharos, or Lighthouse Guide*. Washington, D.C.: Thompson & Homans, 1832. (134 pp.) *Alteration of Hall House of Representatives*, S. Rept. 495, 22d Cong., 1st sess., 1832.
1 8 3 3	Customs House (alterations, renovation), St. Augustine, Fla. Customs House, New London, Conn., 1833–35 Customs House, Middletown, Conn., 1833–35 Customs House, New Bedford, Mass., 1833–35 Customs House, Newburyport, Mass., 1833–35 U.S. Appraisers Stores, Baltimore, Md., 1833–39	Customs House, New York, N.Y. Improvements, Baltimore Harbor, Md.	
1 8 3 4	U.S. Capitol (water system), Washington, D.C.	Railroad to the Pacific Steam carriages on common roadway	*Substitute for Railroads and Canals: Embracing a New Plan of Roadway; Combining with the Operation of Steam Carriages, Great Economy, in Carrying into Effect a System of Internal Improvement*. Washington, D.C.: James C. Dunn, 1834. (12 pp.) *Guide to the Capitol of the United States, Embracing Every Information Useful to the Visitor Whether on Business or Pleasure*. Washington, D.C.: Privately printed, 1834. (64 pp.)
1 8 3 5	Penitentiary, Baton Rouge, La., c. 1835	National foundry, Washington, D.C., 1835–38 Patent for pump	
1 8 3 6	Courthouse (alterations), St. Augustine, Fla. Powers Fountain, Washington, D.C., 1836–37 U.S. Patent Office, Washington, D.C., 1836–40, 1849–51 South Caroliniana Library, Columbia, S.C., 1836–40 Treasury Building, Washington, D.C., 1836–42	Marine barracks	*New Hall House of Representatives*, H. Doc. 266, 24th Cong., 1st sess., 1836, 1–2.

	Works	Projects	Writings
1 8 3 7	White House (heating system), Washington, D.C. Marine Hospital, New Orleans, La., 1837–48	Decorative cast-iron fencing, Governor's Mansion, Milledgeville, Ga. Marine hospital prototype	*Plans and Estimates for Marine Hospitals, Message from the President*, H. Doc. 3, 25th Cong., 2d sess., 1837, 216–19. *Report Commissioner of Public Buildings*, H. Doc. 28, 25th Cong., 2d sess., 1837, 3–6. *Treasury Building*, H. Doc. 38, 25th Cong., 2d sess., 1837, 2–4.
1 8 3 8	Alexandria Courthouse, Alexandria, Va., 1838–39	National foundry, Washington, D.C., 1838–40 Harmer Denny House, Pittsburgh, Pa., 1838–40 Andrew Jackson Monument, 1838–40 Benjamin Pollard House, 1838–40 Seldon House, 1838–40 W. Gibbs "Country Seat," 1838–40 Masonic Hall, Augusta, Ga., 1838–40 Courthouse, Savannah, Ga., 1838–40	*New Treasury and Post Office Buildings*, H. Rept. 737, 25th Cong., 2d sess., 1838, 19–28, 36–38.
1 8 3 9	Library and Science Building, U.S. Military Academy, West Point, N.Y., 1839–41 Jail, Washington, D.C., 1839–41 U.S. Post Office, Washington, D.C., 1839–42		*Post-Office Building, &c*, H. Rept. 129, 25th Cong., 3d sess., 1839, 2–3. *National Foundry*, H. Rept. 168, 25th Cong., 3d sess., 1839, 73–76. *Public Buildings—Marble or Granite*, H. Rept. 305, 25th Cong., 3d sess., 1839, 15. *Expenditure—Public Buildings*, H. Doc. 32, 26th Cong., 1st sess., 1839, 4–7.
1 8 4 0		Joseph Hand Villa, Bristol, Pa., c. 1840 Lighting public buildings with gas	*Foundation for Statue of Washington*, H. Doc. 124, 26th Cong., 1st sess., 1840, 1–3. *Lighting the Capitol and President's Squares [with] Carburetted Hydrogen Gas*, S. Doc. 434, 26th Cong., 1st sess., 1840, 1–3.
1 8 4 1	Charles Bennett Monument, Alexandria, Va. Fireproof Stores, Harper's Ferry, Va., c. 1841	Smithsonian Institution, Washington, D.C. Fireproof Navy and War Department wings, Washington, D.C. Barracks on western frontier, c. 1841	*Treasury and Patent Office*, S. Doc. 123, 27th Cong., 1st sess., 1841, 14–21, 25. *Statue of Washington by Greenough*, H. Doc. 45, 27th Cong., 1st sess., 1841, 15. *Guide to the National Executive Offices and the Capitol of the United States.* Washington, D.C.: P. Force, 1841. (57 pp.)

	Works	Projects	Writings
1 8 4 2	Marine Hospital, Mobile, Ala., 1842–49	St. John's Church, Washington, D.C. [?] Statistical history of Virginia	*Superintendent and Architect of Public Buildings,* H. Rept. 460, 27th Cong., 2d sess., 1842, 7–8, 10–11, appendix 1–15. *Memorial of Robert Mills of Injustice Done Him in Report of the Commissioner of Public Buildings,* H. Rept. 460, 27th Cong., 2d sess., 1842, 1–15.
1 8 4 3		War and Navy Departments, Washington, D.C., 1843–46	*Buildings for War and Navy Departments,* H. Doc. 85, 27th Cong., 3d sess., 1843, 8–17.
1 8 4 4	Marine Hospital, Key West, Fla.	Hall of Representatives, Washington, D.C.	
1 8 4 5	Washington National Monument, Washington, D.C., 1845–52, completed 1879–84		*The American Light-house Guide: with Sailing Directions, for the Use of the Mariner.* Washington, D.C.: Wm. M. Morrison, 1845. (189 pp.) *Public Buildings,* H. Rept. 89, 28th Cong., 2d sess., 1845, 8–10. *Marine Hospitals,* H. Rept. 124, 28th Cong., 1845, 10–13.
1 8 4 6	City (Willard) Hotel (addition), Washington, D.C.	East facade of U.S. Capitol (alteration), Washington, D.C. City (Willard) Hotel (alteration), Washington, D.C.	*Memorial of Robert Mills, Submitting a New Plan of a Roadway,* H. Doc. 173, 29th Cong., 1st sess., 1846, 1–27.
1 8 4 7	Smithsonian Institution (supervising architect), Washington, D.C., 1847–49 Marine Hospital, Pittsburgh, Pa., 1847–50	Gaslight, dome of U.S. Capitol	*Guide to the Capitol and the National Executive Offices of the United States.* Washington, D.C.: Wm. Greer Printer, 1847–48.
1 8 4 8			*Memorial of Robert Mills Respecting a new route to the Pacific ocean,* S. Doc. 51, 30th Cong., 1st sess., 1848 (7 pp.).
1 8 4 9		Waterworks, Washington, D.C., 1849–54	
1 8 5 0		Washington Monument, Richmond, Va. U.S. Capitol (extension), 1850–51 National mausoleum, Washington, D.C., 1850–53 Washington Monument, Fort Necessity, Uniontown, Pa., 1850–54	*Enlargement of the Capitol,* S. Rept. 145, 31st Cong., 1st sess., 1850, 2–20.
1 8 5 1			*Enlargement of the Capitol Building,* S. Rept. 273, 31st Cong., 2d sess., 1851, 3–4.

	Works	Projects	Writings
1 8 5 2	Washington Monument Base, Richmond, Va. University of Virginia Library (addition, renovation), Charlottesville, Va.	Robert W. Johnson House Customs house, Norfolk, Va. Potomac River Bridge, Washington, D.C. Balloons for aerial reconnaissance, 1852–53	*Memorial by Robert Mills proposing railroad and telegraphic communication with the Pacific,* S. Rept. 344, 32d Cong., 1st sess., 1852 (17 pp.). Letter concerning the "Steamer Henry Clay," *Scientific American* 5 (August 21, 1852), p. 387.
1 8 5 3		York River Railroad, Richmond, Va. Waterworks, Washington, D.C. Post Office (extension), Washington, D.C. Elevated railroad to the Pacific Monument to Jefferson, c. 1853	"Architecture in Virginia." *Virginia Historical Register* 6 (1853): 37–42. *Water-works for the Metropolitan City of Washington.* Washington, D.C.: Lemuel Towers, 1853. (36 pp.)

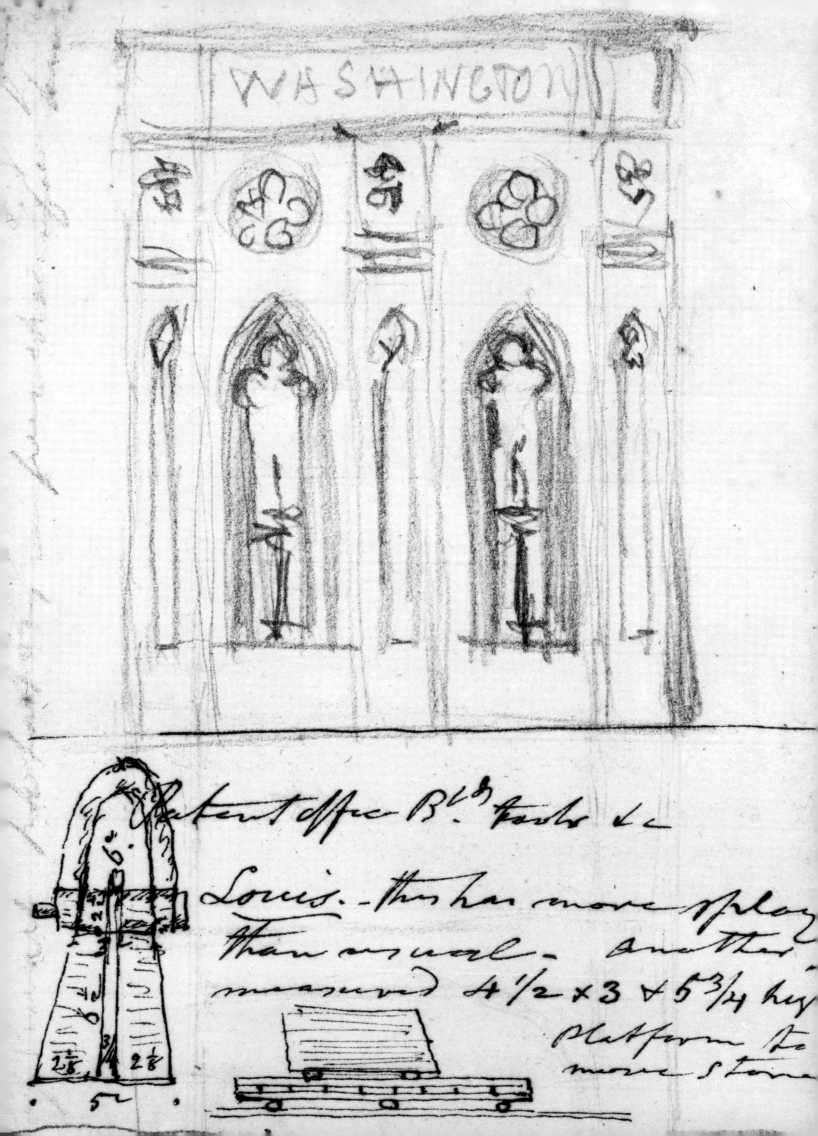

WASHINGTON

INDEX

This index includes persons, places, and buildings discussed in the text. References to illustrations are in italics. Buildings and other structures designed by Mills are indexed by name and by location.